PENSIONS HANDBOOK

9th edition

by

Anthony M Reardon, ACII

PEARSON EDUCATION LIMITED

Edinburgh Gate
Harlow CM20 2JE
Tel: +44(0)1279 623623
Fax: +44(0)1279 431059
Website: www.pearsoned-ema.com

This edition first published in Great Britain in 2003

© Zurich Financial Services Ltd 2003
www.zurichadvice.co.uk

The right of Anthony Reardon to be identified as author of
this work has been asserted by him in accordance with the
Copyright, Designs and Patents Act 1988.

ISBN 0 273 67541 9

Typeset by Land & Unwin (Data Sciences) Ltd
Printed and bound in Great Britain by
Biddles Ltd, Guildford, Surrey

*The Publishers' policy is to use paper manufactured
from sustainable forests.*

CONTENTS

PREFACE

Since the publication of the last edition of this handbook in December 2001 many changes to pensions have been made and proposed. The biggest change has been the introduction of the State Second Pension from 6 April 2002 to replace the State Earnings Related Pension. This is designed to provide a better second pension (in addition to the basic old age pension) for low earners and non-earners such as carers.

Attempts to encourage others, including employers, to set up privately funded arrangements – stakeholder pensions – have been less successful. Although many stakeholder schemes have been set up, the number of people contributing to them has been disappointing, so far. According to statistics published by the Association of British Insurers in August 2003 over 1.5 million stakeholder pensions have been set up but 82 per cent of them have no members: 350,000 employers have met their obligations to designate a scheme but the vast majority are 'shell schemes'. Only 9 per cent of employers are making contributions to these schemes.

Many other pensions changes have been proposed. Alan Pickering's independent report 'A simpler way to better pensions' was published in July 2002 the main emphasis of which was to propose changes that would encourage employers to continue with their pension schemes and to make it easier for them to do so through changes in legislation, especially the tax structures and the complexities of contracting out. The Government followed up the Pickering Report with its Green Paper in December 2002, 'Simplicity, security and choice: working and saving for retirement', responding to Alan Pickering's proposals and asking for further comments from the pensions industry.

In June 2003, the Government published an action plan on how it intends to take forward a number of changes most of which will become law in April 2005 (this is covered in Chapter 20 – The Future). Probably the most controversial initiative is its intention to set up an insurance scheme in the form of the Pension Protection Fund to protect the pensions of members of defined benefit schemes should their employers become insolvent and leave their schemes with fund deficits.

In December 2002, the Treasury and Inland Revenue published radical proposals to simplify pensions tax rules in a consultation document, 'Simplifying the taxation of pensions: increasing choice and flexibility for all', asking for responses by April 2003. Pension providers, employers and other interested parties expected that the Inland Revenue would publish a second document in October 2003. This would take account of their comments on the December 2002 consultation document and provide detailed answers to questions raised. This second document, possibly a White Paper, is now expected in December 2003. Chapter 1 of this book contains a summary of the Treasury and Inland Revenue proposals. References to the far-reaching proposals are also made in other chapters throughout the book.

While these proposals for change were being discussed against a background of falling stock markets worldwide, household-name UK employers continued the flight from defined benefit schemes to defined contribution schemes. Many employers are not prepared to continue to carry the investment risk inherent in defined benefit schemes alone and prefer to share it with scheme members through the defined contribution method. Unfortunately, people with individual pensions have seen their pension funds and other investments fall in value: overall the poor investment performance of UK pension funds has made for a gloomy outlook for private and corporate pension provision although there has been a small recovery in recent months. The National Association of Pension Funds has published information showing that over 40 per cent of companies operating defined benefit schemes closed them to new members within the past year.

I acknowledge with thanks the valuable assistance given to me by the following staff at Zurich Financial Services: Stuart Reynolds LLB, Kate Griffin, Lynn Stewart, LLB FCII and Helen Mosley MMath.

A M Reardon
October 2003

Note: To save endless repetition of 'he' or 'she' we have mainly used the male gender indiscriminately to denote both genders.

ACKNOWLEDGEMENT

The following is Crown copyright and parts have been reproduced, with permission of the Controller of HMSO.

Inland Revenue Personal Pension Scheme Guidance Notes IR 76 (2001)

Inland Revenue Occupational Pension Scheme Practice Notes IR 12 (2001)

ZURICH

Other titles in the Zurich Handbook series

RETIREMENT PLANNING HANDBOOK (9th Edition)

The Retirement Planning Handbook focuses on the financial mechanics of planning a stress-free retirement with no financial worries. It enables you to implement a retirement plan successfully and ensures that you are fully aware of the long- and short-term investment opportunities.

ZURICH INVESTMENT & SAVINGS HANDBOOK 2003/2004

The *Investment & Savings Handbook 2003/2004* guides you through the complexities surrounding the abundance of financial products available so that you can make informed choices for your investment strategy. Completely up to date with the latest legislation, it highlights the significant changes in the law and how they will impact on your investments and savings.

TAX HANDBOOK 2003/2004

Whether you are a financial adviser, accountant, solicitor, company secretary, finance director or private individual who wants to find out about your own tax situation, this thorough guide has to be your first choice for shrewd advice and tax saving hints. Fully revised and updated, this edition incorporates all the latest changes following the Finance Act 2003. It offers sound advice on how to cope with self assessment, as well as offering detailed information on the complete range of taxes including CGT, VAT, stamp duty, inheritance tax, life assurance and national insurance.

—————— AVAILABLE SOON ——————

ESTATE PLANNING & TAXATION OF CAPITAL HANDBOOK (4th Edition)

This is an invaluable guide to estate planning, whether you are an individual wishing to control who benefits from your estate, or a professional adviser. It enables you to grasp the implications of capital taxation on personal business and family wealth and how, by careful planning, its impact can be legally mitigated.

ZURICH BUSINESS TAX AND LAW HANDBOOK (5th Edition)

The ultimate business tax reference, this handbook details the tax obligations and legal considerations facing businesses and their advisers. For business proprietors, financial advisers, company secretaries, directors and executives, this book will become the first point of reference for addressing legal questions and limiting tax obligations.

ZURICH EXPATRIATE TAX & INVESTMENT HANDBOOK (9th Edition)

For British citizens living abroad this book offers essential guidance on how to manage their financial affairs to their greatest possible advantage. It provides comprehensive coverage of every aspect of expatriate tax and investment from the effect of the single currency to advice on working abroad.

**For further information, contact your local bookseller,
telephone Pearson Education Ltd on 02379 623333,
or visit our website www.pearsoned.co.uk/**

1

PENSIONS SIMPLIFICATION – NEW PROPOSALS

1.1 INTRODUCTION

The consultation document that the Inland Revenue and Treasury published in December 2002 proposed far-reaching changes to UK pensions law and practice. The main proposal is a completely new tax regime that will replace all the previous regimes that have accumulated over the years. There will be a single regime covering all pensions (defined benefit, defined contribution, personal and occupational). In the past, changes in the law and practice have usually applied to new pensions schemes or to new members joining schemes from a given date but not to old schemes or to members who joined before the given date. This method of maintaining different, usually more favourable, rules for old schemes is known as 'grandfathering' and has been at the root of the considerable complexity that now represents the UK pensions scene.

Under the new tax regime proposed by the Inland Revenue there will be no grandfathering in future. Instead, there will be one new tax regime that will apply to all types of pension arrangement and will replace all the previous regimes. This chapter sets out the proposals and their impact. The following chapters also contain references to the proposed changes.

The result of the proposed changes is that favourable benefits of existing members are not necessarily preserved so that there will be winners and losers, except perhaps that pension scheme administrators and pension providers may find the new rules easier to follow and implement. The main losers will be those who hoped to build up a pension fund of more than £1.4 million, or a pension of around £70,000 a year.

Much of the criticism from employers about the proposed new tax regime has related to the lifetime limit (see 1.5) of £1.4 million, the amount set out in the December 2002 consultation document. The lifetime limit is seen as too low and the recovery tax charge on funds exceeding it too high (see 1.15). It is possible that when the proposals are enacted the lifetime limit will have increased, if only to allow for inflation between December 2002 and the date the law takes effect.

1.2 START DATE FOR THE CHANGES

The Inland Revenue's original preferred target date was 6 April 2004 but pension providers considered this to be too soon, giving insufficient time to change systems and make the necessary alterations to information sent to existing customers. The Government has announced that it intends that the new regime will be legislated in 2004 but will carry an effective date for all changes of 6 April 2005. An update on the Revenue's views on its December 2002 proposals is expected in December 2003.

1.3 MAIN FEATURES

(1) Most employees will not pay tax on contributions paid by their employers into their schemes and will obtain tax relief on their own contributions, including higher-rate relief where appropriate.
(2) Contributions can be made by the member, the current employer or former employer. A third party can pay a contribution on behalf of the member and any third party contribution will be treated as having been paid by the member.
(3) There will be an overall annual contribution limit of £200,000.
(4) The investment growth of pension schemes will be largely tax-free as now.
(5) The individual's pension fund at retirement must not exceed £1.4 million (the lifetime limit).
(6) The member can take a tax-free cash sum of up to 25 per cent of the capital value of the pension. This is the system used today under personal pension schemes but is different to the many different methods that are used under the other tax regimes relating to occupational schemes and which are being replaced.
(7) There will be limited transitional rights for members of existing schemes to protect large pension rights already accrued and rights to cash lump sums.

1.4 THE CONTRIBUTION LIMIT

(1) Employees, employers and self-employed will receive tax relief on contributions to pension schemes of all kinds up to the higher of 100 per cent of earnings or £3,600 a year. Higher-rate tax relief will remain.
(2) There will be an overall contribution limit of £200,000 which will be indexed. This limit is an 'inflow' limit to an individual's pension

fund, or notional fund in the case of members of a common trust fund where funds are not earmarked for individuals. The 'inflow' includes the increase in value of the individual fund over the year, for example after investment growth and can also apply to pensions in payment, for example where pension increases are granted.

(3) Under defined contribution schemes the annual inflow into a person's fund is easy to establish as it amounts to the difference between the funds at the beginning and end of the year. Under defined benefit schemes the increase in the value of defined benefit rights in the employer's scheme must be included when establishing whether the member's annual contributions has been breached. The Inland Revenue will publish actuarial tables valuing increases in defined benefit pensions.

(4) Scheme members wishing to have a more exact valuation of their benefits will need to agree the terms of the valuation with the Inland Revenue.

(5) The method for enforcing the annual contribution limit will be through the self-assessment tax system which will apply a new income tax charge on any inflow above the annual limit.

(6) The Inland Revenue states that only about 1,000 people will be affected by the annual limit (about 90,000 people earn more than £200,000 a year).

1.5 THE LIFETIME LIMIT

(1) The individual's pension fund at retirement must not exceed £1.4 million, known as the 'lifetime limit'. This limit will be indexed to keep pace with inflation.

(2) The reasoning behind the limit is that £1.4 million is the amount approximately equivalent in value to a maximum pension of two-thirds of the current earnings cap under an occupational pensions scheme for a man aged 60 drawing an indexed pension and with a surviving spouse's pension of one-half of the member's pension. (The earnings cap is the limit, introduced in 1989, on pensionable earnings under approved pension schemes.)

(3) The Inland Revenue will publish tables to determine the capital value of defined benefit schemes for people of different ages and in different types of scheme.

(4) The Inland Revenue states that only about 5,000 people have personal pensions schemes valued above £1.4 million.

(5) The £1.4 million lifetime limit is the *tax-favoured* limit: it will be possible to fund for an amount over this limit but punitive tax will be incurred.

1.6 TESTING AGAINST AND COMPLYING WITH THE LIMITS

The rules are as follows:

(1) If the value of the total pension from all sources is less than the lifetime limit then it can be paid out according to the new tax regime.

(2) If the value of the total pension is more than the lifetime limit a recovery charge of one-third of the excess will be applied before any income can be drawn. The recovery charge is supposed to neutralise the tax relief previously given on pension contributions and on investment growth within the fund. Any amount drawn from the slice above the lifetime limit will then be taxed as income.

(3) Where people do not take all their pension benefits at once there will be a need to test against the lifetime limit each time benefits are taken.

(4) When pension schemes pay out benefits they will have to test against the lifetime limit and notify the Inland Revenue what percentage of the lifetime limit the member has used and also notify the scheme member.

(5) Scheme members will have to monitor the annual contribution limit and the lifetime limit. This means that schemes will have to provide the necessary information to members, including valuations of benefits, to enable them to meet their obligations to the Inland Revenue (probably through the income tax self-assessment return).

1.7 THE IMPACT ON EXISTING SCHEMES

(1) Everyone saving for pensions will be subject to the new rules from 6 April 2005 (the start date of the proposed new regime). Pension rights already accrued will be honoured subject to the limits in place at A-Day but members and employers cannot continue to save and operate under the previous rules.

(2) Provided members are within the pre 6 April 2005 tax rules pensions rights above the lifetime limit will be honoured, and indexed (the method of indexation is not yet known). Any further rights built through savings after 6 April 2005 will be calculated according to the new rules.

(3) One-off valuations of pension funds will be needed for those above the lifetime limit at 6 April 2005. Members will have three years from that date to register their pre 6 April 2005 rights. Those regis-

tered rights may be paid out later as pensions benefits even though they have a value more than the lifetime limit without the recovery tax charge being made.

(4) In order to protect the pre 6 April 2005 tax-free lump sum it is proposed that the tax-free lump sum is the higher of:
   – 25 per cent of total pension rights pre and post 6 April 2005;
   – an exact valuation of pre 6 April 2005 lump sum rights within three years of that date and indexed, or $3/80$ for each year of service of P60 earnings subject to the limits under the relevant tax regime, and indexed.

(5) If a scheme's administrators do not want to be subject to the new rules they will have a notice period of three months before 6 April 2005 to register their position and have it acknowledged by the Inland Revenue.

(6) Pension schemes which opt-out of the new tax rules will be treated as funded unapproved retirement benefits schemes (FURBS) and all pension rights paid after 6 April 2005 will be taxed.

1.8 TAX RELIEF ON MEMBER CONTRIBUTIONS

The rules are as follows:

(1) The current system used by occupational pensions schemes will continue. This is known as the 'net pay arrangement' in which contributions by members are deducted from gross pay before applying tax under PAYE (this method also gives higher-rate taxpayers immediate tax relief).

(2) The method used by individuals paying contributions to personal pension schemes, including group personal pensions and stakeholder schemes – pension relief at source (PRAS) – will continue and also be available to employers. Under the PRAS system only basic rate tax relief is given at source and higher-rate taxpayers have to claim a refund of higher-rate tax through their tax returns.

(3) It appears that the above methods of giving tax relief will also apply to retirement annuities: currently contributions to these contracts are paid without any form of tax relief at source with policyholders having to claim tax relief through their tax returns. This is likely to cause problems to insurers who may find it difficult to change old computer systems to apply PRAS.

(4) Pension schemes will make the choice as to adopting either methods (1) or (2) above.

5

1.9 CONTRIBUTION RULES FOR PEOPLE WHO ARE NON-RESIDENT

The rules are as follows:

(1) Individuals who are not resident and ordinarily resident in the UK and who are not chargeable to UK tax on their earnings but who wish to contribute to UK pensions under the new regime but on less favourable terms than today:
   – will be able to pay unlimited personal contributions but without tax relief;
   – their employers (current or former) will be able to make unlimited contributions but only UK tax resident employers will be able to obtain tax relief.

(2) For other individuals who are not resident and ordinarily resident in the UK, and who are not chargeable to UK tax on their earnings, but who have been resident and ordinarily resident or have had UK chargeable earnings in the last six years the rules are slightly more generous:
   – they will be able to make unlimited personal contributions with the first £3,600, gross, eligible for tax relief at the basic rate provided the scheme operates pension relief at source; and
   – their employers will be able to make unlimited contributions, but only UK tax resident employers will be able to obtain tax relief.

1.10 RETIREMENT BENEFITS

The complex rules that apply today relating to the maximum pension that can be paid as a proportion of 'final pay' will not appear under the new rules. Subject to what scheme rules allow, in future all pension schemes will be able to provide benefits in stages (known as 'staggered vesting') until age 75, more flexible income patterns, the payment of a limited taxable death benefit if the member dies before age 75 while the pension or income is being paid, and survivors' benefits. However, there are some conditions, as follows:

(1) The pension or income must start no later than age 75. Where income benefits are being paid from 'unsecured funds' (the new version of income withdrawal or income drawdown – see Chapter 19) there is no requirement for an annuity to be bought by the age of 75.

(2) The pension or income may not start before age 50 until 2010 or from 2010 not before age 55, except though ill-health.

(3) The pension must last for the member's life, be paid in instalments at least annually, not be assigned to anyone other than permitted

beneficiaries, not be guaranteed for more than ten years and be taxed as earned income.

(4) The pension can only provide a lump sum on the death of the member up to age 75 in accordance with 'value protection' (see below).

(5) If the pension is not underwritten by a life company or promised by an occupational scheme, i.e. it is 'unsecured', the income must lie between minimum and maximum levels each year (see *Unsecured funds* below).

(6) Members age 60 and over whose pension funds are no more than £10,000 will be able to take all of it as a lump sum: the first 25 per cent will be tax-free with the rest taxed as income. The fund includes 'protected rights', which currently must be taken as a pension ('protected rights' is the term that applies to the pension fund secured by rebates in national insurance contributions where schemes are used to contract out of the State Second Pension, previously the State Earnings Related Pension).

All pension schemes will be allowed to permit members to take retirement benefits while continuing to work for the employer.

1.11 NEW TYPES OF ANNUITY

There are two new types of annuity:

(1) Limited period annuity: this allows the scheme members to use their pensions fund to buy a short-term annuity and at the end of the period another short-term annuity or a lifetime annuity. This gives the member some flexibility over having to commit to buying a lifetime annuity at the outset.

(2) Value protected annuity: if on the death of the annuitant before age 75 the amount paid for the annuity – the purchase price – is more than the annuity instalments made, the remainder may be paid as a lump sum subject to deduction of tax at 35 per cent.

1.12 UNSECURED FUNDS

Most income drawn from pension rights is likely to continue to take the form that applies today: the scheme promises to pay an income for the rest of the member's life, or a lifetime annuity is purchased from a life office. These are called 'secured funds' in the Inland Revenue's consultation document. There will also be an option to take 'unsecured benefits' where there is no guarantee that the benefits will continue for life. This is a successor to the income drawdown or income withdrawal plans available today (see Chapter 19). Income from unsecured funds will be subject to the following conditions:

(1) a minimum annual income of £1;
(2) a maximum annual income related to the annuity that the funds supporting the pension could achieve on the open market;
(3) the maximum income must be reviewed every five years, or annually after age 75;
(4) there is no requirement to buy an annuity at age 75 (as applies under current rules on income drawdown plans) but no death benefit, including 'value protection' benefit, may be paid on death after age 75.
(5) Only survivors' pensions may be paid on death after age 75.

1.13 DEATH BENEFITS BEFORE TAKING RETIREMENT BENEFITS

The details are as follows:

(1) A tax-free lump sum may be paid. If the amount exceeds the lifetime limit the excess will be subject to the recovery tax charge of one-third of the excess.
(2) All or part of the member's fund may be used to provide a taxable income to the member's dependants, without limit.

The value of the death benefits, including life assurance, must be tested against the lifetime and annual limits.

1.14 DEATH BENEFITS WHILE RECEIVING BENEFITS

The details are as follows:

(1) On death before age 75, a limited lump sum benefit may be paid where the member has opted for 'value protection'. The amount will be equal to the value of the fund used to provide the income to the member less the actual amounts of pension or income paid to the member before death subject to a tax charge of 35 per cent.
(2) An income may be guaranteed for a minimum period, for example where it is paid under an occupational pension scheme or under an annuity purchased from a life company (typically for five or ten years). On death, the remaining instalments may continue for the remainder of the guarantee period although a capital sum equal to the outstanding requirements may not be paid. There is no recovery tax charge in these circumstances.

1.15 THE RECOVERY TAX CHARGE

The tax charge on funds above the lifetime limit will be calculated as follows:

Example 1.1

> If when benefits are drawn the member has an excess fund of £100,000 over the lifetime limit this will be taxed at 33% = £33,333 leaving a fund of £66,667. This is then taxed as income (but can be paid as a lump sum). Assuming income tax at 40% this amounts to another £26,666. Thus the total tax amounts to £60,000, which represents 60% of the excess fund of £100,000.

1.16 UNAPPROVED SCHEMES

It appears that the tax treatment of funded unapproved retirement benefits schemes (FURBS) and unfunded unapproved retirement benefits schemes (UURBS) will change. The new tax regime is intended to replace all previous regimes including unapproved as well as approved schemes. With the lifetime limit likely to catch many high earners, employers wishing to provide retirement benefits for them will inevitably have to use what have been termed 'unapproved schemes' in the past. However, at this stage it is not known how unapproved schemes will be affected by the new proposals.

However, the new proposals outlined above will end the distinction between employed and self-employed pensions. The rest of this chapter looks at the differences and similarities between pensions for these two categories although when the changes take effect from 6 April 2005 one new tax code will apply to all pensions for the future and the past. The different contributions that can be invested for the self-employed and employed, as shown in Tables 1.1 and 1.2, will cease to be relevant.

1.17 EMPLOYED V SELF-EMPLOYED – CLOSING THE GAP

Currently, pensions for these two categories differ considerably. If you are employed, you may join a pension plan set up by your employer where the only limits on the benefits relate to your salary: if you are self-employed, you may contribute to a pension plan where the limits are related not to your salary, but to the contributions that you may pay. The potential for pension provision is generally far greater if you are employed.

Pension arrangements available to the employed, including directors, are usually known as executive pension plans, occupational pension schemes, company pension schemes, superannuation funds or variations on that theme. Such schemes can be introduced for the benefit of employees of not only companies, but also sole traders, partnerships, charities and other bodies.

If you are self-employed you are eligible for a personal pension scheme. The eligibility for personal pension schemes is extended to employed persons who are not members of a company scheme. The forerunner of the personal pension scheme was the retirement annuity contract, also commonly known as the self-employed retirement annuity. It is still possible to contribute to these contracts although new ones have not been allowed since 1988.

Company pension schemes and personal pension schemes enjoy considerable tax concessions which are broadly similar. The surrounding legislation, however, is separate and differs in many ways.

Provided a company pension plan or personal pension scheme is approved by the Inland Revenue, contributions paid by the employee are tax deductible. Employer contributions are also tax deductible although the question of whether tax relief is allowable is a matter for the Tax Office to decide. The fund is exempt from income tax on investments and deposits and capital gains tax on the disposal of investments. The benefits may be taken in the form of a tax-free lump sum and a pension which will be treated as earned income.

Benefits under new occupational pension schemes are restricted for high earners through the application of an earnings limit which stands at £99,000 for the tax year 2003/04. Under personal pension schemes (including stakeholder pension schemes) higher contributions, as a percentage of earnings, can be paid, compared with contributions to retirement annuities, although earnings are also restricted to £99,000. The basis for calculating maximum benefits under 'earmarked' pension schemes such as executive pension plans set up for a few members, usually directors and senior executives, was changed in September 1994 and June 1996. This reduced the advantage previously enjoyed by employed people of being able to accelerate the funding of their pensions.

A comparison of the contributions that may be invested at intervals throughout the term to retirement, if salary increases at 6.9 per cent per annum compound, is set out in Tables 1.1 and 1.2.

The changes in 1994 and 1996 reduced the gap between maximum contributions that may be paid under arrangements of the self-employed as

Table 1.1

Male aged 30, initial salary £30,000, retirement at 60.

Future age	Salary progression	Personal Pension Scheme		Executive Pension Plan	
		% Salary	Amount	% Initial salary	Amount
30	£ 30,000	17.5	£ 5,250	26	£ 7,800
40	£ 58,465	20.0	£11,693	26	£15,201
50	£113,940	25.0	£28,485	26	£29,624
55	£159,061	30.0	£47,718	26	£41,356

Table 1.2

Male aged 40, initial salary £40,000, retirement at 60.

Future age	Salary progression	Personal Pension Scheme		Executive Pension Plan	
		% Salary	Amount	% Initial salary	Amount
40	£ 40,000	20.0	£ 8,000	42	£16,800
50	£ 77,954	25.0	£19,488	42	£32,740
55	£108,824	30.0	£32,647	42	£45,706

Notes:
(1) Under the Executive Pension Plan, allowance is made at outset for future salary increases, assumed to be 6.9 per cent per annum compound, and fund growth, assumed to be 8.5 per cent per annum. If the salary increases at a greater level and/or fund growth is lower, higher contributions may be paid in future. The cost of providing dependants' pensions and life assurance benefits has been excluded. The nominal rates of 6.9 and 8.5 per cent are high in today's environment of low interest rates. However, the real rate of growth of 1.6 per cent is a cautious assumption and is of more importance.
(2) Under the Personal Pension Scheme, the amount that can be paid is based on the actual salary and the percentage contribution which applies at that age.

compared to employees. However the differences in the underlying systems remain unchanged until 6 April 2005:

(1) For the self-employed there are no specific limits on benefits. The restrictions on contribution input, however, make it imperative that contributions are started as early as possible.
(2) For employees, whilst contributions are now restricted, the underlying limits on benefits remain. If, for example, there are substantial

salary increases close to retirement, and the fund is insufficient to provide maximum benefits, then a further single contribution may be made just prior to retirement to bridge the shortfall.

The two different forms of pension arrangements, occupational pension schemes and personal pension plans, are considered in detail in the following chapters.

2

HISTORICAL NOTES

2.1 EARLY SCHEMES AND LEGISLATION

One early example of a scheme is seen in the famous case of *Hancock v General Reversionary and Investment Company Ltd* [1919] 1 KB 25, which established the important principle that a company which purchases an annuity for a retiring employee may set the cost against its profits for tax purposes as a business expense.

The Income Tax Act 1918 gave life assurance tax relief to employees contributing to a retirement benefit scheme using insurance policies. The Finance Acts of 1921 and 1930 provided, amongst other things, for the approval of superannuation funds set up under irrevocable trust and for the Commissioners of Inland Revenue to regulate such schemes.

New pensions legislation was introduced by the Income Tax Act 1952 and re-enacted in the consolidating Income and Corporation Taxes Act 1970. By 1970, however, the conditions for approval of pension schemes derived from a combination of legislation, case law and Inland Revenue practice. The Civil Service Superannuation Scheme was the model by which all private schemes were judged. The tax treatment of pension fund investments varied from total freedom to partial exemption from capital gains tax but no exemption from income tax, depending entirely on the type of benefit being provided, for example cash, pension or death benefit. It was common for trustees of these old pension schemes to seek approval of three-quarters of the benefits under s 208 of the Income and Corporation Taxes Act 1970 (giving complete tax-free treatment but requiring all benefits to be taken in pension form) and one-quarter of the benefits under s 222 (allowing benefits to be taken in cash but giving limited relief) – giving rise to the expression '¾, ¼ Schemes'.

2.2 OLD AND NEW CODES

The case for simplification was recognised in the late 1960s resulting in a 'New Code' of approval introduced by the Finance Act 1970 (FA 1970) Pt II, Chap II. The New Code introduced a concept of one single fund with total freedom from tax on both contributions and investment income.

By April 1980 all schemes, including existing Old Code schemes, had to be approved by the Inland Revenue under the New Code.

Section 15 of FA 1973 extended FA 1970 by allowing 'controlling directors' to be included in New Code pension schemes.

The F(No 2)A 1987 brought in a number of significant changes to pension scheme practice. In some ways the changes meant a reversion to the Old Code regime in that:

(1) Maximum pensions for persons joining pension schemes on or after 17 March 1987 could be provided only if 20 years' service with the employer could be completed by retirement, rather than ten.
(2) Pension schemes set up to provide only tax-free cash sums on retirement are restricted. Generally, if the *maximum* tax-free cash sum is required the *maximum* pension benefit has to be provided under the scheme.
(3) Measures were introduced to restrict the benefits which may be enjoyed by high earners, including 'controlling directors'.

Schedule 6 to FA 1989 introduced further limitations to all members of new occupational pension schemes set up from 14 March 1989 and, in respect of new members joining from 1 June 1989, schemes set up before that date. Details are given in later chapters but the principal change was the maximum level of earnings on which retirement benefits could be based. This was set at £60,000 in 1989/90 and is increased each year in line with increases in the Retail Prices Index (RPI), except in 1993/94 when no increase was applied. The maximum level stands at £99,000 in 2003/04.

2.3 TOP HAT SCHEMES

The top hat scheme first gained prominence in the late 1940s as a simple but effective means of reducing the burden of income tax; in those days the top rate was 97.5 per cent. The proceeds of endowment schemes could be taken completely tax free at the end of a period of employment. The FA 1947 was an attempt to make top hats less attractive by restricting the amount of pension which could be commuted for a tax-free lump sum to 25 per cent but in fact it only succeeded in boosting their popularity by giving them respectability.

Following the passing of FA 1973, which allowed controlling directors to join New Code schemes, top hat schemes found a new lease of life. Because of the changes which were brought about by the New Code, the modern top hat policy became a much more sophisticated vehicle than its predecessor, offering maximum flexibility in terms of benefits and investment options. Indeed, executive pension plans, as they are now called, became essential tools of tax planners with their ability to reduce the impact of income tax, capital gains tax, inheritance tax and corporation tax.

2.4 GROWTH OF EXECUTIVE PENSION PLANS

The creation and growth of the executive pension plan for the controlling director coincided with the development of unit-linked life assurance policies, pioneered by such companies as Hambro Life Assurance and Allied Dunbar Assurance plc (now Zurich Financial Services). By the end of the 1970s these companies had been joined by many other new companies and also very old established life assurance companies, all offering unit-linked as well as with-profits policies.

The essential attraction of the unit-linked policy is the option given to the policyholder to decide his own investment strategy. He may choose to invest his contributions in a variety of sectors ranging from properties, equities, cash, gilts and overseas funds. Alternatively, the policyholder may leave the investment strategy to the insurance company under what is known as a 'managed fund'.

The introduction of personal pension plans in 1988 and the earnings cap in 1989 put a brake on the popularity of executive pension plans. The ability to pay large contributions into executive pension plans in the early years of a plan's existence (accelerated funding) became more restricted. Individuals, including directors of family-owned companies, became attracted to the greater flexibility available under small self-administered schemes.

2.5 SMALL SELF-ADMINISTERED PENSION SCHEMES

The late 1970s saw the development of small self-administered pension schemes, where the employer sets up a pension scheme himself, with the assistance of various experts, rather than using an insurance company. The trustees have wider powers of investment compared with those allowed under a straightforward insured arrangement, in particular the ability to lend part of the pension fund back to the employer to assist the expansion of the business, to purchase shares in the employer's business and to purchase property which is leased to the employer. However, the Social Security Act 1990 limited such 'self-investment' to 5 per cent of the value of the pension fund unless the scheme membership is limited to '20 per cent directors' of the company, and provided other conditions are met (see Chapter 9).

Insurance companies offer small self-administered schemes, usually providing all the necessary services and investment management if required but normally on the basis that a portion of the pension fund is invested in an insurance policy.

2.6 DEVELOPMENT OF STATE BENEFITS

The 1960s and 1970s were notorious for the frequency with which governments invented new state schemes. Some never reached the statute book while others were overturned by an incoming administration. All tended to bear the name of their creators – the Boyd-Carpenter Graduated Pension Scheme, the Crossman Plan, the Keith Joseph Funded Pension Scheme and the Barbara Castle State Earnings Related Scheme (SERPS).

Although there was all-party consensus on the Castle Scheme, Norman Fowler, as Secretary of State for Health and Social Security, introduced measures in the Social Security Act 1986 which reduced benefits under the earning-related part of the state scheme (see Chapter 11).

Recent commentaries on welfare provision have tended to question the continuation of the current universal nature of the state pension, suggesting that any future improvements should be targeted on the most needy.

The current Labour Government, through the Child Support, Pensions and Social Security Act 2000, replaced SERPS with the State Second Pension, known as S2P, with effect from April 2002. S2P provides pensions on an earnings-related basis but this is expected to become a flat-rate pension in the future.

From the corporate viewpoint, the main concern is the relationship between SERPS/S2P and schemes sponsored by employers. Members of schemes which provide benefits to a specified level may be contracted out of SERPS/S2P.

2.7 SEX EQUALITY IN PENSIONS

The 1970s saw the start of legislative changes to improve the benefits of early leavers and provide for greater transferability between schemes. This continued into 1990 which saw further legislation to improve early leavers' benefits. The late 1980s saw significant changes to both occupational and personal pension schemes (see 2.9 below and later chapters), increased the awareness of 'unapproved pension schemes' (see Chapter 5) and saw the beginning of anti-sex discrimination law in the field of pensions. Under the Sex Discrimination Act 1986, it is unlawful for employers to require female employees to retire at an earlier age than male colleagues. European law has affected sex equality in pensions considerably over the past decade. In its judgment on the *Barber v Guardian Royal Exchange* case in May 1990 the European Court ruled that redundancy pay and membership of a contracted-out pension scheme are 'pay' for the purposes of equal treatment directives of the European Community Council and Article 119 of the Treaty of Rome and that Mr Barber had been discriminated against by his employer even though the reason for the different treatment between him and his female colleagues was the different state retirement ages for men and women.

In the *Coloroll Pension Trustees* case the court ruled that scheme trustees as well as employers are bound by Article 119. It also ruled that actuarial factors which vary according to sex do not fall within the scope of Article 119 where such factors are used by employers in establishing the funding levels of defined benefit schemes and in determining matters which are linked to those funding arrangements, for example commutation factors and the calculation of transfer values.

In the event of a transfer of pension rights from one occupational scheme to another, owing to a worker's change of job, the second scheme is obliged, on the member reaching retirement age, to increase the benefits it undertook to pay him when accepting the transfer. This increase in benefits is required in order to eliminate the effects which may have been suffered by the worker in consequence of the inadequacy of the cash equivalent transferred (this being due in turn to discriminatory treatment suffered by the worker by the first scheme in relation to benefits payable in respect of period of service, subsequent to the *Barber* judgment of 17 May 1990).

The court also ruled that in equalising pensions, scheme trustees are allowed to equalise down the benefits of men and women. However, scheme trustees have to improve benefits for men accruing between May 1990 (the date of the *Barber* judgment) and the date when the company took whatever action was required to implement equal pension rights.

In *Smith v Advel Systems*, five women, backed by the Equal Opportunities Commission, brought claims before the Industrial Tribunal in the United

Kingdom arguing that they were financially worse off as a result of the employer raising their retirement age from 60 to 65 following the *Barber* ruling. The court ruled that it was legitimate for employers to worsen pension provision for women for the period of service after implementation of equal pension rights. However, for the period of service between 1990 and implementation of equal pension rights the benefits enjoyed by women as a result of lower retirement ages may not be reduced.

In *Vroege v NCIV* (a Dutch case) about the rights of access to pension schemes by part-time workers, the court ruled that the right to join an occupational pension scheme falls within the scope of Article 119 of the Treaty of Rome. The right is not time-limited by the *Barber* judgment and therefore stretches back to April 1976.

In *Fisscher v Voorhuis Hengelo* (another Dutch case), the court ruled that equal pay rules applied to access to a pension scheme which excluded married women. The court also ruled that a worker wishing to join a scheme retroactively must pay back contributions if the scheme is a contributory scheme.

In *Van Den Akker v Shell* the court ruled that, for a period between the *Barber* judgment in May 1990 and equalisation, conditions for male workers have to be improved to equal the benefits for female workers.

In *ABP v Beune*, the court ruled that the Dutch civil service occupational pension scheme is also covered by equal treatment rules and it is not permissible for such a scheme to discriminate against married men. This case also affects other national public service schemes.

Doubt about the use of actuarial factors under money purchase schemes still exists: we still do not know whether it is sufficient for employers to pay *equal* contributions for men and women or whether equal pensions have to be paid. In the future, it is possible that developments in the European Court will result in the use of unisex annuity rates.

In *Allonby v Accrington and Rossendale College* the Advocate General's opinion was that it is unlikely that a part-time lecturer's claim for equal pay against a college that dismissed her and re-employed her on a self-employed basis will succeed when the European Court of Justice makes its judgment. However, the lecturer may succeed in the related matter concerning her inability to join the Teachers Pension Scheme: there may be indirect discrimination if the prohibition on self-employed lecturers joining the scheme affects more women than men.

In *Beckmann v Dynamo Whicheloe Macfarlane Ltd* an employee was made redundant after her job was transferred from a public health authority in the UK to a private company. If she had remained with her former employer she would have been entitled to a redundancy package including an early retirement pension. Under the Transfer of Undertakings

(Protection of Employment) Regulations occupational pensions are currently excluded from the protection provided for other employment conditions on a business transfer. The European Court of Justice held that early retirement pensions are not excluded and are therefore protected. This ruling will have major implications for business transfers. Some aspects of this case have been referred back to the High Court in England.

2.8 PENSIONS LAW REFORM

2.8.1 Pensions Act 1995

This Act brought in many of the proposals of the Pension Law Review Committee to improve the security of occupational pensions. The main effects of the Act are as follows:

(1) The Occupational Pensions Regulatory Authority, known as OPRA, has wide-ranging powers. It may impose civil penalties of up to £5,000 in the case of individuals and £50,000 in the case of companies for breaches in their statutory duties by trustees, employers and their advisers. OPRA may prohibit a person from being a trustee of a scheme and appoint new trustees. It has the power to wind up a scheme and apply to the court for an injunction if it is likely that someone will misappropriate scheme assets. OPRA regulates stakeholder pension schemes and also provides accreditation to providers seeking to market them.

(2) Member-nominated trustees – existing trustees were responsible for putting in place and obtaining the scheme members' approval to procedures for members to select one-third of the trustee board. Employers may decide that they wish to opt out of the requirement to have member-nominated trustees and introduce alternative arrangements for selecting trustees. Members must be given the opportunity to object to the employer's proposals.

(3) General aspects of trusteeship – a trustee and any person who is connected with the trustee cannot act as the auditor or actuary of the same scheme. A trustee will be disqualified from being a trustee of any scheme if he has been convicted of an offence (including deception or dishonesty), has been made bankrupt, has made an arrangement with his creditors, is subject to a disqualification order as a company director, and in the case of a corporate trustee, if any of the directors is disqualified from being a trustee. Trustees cannot be indemnified out of scheme assets for fines or penalties.

(4) Functions of trustees – the trustees must maintain a written statement of investment principles, including the kinds of investments

to be held, risk, expected return and the balance between different kinds of investments. They must consider the advice of a suitable expert and consult the employer.

(5) Advisers – the trustees must appoint a scheme auditor and actuary, although most money purchase schemes are exempt from the requirement to appoint an actuary.

(6) Minimum funding requirement – every scheme, except money purchase schemes, is subject to a minimum funding requirement (MFR) that the value of its assets is not less than the amount of its liabilities. The trustees must maintain a schedule showing the contribution rates payable by the employer and members, and the due dates for payment. Contribution rates must be certified by the actuary. If the contributions schedule cannot be agreed between the trustees and the employer, the schedule must show the contribution rates decided by the trustees as adequate for MFR purposes. The trustees must notify OPRA and the scheme members of any unpaid contributions which will then be a debt on the employer. The minimum funding requirements will be replaced with 'scheme specific funding' for defined benefit schemes under new proposals set out in the Government publication, 'Working and saving for retirement: Action on occupational schemes', published in June 2003.

(7) Equal treatment – all schemes will be treated as if they have a rule providing for equal treatment between men and women relating to eligibility and scheme benefits (the latter relating to pensionable service from 17 May 1990). Sex-based factors, however, are permitted in calculating benefits in money purchase schemes and optional benefits in defined benefit scheme such as transfer values.

(8) Compensation scheme – a Pensions Compensation Board and scheme has been set up to cover schemes where the employer is insolvent and in the case of a defined benefits scheme, the value of the assets is less than 90 per cent of liabilities.

(9) Transfer values – the Act extended the right to receive a cash equivalent to those members whose pensionable service ended before 1 January 1986.

(10) Modification of schemes – any power to modify a pension scheme cannot be exercised if it would reduce or prejudice members' benefits and the members' consents have not been obtained.

(11) All occupational pension schemes, including money purchase, must provide pensions in payment which increase by 5 per cent per annum or RPI if lower, in respect of benefits arising from service after April 1997.

(12) A new scheme-based test (the 'reference test') replaced Guaranteed Minimum Pensions under contracted-out final salary schemes: the scheme must provide an accrual rate of at least $\frac{1}{80}$ of final average salary based on 90 per cent of band earnings for each year of

service after April 1997, and payable at a normal pension age of 65.

(13) The rebate payable under contracted-out money purchase schemes, and personal pension schemes, moved to an age-related basis from April 1997.

2.8.2 Welfare Reform and Pensions Act 1999

This wide-ranging piece of legislation covers, amongst other matters:

(1) the legal framework for stakeholder pension schemes;
(2) the extension of OPRA's role in relation to the registration and regulation of pension schemes;
(3) the removal of pension rights from the estate following personal bankruptcy;
(4) the introduction of an option to transfer pension credits from one spouse to another as part of a divorce settlement (pension sharing).

2.8.3 Child Support, Pensions and Social Security Act 2000

Most recently, this Act:

(1) sets out the base legislation for the new State Second Pension (S2P);
(2) changes the rules relating to the appointment of member-nominated trustees and directors;
(3) enhances the powers of the Pensions Ombudsman.

2.8.4 Income Tax (Earnings and Pensions) Act 2003

This Act came into force from 6 April 2003. The expression 'Schedule E', much used in pension law and practice, and throughout this book, will cease to exist and income and benefits previously assessed under Schedule E will be called 'employment income'.

2.9 PERSONAL PENSIONS AND STAKEHOLDER PENSIONS

The introduction of personal pensions in 1988 resulted in a considerable increase in pensions coverage, albeit at modest contribution levels. Around 6 million people have taken out personal pensions, of whom the vast majority are using these plans to contract out of S2P.

These plans can also take contributions from individuals (employed and self-employed) and from employers, as well as from the Government where the plans are used for contracting out.

Personal pensions are truly portable, with no employer control, although many employers are prepared to contribute to employees' personal pensions.

2.10 STAKEHOLDER PENSION SCHEMES

The introduction of stakeholder pensions schemes on 6 April 2001 (covered in detail in later chapters) has had an impact on the differences in approach to pensions for the employed and self-employed. Stakeholder pension schemes are a form of personal pension with restrictions on the levels and types of charges that the provider can deduct from the scheme. Stakeholder schemes, and personal pensions can be set up by individuals and by employers.

Schemes set up by employers are known as 'Chapter IV schemes'. The structure of these schemes is similar to that of traditional occupational pension schemes set up by employers in that they will be governed by a trust created by the employers and administered by trustees. However, in other respects these schemes will be the same as individual personal pension schemes. There are restrictions on the amount that may be contributed but no limits on the emerging benefits. Sometimes these schemes are known as 'DC tax regime schemes'.

Stakeholder pension schemes have been set up for employed affinity groups, for example individuals working in the same industry but for different employers. It is likely that similar schemes will be set up for self-employed affinity groups.

Alongside the employed and the self-employed is another group – the non-employed. Since 6 April 2001 it has been possible for people without earned income to contribute to a pension.

Stakeholder pensions are a form of personal pension where there is a limit of 1 per cent a year on the charges that the provider may deduct from the fund. Stakeholder pensions became available to individuals and to employers on 6 April 2001. Employers with five or more employees have to designate a stakeholder pension scheme if they do not already run an occupational pension scheme, or contribute to a group personal pension for employees. The vast majority of stakeholders schemes set up since 6 April 2001 are still 'shell schemes' – schemes that have been designated by employers to meet their employment obligations but without any employer contributions.

2.11 PART-TIME WORKERS

The European Court decided in *Fisscher v Voorhuis Hengelo* and *Vroege v NCIV* (see 2.7) that the exclusion of part-time workers from occupational pension schemes could constitute indirect sex discrimination in contravention of Article 119 of the Treaty of Rome (see also 2.7). The court held that this could relate back to 8 April 1976. Subsequently, many claims from part-time workers who had been excluded from occupational schemes were lodged at industrial tribunals to clarify various issues, particularly in relation to the time limits for bringing actions against employers.

An industrial tribunal, in December 1996, presiding over various test cases, decided that the time limits of the Equal Pay Act 1970 do apply to claims for access to pension schemes and therefore applications from part-timers should have been made within six months of the end of the employment giving rise to the claims. The industrial tribunal also stated that access to schemes retrospectively can only be ordered by the tribunal for the two years before the application was made.

In July 1996 the Employment Appeal Tribunal stated that the six months' time limit applies to all part-timers' claims. As a result the vast majority of claims from part-timers will be ineffective under the six-month rule. Claims for those cases which are valid will be restricted by the overall two-year limit.

In February 2001, the Law Lords handed down their judgment in the case of *Shirley Preston and Others v Wolverhampton Healthcare NHS Trust and Others*. Confirming the decision of the European Court in the previous year, the Lords confirmed that part-time employees are entitled to backdate claims to pension scheme membership to 8 April 1976, or the commencement of employment, if later. For a claim to succeed, however, it must have been lodged while the employee was still in the relevant employment, or within six months of leaving it.

2.12 MATERNITY LEAVE

The European Court of Justice in *Boyle v Equal Opportunities Commission* ruled that women are entitled to build up their full pension benefits during 14 weeks of maternity leave, and that employers are not allowed to restrict the period during which occupational pension rights accrue to the period of paid leave.

3

OCCUPATIONAL PENSION SCHEMES – INLAND REVENUE APPROVAL

3.1 INLAND REVENUE SAVINGS, PENSIONS, SHARE SCHEMES (IR-SPSS)

All pension schemes, to be tax effective, must be approved by the Inland Revenue. The United Kingdom is fortunate in the system of tax approval for pension schemes administered by the Inland Revenue in accordance with the broad discretionary powers conferred on it by the Income and Corporation Taxes Act 1988.

The IR-SPSS has built up a unique relationship with the pensions industry over many years and gives guidance and offers comment on proposals put to it by interested organisations.

Those aspects of pension schemes relating primarily to tax approval are regulated by a flexible code of practice, which can quickly accommodate changes in legislation and social custom, as well as react swiftly to counter tax avoidance. In recent years, however, the IR-SPSS has found it necessary to seek additional powers in the form of statutory regulation.

3.1.1 The purpose of approval

It is often forgotten by directors when drawing up their service agreements or contracts of employment that the mere promise of a pension constitutes a 'retirement benefits scheme' in the eyes of the Inland Revenue who will tax it as a benefit in kind in the hands of the director.

There are many directors who have service agreements which promise pension benefits but which have never been seen by the Inland Revenue and are potential tax traps: such agreements normally only come to light following a takeover or the merger of companies. These agreements will almost certainly be unapproved pension schemes requiring careful examination following FA 1989 (see Chapter 5).

One of the purposes of seeking approval from the IR-SPSS is to remove the liability for income tax from the employee. If the scheme is approved by the IR-SPSS as an exempt-approved scheme, further advantages flow from this. If the promise to provide retirement benefits is funded by means of an exempt approved pension scheme the employer can claim tax relief on the payment as a business expense. Exempt approval also enables the trustees of funded schemes to invest fund monies without liability to income tax or capital gains tax.

Following a change of practice in October 1991, the Inland Revenue now maintains that an *ex gratia* payment can also constitute a retirement benefit scheme where the payment is made on retirement. Although many genuine redundancy payments are free from tax as 'golden handshakes' (if they are up to £30,000 in value), other *ex gratia* benefits need to be restricted to the normal limits and formal approval obtained.

3.1.2 Conditions for approval

The basic conditions which must be met before the IR-SPSS approves a scheme as an exempt approved scheme are:

(1) That the scheme is established under irrevocable trusts for the sole purpose of providing relevant benefits in respect of service as an employee: 'relevant benefits' is defined in ICTA 1988, s 612(1) (see Appendix 4) in very wide terms, and covers any type of financial benefit given in connection with the termination of an employee's service with a particular employer, including termination by reason of death, with the sole exception of benefits receivable only in the event of death by accident or disablement by accident during (though not necessarily arising out of) service.

(2) That the scheme is recognised by the employer and employees to whom it relates and that every employee who is or who has a right to be a member of the scheme has been given written particulars of all essential features of the scheme which concern him (sometimes known as an 'announcement letter').

(3) That there is a person resident in the United Kingdom who is responsible for the discharge of all duties imposed on the scheme's administrator.

(4) That the employer is a contributor to the scheme. (Generally, the level of contribution must be at least 10 per cent of the total contribution to the scheme.)

(5) That the scheme is established in connection with some trade or undertaking carried on in the United Kingdom by a person resident in the United Kingdom.

(6) That in no circumstances, whether during the subsistence of the scheme or later, can any amount be paid by way of repayment of an employee's contributions under the scheme (although this condition may be overridden by preservation provisions).

(7) That any benefit for an employee is a pension on retirement at a specified age not earlier than 60 and not later than 75, which does not exceed ¹⁄₆₀ of the employee's final remuneration for each year of service up to a maximum of 40 years.

(8) That any benefit for any widow of an employee is a pension payable on his death after retirement such that the amount payable to the widow by way of pension does not exceed two-thirds of any pension or pensions payable to the employee.

(9) That no other benefits are payable under the scheme.

(10) That no pension is capable in whole or in part of surrender, commutation or assignment except so far as the scheme allows an employee on retirement to obtain by commutation of this pension, a lump sum or sums not exceeding in all ³⁄₈₀ of his final remuneration for each year of service up to a maximum of 40 years.

These are the primary conditions which, if met, entitle the scheme to all the tax advantages which approval can confer as of right and are contained in ICTA 1988, s 590 (see Appendix 4). Very few schemes, however, exist which do not infringe one or more of these primary conditions, and approval under s 590 is normally only sought in very limited circumstances such as where a scheme is to be set up for directors of investment companies (of which more is said in Chapter 18).

To cope with the vast majority of occupational pension schemes, the IR-SPSS relies on its discretionary powers which are extremely wide ranging and are set out in the Inland Revenue's Practice Notes on approval of Occupational Pension Schemes (IR 12 (2001)). Previous Practice Notes, IR 12 (1979) as amended, may continue to apply to schemes approved before 29 November 1991, although these may not necessarily be more advantageous. The Practice Notes have to be interpreted alongside separate Updates, and other notification of change of practice, published by the IR-SPSS.

In effect approval can be given to a scheme:

(1) which exceeds the limits imposed by the primary conditions as respects benefits for less than 40 years' service;

(2) which provides pensions for the widows or widowers of employees on death in service or for children or dependants of such employees;

(3) which provides, on death in service, a lump sum of up to four times the employee's final remuneration (exclusive of any refund of contributions);

(4) which allows benefits to be payable on retirement within ten years of the specified age, or on earlier incapacity;

(5) which provides for the return in certain contingencies of the employee's contributions;

(6) which relates to a trade or undertaking carried on only partly in the United Kingdom and by a person resident in the United Kingdom;

(7) which provides in certain contingencies for securing relevant benefits (but no other benefits) by means of an annuity contract approved by the Board and made with an insurance company of the employee's choice (ie a 'Section 32 annuity'); or

(8) to which the employer is not a contributor and which provides benefits additional to those provided by a scheme to which he is a contributor (ie a 'freestanding AVC').

The much wider benefits set out above are contained in ICTA 1988, s 591 (see Appendix 4).

The Inland Revenue has the power to withdraw approval at any time should it feel that the scheme is no longer meeting its requirements. The consequences of withdrawal of approval are penal since the contributions paid by the employers would be regarded as income in the hands of the members, tax relief on employees' contributions would be withdrawn, the fund itself would lose its tax exempt status and tax is charged at 40 per cent on an amount equal to the value of the assets immediately before the date of cessation of approval.

A scheme which meets all the other conditions of approval set out above but which is not established under irrevocable trust may be approved by the Inland Revenue, but not exempt approved. The effect of this is to avoid a charge to income tax on the employee or director, but none of the other tax advantages apply.

The Inland Revenue's proposals to simplify pensions contained in its consultation document, 'Simplifying the taxation of pensions: increasing choice and flexibility for all', will have a major impact on the approval process. The replacement of the current complex benefit structure set out in this paragraph with a lifetime limit on the value of a member's pension fund, and a limit on the annual inflow of value into the fund (£1.4 million and £200,000 respectively, in 2002 terms) will greatly simplify administration for the Inland Revenue, scheme administrators and pension providers.

3.2 TRUSTS

In order to obtain exempt approval, the scheme must be established under trust so that the pension scheme's assets are legally separated from those of the employer.

The employer establishes the trust, appoints the first trustees and lays down the conditions under which employees and their dependants will benefit.

3.2.1 Setting up the trust

For the purposes of approval a trust can be created in a number of ways, all of which are acceptable to the Inland Revenue.

Formal deed

This method is generally used for large group pension schemes and consists of a formal deed under which the employer creates a trust and appoints trustees giving them various powers of investment, and also adopts formal rules. Often the trust is established by an interim deed and is followed by a definitive deed at a later stage.

Declaration of trust

This is similar to, though much shorter than, a formal deed, and is normally used in connection with discretionary individual pension arrangements, for example executive pension plans, where benefits are to be provided by an insurance company.

Board resolution

Providing a company's memorandum and articles of association permit it, the Board of Directors may pass a board resolution which has the effect of creating a trust.

Employer trust

Sometimes a trust is created by an exchange of letters between the employer and the employee who is to benefit from the pension scheme. This is only used for individual pension arrangements where the scheme is being established for one employee or director.

The legislation requires the appointment of a UK resident person as scheme administrator who is liable for tax matters relating to the scheme. It is usual to appoint the scheme trustee(s) as administrator. The scheme's actual day-to-day administration is normally carried on by either an in-house office with the assistance of external advisors or, where the scheme is insured, by the insurance company.

3.3 HOW TO OBTAIN INLAND REVENUE APPROVAL

Applications for approval to schemes must be sent in writing to the IR-SPSS within at least six months from the scheme's establishment, possibly longer, depending on the date of establishment, as follows:

Date scheme established		*Date by which application must be received by IR-SPSS*	
In the 6 months ending	5 October	By the following	5 April
In the month ending	5 November	By the following	5 May
	5 December		5 June
	5 January		5 July
	5 February		5 August
	5 March		5 September
	5 April		5 October

Subject to provisions for spreading tax relief forward (see Chapter 7) employer's contributions are relieved for tax purposes in the accounting year in which they are paid.

The application for approval must be accompanied by the appropriate forms. There are three types of form prescribed by the IR-SPSS: one for the schemes open to more than one employee; one for individual arrangements; and one for 'Hancock annuities'.

Standard forms must be completed fully and accurately otherwise they will not be treated as valid applications for approval. The following information is included in the forms, but is not exhaustive.

(1) The employer's full name, address and registered number.
(2) The employer's status, eg limited company, partnership, sole trader.
(3) The nature of the employer's business.
(4) The name of the scheme.
(5) The tax districts dealing with the employer's PAYE and corporation tax and the employer's reference numbers in those districts.
(6) A copy of the document establishing the scheme, for example the trust deed, exchange of letters or declaration of trust if not already agreed as standard.
(7) A copy of the letter to employees describing the scheme's main features.
(8) The scheme's commencement date.
(9) Where appropriate (eg in the case of small self-administered schemes) actuarial reports concerning the scheme's funding.
(10) Details of any existing schemes and their interaction with the new scheme which has been set up.
(11) The name and address of the administrator and trustee.

(12) Details of the person or persons who will be responsible for paying pensions. This is normally the trustees but in insured schemes the insurance company often pays pensions as agent for the administrator.
(13) The employer's financial year end.
(14) The number of members.
(15) The amount of ordinary annual contributions and date of first payment.
(16) The method of funding, for example insured or self-administered, together with full details of the employer's ordinary annual contributions and any special contributions to any other schemes.
(17) The names of any directors joining the scheme who either on his own or with one or more associates beneficially owns or is able to control directly or indirectly or through other companies 20 per cent or more of the ordinary share capital of the company.
(18) Details of controlling directors including national insurance number, current pensionable earnings and whether they have retained benefits.

3.4 TAX RELIEF FOLLOWING INLAND REVENUE APPROVAL

The Inland Revenue does not authorise provisional income tax relief on members' personal contributions until they have received the above items. Most insurance companies have agreed standard documents with the Inland Revenue so that approval is normally a matter of waiting for the Inland Revenue to rubber stamp the documents.

After receipt of confirmation of the scheme's approval from the IR-SPSS it is the responsibility of the employer(s) or their agents to forward a copy to the appropriate tax district to support the initial claim for relief in respect of an employer's pension scheme contribution. This procedure ensures that tax inspectors have evidence of the entitlement to relief before them at a time a participating employer's accounts are examined for Schedule D or corporation tax liability.

If employees are contributing towards the cost of the pension scheme, they receive tax relief under PAYE: this means, for example, that if an employee's salary amounts to £800 per month and is proposing to pay £50 per month to the pension scheme the employer calculates tax by applying the employee's PAYE code to £750. This is known as the 'net pay arrangement' but an employer should not operate this until the local inspector has been notified that provisional tax relief has been allowed.

Until formal approval is granted no relief can be given on the employer's contributions, nor can tax suffered on investments be repaid. If approval is not granted from the commencement of the scheme relief will not be allowed in respect of contributions made by employees prior to the date of approval and any provisional tax relief will be withdrawn. The employer's contribution to the scheme prior to approval will be assessed on the employees. Relief in respect of income and gains to the scheme will not be allowed.

3.5 SIMPLIFIED DEFINED CONTRIBUTION SCHEMES (SDCSs)

SDCSs were launched by the government in 1987 and were intended to provide an occupational scheme for employees without the usual complexity involving funding and aggregate limits on emerging benefits. SDCS limits on both contributions and benefits resemble those applicable to personal pensions.

Employers, however, found SDCSs unattractive in comparison to grouped personal pension schemes. Also, the facility both to establish and convert an existing occupational pension scheme on a stakeholder basis renders SDCSs effectively redundant.

Accordingly, with effect from 1 April 2001 the Inland Revenue ceased to consider new applications for approval of SDCSs.

3.6 UNAPPROVED SCHEMES

Since the introduction of the limit on the benefits which can emerge from new occupational pension schemes there has been increasing interest in unapproved schemes. These are not subject to Inland Revenue limits; for example an employer could provide a pension equal to an employer's retiring salary.

Under the current legislation however, the major drawback is the choice forced on the employee between an immediate charge to income tax and national insurance on employer contributions (treated as a taxable benefit in kind) and an unsecured benefit (if the arrangement is unfunded). (Full details are contained in Chapter 5.)

These arrangements may be either funded (in which case the employer contributions attract a Schedule E charge payable by the member) or unfunded (in which case the payment of the benefit will be tied closely to the financial position of the employer several years hence).

4

MAXIMUM PERMITTED BENEFITS

This chapter looks at the maximum levels of benefits which the Inland Revenue will approve for an employee including the considerable changes brought about by F(No 2)A 1987 and FA 1989. The restrictions which apply to company directors are contained in Chapter 6.

This chapter also sets out the current position on maximum benefits under occupational schemes. However, as will be seen from Chapter 1 the rules on maximum benefits are set to change significantly from 6 April 2005 assuming that the Government's proposals as set out in the Inland Revenue's consultation document, 'Simplifying the taxation of pensions: increasing choice and flexibility for all', become law. However, the current complex rules will continue until that date. After that date a new tax regime will apply replacing the current rules, not sitting alongside them.

4.1 WHO CAN QUALIFY?

Any person who is an employee of an employer and therefore liable to pay tax under Schedule E may be provided with retirement and death benefits under an approved retirement benefit scheme. The term 'employee' includes:

(1) directors, whether controlling or not, whose income is assessable under Schedule E;
(2) part-time or temporary employees;
(3) genuinely employed spouses of professional persons such as accountants, solicitors, doctors and dentists;
(4) genuinely employed spouses of the self-employed;
(5) salaried, not equity, partners in a partnership;
(6) UK-resident employees of overseas employers;
(7) domestic servants.

4.2 WHO CANNOT QUALIFY?

It is not possible to provide benefits under an approved retirement benefit scheme for anyone whose income is assessable under Schedule D, for example:

(1) self-employed persons, whether sole proprietors or equity partners;
(2) consultants whose only source of income is assessable under Schedule D;
(3) directors of an investment company, although they are often entitled to receive low levels of Schedule E income from the company (see Chapter 18).

The categories listed above may, however, pay contributions to personal pension schemes (see Chapter 14).

4.3 RESTRICTIONS ON BENEFITS

By the mid-1980s there was concern in Treasury circles about the abuse of pension schemes by high-earning individuals. In March 1987 the Chancellor of the Exchequer, Nigel Lawson, caught the pensions industry by surprise by including a number of measures in his Budget which restricted, in particular, the commutation of pensions for cash lump sums. Two years later, in March 1989, further restrictive measures were announced, most importantly the cap on the level of earnings that could be pensioned, set initially at £60,000. The earnings cap in the tax year 2003/04 is £99,000.

Membership categories

In broad terms the maximum benefits that may be provided depend on the date of joining the scheme, which categorises membership as follows.

4.3.1 Pre-1987 members

Pre-1987 benefits may be provided under schemes which were established before 17 March 1987 for members who joined before that date.

4.3.2 1987–89 members

1987–89 benefits may be provided under schemes which were established before 14 March 1989 for members who joined on or after 17 March 1987 and before 1 June 1989.

4.3.3 Post-1989 members

Post-1989 benefits may be provided for members joining schemes from 1 June 1989, regardless of when the scheme was established and also for members who joined, before 1 June 1989, schemes established on or after 14 March 1989.

In general terms each category is subject to more restrictions on the benefits which may be provided than its predecessor: pre-1987 pension benefits are better than 1987–89 pension benefits which in turn are better than post-1989 pension benefits. However, it is possible to opt for post-1989 benefits where the result would be beneficial in certain circumstances, for example where enhanced early retirement benefits are required.

The benefits relating to the three categories are described later in this chapter.

4.3.4 Maximum funding

Inland Revenue concern about over-funding of money purchase schemes resulted in the imposition of age-related contribution limits, at first on insured schemes from 1 September 1994, and then on small self-administered schemes from 1 June 1996. These contribution limits, based on assumptions which are more stringent than hitherto, have the effect of reducing funding rates, particularly at the lower end of the age scale. Accordingly, money purchase schemes are limited both in relation to contributions and emerging benefits.

4.4 RETIREMENT AGES

To obtain Inland Revenue approval of scheme membership it is necessary to stipulate a normal retirement age, which should be the best estimate of an employee's retiring age.

Under schemes approved on or after 29 November 1991, the permitted age range for both men and women is normally 60 to 75, although an earlier or later normal retirement age is possible in individual cases at the Inland Revenue's discretion, for example in the case of a member who joins the scheme as a post-1989 member with the right to benefits on a pre-1987 basis.

Under schemes approved before 29 November 1991, post-1989 members of either sex are restricted to the age range 60 to 75. However, the permitted ranges for pre-1987 and 1987–89 members are 60 to 70 for men and 55 to 70 for women (subject to the special restrictions for controlling directors – see Chapter 6). Where it can be demonstrated that such a member is likely to continue working beyond age 70 it is possible to obtain approval of a later normal retirement age.

The Government has stated that state pension age will remain at age 65. However, scheme members will have greater flexibility over retirement and the taking of benefits from their occupational pension schemes. The earliest age from which a pension may be taken (under an occupational or personal pension scheme) is being increased from 50 to 55 by 2010 (including existing schemes with retirement ages at or below age 50).

4.5 MAXIMUM BENEFITS

The maximum benefits available to an employee or director from a pension scheme normally depend on his years of service with the employer and his salary at or around retirement. Generally, the maximum pension which an employee can receive at his normal retirement date under Inland Revenue rules is two-thirds of his final salary ('final salary' is explained below), of which he may be able to commute up to a maximum of 1.5 times final salary for a lump sum.

There is, however, a distinction between what the Inland Revenue permits and what a particular pension scheme might provide: even if the pension fund has accumulated substantial amounts it is not possible to provide retirement benefits in excess of Inland Revenue limits. Conversely a pension scheme may provide benefits well below the maximum permitted by the Inland Revenue.

In the case of a post-1989 member who is a controlling director (see Chapter 6) and who retired on or after 31 August 1991, the Inland Revenue also requires that the limits described below apply to the *aggregate* of the member's occupational scheme benefits and those derived from retirement annuity contract/personal pension schemes relating to earnings with the same employer.

4.6 MAXIMUM PENSION

4.6.1 60ths scale

The Inland Revenue will always permit a pension benefit of up to $\frac{1}{60}$ of final salary for each year of service (this is known as the '60ths scale' or 'straight 60ths') so that a maximum pension of two-thirds of final salary is obtained only after completing 40 years' service with the employer – an unlikely event for most people. If the period of service is less than 40 years the pension on retirement is calculated by multiplying the number of years of service with the employer by $\frac{1}{60}$ of final salary.

Example 4.1

An employee retires after 27 years' service with his employer: his final salary is £20,000: the rules of the group pension scheme provide for a pension of $\frac{1}{60}$ of final salary for each year of service: his retirement pension from the scheme will therefore be £9,000:

$$\frac{27}{60} \times £20,000 = £9,000 \text{ pa}$$

Very few employees and directors will complete 40 years' service with the same employer. It is still possible, however, for them to receive the maximum pension of two-thirds of final salary under an enhanced accrual rate (if permitted by the rules of the scheme) depending on their category of membership.

4.6.2 Uplifted 60ths scale (pre-1987 members)

Under this scale the two-thirds maximum is permitted if at least ten years' service has been completed with the employer at normal retirement date. Provided at least five years' service can be completed with an employer, higher benefits can be provided than under the straight 60ths scale.

The following table shows how pension entitlement can be accelerated.

Table 4.1

Years of service normal retirement age	Maximum pension as a fraction of final salary
1–5	1/60th for each year
6	8/60
7	16/60
8	24/60
9	32/60
10 or more	40/60

Example 4.2

An employee retires after eight years' service with his company. His final salary is £28,000. The rules of the pension scheme provide for a pension calculated on the uplifted 60ths scale.

His retirement pension from the scheme will therefore be £11,200, calculated as follows:

$$^{24}\!/_{60} \times £28,000 = £11,200 \text{ pa}$$

If, as is usually the case, the period of service includes a part of a year, the uplifted 60ths scale is increased proportionately to reflect the service in the last year.

Example 4.3

The employee in the previous example retires after seven years and six months. His retirement pension from the scheme will be calculated as follows:

Number of 60ths after eight years	24
Number of 60ths after seven years	16
Increase obtained during twelve months	8
Increase obtained during six months	4
Number of 60ths after seven years and six months	16 + 4 = 20
Pension $^{20}\!/_{60} \times £28,000 = £9,333$ pa	

In arriving at the maximum pension obtainable on the 'uplifted 60ths scale', it is necessary to include a restriction to take account of additional pensions arising from any voluntary contributions and any 'retained benefits' (see below).

4.6.3 Accelerated scale (1987–89 members and post-1989 members)

In respect of members joining schemes on or after 17 March 1987 or where a new scheme was established on or after that date, the maximum pension is one-thirtieth of final salary for each year of service. The two-thirds maximum is therefore permitted only on completion of at least 20 years' service with the employer at normal retirement date (compared with ten under the uplifted 60ths scale).

Thus, the pension on the new accelerated scale is better than the maximum pension set out in Table 4.1 where the years of service to normal retirement age are seven or less. Where the years of service to normal retirement age are greater than seven the old uplifted 60ths scale is significantly better.

The following is a comparison of the two scales:

Table 4.2

	Pre-1987 members		1987–89 members and post-1989 members	
Years of service	Fraction of final salary	Percentage of final salary	Fraction of final salary	Percentage of final salary
1	1/60	1.66	2/60	3.33
2	2/60	3.33	4/60	6.66
3	3/60	5.00	6/60	10.00
4	4/60	6.66	8/60	13.33
5	5/60	8.33	10/60	16.66
6	8/60	13.33	12/60	20.00
7	16/60	26.66	14/60	23.33
8	24/60	40.00	16/60	26.66
9	32/60	53.33	18/60	30.00
10	40/60	66.66	20/60	33.30
11	40/60	66.66	22/60	36.60
12	40/60	66.66	24/60	40.00
13	40/60	66.66	26/60	43.33
14	40/60	66.66	28/60	46.66
15	40/60	66.66	30/60	50.00
16	40/60	66.66	32/60	53.33
17	40/60	66.66	34/60	56.66
18	40/60	66.66	36/60	60.00
19	40/60	66.66	38/60	63.30
20	40/60	66.66	40/60	66.66

4.7 DEFINITIONS OF 'FINAL SALARY'

The bases for calculating final salary permitted by the Inland Revenue are as follows:

(1) Remuneration (on which Schedule E income tax liability has been assessed as final and conclusive) for any one of the five years preceding the normal retirement date: remuneration includes basic salary for the year in question together with the average of fluctuating emoluments, such as bonus or commission, earned over a period of at least three consecutive years ending in the year in question.

(2) The annual average of total earnings (on which Schedule E income tax liability has been assessed as final and conclusive) over a period of at least three consecutive years ending not earlier than ten years before normal retirement date.

In the case of a controlling director, however, only definition (2) is acceptable.

'Fluctuating emoluments' means any earnings not paid on a fixed basis which are additional to basic wage or salary and, depending on the rules of the scheme, can include:

(a) profit related pay (whether or not taxable);
(b) overtime, commission, bonuses assessable to income tax under Schedule E;
(c) benefits in kind which are assessable to income tax under Schedule E such as company car, company paid petrol, rent-free accommodation.

Where fluctuating emoluments have been paid for less than three years they should (when calculating final salary in accordance with definition (2) above) be averaged over the period starting with the date they commenced or, if later, the beginning of the three-year period and ending on the last day of the basic salary year in question. Inland Revenue permission must, however, be sought if it is intended to include a fluctuating emolument paid only once.

The F(No 2)A 1987 and FA 1989 brought about changes to the definition of 'final salary'. The changes apply to all members of occupational schemes, as follows:

(1) Income or gains from the acquisition or disposal of shares or interests in shares or options over shares acquired through share option, share incentive and profit sharing schemes, or from shares which give rise to a Schedule E tax liability, are excluded from the calculation of 'final salary'. However this exclusion does not apply:
  (a) where the shares or the option or other interest in shares which give rise, on or after 17 March 1987, to a Schedule E tax liability were acquired or granted before that date; or
  (b) where 'final salary' is determined for calculating maximum benefits on death in service (see below).
(2) Also excluded from 'final salary' is anything in respect of which tax is chargeable by virtue of ICTA 1988, s 148 (payments on termination of employment, for example golden handshakes) except where final salary is being used to calculate maximum benefits on death in service.
(3) In the case of a pre-1987 or 1987–89 member, if the 'final salary' calculated in accordance with definition (1) exceeds £100,000 (or such other figure as may be prescribed by the Treasury) in any year from 6 April 1987 onwards, actual 'final salary' must be restricted to the amount calculated in accordance with definition (2) or, if greater, £100,000.
(4) In the case of a post-1989 member, 'final salary' under either definition is restricted to a maximum of £99,000 (for the 2003/04 tax

year). It is intended that this maximum will be adjusted annually in line with increases in the RPI (measured from September to September) and rounded up to the next highest multiple of £600. A member who is subject to this upper limit may therefore be provided with a maximum pension of £66,000 per annum on normal retirement in the 2003/04 tax year.

(5) Final remuneration may now also include:

    (a) remuneration received after termination of employment or retirement but on which the tax liability has been determined, provided that it was earned prior to termination and is treated as a fluctuating emolument;

    (b) remuneration assessable to tax under Schedule E but on which the tax liability has not yet been determined, provided that final remuneration is recalculated once the tax liability has been determined, but only for calculating immediate benefits.

4.8 DYNAMISED OR INDEXED FINAL REMUNERATION

Final salary may be recalculated as a notional figure known as dynamised final remuneration or indexed final remuneration by increasing the actual salary earned in a particular year by the increase in the RPI between the end of the year in question and normal retirement date. The result is to produce a pension which is related to the salary which an employee would have received if his previous years' salaries had kept pace with the cost of living. Dynamisation, however:

(1) may not be used to increase the tax-free lump sum (see below) payable to a pre-1987 member unless the pension is increased to the same proportionate extent – that is dynamisation must be justified by the increase to the overall entitlement to benefits;

(2) may not cause the final salary of a 1987–89 member used to calculate the tax-free lump sum to exceed £100,000 (or such other figure as may be prescribed by the Treasury although in 2003/04 the figure of £100,000 still stands);

(3) may not be used to increase the final salary of a post-1989 member beyond the value of the 'earnings cap' as at the date of retirement.

4.9 RETAINED PENSION BENEFITS

Depending on the context in which maximum permitted benefits under the current employer's scheme are being calculated, retained benefits can include:

(1) Deferred pensions and pensions in payment, in respect of previous employment, from:
  (a) any UK scheme which is approved or seeking approval, including any free standing additional voluntary scheme;
  (b) any statutory scheme (eg the Teacher's Superannuation Scheme);
  (c) any overseas scheme which the Inland Revenue regards as approved for UK tax relief purposes.
(2) The annuity equivalent of lump sums received or receivable from previous pension schemes defined under (1) above.
(3) Pensions and/or the annuity equivalent of lump sums arising from personal pension schemes or retirement annuity contracts relating to service with the same or a former employer, or to previous self-employment.
(4) Benefits relating to transfer payments from overseas schemes made to any of the arrangements defined in (1), (2) or (3) above.
(5) Funds to which s 608 of ICTA 1988 (see Appendix 4) applies (ie 'Old Code' funds).
(6) Benefits arising from transfer payments received by the current employer's scheme.

Benefits which would otherwise have to be taken into account may however be disregarded as retained benefits in the following circumstances:

(1) If the member retires and
  (a) his earnings in the first year of membership of the scheme do not exceed one-quarter of the earnings cap in force at the date of entry (for the 2003/04 tax year £99,000 ÷ 4 = £24,750), and
  (b) he is not, and has not been in the ten years prior to joining the scheme, a controlling director in respect of the employment being pensioned,
  although if the member is or was a member of more than one scheme of the employer it is the date of entry to the first of those schemes which determines if the exemption applies, so that there is no exemption if the member joined the first scheme before 31 August 1991.
(2) Where the benefits in question relate to a wholly concurrent employment/occupation.
(3) If the total retained benefits are equivalent to or less than a pension of £260 per annum.
(4) Where the benefits relate to a transfer value received from an occupational pension scheme of the same employer.

Effect of retained pension benefits on maximum benefits

If a member's benefits are calculated on the 'straight' 60ths scale it is not in any event necessary to take retained benefits into account, *unless* that member is a controlling director in which case:

(1) If the controlling director is:
    (a) a pre-1987 member; or
    (b) a 1987–89 member; or
    (c) a post-1989 member who retired before 31 August 1991;
    the value of all personal pension scheme/retirement annuity contract benefits has to be deducted from the straight 60ths scale benefits in order to arrive at the occupational scheme maximum.

(2) If the controlling director is a post-1989 member who retires on or after 31 August 1991, the value of personal pension scheme/retirement annuity contract benefits are required to be taken into account by treating such benefits which relate to earnings from the same employer as if they were benefits which had been provided by the occupational scheme (other retained personal pension scheme/retirement annuity contract benefits relating to previous employment can be ignored).

Whenever pension benefits are to be provided on the pre-1987 member 'uplifted 60ths' scale or 1987–89/post-1989 member accelerated scale, the sum of the member's retained benefits and pension benefits from his current employment must not exceed two-thirds of his final salary. In this context the pension benefit of a post-1989 controlling director member from his current employment is the aggregate of that payable from the occupational scheme and from personal pension schemes/retirement annuity contracts relating to earnings from the same employer.

4.10 PENSION INCREASES (ESCALATION)

Pensions which have been paid to a retired employee or to his dependants may be increased to reflect increases in the RPI since retirement or up to the level of the maximum approvable pension payable on retirement and then subsequently increased in line with the RPI.

Example 4.4

An employee retires from the company on a final salary of £15,000 but receives only £4,000 from his pension scheme. It would be possible for his employer subsequently to increase his pension up to £10,000, ie two-thirds of his final salary (assuming that he had completed at least 20 years' service with the employer) with subsequent RPI increases on the pension of £10,000.

For members who retired before 31 August 1991, the maximum approvable pension at retirement includes any amount commuted for a lump sum. On retirement on or after 31 August 1991, however, the pension cannot be increased beyond the maximum residual pension as at the date of retirement, ie after deducting the annuity equivalent of any lump sum and any spouse's/dependant's pension provided by surrender of the member's pension from the maximum approvable before either or both of those events. The maximum residual may be subsequently increased in line with the RPI.

After 6 April 1997, the provisions of the Pensions Act 1995 require schemes to increase pensions by at least the lower of 5 per cent per annum or the increase in the RPI (known as Limited Price Indexation (LPI)). In its Action Plan on occupational pensions, published in June 2003, the Government signalled its intention to reduce the cap on mandatory indexation from 5 per cent to 2.5 per cent a year.

4.11 CASH LUMP SUMS

4.11.1 80ths scale

Most pension schemes allow an employee to give up part of his pension on retirement for a tax-free cash lump sum. Even if income is of paramount importance the tax-free lump sum should still be taken and then if necessary converted into an income which would be taxed more favourably (see Chapter 19).

The maximum tax-free lump sum that can be provided for an employee is 1.5 times his final salary after completing 40 years' service at normal retirement date: this represents three-eightieths of his final salary for each year of service.

Example 4.5

> If an employee retires after 27 years' service with his employer on a salary of £20,000, and his pension scheme provides that part of his pension may be given up for a tax-free cash sum of three-eighths of his final salary for each year of service, his lump sum will therefore be £20,250.

14.11.2 Uplifted 80ths scale for pre-1987 members

Under Inland Revenue limits pre-1987 members can obtain the maximum lump sum after 20 years' service with the same employer if the pension scheme provides lump sum benefits at an enhanced accrual rate known as the 'uplifted 80ths' scale. There is no advantage in using this scale unless the employee has achieved eight years' service before normal retirement age because the accrual rate is the same as the '80ths' scale, ie $3/80$ of final salary per year of service. Thereafter the lump sum accrual rate increases progressively until a lump sum of $1/128$ of final salary is obtained after 20 or more years' service.

Table 4.3

Years of service to normal retirement age	Maximum lump sum as a fraction of final salary
1–8	3/80ths for each year
9	30/80
10	36/80
11	42/80
12	48/80
13	54/80
14	63/80
15	72/80
16	81/80
17	90/80
18	99/80
19	108/80
20 or more	120/80

Example 4.6

An employee retires after 15 years' service with his employer. His final salary is £18,000. The rules of the pension scheme provide for a tax-free lump sum calculated on the uplifted 80ths scale.

His tax-free lump sum from the scheme will therefore be £16,200, calculated as follows: $72/80 \times £18,000 = £16,200$.

If, as is usually the case, the period of service includes a part of a year, the uplifted 80ths scale is interpolated to reflect the service in the last year but the result must be a whole eightieth.

4.11.3 Accelerated scale (1987–89 members)

It is not possible for a 1987–89 member to be provided with a tax-free lump sum on the uplifted 80ths scale in isolation, although a lump sum on the 80ths scale is always permitted (ie $3/80$ of final salary for each year of service) regardless of the amount, if any, of pension benefit.

Even where the occupational scheme provides for both pension and tax-free lump sum it is only possible to provide the maximum lump sum cash on the uplifted 80ths scale if the scheme provides the maximum approvable pension benefits on the accelerated scale for pensions, ie $\frac{1}{30}$ of final salary for each year of service. However, where the pension provided is between $\frac{1}{60}$ and $\frac{1}{30}$ of final salary for each year of service an enhanced cash lump sum may be payable. The formula and examples are shown below.

In calculating the maximum tax-free lump sum, final salary is still capped at a figure of £100,000 (although this may be increased by Treasury Order). For an individual who could complete 20 years' service by retirement and whose scheme provides him with a maximum approvable pension, his tax-free lump sum will be limited to £150,000 even though his final salary might be, say, £200,000.

The formula for calculating the amounts of tax-free cash on the new accelerated scale is as follows:

Formula

Step 1

$$\frac{\text{Actual pension} - \text{basic pension (on 60ths scale)}}{\text{maximum pension (30ths scale)} - \text{basic pension (60ths scale)}}$$

$$= \%$$

Step 2 Maximum Tax-Free Cash – basic Tax-Free Cash × % in Step 1 above.

Step 3 Add result of Step 2 to basic Tax-Free Cash = Total Tax-Free Cash permitted

Example 4.7

Service 20 years
Final Salary £30,000
Actual Pension Provided £19,000 pa

Actual pension			=	£19,000
Basic pension ($\frac{1}{60}$ scale)	=	$\frac{20}{60} \times$ FS	=	£10,000
Maximum pension	=	$\frac{40}{60} \times$ FS	=	£20,000
Basic cash ($\frac{3}{80}$ scale)	=	$\frac{60}{80} \times$ FS	=	£22,500
Maximum cash	=	$1\frac{1}{2} \times$ FS	=	£45,000

(a) $\dfrac{19,000 - 10,000}{20,000 - 10,000}$ $=$ $\dfrac{9,000}{10,000}$ $=$ 90%

(b) $45,000 - 22,500$ $=$ $22,500 \times 90\%$ = £20,250

(c) $22,500 + 20,250$ $=$ £42,750 = Tax-Free Cash permitted

45

Example 4.8

Service 15 years
Final Salary £30,000
Actual Pension Provided £10,000 pa

Actual pension			=	£10,000
Basic pension ($\frac{1}{60}$)	=	$\frac{15}{60} \times FS$	=	£ 7,500
Maximum pension	=	$\frac{30}{60} \times FS$	=	£15,000
Basic cash ($\frac{3}{80}$)	=	$\frac{45}{80} \times FS$	=	£16,875
Maximum cash	=	$90\% \times FS$	=	£27,000

(a) $\dfrac{10,000 - 7,500}{15,000 - 7,500}$ $=$ $\dfrac{2,500}{7,500}$ $=$ $33\frac{1}{3}\%$

(b) $27,000 - 16,875$ $=$ $10,125 \times 33\frac{1}{3}\%$ $=$ £3,375

(c) $16,875 + 3,375$ $=$ £20,250 = Tax-Free Cash permitted

Example 4.9

Service 18 years
Final Salary £75,000
Actual Pension Provided £40,000 pa

Actual pension			=	£40,000
Basic pension	=	$\frac{18}{60} \times FS$	=	£22,500
Maximum pension	=	$\frac{36}{60} \times FS$	=	£45,000
Basic cash	=	$\frac{54}{80} \times FS$	=	£50,625
Maximum cash	=	$123.75\% \times FS$ =		£92,812

(a) $\dfrac{40,000 - 22,500}{45,000 - 22,500}$ $=$ $\dfrac{17,500}{22,500}$ $=$ 77.77%

(b) $92,812 - 50,625$ $=$ $42,187 \times 77.77\%$ $=$ £32,808

(c) $50,625 + 32,808$ $=$ £83,433 = Tax-Free Cash permitted

Example 4.10

Service 15 years
Final Salary £200,000
Actual Pension Provided £90,000 pa

Actual pension			=	£ 90,000
Basic pension	=	$\frac{15}{60} \times FS$	=	£ 50,000
Maximum pension	=	$\frac{30}{60} \times FS$	=	£100,000
Basic cash	=	$\frac{45}{80} \times £100,000$	=	£ 56,250
Maximum cash	=	$90\% \times £100,000$	=	£ 90,000

(a) $\dfrac{90,000 - 50,000}{100,000 - 50,000}$ $=$ $\dfrac{40,000}{50,000}$ $=$ 80%

(b) $90,000 - 56,250$ $=$ $33,750 \times 80\%$ $=$ £27,000

(c) $56,250 + 27,000$ $=$ £83,250 = Tax-Free Cash permitted

4.11.4 Scale for post-1989 members

The maximum lump sum is the greater of $\frac{3}{80}$ of final salary (capped at £99,000 in 2003/04) for each year of service and the pension multiplied by 2.25: 'Pension' is the amount before commutation or any reduction in favour of widows/dependants and is calculated on the basis on which it will actually be paid, for example in monthly instalments, increasing in payment at 5 per cent per annum compound.

In the case of a controlling director who retires on or after 31 August 1991 it is also required that the $\frac{3}{80}$ limit applies to the aggregate benefit payable from the occupational scheme and any personal pension scheme/retirement annuity contract relating to earnings from the same employer. Similarly such benefits are aggregated for the purposes of the '2.25 × ' calculation.

4.12 RETAINED LUMP SUM BENEFITS

The retained lump sum benefits which it might be necessary to take into account are those arising from the arrangements described under retained pension benefits above, as are the circumstances in which retained lump sums may be disregarded.

If a member's benefits are calculated on the $\frac{3}{80}$ scale it is not necessary to take retained benefits into account, unless that member is a controlling director in which case:

(1) If the controlling director is:
    (a) a pre-1987 member, or
    (b) a 1987–89 member, or
    (c) a post-1989 member who retired before 31 August 1991,
    the $\frac{3}{80}$ scale benefits cannot exceed a maximum of 1.5 × final salary minus the value of all personal pension schemes/retirement annuity contract retained benefits.
(2) If the controlling director is a post-1989 member who retires on or after 31 August 1991, the value of personal pension scheme/retirement annuity contract benefits is required to be taken into account by treating such benefits which relate to earnings from the same employer as if they were benefits provided by the occupational scheme (other retained personal pension scheme/retirement annuity contract benefits relating to previous employment can be ignored).

Where the date of retirement is before 31 August 1991 and lump sum benefit is to be provided for a pre-1987 or 1987–89 member on the 'uplifted 80ths' scale or is to be enhanced in the case of a post-1989 member, the sum of the member's retained benefits and lump sum benefits from his current employment must not exceed 1.5 × final salary. On retirement on or after 31 August 1991, however:

(1) Retained benefits of any 1987–89 non-controlling director can be disregarded in calculating benefit on the 'uplifted 80ths' scale.

(2) The 'uplifted 80ths' scale benefit for a 1987–89 controlling director is subject to a maximum of 1.5 × final salary minus retained benefits from personal pension schemes/retirement annuity contracts *only*.

(3) All retained benefits of any post-1989 member can be disregarded.

The lump sum benefit of a post-1989 controlling director, who retires on or after 31 August 1991, from his current employment is in any event the aggregate of that payable from the occupational scheme and from personal pension schemes/retirement annuity contracts relating to earnings from the same employer.

4.13 PENSION VALUES OF LUMP SUMS

If a lump sum is taken under a pension scheme, any pension benefit to which the employee would be otherwise entitled is reduced. For pre-1987 and 1987–89 members and post-1989 members retiring before 31 August 1991, the amount by which the member's pension is reduced depends on the member's age at retirement; the following table of factors was agreed between the Inland Revenue, the Association of British Insurers and the Association of Consulting Actuaries.

Table 4.4

	Age	Factor
Men	60	10.2
	65	9.0
	70	7.8
Women	55	12.2
	60	11.0
	65	9.8

Factors for intermediate ages are calculated by an increase or decrease of 0.02 per month of age difference.

The amount by which a pension reduces is obtained by dividing the factor into the cash available. For example, a male employee retiring at age 65 and accepting a tax-free lump sum of £18,000 will have his pension reduced by £2,000 per annum.

Where pensions increase at a greater rate than 5 per cent per annum compound, the Inland Revenue insists that different factors are used to reflect this. Thus, if a pension increases at, say, 8.5 per cent per annum compound automatically, the factor used for commutation purposes must incorporate an interest yield assumption of at least 11.5 per cent. In other words, the difference between the rate of increase in the pension and the yield assumed on investments must be 3 per cent at least.

Trustees of pension schemes are not bound by any of these factors and may use less generous ones reflecting economic conditions from time to time. Insurance companies may agree tables of commutation factors with the Inland Revenue.

However for post-1989 members retiring on or after 31 August 1991 the commutation factor which must be used in calculating Inland Revenue limits is a unisex 12:1 regardless of escalation.

It is sometimes difficult for a retiring employee to decide whether he should take a tax-free lump sum or opt for a pension which will increase in payment. Chapter 19 deals with some of the considerations which should influence his decision.

4.14 DEATH BENEFITS

4.14.1 Benefits on death after retirement

A pension can be provided for the widow or dependants of a former employee who dies in retirement. The maximum amount is two-thirds of the maximum approvable pension which could have been provided for the employee himself ignoring his retained benefits from earlier occupations. As the maximum will normally be two-thirds of the employee's final salary, the widow or dependant's maximum pension is two-thirds of two-thirds of the employee's final salary (four-ninths).

If the member retired before 31 August 1991 then any widow's/ dependant's pension payable from the arrangements described under retained pension benefits above must be deducted from the four-ninths maximum.

Whether or not retained benefits have to be taken into account, the widow's/dependant's maximum may be increased in line with the increase in the RPI since the date of the member's retirement.

The reduction in the maximum approvable member's pension for short-serving employees, which applies to 1987–89 members and post-1989 members, also has the effect of reducing dependants' pensions.

Where pensions are paid to a widow and one or more dependants (or if there is no widow, to more than one dependant) no individual pension can exceed the above maximum, nor can the aggregate of all the pensions exceed the maximum pension which could have been provided for the employee.

It is possible for these pensions to increase in line with the RPI calculated from the date at which the employee would have retired (rather than from the time the widow's or dependant's pension commences).

A widow's or dependant's pension can start at the date of the employee's death (unless the employee's pension was guaranteed to be paid for a period exceeding five years, when the pension cannot start until the end of the guarantee period). The widow's pension and dependant's pension can continue for life or can cease or reduce on remarriage. Any pension received by a child must cease when the child ceases to be a dependant. A dependant is someone who is financially dependent on the employee. A widow's or dependant's pension must cease on death: no guaranteed period may apply as in the case of an employee's own pension, unless the pension has been provided by surrender.

An employee may surrender part of his own pension to provide one for his widow or dependant on his death in retirement, either because the widow/dependant has no pension entitlement in his or her own right or because the employee wishes to enhance an own right pension. The maximum pension which is allocated in this way must not exceed the amount of the reduced pension (either before commutation, or including the annuity equivalent of any separate lump sum) which is payable to the employee and if more than one allocated pension is provided, the limit applies to their aggregate value. A widow's or dependant's pension provided by this method can start at the date of the employee's death, even if his residual pension continues to be paid under a guarantee not exceeding five years.

The employee's pension can be guaranteed for a period of up to ten years, even though he dies during that period. If the guaranteed period is five years or less the balance of the pension payable following the death of the retired employee in that period can be paid as a lump sum. For example, if the employee's pension amounted to £1,000 per annum, commencing at age 65 and the employee died at age 67, having received two instalments of pension, a lump sum could be paid to his dependants amounting to £3,000. The destination of these payments can be at the discretion of the scheme trustees to a wide range of beneficiaries and are normally exempt from income tax and inheritance tax.

Widowers' pensions can be provided on a similar basis to widows' pensions as set out above.

4.14.2 Benefits on death in service

If death occurs in service the following maximum benefits may be provided.

Lump sums

A lump sum may be provided not exceeding the greater of £5,000, and four times the final remuneration of the employee at the date of death (minus any retained benefits), together with a refund of any personal contributions paid by the employee with or without interest: the interest may represent the actual rate of growth on those contributions. For post-1989 members, final remuneration is subject to the earnings limit of £99,000 in 2003/04. Thus the maximum lump sum is £396,000 (plus a refund of personal contributions with growth, as before).

The retained benefits are those payable on death in service from the arrangements described under retained pension benefits above, but lump sum death benefits may be disregarded under the following conditions:

(1) where the member satisfied the one-quarter earnings cap exemption;
(2) if the benefits total £2,500 or less;
(3) where they represent a return of fund under a personal pension scheme or retirement annuity contract;
(4) when payable from a personal pension scheme providing contracted-out benefits only;
(5) when they are a refund of member contributions under an occupational scheme (other than a Free Standing Additional Voluntary Contribution (FSAVC) scheme);
(6) where the benefits in question relate to a wholly concurrent employment/occupation.

The destination of lump sum death-in-service payments can be at the discretion of the scheme's trustees in which case they are normally free of inheritance tax. The rules of the pension scheme will specify the classes of individual to whom such payments may be made. Normally the employee will have notified the trustees of his wishes regarding the person or persons to whom he would like the monies to be paid although the trustees are not bound by this nomination.

Spouses' and dependants' pensions

A pension for a spouse or dependant may be provided equal to two-thirds of the maximum pension that could have been approved for the employee assuming he or she had not died but had continued in employment to normal retirement age with the same final salary as he or she was earning at the time of death. The maximum pension, therefore, is four-ninths of the employee's salary at the date of death (subject to the earnings limit in the case of a post-1989 member).

Where the deceased member was a 1987–89 member the maximum pension for a spouse or dependant may again be lower, as a result of the reduction in the maximum approvable member's pension for short-serving employees.

In the same way as on death in retirement, pensions can also be provided for other dependants, including children, provided the total income payable to spouses and dependants does not exceed the maximum level of pension which could have been provided for the deceased, had he or she remained in service to normal retirement age. A widow's or widower's pension is normally payable for life but could cease or reduce on remarriage. Pensions for children must cease at the age of 18 or completion of full-time education or training, if later.

Escalation of death-in-service benefits

Spouse's and dependant's pensions may automatically increase in payment in a similar manner to that described above for members' pensions.

Dynamised final remuneration

In calculating maximum benefits on death in service, use may be made of dynamised final remuneration, as explained in 4.8 above.

Final remuneration need not be defined in the same terms as for the calculation of other benefits. It may be defined in the following ways:

(1) where basic salary only is involved, the annual rate of salary being received immediately before death;
(2) basic salary as above, plus the average of fluctuating emoluments during the three years (or the whole period of the employment if less) up to the date of death;
(3) the total earnings (fixed plus fluctuating) paid during a selected period of 12 months prior to death (the selected period may end either at the date of death, or on some convenient date, such as 5 April, or the end of the pension scheme year, falling not earlier than 36 months prior to the date of death).

Death in service after normal retirement date

Where an employee has deferred his retirement and dies during his extended service, benefits may be paid on either of the following bases:

(1) that he died before normal retirement date and therefore normal death-in-service benefits may be provided; or

(2) that he retired the day before he died and is, therefore, entitled to death-in-retirement benefits.

If an employee has taken any benefit at normal retirement date, for example the tax-free cash sum, and subsequently dies in service, any death benefits are limited to those payable on death after retirement.

The rules of the scheme will specify which method is to be used in the event of death during deferred retirement.

4.15 RETIREMENT

4.15.1 Retirement before normal retirement date

An employee can take an immediate pension and lump sum if his employment is terminated or if he retires early, from age 50. Female employees who joined schemes approved before November 1991 can take immediate benefits at age 45, provided they are within ten years of their normal retirement date.

4.15.2 Early retirement (not through ill-health)

Pre-1987 members and 1987–89 members

As an alternative to using the straight $\frac{1}{60}$ and $\frac{3}{80}$ scales, maximum benefits can be calculated in accordance with the formulae:

$$\frac{N}{NS} \times P \text{ or } \frac{N}{NS} \times LS$$

where: 'N' is the number of years which have been completed in service to the point of early retirement (maximum 40);

'NS' is the number of years which could have been completed from the date of joining service to normal retirement date;

'P' and 'LS' are, respectively, the maximum pension and tax-free lump sum which could have been approved had the employee retired at his normal retirement date but based on his final remuneration at the date of his early retirement.

For example, a pre-1987 member who joined the scheme at the age of 25, expecting to retire at age 60 but who retires early at the age of 50 on a salary of £9,000 per annum, may be provided with a maximum early retirement pension of £4,285, calculated as follows:

$£9,000 \times \frac{2}{3} \times \frac{25}{35} = £4,285$ pa

He could exchange part of the above early retirement pension for a lump sum calculated on a similar basis as follows:

$£9,000 \times 1.5 \times \frac{25}{35} = £9,642$

These are the overall limits and include the value of any retained benefits (see above) which must be deducted from the value of 'P' and 'LS' before applying N/NS. Any dependants' benefits are then directly related to the reduced pension.

Post-1989 members

The method of calculating the pension is much simpler. The alternative to the straight $\frac{1}{60}$ benefit is normally a maximum of $\frac{1}{30}$ of final remuneration for each year of service completed up to the date of early retirement. Thus, if an employee has completed 20 years' service a maximum pension of two-thirds of final remuneration may be provided from age 50 onwards.

Money purchase schemes

Under money purchase schemes approved before 29 November 1991 whose rules have been suitably drafted and under all money purchase schemes approved on or after 29 November 1991, the 'normal' early retirement pension maxima described above do not apply. The permitted maximum (as an alternative to straight $\frac{1}{60}$) is the same as that on early retirement through ill health (incapacity), ie based on potential service to normal retirement age and final salary at the date of early retirement.

4.15.3 Early retirement through incapacity

If the reason for early retirement is incapacity, the maximum benefits payable are those which could have been payable at normal retirement date but based on the level of final remuneration at the date of early retirement.

Thus, a person with potentially at least 20 years' service to normal retirement date may receive a maximum early retirement pension of two-thirds of his final salary in the event of early retirement through ill health. The same principle applies to his tax-free lump sum.

'Incapacity' means physical or mental deterioration which is bad enough to prevent the individual from following his or her normal employment, or which seriously impairs his or her earning capacity. It does not simply mean a decline in energy or ability.

Where an employee is in exceptional circumstances of ill health such that his life expectancy is undoubtedly very short (ie less than one year) he may be able to exchange the whole of his early retirement pension for an immediate cash sum although this will not be totally free of tax. Commutation on those grounds should not take place unless the administrator is notified by adequate medical evidence that the expectation of life is measured in months rather than years and so short that a pension is not a reasonable provision. The value of the pension which, but for the seriousness of the ill health, would not have been commutable, will be subject to tax at 20 per cent. (See 6.5 for controlling directors.)

4.15.4 Benefits on late retirement

An employee who remains in service after normal retirement date can be provided with such additional pension benefits up to the normal maximum as would be available assuming that his actual retirement date is his normal retirement date.

1987–89 members

If his total service exceeds 40 years, he will be entitled to an additional pension of $\frac{1}{60}$ of his final salary in respect of each year in excess of 40 which occurs after reaching normal retirement date: there is an overall maximum of $\frac{45}{60}$ of final salary at the date of retirement.

As an alternative to accruing additional $\frac{1}{60}$, the maximum benefits available at normal retirement date may be increased by the greater of the actuarial increase reflecting the period of deferment and the growth in the underlying fund, or the increase in the RPI during the period of deferment.

A similar basis is used for calculating the increased tax-free lump sum on late retirement. Where total service exceeds 40 years, each year over 40 occurring after normal retirement date can generate an additional lump sum of $\frac{3}{80}$ of final salary at the date of actual retirement, subject to a maximum lump sum of $\frac{135}{80}$ of final salary. Alternatively the lump sum available at normal retirement date can be increased on a reasonable basis – in line with the increase in the underlying pension funds investments.

Post-1989 membership

No additional benefits may be provided in respect of service completed beyond normal retirement date above the maximum approvable pension at normal retirement date.

14.15.5 **Options on retirement**

At normal retirement date the member is entitled to take pension from the scheme. In addition, the member may choose to give up part of his pension in exchange for a tax-free lump sum.

The scheme rules may allow the member to retire at any time after the age of 50 and take a reduced level of benefit.

Pre-1989 members may decide to defer retirement until after normal retirement date and accrue enhanced benefits. These members may also have the facility to take the tax-free lump sum and defer the pension, or take the pension and defer the tax-free lump sum, while remaining in service.

Some occupational schemes (generally those providing benefits on a defined contribution basis) may allow the member to withdraw an income from the scheme rather than purchasing an annuity (see Chapter 19).

Greater flexibility may be achieved by transferring the fund into a personal pension plan (see Chapter 14).

4.16 TRIVIAL BENEFITS

Where the total annual value of all pensions to an employee from the same employer do not exceed £260 per annum it is possible for the whole of the pension to be commuted for a lump sum. This does not apply where the member who is entitled to a pension which exceeds £260 per annum, commutes part of it for a lump sum and has a residual pension of £260 per annum or less. In the Inland Revenue's consultation document on pensions tax simplification there is a proposal to liberalise this rule: people over age 65 whose total matured pension funds from all sources amount to no more than £10,000 in value will be able to take them as a lump sum. The first 25% of the lump sum will be tax free with the remainder taxed as income.

4.17 COMBINATIONS OF SCHEMES

The changes introduced by F(No 2)A 1987 and FA 1989 have given rise to questions about the levels of benefits which may be provided for members who move to new or reconstructed schemes or join schemes to provide additional benefits. It is the broad intention that members of a scheme who remain with the same employer or who effectively remain members of the same scheme should not be adversely affected by any subsequent changes.

4.18 CONTINUED RIGHTS

Scheme members are entitled to 'continued rights', meaning that the scheme can continue to accrue benefits for them on the basis applying before the statutory restrictions imposed in 1987 and 1989 came into force, if:

(1) they were a member of a scheme before 17 March 1987, in relation to the restrictions announced on that date; or

(2) they were a member on 1 June 1989 of a scheme, which had been established on or before 14 March 1989, in respect of the restrictions announced by the Chancellor of the Exchequer on the latter date; or

(3) they were party to a contract of employment, whereby the employer was bound to provide benefits, but had not established a suitable scheme before a specified date.

Scheme members do not lose their continued rights if they:

(a) become a member of another scheme established by the same employer or an associated employer; or

(b) become a member of a scheme of an employer who has acquired, been acquired by, merged with, or taken over the whole or part of the business of, their employer; or

(c) have a definite expectation that at the end of a secondment or posting to another employer, they will be offered membership of a scheme of their employer; or

(d) rejoin their employer's scheme within one month of returning to work, following a period of absence; or

(e) were members of a scheme of their employer before 17 March 1987 or 1 June 1989, as appropriate, and without benefits ceasing to accrue under that scheme, become members of a scheme providing supplemental benefits; or

(f) were employees in a waiting period before becoming full members of the employer's scheme, provided they were regarded as members before 17 March 1987 for preservation purposes; or

(g) were members before 1 June 1989 of a scheme (established before 14 March 1989) which provided only death-in-service benefits, and are therefore entitled to pre-1 June 1989 continued rights.

Note: Members entitled to death-in-service arrangements under a similar scheme before 17 March 1987 do not acquire pre-17 March 1987 continued rights.

4.18.1 **Transfers by members with continued rights**

These changes to pensions in 1987 and 1989 were imposed on individual schemes by blanket statutory overrides which, for members entitled to continued rights, were subsequently 'disapplied' by regulations (SI 1988 No 1436 and SI 1990 No 2101, as applicable).

If a member with continued rights wishes to transfer to a scheme which is subject to the statutory override, but it is automatically disapplied by the above-mentioned regulations, Inland Revenue agreement to the transfer is not needed.

Where, however, a member with continued rights transfers to a scheme which is not subject to the statutory override, ongoing entitlement to continued rights under the receiving scheme must be agreed with the Inland Revenue.

Specific Inland Revenue agreement to ongoing entitlement to continued rights is required for members who make subsequent transfers, regardless of whether the receiving scheme is subject to the statutory override. The Inland Revenue has indicated, however, that it will generally be prepared to take a sympathetic view, where the subsequent transfer to another scheme of the members' employer is necessitated by a member's promotion, or a reconstruction of the business as described in (b) of 4.18 above.

4.19 OPTING FOR POST-1989 BENEFITS

A pre-1987 member may opt to receive the benefits applicable to a post-1989 member if the scheme's trustees are prepared to allow his benefits to be augmented and if the scheme rules are amended. For example, a pre-1987 member may wish to retire at age 50 on a pension of two-thirds of his final remuneration: this would not be permissible under pre-1987 rules although under post-1989 rules this would be permissible subject to the earnings cap.

A 1987–89 member may opt to be classed as a post-1989 member should the result be beneficial. Once again the member has to accept the earnings cap but in these circumstances there is no requirement for the scheme's trustees to permit the election because the right to make that election is conferred by statute.

4.20 ASSOCIATED EMPLOYMENTS

It is not uncommon for an individual to draw earnings from two or more employments which are associated and for these employments to provide pension benefits for the individual.

The FA 1989 provides that employers are associated if one is controlled by the other (eg parent and wholly-owned subsidiary) or both are controlled by the same third party (eg wholly-owned subsidiaries of the same parent).

4.20.1 Connected schemes

For post-1989 members this means that:

(1) Two or more schemes of such associated employers are connected schemes if:
   (a) there is a period during which the member is an employee of the associated employers;
   (b) that period is one for which benefits are payable under the scheme of each associated employer;
   (c) under each scheme that period counts as service with the relevant associated employer.
(2) Under any occupational scheme the Inland Revenue limits apply to the total benefits payable:
   (a) in respect of all associated employers participating in the scheme; and
   (b) from all connected schemes; and
   (c) if the member is a controlling director who retires on or after 31 August 1991, from personal pension schemes/retirement annuity contracts relating to earnings from associated employers participating in the scheme.
(3) The earnings cap applies to aggregate pensionable remuneration payable from associated employers providing benefits under the scheme and/or under any connected scheme.

For all members moves between such associated employers can (and for post-1989 members must) be regarded as constituting a single unbroken employment. Pre-1987 or 1987–89 members who make that move therefore have, usually, a continued right to benefits calculated on pre-1987 or 1987–89 limits, whether they remain in the same scheme or join another of the associated employers.

4.20.2 Permanent community of interests

The Inland Revenue will also approve the inclusion in a scheme which although not an associated employer in terms of the statutory definition, is associated with the employer who established the scheme through a permanent community of interests, such as common management or shareholders, interchangeable or jointly employed staff or interdependent operations, for example one selling the bulk of the other's products.

Where employers are associated through a permanent community of interests:

(1) Moves between them by pre-1987 and 1987–89 members who are not controlling directors can be regarded as constituting a single unbroken employment with continued benefit rights (ie they are treated the same as those who move between employers who are associated in terms of the statutory definition).

(2) The benefits of pre-1987 and 1987–89 and post-1989 controlling directors must be calculated separately for each employment and the limits applying to each will depend, generally speaking, on the date of joining the relevant employer.

If however the scheme was approved before 27 July 1989 any member will, where appropriate, have continued rights to pre-1989 limits if he joins an employer which participated in the scheme before 14 March 1989, irrespective of the nature of the association between the employers.

4.21 MULTIPLE EMPLOYMENTS

It is not uncommon for people to have two or more completely separate employments, one assessable under Schedule D and the other or others assessable under Schedule E. Examples might be a teacher working for a local authority who also does private tuition work, or an accountant in practice who is also a director in his family firm. In these cases retirement and death benefits may be provided through an approved retirement benefit scheme in respect of the service and income from the Schedule E employment while completely separate pension provision may be made through retirement annuity contracts and personal pension schemes in respect of the Schedule D income.

If the earnings from the multiple employments are classified under Schedule E then retirement benefit schemes may be set up in respect of each separate employment, although complications arise if the employments are neither associated (see above) nor wholly concurrent.

Where the concurrent employment extends to only part of the member's overall service with the employers, the benefits from one scheme relating to a period when the employments are not concurrent must be taken into account under the other as retained benefits, ie as if they were benefits of a previous employer, unless:

(1) In relation to a pre-1987 or 1987–89 member the employers are associated through control (see above) and:
  (a) each participates in the other's scheme; or
  (b) only one employer participates in both schemes, in which case the scheme with the single employer will have to take only the non-concurrent benefits relating to service with the associated employer under the other scheme into account as retained-benefits.
(2) In relation to a post-1989 member, the schemes are connected schemes (see above).

4.22 PENSIONS SIMPLIFICATION

The preceding paragraphs in this chapter illustrate the complexity of today's pension tax laws and practice. Over the years changes have been made to reflect the wishes of governments while at the same time accommodating, to different degrees, the specific circumstances, often merited, of special groups. The current position has become difficult to understand, administer and communicate to prospective and existing scheme members. The simplification changes summarised in Chapter 1, assuming they become law effective from 6 April 2005, will sweep away much of the existing complexity although some transitional arrangements will continue to apply.

5

UNAPPROVED PENSION SCHEMES

5.1 INTRODUCTION

The FA 1989 allowed employers to establish unapproved pension schemes providing benefits in excess of those permitted under approved schemes (see Chapter 4). This change in legislation was partly cosmetic in that it disguised the restrictions placed on new approved occupational schemes by FA 1989. The change also provides opportunities for employers to provide more flexible remuneration packages for high earners who would be restricted by the earnings cap under approved pension schemes and for those with less than 20 years' service to retirement who would be unable to obtain a maximum approvable pension. However, these opportunities are at the expense of the generous tax reliefs available to approved schemes, some or all of which will not be available to unapproved schemes. Guidance Notes on the tax treatment of top-up pension schemes were published in August 1991 by the Inland Revenue: these Notes have been used in parts of this chapter.

The FA 1994 introduced further changes to funded unapproved retirement benefit schemes which invest in assets which are not subject to UK income or capital gains tax, normally by means of an offshore trust.

The FA 1998, whilst having no direct impact on funded unapproved retirement benefits schemes (FURBS), brought about fundamental changes to capital gains tax which had an adverse effect on the financial attraction of FURBS to higher earners. This, together with extension of employers' national insurance contributions on employer contributions to FURBS, means that the financial benefit in having a FURBS rather than cash in hand is finely balanced.

5.2 SUMMARY OF IMPACT OF LEGISLATION

(1) Benefits from 'approved' and 'unapproved' schemes do not need to be considered in aggregate. Before the FA 1989, membership of an

unapproved scheme would render invalid membership of the approved scheme.

(2) The definition of 'retirement benefit schemes' is a key part of the rules: this expression is generally assumed to include a conventional occupational scheme or arrangement set up under trust and approved by the Inland Revenue for tax purposes. However, other arrangements may also fall within the meaning of this expression. For example, an insurance policy taken out by an employer on the life of a 'keyman' in the organisation might be regarded as an unapproved pension scheme if the employee can expect that it will be assigned to him on retirement – a form of 'golden handshake'. (A keyman policy is one which pays out benefits to the employer in the event of the keyman's death to provide a cushion until such time as the employer is able to employ another employee of similar calibre.)

(3) Employees are taxed on contributions to 'funded' schemes at the time the contributions are paid. A scheme is 'funded' for these purposes when the payment is made 'with a view to provision of' benefits for the employee. Employee contributions do not benefit from tax relief and may bring into play the special anti-avoidance rules applicable to trusts where the person establishing a trust can benefit. Most unapproved schemes do not permit employee contributions.

(4) The Budget on 17 March 1998 introduced more changes to the rate of capital gains tax payable on trusts (considered by the Inland Revenue to include a FURBS established under trust). The assets of a FURBS are now generally subject to capital gains tax starting at an initial rate of 34 per cent tapering to an effective rate of 20.4 per cent when the asset in the FURBS is held for more than ten years. The trustees normally benefit from half of the annual exemption from capital gains tax (£3,950 for the tax year 2003/04).

(5) In the case of unfunded schemes employees are taxed on the benefits they receive, but funded schemes can provide a full tax-free lump sum as long as tax has been paid on the underlying fund. Pensions are always taxable, and, for this reason, funded schemes normally pay out their benefits as a lump sum (representing the commuted value of the pension) allowing the employee to buy a purchased life annuity if he needs income. By doing this, at least part (the capital element) of the annuity escapes tax.

(6) The tax treatment of contributions by employers to funded unapproved pension schemes depends on the normal rules for the deductibility of business expenses. It is likely that in some cases these contributions are not deductible expenses particularly where very large contributions are paid by private limited companies to schemes set up for members who are directors of those companies.

(7) In November 1997 the Department of Social Security, now the Department for Work and Pensions (DWP), announced that

employer's national insurance contributions (NICs) would be payable in respect of contributions made by employers from 6 April 1998. However, national insurance contributions are also payable on any extra salary paid to the employee to compensate for the income tax due in respect of the employer's contributions.

(8) As long as the scheme satisfies certain conditions (broadly that the employer bears the running costs of the scheme and any death benefits are distributed at the discretion of the scheme's trustees) it is normally possible to avoid any inheritance tax on the contributions to and the benefits from an unapproved scheme.

5.3 RETIREMENT BENEFITS SCHEME

One feature of the development of unapproved pension schemes is that more attention has to be paid to the definition of 'retirement benefits scheme'. In the past employers generally knew when they were setting up a 'pension scheme' and approval was sought and obtained. However, the greater flexibility permitted by the amendment of FA 1989, s 590(7) permits the establishment of schemes which look less like a true pension scheme.

This focuses attention on what is a 'retirement benefits scheme' and what is not. This distinction is likely to be important as it may determine the tax treatment of both the contributions and the benefits.

A 'retirement benefits scheme' is 'a scheme for the provision of benefits consisting of or including relevant benefits' (see ICTA 1988, s 611(1) in Appendix 4). This definition makes it important to consider the meaning of:

(1) 'scheme'; and
(2) 'relevant benefits'.

Scheme is defined by s 611(2) as including:

'Reference to a deed, agreement, series of agreements, or other arrangements providing for relevant benefits notwithstanding that it relates or they relate only to:

(a) small number of employees, or to a single employee, or,
(b) the payment of a pension starting immediately on the making of the arrangements.'

This definition is wide and is capable of encompassing many arrangements which would not perhaps be regarded as 'schemes' in the accepted sense. However, it is not as wide as it may at first appear because the word 'arrangement' must be read in the light of the preceding words 'deed' or 'agreement'. Both of these words denote a form of binding obligation (on the employer). It is possible that a letter from an employer promising a lump sum at retirement could constitute a scheme and that, theoretically at least, nothing in writing is needed at all. Following an Inland Revenue change of practice in October 1991 it now considers that an *ex gratia* pension or a lump sum may be capable of constituting a retirement benefit scheme.

The difficulty in deciding whether a 'scheme' exists is quite simply how far can the employer go in informing the employee and making any form of commitment without creating a scheme? The answer is not likely to be far, especially where the employee is continuing in employment and is thus working for his potential entitlement.

5.3.1 Relevant benefits

The second part of the definition of retirement benefits scheme is the definition of 'relevant benefits'. These are defined by s 612(1) as:

> 'Any pension, lump sum, gratuity or other like benefit given or to be given on retirement or on death, or in anticipation of retirement, or, in connection with past service, after retirement or death, or to be given on or in anticipation of or in connection with any change in the nature of the service of the employee in question, except that it does not include any benefit which is to be afforded solely by reason of the disablement by accident of a person occurring during his service or of his death by accident so occurring and for no other reason.'

Relevant benefits are defined so widely that they could possibly be stretched to cover practically every kind of benefit paid or provided by an employer except remuneration paid during service.

The only clear feature of the definition is that accidental death and disability benefits are not relevant benefits. However, this only applies to accidental death and disability benefits (although the accident need not have occurred at work). It is clear that ordinary death benefits are relevant benefits although it is not clear whether disablement benefits generally are caught.

The answer probably depends on whether the individual can be said to have 'retired' and the better view is that there is a distinction between 'sick pay' (where the individual expects to return to work) which is not a relevant benefit, and a 'disability pension' or a lump sum disability benefit (where the individual does not expect to return to work) which are likely to be relevant benefits.

Finally it is not necessary for the creation of a scheme for there to be a direct contract between the employer and employee for the provision of the relevant benefits. Section 612(2) provides that references to the provision of relevant benefits include 'the provision of relevant benefits ...

by means of a contract between the Administrator (of the scheme) or the employer or the employee and a third person'. The reference to the employee would appear to make it theoretically possible for an insurance policy effected by the employee himself to constitute a scheme providing relevant benefits. For this to be the case it is probably necessary for some employer involvement but this could be satisfied if the employer promised to pay the contributions for the employee. Of course, whether the Inland Revenue would seek to extend the definition this far is doubtful.

5.4 TAXATION OF CONTRIBUTIONS – THE EMPLOYER'S POSITION

Contributions to an exempt approved scheme attract automatic tax relief for the employer by virtue of ICTA 1988, s 592(4) (see Appendix 4). Contributions paid by the employer to an unapproved scheme do not qualify for relief automatically but *may* be relievable under the ordinary rules of Schedule D.

In order to be deductible, expenditure has to be in broad terms:

(1) incurred wholly and exclusively for the purposes of the business;
(2) not incurred for any other non-business purpose;
(3) expenditure of an income nature and not a capital nature;
(4) the expenditure must actually have been incurred.

These rules impact on expenditure on a pension scheme in the following ways:

(1) It may be difficult to argue that pension schemes for directors are wholly and exclusively for the purposes of the business.
(2) It is easy to imply a non-business purpose (eg a personal benefit) where the employees also have a significant shareholding in the company (or are relatives of such persons).
(3) It is often common to put in a lump sum to start a pension scheme (in order to make provision for past service) which could be regarded as a capital payment.
(4) Merely saving money or investing it may not be expenditure for these purposes.

5.5 OBTAINING TAX RELIEF

As can be seen the test for obtaining tax relief is strict. The key features for schemes are:

(1) There is likely to be a need to put scheme's assets beyond the reach of the company perhaps directly in the hands of the employee or a trust for his benefit (the investment of scheme assets in the employer's business in the form of a loan, or in the purchase of shares, may make the obtaining of tax relief more difficult).

(2) The company should not be a 'long stop' beneficiary of the trust (eg the company should not be in the position where it can benefit from any undistributed funds).

(3) There is likely to be a 'reasonableness' test in the level of benefits (ie it might become more difficult to justify high levels of pension as being wholly and exclusively for the purposes of the trade).

(4) Deductibility is more likely in respect of arm's length employees (ie non-shareholder directors) than employees with a proprietary interest or relatives of such persons.

(5) If the company merely sets up an accounting reserve to meet a liability under an unfunded scheme payments into the reserve are not regarded as expenditure and, therefore, are non-deductible.

(6) Payments of lump sums and the purchase of annuities at retirement under unfunded schemes should be deductible if they satisfy the general rules for deductibility.

5.6 TAXATION OF CONTRIBUTIONS – THE EMPLOYEE'S POSITION

If an employee has an absolute right to benefit from a fund or policy the amounts paid in are taxable under ordinary principles and the specific rules relating to pension schemes do not apply. Those specific rules were introduced to catch a simple dodge. Rather than giving the employee an absolute right to benefit it was possible to make his benefits contingent on reaching retirement. This was actually quite common before FA 1947 imposed the charge to tax on schemes where the employee's benefit was contingent.

This legislation is contained in ICTA 1988, s 595 (see Appendix 4). Subsection (1) deals with 'where, pursuant to a retirement benefits scheme, the employer … pays a sum with a view to the provision of any relevant benefits for any employee (whether or not the accrual of the benefits is dependent on any contingency)'. These are what the Inland Revenue calls 'funded schemes', ie where the employer is actually making payments to provide the benefits.

However, s 595(1) is insufficient on its own to tax all situations where the employer has set up a scheme (ie made a commitment or promise of relevant benefits). If the employer did not fund in advance no tax would be payable.

Prior to FA 1989, s 595(2) and (3), ICTA 1988 provided for the notional cost of providing the relevant benefit, based on actuarial principles, to be taxed in the hands of the employee. Section 596(A) replaced these sections the consequence of which is that no charge arises on 'unfunded' schemes but one would arise where the scheme is 'funded'.

The employee is chargeable to tax where, to reiterate the words of s 595(1), the employer: 'pays a sum with a view to the provision of relevant benefits'. In effect this is the Inland Revenue's definition of 'funded schemes'. This could apply where, say, a trust fund is established for the benefit of an employee to provide him with a pension but the employer can wind up the trust, or if the employee were a director or substantial shareholder of the company.

Where employers make contributions to unapproved pension schemes employees see no immediate benefits, but rather a tax charge, which could lead to pressure to increase employees' salaries. This in itself is taxable and subject to employer's NICs (12.8 per cent) giving considerable extra costs.

If an employer wants to meet the employee's tax liability on the contributions they may agree a grossing arrangement. The grossed-up equivalent of the actual chargeable contribution, and the tax figure, should then be included on the employer's pay record (form P11) for the pay period in which the contributions are paid. Contributions paid by an employer without a grossing arrangement should be notified by the employer at the end of the year to the Tax Office on a form P9D or P11D.

5.7 TAXATION OF THE FUND

In the case of unapproved unfunded schemes, there is by definition no fund but in the case of unapproved funded schemes, the scheme assets do not enjoy tax benefits available to exempt approved pension funds. Prior to 17 March 1998, tax was payable at the basic rate on investment income and on chargeable capital gains. Since then the rate of capital gains tax on trusts has changed to 34 per cent, subject to tapering. Where the asset is held for ten years or more, the effective rate of tax for a FURBS trustee will be 20.4 per cent (as compared with between 13.2 and 24 per cent, depending on the tax position of the individual, where the asset is held outside a FURBS).

A FURBS trustee still has an annual capital gains tax exemption of £3,950 (in 2003/04) but the capital gains tax indexation allowance (which was removed for increases in asset values in line with the price of inflation) is only available up to 5 April 1998. However, this annual exemption applies at the scheme level, not in respect of each individual member of the FURBS. Where a FURBS comprises a number of members, the claiming of the annual exemption and its equitable distribution across members may be costly and time-consuming.

Prior to 30 November 1993, it was attractive to establish a funded scheme using an offshore trust enabling the fund to accumulate free of UK income and capital gains tax (other than any withholding tax on dividends from UK companies). Care had to be taken to ensure that special anti-avoidance rules, designed to prevent the avoidance of tax by transfers of assets outside the United Kingdom, did not apply. For schemes set up from 30 November 1993 onwards, or existing schemes varied after that date (eg by adding a new member) the use of offshore trusts is no longer likely to be attractive (see 5.8 below).

If the fund is invested in a life assurance policy, even if the policy is a qualifying policy, or any annuity policy there is a potential tax charge under new rules introduced in FA 1989 (Sched 9). If the policy is held by a company or under a trust set up by a company any investment profit realised from the policy is liable to corporation tax under the chargeable event legislation contained in ICTA 1988. In any case, the life assurance company's fund is subject to tax as the policy does not form part of its pensions business exempt fund.

5.8 TAXATION OF LUMP SUM BENEFITS

Lump sum benefits from unfunded schemes are subject to income tax. In the case of funded schemes, where the employee can prove that he has already paid tax in respect of the employer contributions, lumps sums can be paid free of tax. From 30 November 1993, the exemption from tax on lump sums from unfunded schemes was removed where the fund was not itself subject to UK income tax.

This provision contained in ICTA 1988, s 596A was primarily directed at situations where the fund is subject to an offshore trust and the assets are likely to consist of investments which are not subject to UK income tax. In effect, these funds could grow tax free, similar to the funds of UK approved pension schemes. This was seen by the Government as an abuse and the legislation now provides that income tax is payable on lump sums payable out of funds which are not themselves subject to income tax.

5.9 TAXATION OF PENSIONS

At present it is unlikely that any funded unapproved scheme would pay out a pension. If a pension is required, the better route for the employee is to take a lump sum and purchase a purchased life annuity. All pensions payable by the scheme are taxed under the ordinary rules of Schedule E.

5.10 INHERITANCE TAX

Unapproved schemes can, like approved schemes, benefit from significant inheritance tax advantages.

Unapproved schemes can be set up as 'sponsored superannuation schemes' because even where the employee is charged to income tax under s 595(1), that tax does not cover the costs of setting up and running the scheme. For inheritance tax (IHT), this means that unapproved schemes set up under trust may be sponsored schemes, if there are separately identifiable setting up and running costs, and such schemes fall within IHTA 1984, s 151. As a result, the normal IHT charges on settled property do not apply. So, for example, benefits paid out under such schemes are free of any IHT trust charges.

Tax may, however, be chargeable if the benefit is expressed to be payable only to the deceased's estate. But commonly, death benefits may be paid at the employer's or scheme administrator's discretion to one or more of a specified group of possible beneficiaries as under approved schemes. In these cases IHT is not generally payable if the employee's estate is excluded from this group. However, there remains the possibility of an inheritance tax gift with reservation (GWR) charge. Unlike tax approved schemes, where the GWR rules do not apply (see Inland Revenue press release of 9 July 1986) there remains the possibility of an IHT charge on benefits from an unapproved scheme if the employee is deemed by the Inland Revenue to have retained a benefit from the scheme. However, so long as the scheme is operated in a similar way to an approved scheme and no employee contributions are made, the GWR rules should not apply.

5.11 NATIONAL INSURANCE CONTRIBUTIONS

National insurance contributions (NICs) are payable on 'earnings'. These are broadly defined as 'any remuneration or profit derived from any trade, business, profession, office or vocation'.

Before November 1997, payments which were regarded as 'benefits in kind' were excluded for NIC purposes and, for example, if the scheme was set up under trust, payments to the trustees would be 'benefits in kind' and not 'earnings' (in the same way as payments to existing approved schemes).

However, the National Insurance Contributions Office (NICO) believed some FURBS had been set up to avoid NICs rather than to provide retirement benefits. A scheme would be set up into which a payment would be made, equivalent to, say, a bonus to which the employee would otherwise be entitled. The trustees of the scheme would pay the benefits out of the scheme shortly afterwards. The payment into the scheme would be regarded as a 'benefit in kind' and not subject to national insurance. To prevent such avoidance, the NICO stated in November 1997 that employer contributions would no longer be regarded as benefits in kind and would be subject to national insurance. The general rule now is that if there is a Schedule E tax charge, NICs are also payable.

5.12 USES OF UNAPPROVED SCHEMES

The Guidance Notes issued by the Inland Revenue suggest that there are three situations where an unapproved scheme is likely to be attractive:

(1) where an employer wants to offer some employees a pension greater than two-thirds of final salary;
(2) where the employee has not completed the full 20 years' service to qualify for a full two-thirds pension;
(3) where the employer wants to pension earnings over £99,000 (in 2003/04).

The first situation is likely to be rare as few employers will want to offer a pension of more than two-thirds final salary as this is likely to be as much as the employer will want to pay or is able to afford. The second situation where employers wish to provide more for employees unable to obtain a full two-thirds final salary pension is marginally more likely. (The maximum pension can now be provided only after 20 years whereas previously it was possible after ten.)

In some circumstances employers may wish to recruit staff who will be affected by the £99,000 (indexed) earnings cap under an approved retirement benefits scheme, initially or at a later date. Employees who are already in existing schemes and are pre-1987 members or 1987–1989 members are less likely to wish to move jobs if they are earning or anticipate earning more than the £99,000 limit.

It remains to be seen, however, the extent to which employers will be forced to provide 'top-ups' to recruit staff. This may be more likely in industries with skills shortages than elsewhere. Also, companies who have one or more key employees whom they wish to tie in (eg computer experts, top salesmen, key executives) may wish to provide top-up schemes. Small private companies could find the prospect of providing pensions for the key directors appealing but the availability of tax relief is crucial. The charge to tax on the employer's contribution as a 'benefit in kind' is a disadvantage for funded schemes (except perhaps in the case of death in service schemes where the premiums are smaller in relation to the emerging benefits). The alternative of an unfunded arrangement – where a lump sum is paid to the employee on retirement – while much more financially attractive offers little security for the employee.

5.13 DEATH-IN-SERVICE BENEFITS

The unattractiveness of unapproved as compared with approved pension schemes in relation to tax benefits is not so evident where the employer wishes to provide additional death-in-service benefits for an employee where there is a possibility of a substantial benefit compared with the tax liability.

Take an employee, aged 45, earning £150,000 who is a post-1989 member of an approved pension scheme and is subject to the earnings cap of £99,000. The scheme provides maximum approved death-in-service benefits on death before retirement, assumed to be at age 60, as follows:

(1) A lump sum of four times capped earnings, ie £396,000.
(2) A pension for his widow payable on his death before retirement of £44,000 (two-thirds of his maximum approvable pension which is assumed to be £66,000). The widow's pension is assumed to be capitalised at a lump sum of £704,000 so that the total value of the death-in-service benefit amounts to £1,100,000.

The employer wishes to provide the above scale of death in service benefits in relation to total earnings of £120,000 which would have a capitalised value of £1,333,333. The difference which could be provided by an ordinary term life assurance policy with a sum assured of £233,333 would be payable by the employer by means of an unapproved funded scheme written under a discretionary trust. The annual premium would amount to around £770, increasing each year in line with the Average Earnings Index, assumed to be at 4 per cent a year (assuming that the employee is male and is a non-smoker). The premium would be regarded as income in the hands of the employee and subject to income tax. The contribution, however, could no longer be regarded as a 'benefit in kind' and would be subject to national insurance. The employer would obtain tax relief on the premiums.

On death the benefits would be paid to the trustees and distributed according to the trust provisions. Inheritance tax would not be payable as long as the unapproved scheme is seen to have been 'sponsored' by the employer. However, 'sponsorship' requires more than payment of the premium by the employer: it is likely that this will be satisfied by separate and identifiable payments to meet expenses in setting up and administering the scheme.

The FA 1989 charges to tax gains made by companies in respect of company-owned life policies and annuity contracts and those held in trusts set up by companies. The gain is the difference between the premiums paid and the proceeds of the policy and in the case of a life assurance policy the gain on death is calculated by deducting total premiums paid. If a group policy is used, say, for a group of members, death benefits paid in respect of previous deaths may come into the computation for calculating the surrender value on a subsequent death. To avoid this, individual assurance policies should be used for each member.

5.14 UNFUNDED SCHEMES: ACCOUNTING FOR COSTS

Provisions for unfunded schemes made in company accounts are not allowable as business expenses but it may be possible to obtain allowance for deferred tax relief. From a member's point of view the lack of security is the main drawback of an unfunded scheme. However, it may be possible to obtain a charge over employer assets where the charge could only be taken on the default of the employer (eg on insolvency) but the Inland Revenue may treat this as amounting to funding for the scheme, giving rise to a tax charge.

Leaving service benefits

Unfunded schemes are not subject to preservation requirements, following a High Court ruling in December 2000. However, this will be unsatisfactory for the member although the member's contract of service with the employer and the scheme rules could specify the preservation of benefits on leaving the employer. On leaving the employer's service the member is likely to prefer a physical transfer of funds from the unfunded unapproved retirement benefits scheme (UURBS) representing his preserved benefits rather than continuing to have a promise of unfunded benefits from an ex-employer. However, before the transfer can take place the UURBS will have to become a FURBS: this crystallisation of the UURBS into a FURBS will give rise to tax and national insurance.

5.15 RECENT TRENDS

A common approach by employers to unapproved pension schemes is beginning to emerge. The earnings cap becomes more significant each year as wages inflation, which exceeds price inflation (by which the earnings cap is increased), catches more employees. Large employers are becoming more interested in setting up unapproved pension schemes as they are keen to be able to offer an attractive financial package to high-flyers whom they may wish to recruit. Equally, smaller employers, attracted by the flexibility of unapproved schemes, are becoming more interested in the tax planning opportunities presented by them (including the opportunity of a 'self-invested' option). In the last few years, changes to national insurance contributions and the taxation of FURBS investments have reduced the financial benefits in receiving part remuneration by means of a FURBS investment. However, some employers will prefer to use FURBS for high earners in order to complement approved schemes and to ensure a discipline of retirement saving which would disappear if remuneration were to be paid wholly as salary. However, as seen from this chapter, the taxation of unapproved pension schemes can give rise to considerable complexity. Other options worth considering are as follows:

(1) By maximising the benefits under approved pension schemes in relation to earnings up to the cap, for example providing a maximum pension of two-thirds of final remuneration after completion of 20 years' service, together with cost of living increases in pensions in payment: these benefit scales may be more generous than those for employees who are not subject to the cap.

(2) High earners could pay Additional Voluntary Contributions (AVCs) of up to 15 per cent of their remuneration (subject to a cash limit of £14,850 in 2003/04) in order to maximise benefits up to the cap.

(3) Rather than using a combination of approved occupational schemes and unapproved pension schemes (whether funded or unfunded), it may be worthwhile considering a personal pension scheme for the employee. Where earnings are high and the employee is young it is possible that personal pension plans might provide higher benefits than under an approved pension scheme in any case, without having to resort to an unapproved scheme.

(4) Other 'benefits in kind' could be considered, such as share option schemes or increased remuneration which gives the employee the

means to maximise contributions to personal investment arrangements like an individual savings account (ISA).

(5) Salaries could be increased to allow contributions to be paid into personal pensions for spouses and/or children (contributions of up to £3,600 a year may be paid without the need for earnings).

Table 5.1 Summary of tax position

	Funded	Unfunded
Employer's contributions	allowable as business expenses subject to NI taxed in hands of employee	allowable as business expenses
Employee's contributions	paid out of taxed income, so no tax relief	not applicable
Growth of fund	subject to income tax and capital gains tax in excess of annual exemption after taking into account indexation allowance to April 1998 less tapering relief. No further tax to pay on investment income accompanied by tax credit	not applicable
Benefit payments	if lump sum, tax free, provided that the fund has suffered tax as above. If the fund is established offshore, and tax has not been paid on the investment growth, tax will be paid on the emerging lump sum. If pension, subject to income tax (therefore an ineffective alternative)	lump sum or pension paid subject to income tax
Death benefits	free of inheritance tax under a 'sponsored' superannuation scheme	as for funded

5.16 PENSIONS SIMPLIFICATION

The Inland Revenue's consultation document, 'Simplifying the taxation of pensions: increasing choice and flexibility for all', refers to unapproved pensions in a diagram illustrating the complexity of the various regimes that govern pensions. Although the Inland Revenue has amplified its thinking in many ways since the publication of the consultation document in December 2002 the impact the new tax proposals will have on unapproved schemes is not clear. However, the introduction of a lifetime limit on pension funds, to be set initially at £1.4 million in 2002 terms, will undoubtedly affect high earners who will look for alternative means to top up their pensions. This could increase the popularity of unapproved schemes.

The likelihood is that funded unapproved schemes will be curtailed significantly, otherwise the complexity currently present in approved schemes will simply transfer across to the unapproved regime. However, UURBS are likely to continue.

6

COMPANY DIRECTORS

6.1 INTRODUCTION

The Inland Revenue has long regarded company directors – especially those with a controlling interest – as a special category for whom membership of an approved pension scheme is permitted only subject to certain restrictions. In recent years, the Inland Revenue has increased its monitoring of pension schemes with controlling director members.

The earnings cap (£99,000 in 2003/04) has hit this particular group more than others. In addition, from 1 September 1994, the Inland Revenue announced further limitations on levels of contributions to 'earmarked' money purchase schemes. Although there has been no restriction on the benefits which can be provided for directors, the funding of those benefits has to take place uniformly, without the scope for accelerated funding as had been possible previously. A similar limit on contribution levels has been applied to small self-administered schemes from 1 June 1996.

Directors of companies which are regarded for tax purposes as investment companies are ineligible to become members of a pension scheme approved by the Inland Revenue under its discretionary powers if they are controlling directors (see below) or are members of a family who together control more than 50 per cent of the company (see Chapter 18). The Inland Revenue does not, however, object to such schemes for these directors if the investment company is the holding company for a group of trading companies for which it acts as coordinator.

The benefits which may be provided for a director who is described by the Inland Revenue as a *controlling director* are restricted as follows.

6.1.1 All members

The definition of 'final remuneration' and 'dynamised final remuneration' must not be based on one year only but must be averaged over a period of at least three consecutive years.

6.1.2 **Pre-1987 and 1987–89 members only**

(1) The earliest normal retirement age is 60. This means that female controlling directors of schemes approved before 29 November 1991 are restricted to a normal retirement range of 60–70 and cannot retire on maximum benefits at age 55 (see 4.4).

(2) If the director defers drawing benefits beyond his normal retirement date the limits on pension and tax-free cash up to age 70 are the same limits as would have applied had he chosen the actual date of his retirement as his normal retirement date and there is no entitlement to the additional benefits described in 4.15.4.

(3) For deferment beyond age 70, benefits based on final remuneration and service determined at age 70 may be increased by the greater of an actuarial increase and the increase in the Retail Prices Index (RPI). Alternatively, full service to and final remuneration at the actual date of retirement can be taken into account, with an extra $\frac{1}{60}$ of final remuneration given for each year of service after age 70 in excess of 40 years, up to a maximum of $\frac{45}{60}$.

(4) If the cash lump sum is taken at the normal retirement date or later (but before age 70) during deferred retirement, the maximum deferred residual pension may only be increased by reference to the RPI up to age 70. Thereafter, it may be increased by the greater of an actuarial increase and the increase in the RPI.

(5) Normally lump sum death in service payments from a pension scheme are made at the discretion of the trustee of the scheme to a wide range of beneficiaries, free of inheritance tax. However, in the case of a controlling director with continued rights, remaining in service on or after age 75, the rules of the pension scheme may provide only that any death in service payment should be made either to the surviving spouse or to the director's estate.

(Death benefits for scheme members (including controlling directors) *without continued rights* must be provided on a death-after-retirement basis, and a lump sum benefit will take the form therefore of a guarantee payment, which may be made subject to the trust's discretionary disposal provisions.)

6.2 CONTROLLING DIRECTOR – DEFINITION

There are currently two operative definitions of controlling director. The definition applicable to an individual director depends on the date on which he joins the pension scheme. Therefore:

(1) A director joining a pension scheme on or after 1 December 1987 is treated as a controlling director to whom the relevant above-mentioned restrictions apply if he has at any time after 16 March 1987 and within ten years of retirement or leaving (pensionable) service been a director and either on his own or with one or more associates beneficially owned or been able to control directly or indirectly or through other companies 20 per cent or more of the ordinary share capital of the company. 'Associate' means:
   (a) any relative or partner;
   (b) the trustees of any settlement in relation to which the director is a settlor;
   (c) the trustees of any settlement in relation to which any relative of the director (living or dead) is or was a settlor;
   (d) if the director has an interest in any shares or obligations of the company which are subject to any trust (or are part of the estate of a deceased person) the trustees of that trust (or the personal representatives of the deceased as the case may be).
'Either on his own or with one or more associates' means a director is treated as owning or controlling what any associate owns or controls, even if the director in question does not own or control any share capital himself. Benefits for a director who joined a pension scheme *before* 1 December 1987 to whom the above definition applies are restricted to the definition of final remuneration which is based on an average of three or more consecutive years. None of the other restrictions, however, are effective unless (2) below applies.

(2) A director who joined a pension scheme *before* 1 December 1987 is only treated as a controlling director to whom all the relevant restrictions apply if he could at that date be described as a director who, either alone or together with his or her spouse and minor children, is or becomes the beneficial owner of shares which when added to any shares held by the trustees of any settlement to which the director or his or her spouse had transferred assets carry more than 20 per cent of the voting rights in the company providing the pension or in a company which controls that company.

Regulations relating to transfers to personal pension schemes, and early retirement of members on ill-health grounds, apply the definition in (1) above to all members.

6.3 RETAINED BENEFITS

6.3.1 Controlling directors

Retained benefits cannot always be disregarded for a controlling director, or a person who has been a controlling director in the ten years prior to first joining a scheme of the employer, even if earnings in the first year of scheme membership do not exceed one-quarter of the earnings cap at the date of entry.

Pre-1987 and 1987–89 controlling directors

Unless benefits from the company scheme are to be provided on an uplifted/accelerated accrual basis, the maximum can be calculated ignoring retained benefits from:

(1) occupational schemes of previous employment;
(2) retirement annuity contracts and personal pension schemes of previous self-employment;
(3) retirement annuity contracts and personal pension schemes of the same employment.

Post-1989 controlling directors

Benefits from retirement annuity contracts and personal pension schemes relating to earnings from the same employment must always be taken into account, and treated as if they were further benefits provided by the company scheme. Retained benefits from occupational schemes, retirement annuity contracts and personal pension schemes relating to previous employments or self-employment can be ignored unless benefits from the company scheme are to be provided on an uplifted/accelerated accrual basis.

6.4 PENSIONABLE SERVICE

It may be possible by prior application to the Inland Revenue to pension the service of a director even though no remuneration is paid by the company. The reasoning appears to be that directors are included in the definition of 'employee' under ICTA 1988, s 612(1) (see Appendix 4) and any employee can become a member of a retirement benefit scheme. Obviously the director has to receive at least one year's remuneration on which to base the calculation of final remuneration.

6.5 SERIOUS ILL-HEALTH AND INCAPACITY

Full commutation of a member's benefits for a cash lump sum may be permissible where the member is in serious ill-health such that the expectation of life is so short that it is measured in months rather than years. In the case of controlling directors, the prior agreement of the Inland Revenue must be obtained before a member's benefits are commuted on these grounds.

Similarly, if retirement is caused by incapacity, a scheme member may take benefits immediately, but calculated on the assumption that service with the employer has continued to the normal retirement date. Again, the prior agreement of the Inland Revenue must be obtained.

In a 2002 court case, *Venables v Hornby*, the Court of Appeal overturned a High Court decision that benefits could be paid out of an approved pension scheme to an individual who remained as a non-executive director of a company after retiring from his job with the company as an executive director through ill health. According to the court "retirement" means cessation of service as an employee including service as a director.

6.6 CONTINUOUS SERVICE/CONTINUED RIGHTS

Where a controlling director is a member of a scheme set up by an employer which is later reconstructed (eg on a company takeover) there may be implications for the way in which 'pensionable service' is calculated. Neither continuous service nor continued rights are granted on a move to employers associated only by a 'community of interest'. Continuous service may not be granted following a takeover unless continuity of trade, involving the assumption of at least 75 per cent of the vendor's liabilities, can be demonstrated.

Also, in a centralised scheme for employers associated only by a community of interests, cross-subsidy is not permitted in relation to controlling directors: each employer must contribute only in respect of the controlling director's salary and service with that employer, and the benefits payable must also be calculated separately in respect of each employer, the applicable limits usually depending on the date of joining the relevant employer.

Claims for continuous service where the individual is a controlling director of either or both the employers concerned must be submitted to the Inland Revenue for approval on a special form, PS 155. This form has been updated and the Inland Revenue requirements are now more extensive and rigorous.

6.7 RULES ON TRANSFERS

As will be seen from the above paragraphs, the Inland Revenue has always wanted to ensure that controlling directors do not obtain excessive pension tax reliefs through manipulation of the various tax regimes, in particular the ability to provide high levels of retirement benefits from occupational pension schemes. The ability to transfer benefits between different types of scheme governed by different tax regimes has caused the Inland Revenue to look very closely at transfers by controlling directors. A controlling director is more likely than an ordinary employee to fund for maximum benefits under an occupational scheme or even to manipulate his earnings so that his benefits might exceed Inland Revenue limits. Having funded to the maximum, or in excess of the maximum, in the occupational pension scheme the controlling director might then try to transfer his benefits out into a personal pension scheme where there is no check on the final benefits that can be paid. As a result there are special controls on transfers to personal pension schemes as follows.

6.7.1 Overfunding certificate

Where a transfer is to be made from an occupational pension scheme to a personal pension scheme the administrator of the former must provide a certificate to the administrator of the personal pension scheme if the person transferring is, or has been at any time leading up to his right to that transfer payment, a controlling director (as defined above).

The certificate, signed by the administrator of the transferring scheme must show that the benefits secured by the transfer payment, together with any other schemes of that employer, do not exceed the maximum benefits permitted in the formula $N/NS \times P$, assuming that the pension increases by 5 per cent between the date of leaving and normal retirement date, and that the pension increases in payment at 3 per cent a year. If the certificate cannot be provided the transfer cannot take place: the only other option is for the member to transfer to another occupational pension scheme or to a s 32 policy (or buy-out bond).

6.7.2 The ten-year rule

A s 32 policy (buy-out bond) operates according to occupational pension scheme rules and so if a transfer is made from a s 32 policy set up after 1 July 1988 to a personal pension then a certificate is required if the individual was a controlling director of the employer whose pension scheme bought out the benefits. A controlling director who wishes to have the benefits of an individual policy could consider transferring into a s 32 policy, avoiding the need for an overfunding certificate, then to wait for up to ten years before transferring into a personal pension (the exact period being the number of years that have elapsed since the individual was a controlling director).

Example 6.1

> An individual who is a controlling director wishes to transfer into a personal pension in 1 June 2003. An overfunding certificate is only required if he is or was a controlling director of the employment which gave rise to the s 32 policy after 1 June 1993. If he was still a controlling director in that employment on 1 June 1994 the individual would have to wait until 1 June 2004 before transferring into a personal pension without an overfunding certificate.

6.7.3 Cash certificate

The lump sum entitlement under the transfer must also be certified if the individual has, at any time in the ten years before the right to a transfer payment arises, been a controlling director. No part of the transfer can be taken as a lump sum under the personal pension scheme unless the administrator certifies the amount, according to the rules of the transferring scheme. The amount certified can be the maximum allowable by the Inland Revenue though the cash lump sum under the scheme may be on a smaller formula: if the administrator certifies the lower amount that is all that can be paid under the receiving personal pension. The certified cash lump sum may be increased in line with the increase in the RPI between the date of leaving the scheme and the date of the transfer and at the same rate between the date of transfer and when the benefits are eventually taken. When the benefits are taken from the personal pension scheme the maximum lump sum will be the lower of 25 per cent of the non-protected rights fund and the certified amount increased in line with the RPI.

6.8 PENSIONS SIMPLIFICATION

The special conditions that apply to controlling directors and the resulting complexities, as described in this chapter, demonstrate why there is a need for simplification of the pensions tax rules. The lifetime limit (£1.4 million in 2002 terms) will replace the current need for complicated testing of Inland Revenue limits on retirement. Transfers between schemes will also be much simpler, obviating the need for close monitoring of transfers between the different tax regimes as set out above. Nevertheless controlling directors, and other high-earning individuals, will need to take action before the start of the new tax regime in order to safeguard, as far as is possible, the benefits accumulated under today's law and practice in order to avoid or mitigate the impact of the recovery tax charge (one-third of any fund above the lifetime limit) (see Chapter 10).

Where the lifetime fund is taken after the start of the new tax regime and the individual had already accumulated a fund of £1.4 million this amount should be registered with the Inland Revenue. The proportion of the fund that can be taken as a tax-free lump sum should also be registered. This will be calculated according to the tax regime governing that individual's own pension scheme and could be more than 25 per cent of the fund – the maximum under the new tax regime rules. However, the recovery tax charge will apply to any amount generated by fund growth above the RPI.

If the fund built up before the start of the new tax regime is less than but close to the lifetime limit the individual again should register the amount. Any fund eventually taken in excess of the indexed lifetime limit will be subject to the recovery charge.

Individuals will have to monitor closely the build up of their funds if they are close to the lifetime limits: the need to adjust investment strategy to limit investment growth will be essential, however perverse. Substantial investment growth in the pension fund could result in the recovery tax charge. Consequently, asset allocation will be an important consideration. Equity investment with its potential for high returns may be better used for personal investments, outside pensions, with a more cautious investment strategy for the pension itself such as deposits.

7

FUNDING METHODS

The techniques used for funding group pension schemes and individual pension arrangements differ considerably. Although this book is aimed primarily at the personal position of a company director or self-employed person whose benefits will normally be provided by means of an individual arrangement it is important to be aware of the differences in the techniques used as it is not uncommon for a director to receive benefits from a group pension scheme and also an individual pension arrangement.

7.1 FUNDING OF GROUP SCHEMES

Most existing group schemes promise benefits related to final salary so that as salaries increase, so do prospective pensions: it is obvious therefore that it is difficult to quantify in advance the exact pension benefit and therefore the cost of providing it. Under group pension schemes, it is usual for employers to pay contributions which are expressed as a percentage of the total pensionable salaries of employees. This percentage, known as the 'funding rate', will be calculated by the actuary after making various assumptions of which the most important are that:

(1) salaries will increase uniformly at, say, 5 per cent per annum compound;
(2) the yield on the fund will be, say, 6 per cent compound after expenses;
(3) mortality will be experienced in line with an appropriate mortality table;
(4) the salary/age profile of the group will remain more or less constant;
(5) the ratio of males and females in the scheme will remain constant;
(6) persons retiring will be replaced by new entrants within a certain age range, usually at the younger ages.

In recent years funding rates have been affected by external factors not allowed for in actuarial calculations: legislation changes, which have usually benefited scheme members or have increased the compliance burdens on trustees but have resulted in increases in funding rates.

At least every three years, the actuary checks the actual performance of the fund against the assumptions made originally. If the assumptions have not been borne out in practice, an adjustment may have to be made to the funding rate.

If salaries have increased substantially without corresponding increases in the yield on the fund, there will be a deficit which may have to be made good by the injection of a lump sum.

During the 1990s, two factors generated surpluses in some pension schemes, particularly those of large, public companies:

(1) The rate of pension fund growth outstripped the growth in earnings.
(2) Pension schemes made a profit out of early leavers. As redundancy often works on the basis of 'last in, first out,' pension schemes gained by having to provide minimal benefits for persons leaving service after a short period. However, legislation has improved the benefits of the 'early leaver' by providing for inflation-proofing of preserved benefits in line with price, but not earnings, inflation.

In recent years, inflation and pension fund investment returns have fallen and the cost of providing pensions – either directly from the fund or by purchasing annuities from an insurance company – has increased. As a result, many large companies have closed their final salary schemes. Instead they offer money purchase schemes to new entrants, leaving them to take on the investment risks.

7.1.1 Minimum funding requirement

The existing minimum funding requirement (MFR) sets out the minimum level to which employers must fund their defined benefit pension scheme and the time period over which they should make good any shortfall. The MFR also forms the basis for calculating transfer values. The MFR was introduced after the Robert Maxwell affair to help improve the funding of defined benefit schemes. There has been criticism of the MFR mainly because it is seen as a straitjacket by many schemes and does not take into account the special circumstances of individual schemes. The MFR has also caused some schemes to focus on short-term market conditions and influenced the investment conditions of the trustees. It has also lead to additional administrative costs.

In June 2003 the Government published a document, 'Simplicity, security and choice: working and saving for retirement – action on occupational pensions', in which it confirmed that it will replace the MFR with scheme-specific funding requirements which will enable employers, trustees and the scheme actuary to work together to develop an appropriate funding strategy for a scheme. There are also related proposals to improve the security of scheme members by creating a Pensions Protection Fund to guarantee members a specified minimum level of pension if the sponsoring employer becomes insolvent.

7.2 FUNDING INDIVIDUAL ARRANGEMENTS

The funding of individual pension arrangements or executive pension plans also involves making assumptions about salary growth and investment return, but these are related directly to the individual member concerned. The benefits to which he will be entitled will normally represent the proceeds of the fund at the end of the day and will therefore be a function of the contributions paid and the growth thereon: this differs from the final salary type scheme where the employer promises that benefits will be directly related to salary.

7.2.1 Funding for capital

The principle behind executive pension plans is to accumulate capital in the hands of the trustees which can be used to purchase an annuity on retirement. The trustees purchase annuities at the most competitive rates available at the time of retirement from any life office – not necessarily the one which has been used to accumulate the capital before retirement. Thus the executive pension plan can be split into two parts: the first part relates to the period when contributions are paid and invested in order to accumulate the maximum amount of capital, within Inland Revenue limits, and the second part consists of buying an annuity with the accumulated capital.

The various ways in which capital can be accumulated are explored in Chapter 8.

The amount of capital needed at retirement depends on the annuity rates available at that time.

7.2.2 Annuity rates

The actual rate of annuity – or periodical payment by an insurance company in return for a capital investment – depends not only on the age of the person retiring, but on the following factors:

(1) whether the annuity is payable monthly, quarterly, or yearly;
(2) whether the annuity is level or increases (or 'escalates') in payment;

(3) whether it will be guaranteed for a minimum period of five or ten years or not guaranteed; and

(4) whether or not the annuity continues to be paid to the surviving spouse on the prior death of the annuitant.

With regard to (1) above, under the Pensions Act 1995, pensions accruing after 5 April 1997 in occupational pension schemes must increase payment in line with the Limited Prices Index (RPI with a ceiling of 5 per cent per year).

Annuity rates are also volatile as they relate directly to interest rates and also on the desire of an insurance company to come in or out of the annuity market. The following table is an example of annuity rates per annum for males and females based on a purchase price of £1,000 available in July 2003, although it does not represent the most competitive available at that time. It is assumed that the annuity is payable by quarterly instalments in advance and is payable for a minimum of five years and is based on an underlying interest rate of 3.15 per cent. The table shows annuities which are level throughout and annuities which escalate each year at 5 per cent compound.

Table 7.1

Age next birthday	Male level (£)	Male 5% esc.	Female level (£)	Female 5% esc.
55	51.11	24.87	47.77	21.59
56	52.23	25.94	48.68	22.45
57	53.42	27.07	49.64	23.36
58	54.69	28.28	50.67	24.33
59	56.03	29.55	51.75	25.36
60	57.46	30.92	52.91	26.46
61	58.97	32.36	54.15	27.62
62	60.57	33.90	55.46	28.85
63	62.26	35.53	56.85	30.17
64	64.03	37.26	58.33	31.56
65	65.89	39.09	59.90	33.05
66	67.84	41.03	61.57	34.64
67	69.90	43.08	63.34	36.33
68	72.08	45.27	65.23	38.13
69	74.39	47.59	67.24	40.05
70	76.83	50.05	69.39	42.10
71	79.76	52.94	71.72	44.32
72	82.90	56.05	74.21	46.71
73	86.29	59.41	76.86	49.26
74	89.95	63.04	79.69	51.98
75	93.90	66.99	82.70	54.90

Annuities purchased by trustees of pension schemes are known as 'compulsory purchase annuities' and are treated as earned income. These contrast with 'purchased life annuities' which are available to individuals to purchase with their own money and which receive different tax treatment in that they are regarded as partly a return of capital which is tax free with the balance being taxed as unearned income.

7.2.3 Salary increases

In order to calculate how much capital would be required at retirement, it is necessary to project current salary forward to retirement.

In March 1994 the Inland Revenue announced through the Association of British Insurers a revised method of calculating maximum contributions, to take effect from 1 September 1994 and updated from 1 June 1996. The latest (1996) method applies to 'earmarked insurance policies'. For schemes commencing from that date salaries should be assumed to increase at no more than 6.9 per cent per annum compound. The earnings cap, £99,000 in 2003/04, should be assumed to increase at 5.3 per cent.

Example 7.1

A director, aged 30, proposing to retire at age 60, currently earning £80,000, may have the cost of his benefits calculated on a projected final salary of £449,000 (actual final salary would be £592,000 assuming increases at 6.9% pa but limited to the earnings cap increased at 5.3% pa).

7.3 YIELD ASSUMPTION

Having established the amount of capital required at age 60, it is then necessary to make an assumption about the return which will be earned on the investment to achieve that capital sum.

For schemes set up from 1 September 1994 the yield assumption is 1.5 per cent in excess of that assumed for salary inflation and 3 per cent in excess of that assumed for the increase in the earnings cap. In consequence, based on an 8.5 per cent per annum yield, the salary inflation rate is 6.9 per cent per annum ($1.085 \div 1.015$) and the earnings cap increase rate is 5.3 per cent per annum ($1.085 \div 1.03$). For schemes set up before then a yield assumption of 0.5 per cent per annum above salary inflation was acceptable, but that method ended in September 1999.

7.3.1 Maximum permissible contributions – Inland Revenue changes

As stated above, in 1994 the Inland Revenue introduced more realistic assumptions to be made about future salary increases and pension fund growth. It is now permissible to fund for pensions increasing in payment at only 5.3 per cent per annum: prior to the introduction of the changes it was possible to fund for pensions increasing in payment at 8.5 per cent per annum. The increase in the real rate of fund growth over salary inflation to 1.5 per cent per annum and the reduction in the assumed increase in pensions in payment had the effect of reducing the input needed to fund maximum benefits at retirement. There is another change which has a considerable impact: before 1994 maximum contributions were calculated on a 'level' basis. Under the current basis, contributions are assumed to increase in line with earnings, again reducing the initial contribution.

The following table shows a comparison of the previous and current contribution levels in respect of males and females retiring at age 60, with 20 years' service completed at retirement, with no provision for widow(er)s' pensions and where earnings are not affected by the earnings cap. The previous basis ended in September 1999 and any scheme which benefited from it should have recalculated contributions on the current basis by now.

Table 7.2

	Previous basis %	Current basis %
Males Aged		
30	88	26
35	94	33
40	102	42
45	117	59
50	151	92
55	261	190
Females Aged		
30	103	31
35	109	38
40	119	50
45	137	69
50	176	108
55	306	223

7.3.2 New schemes

The following examples show the contribution levels for a director or key executive.

Example 7.2

> Male aged 40 with a salary of £55,000 and a retirement age of 60. The maximum regular annual contribution payable on the current basis (42%) starts at £23,100 and, if earnings grow in line with the assumed rate of salary inflation of 6.9% per annum, rises to £87,733 just before retirement.

Example 7.3

> Female aged 35 with a salary of £50,000 and a selected retirement age of 60. The maximum regular annual contribution payable on the current basis (38%) starts at £19,000 and, if earnings grow in line with the assumed 6.9% per annum, rises to £100,738 just before retirement.

Whilst the two bases are quite different the objective remains the same, to build up a fund sufficient to provide a two-thirds pension at retirement. However, the scope for accelerated funding under the previous basis is no longer available.

7.3.3 *De minimis* rule

There is a *de minimis* contribution limit below which the initial benefit testing does not have to be carried out.

The *de minimis* limit applies where the aggregate contributions to all schemes, excluding contributions for death in service benefits, for the same employment do not exceed 17½ per cent of earnings provided contributions to all schemes of the employer have always been below this limit.

Before 31 March 1998 the limit was higher than this. Pension schemes set up on the higher basis had to be reviewed by 31 March 2001 and, if necessary, contributions reduced.

7.4 ANNUAL AND SPECIAL/SINGLE CONTRIBUTIONS – TAX RELIEF

7.4.1 The employer – regular contributions

Regular contributions to approved executive pension plans (being an exempt approved scheme) are deductible for tax purposes in the year of payment provided that they can be classified as 'ordinary annual contributions'. As a rule of thumb this means that the rate of contribution (eg a fixed amount or a fixed percentage of payroll) should continue for no less than three consecutive years.

There are, however, circumstances in which regular contributions may be treated as single contributions (see 7.4.2 below) in which case tax relief could be spread for up to four years. Where a regular contribution plan is set up and the contribution is either reduced or stopped in a later year, the Inland Revenue has discretion to go back and treat the previous contribution as single instead of regular.

7.4.2 The employer – special single contributions

The tax relief on single or 'special' contributions (usually paid in respect of past service) to an occupational pension scheme is determined as follows:

(1) The maximum term over which tax relief on single contributions will be spread is four years.
(2) The period of the spread is determined solely by the size of the aggregate special contributions to that scheme.

Special contributions which amount to £500,000 or over and exceed the total of other contributions made by the employer to that scheme in the same chargeable period will normally be spread on the basis set out below. Aggregate special contributions amounting to less than £500,000 will not be spread for tax relief purposes:

£500,000 or over but less than £1m	2 years
£1m or over but less than £2m	3 years
£2m or over	4 years

The allowance of the contribution(s) will be spread evenly over the period (eg an aggregate *special contribution* of £800,000 will be allowed on the basis of £400,000 in year 1 (the chargeable period in which it was paid) and £400,000 in year 2 (the next chargeable period)). Where a chargeable period is not a period of 12 months, allowance will be given on a *pro rata* basis.

Where there is evidence of manipulation to reduce the period of spread, the Inland Revenue reserves the right to determine the spread on some other basis.

Once the period of spread has been determined, it will not be changed subsequently, even if the underlying ordinary annual contributions were to be reduced.

In arriving at this spread of relief, all single contributions paid to the scheme are aggregated.

The period of spread may be changed if the employer ceases to trade or its trade is taken over by another employer. In these circumstances the unrelieved balance of the single contribution will normally be allowed against the profits of the employer whose trade has ceased in the final chargeable period before cessation. Alternatively the single contribution may be re-apportioned over the period between the date of payment and cessation.

7.5 DEPENDANT'S DEATH IN RETIREMENT BENEFITS

The amount of additional capital required to provide a widow(er)'s death in retirement pension varies according to the difference in ages between husband and wife and retirement age. For example, if the wife is three years younger than her husband, between 21 per cent and 25 per cent additional capital would be required to provide the maximum widow's pension on the husband's death after retirement ages of 60 and 65 respectively. If a female director wishes to provide a widower's death in retirement pension for her husband, who is three years older, around 5–6 per cent additional capital would be required to provide the maximum widower's pension on the wife's death after retirement ages of 60 and 65 respectively.

7.6 PERSONAL CONTRIBUTIONS

The maximum levels of contribution given above include any contributions paid personally by the employee or director from his own remuneration as follows:

(1) any personal contributions which the employer requires the member to pay towards the cost of his benefits;
(2) any additional voluntary contributions (AVCs) which the member chooses to pay to top up his benefits within the employer's scheme;
(3) any free-standing additional voluntary contributions (FSAVCs) with which the member choses to top up his benefits outside the employer's scheme.

Contributions in (1) and (2) above are fully tax deductible through the PAYE system but contributions under (3) above are paid net of basic rate tax with any higher relief given through the individual's tax assessment.

There is an overall limit on personal contributions of 15 per cent of remuneration (subject to the earnings cap in the case of post-1989 members) in any one tax year.

Where the employee earns less than £30,000 (excluding any PIID benefits) a contribution to a stakeholder pension scheme of up to £3,600 may be paid. (This option is not available to directors.) This contribution is *in addition* to the maximum levels of contribution shown above.

7.7 OVER-FUNDING

As the maximum levels of contribution at the outset incorporate a projection of future salary, it is necessary to monitor the performance of the fund in relation to actual increases in salary, especially as retirement draws near, when a change in annuity rates upwards or downwards can seriously affect the provision of maximum benefits. If there is too much capital in the fund to provide the benefits promised, or the maximum levels of benefit, any excess must be returned to the employer and will be taxed as a trading receipt at a special rate of 35 per cent. Alternatively, if there are other members in the fund it may usually be re-applied to purchase pensions for those other members. The changes in the basis of calculating the maximum contribution levels will reduce the likelihood of a build up of too much capital in the fund.

7.8 DEATH-IN-SERVICE BENEFITS

Under executive pension plans, lump sums and dependants' pensions are provided by means of a straightforward term assurance which normally ceases at retirement age.

The cost of death-in-service benefits are in addition to the maximum contribution for retirement benefits shown in Table 7.2.

Table 7.3 shows the approximate multiple of salary that can be provided at outset as a lump sum for a widow(er)'s death-in-service pension in addition to the four times salary life assurance benefit.

Table 7.3

Age of wife on next birthday	Multiple of salary	Age of husband on next birthday	Multiple of salary
up to 29	12	up to 23	12
30 to 38	11	24 to 32	11
39 to 45	10	33 to 39	10
46 to 51	9	40 to 45	9
52 to 57	8	46 to 51	8
58 to 62	7	52 to 56	7
63 to 67	6	57 to 61	6
68 to 70	5	62 to 67	5
		68 to 70	4

On death in service, any life assurance in excess of four times final salary is used to purchase a widow(er)'s death-in-service pension.

These multiples assume the member can complete at least 20 years' service to retirement age and are subject to the following funding limits.

7.9 ANNUAL AND SINGLE PREMIUMS

Some insurance companies quote death in service benefits on the basis of single premiums. Thus, a premium paid at the beginning of a year will be sufficient to cover the cost of the risk for 12 months only. The following year, the same amount of cover will be slightly more expensive because the member will be one year older. Single premiums, therefore, involve an increase in cost for the same amount of cover.

Annual premiums, however, are level amounts paid throughout the term of the policy irrespective of any change in health and will be higher than single contributions in the early years, but less in later years.

7.10 DECREASING TERM ASSURANCE

Because the capital fund which is building up for retirement is normally returned in the event of death this itself will provide part of the required level of death in service benefit: some companies, therefore, are prepared to insure death in service benefits on the basis of a decreasing term assurance which provides the difference between the total desired level of death in service benefit and the amount building up under the fund.

7.11 PENSIONS SIMPLIFICATION

The Inland Revenue proposals to simplify pensions tax will have a significant impact on the funding of schemes especially individual arrangements (see Table 7.2). The contribution payable by individuals will be the higher of £3,600 or 100 per cent of UK chargeable earnings in each tax year. The current practice of having different maximum contribution levels depending on age, with the need to adjust those contributions to take account of salary changes and the value of the underlying fund, will no longer apply. There will be no limit to the contributions that can be paid by an employer or former employer although there will be an annual limit on inflows of value to an individual's pension fund of £200,000 (to be indexed in line with price inflation).

The lifetime limit, £1.4 million in 2002 terms, will be the maximum capital sum that can be funded for retirement and death benefits. It will be important not to exceed the lifetime and annual inflow limits as otherwise a penal tax recovery charge will be levied on the excess. However, these limits will affect only a small proportion of scheme members, mainly high earners whose benefits are likely to come from a number of sources including group defined benefit schemes and individual pension arrangements.

8

INSURED PENSION ARRANGEMENTS

Insured pension arrangements can be divided into four broad categories, as follows, although categories (1) and (3) are largely historical relics:

(1) with-profits policies;
(2) unit-linked policies;
(3) deposit administration policies;
(4) unitised with-profits policies.

8.1 WITH-PROFITS POLICIES

Many old insurance plans on the market fall into this category. Typically they are operated by traditional life offices, many of which have been in existence for over a century, although these companies, particularly mutuals, have undergone considerable structural change in recent years as a result of takeovers and mergers. The pension policies are similar to with-profits endowment life assurance policies although life cover is generally optional. The policy is either a pure endowment where a guaranteed capital sum is payable on retirement, or a deferred annuity with a guaranteed annuity payable on retirement.

The pure endowment policy is converted into an annuity at an annuity rate that may be guaranteed in the policy, whereas the deferred annuity policy may provide a guaranteed cash option. Most with-profits policies, however, offer an 'open market option' whereby the trustees may purchase an annuity on the open market from another insurance company.

An individual who is considering investing in a conventional with-profits policy is normally offered a 'projected capital fund per £1,000 of annual contribution' made up of three elements:

(1) a minimum guaranteed amount payable at retiring age, plus
(2) an additional sum, which is not guaranteed, and which depends on the actual results achieved over the full investment period; this additional 'bonus' (known as a reversionary bonus) is normally expressed as a percentage of the minimum guaranteed amount in (1) above and usually benefits from a compounding effect, plus

(3) a final additional amount which depends on economic and financial conditions prevailing at the time of retirement – known as a 'terminal bonus'.

Once a reversionary bonus has been declared by the insurance company, it cannot be subsequently removed even if future investment results fail to match expectations.

In recent years there has been a reduction in reversionary bonuses declared by life offices and much more emphasis on terminal bonuses. There is no guarantee with terminal bonuses, however, as these are discretionary payments depending upon investment conditions when the policy matures.

In the event of the member's death before retirement the policy may provide one of the following:

(1) no return of premiums paid;
(2) a return of the premiums paid without interest;
(3) a return of the premiums paid together with compound interest at around 3–6 per cent per annum;
(4) a return of the fund up to the date of death.

Obviously to the extent that the return on death is improved then the eventual benefits which may be received on retirement will be smaller. The fourth option set out above does not, of course, necessarily represent the face value of the policy including attaching bonuses but represents the 'value' of the policy as determined by the actuary. Options (1), (2) and (3) are rare nowadays: most of these policies will have been converted to option (4)-type policies in order to give an improved potential death benefit.

The management charges made by the insurance company for issuing a with-profits policy and running the pension plan are not disclosed in the policy document, although sometimes a separate policy fee is specified in addition to the contributions.

It is only possible to monitor the performance of this type of contract when the policy is determined, for example, by analysing the amount paid in the event of death or the policy's surrender value should it be discontinued on, say, early retirement or should the policy actually mature at retiring age.

The guarantees inherent in these old policies may be very valuable in the current environment where annuity rates are very low. It may be advantageous to convert the accumulated fund at retirement into an annuity at the rate guaranteed in the policy rather than transferring the fund to another provider under an open-market option where current annuity rates would be used. However, the guaranteed route may not offer so many options as to the *type* of annuity that may be taken, for example level, joint level, with or without escalation.

The prime example of the value of guaranteed annuity rates for policy-holders, and the financial strains on an insurer having to meet those guarantees is Equitable Life.

These traditional with-profits polices are no longer marketed.

8.2 UNIT-LINKED POLICIES

The 1970s saw an upsurge of insurance companies offering policies on unit-linked principles. The FA 1973 allowing controlling directors to have executive pension plans gave a timely boost to this business and today, life offices offer unit-linked policies almost exclusively although some also offer unitised with-profits policies (see 8.6 below)

Under a unit-linked policy, the investor is able to choose the investment sector in which he would like his contributions to be invested and he may switch between sectors from time to time. The contributions paid are used to buy units in one or more of the chosen investment sectors and the value of the units at any time is dependent on the value of the underlying assets.

On retirement, the units are encashed and the proceeds are used to pur-chase an annuity on the open market. No bonuses are declared and no guarantee attaches to the value of the units.

8.3 CHARGING STRUCTURES

The methods by which insurance companies historically have taken their charges for administering a unit-linked policy vary from one to another but will normally have been based on one or more of a combination of the following principles. In recent years charging structures have become more transparent (see 8.3.7 below), although the following principles will often still apply to old policies.

8.3.1 Allocation to units

In most plans up to 100 per cent of each contribution is allocated to units but sometimes there is a smaller allocation in respect of investment terms of ten years or less. The following table was fairly typical under old policies.

Table 8.1

Years to pension age from commencement of the contract	Allocation to units (%)
10 or more	100
9	99
8	98
7	97
6	96
5 and less	95

Some insurance companies offer allocations in excess of 100 per cent but often with the requirement that contributions have to be paid throughout the term, some give an increased rate of allocation, provided a proportion of the contributions payable within, say, the first ten years have actually been paid, and some companies give a higher allocation to units in respect of contributions paid towards the end of the term of the contract.

Many contracts have a reduced allocation to units in the first two years, although in recent years there has been a trend away from these front-end-loaded structures towards ones with level allocation to units throughout the term of the contract. It is common for investors who have been contributing to insured pension arrangements for many years to have a number of policies each with slightly different charging structures.

8.3.2 Type of units

Traditionally, it was common to find the first one or two years' contributions allocated to 'capital' or 'initial' units, under which the insurance company takes an additional charge of between 3.5 and 6 per cent per annum of the units' value. Subsequent contributions purchase 'accumulation' or 'ordinary' units under which all the income and growth from the underlying investment accrues to the planholders (except for the 'annual management' charge – see 8.3.3 below).

Another method of charging is where insurance companies allocate a reduced percentage of the first one or two years' contributions to 'accumulation' or 'ordinary' units. As an example, the insurance company may allocate between 25 and 85 per cent of the first year's contribution depending upon the contract's term. Both of these methods are examples of front-end-loaded structures.

Yet another method is for no explicit charge to be made in the first one or two years' contributions. Instead all contributions are allocated to accumulation or ordinary units, but if contributions stop or reduce (a frequent occurrence under pensions plans) a reduction is made to the fund at that time.

8.3.3 Management charges

In addition to the charges mentioned above, most insurance companies make a management charge which is expressed as a percentage of the total value of the units and might lie anywhere between 0.75 and 1.0 per cent per annum, although insurance companies market unit-linked policies which have unlimited annual management charges or have the ability to increase management charges from, say, 0.75 to 1.5 per cent per annum at some stage in the future. Also, it is not uncommon particularly in the case of property investments for the cost of buying, selling and managing properties, fees to independent valuers and other dealing costs to be borne by the fund.

8.3.4 Bid/offer prices

As with unit trusts, units are allocated on the basis of offer prices and are subsequently sold at lower bid prices when the policyholder takes his benefits. The difference between bid and offer prices is usually around 5 per cent.

8.3.5 Policy charges

In addition some companies take an initial instalment charge and a fixed policy amount in real terms every year (the initial amount is thus increased every year in line with an index such as the National Average Earnings Index or Retail Prices Index) which actually reflects the cost of servicing the policy.

8.3.6 Disclosure of charges

The Financial Services Authority (FSA) specifies the basis on which insurers disclose charges taken under pension contracts. The basis, which came into effect from January 1995, includes the following:

(1) Disclosure of the actual deductions taken from the policy by the insurer in certain years throughout its term.
(2) The policy's surrender value (or transfer) during each of the first five years, every five years thereafter and during each of the last five years. A comparison of these surrender values gives an indication of the charges under different contracts.

Under FSA rules on illustrations pension benefits must be illustrated assuming rates of return of 5 per cent per annum, 7 per cent per annum and 9 per cent per annum based on the insurer's own charging structure. This enables investors to compare the contracts of competing pension providers.

The PIA rules require insurers to show the reduction in investment yield brought about by the charges under unit-linked contracts. (Under with-profits and unitised with-profits contracts only the effect of expenses need to be shown; expenses do not include the profits which accrue to the insurer.)

Illustrations are shown in future monetary terms for plans taken out today. However, illustrations for existing pension schemes that operate on a money purchase basis, like personal pensions, are shown in today's terms, from April 2003. Currently it is impossible for pension planholders to understand the working of their plans when they receive statements showing benefits on inconsistent bases.

From 2004, illustrations for new plans will be consistent with benefits shown in today's terms, and on a real rate of return of 2.5 per cent. This is also in line with the basis on which the Government will provide regular illustrations or forecasts of state pensions.

8.3.7 The stakeholder environment

Personal pension schemes that are designed and marketed as stakeholder pension schemes and which comply with stakeholder regulations have simple and transparent charging structures: an annual management charge not exceeding 1 per cent of the value of the fund (calculated at a daily rate) and no other charges. This means that the types of charges outlined in 8.3.2 to 8.3.5 above are not permitted. One effect of the stakeholder regulations has been to simplify charges for pensions not classified as stakeholder plans.

Another effect has been to reduce the amount of the charges available to providers to pay to financial advisers, in the form of commission, for advice given to potential policyholders. This may, in time, lead to a greater incidence of independent financial advisers charging separate fees for advice.

8.4 TYPES OF INVESTMENT FUNDS

Most companies offer separate property, equity, gilt-edged and cash funds, but the majority of investors choose the 'managed' approach where the insurance company itself invests each contribution in whatever proportions and between whichever different investment sectors it feels appropriate for the longer term. This normally means a mixture of property, equities and gilt-edged investments. Cash deposit funds or building society related funds are usually intended to be used as a means of consolidating gains (or losses) at or near retirement age. Policyholders need not direct all their contributions into one fund but normally have the choice of investing in all funds or in any combination. Investment choice extends to overseas areas such as the United States and Canada, Japan, Hong Kong, Australia, Europe and South America. An international managed fund may be available incorporating all these areas.

Policyholders may also invest in tracker funds where the fund tracks an index, such as the UK Financial Times Stock Exchange (FT-SE) All Share Index, which contains a broad spread of companies that aims to be fully representative of the UK market as a whole.

In recent years, ethical funds have become popular where investment managers invest in businesses that conform to a range of ethical and environmental guidelines.

8.5 DEPOSIT ADMINISTRATION

Deposit administration contracts sought to combine the best features of conventional with-profits and unit-linked policies although these are now rarely used. The principle behind deposit administration is that, after deducting charges for administration, the policyholder has a deposit account with the insurance company – similar to a bank account – to which interest is added from time to time. The amount of interest that is actually guaranteed (if any) in the contract varies widely with some offices linking the rates to the building society lending rate and others crediting interest on a basis reflecting interest rates generally.

There are considerable variations in the method of charging expenses. For example, the credited interest rate may take account of expenses or a fixed policy amount may be deducted from the contribution before interest is credited, an annual charge may be made, or a lower interest may be applied to the initial contributions. The pension obtained from the accumulated fund at the time of retirement depends on annuity rates prevailing at the time and therefore it is not normally guaranteed.

These contracts are rarely marketed except for some existing group pension schemes.

8.6 UNITISED WITH-PROFITS POLICIES

The unitised with-profits policy is a variation on the conventional with-profits policy, although it has the hallmarks of a unit-linked policy. However, there are a number of important differences: under unitised with-profits, the unit prices are generally guaranteed to increase at a minimum rate of growth, for example a value equal to the contributions paid into the plan together with regular bonuses added to the plan although this price guarantee normally only applies at maturity or on early death. At any other time the unit price is not guaranteed and may be reduced by the actuary.

Investment performance is not reflected immediately but is smoothed over a period of years. The regular, annual bonus is set at a level that is lower than the insurance company expects to earn over the long term leaving the insurance company with freedom to invest in company shares and property. A final bonus, not guaranteed, may also be paid, representing a fair return (after smoothing) of the total fund value.

The benefits are expressed in the form of units with bid and offer prices, allocation rates and initial charges, similar to unit-linked contracts.

Policyholders are permitted to switch into and out of the unitised with-profits fund although companies normally reserve the right to reduce the unit price on a switch-out by applying a Market Value Reduction and some do not allow switches-in within five years of the retirement date.

In recent years unitised with-profits annuities have become popular, giving annuitants the combination of a guaranteed amount of income (albeit lower than in the past) together with exposure to equity investments through annual bonuses (see also Chapter 19).

In July 2001 the Treasury commissioned an independent review of medium and long-term retail investment, led by Ron Sandler who published his report in July 2002. The recommendations included:

(1) a set of safer, good value, easy to understand products (called 'stakeholder' products, along the lines of stakeholder pension products);
(2) tax measures aimed at simplifying the current regime for retail savings products;
(3) reforms to with-profits policies to make their structure and management simpler and more transparent.

Sandler was concerned at the lack of transparency of with-profits contracts. Investors are unable to obtain proper scrutiny of these contracts and underlying investment performance. To ensure simplicity Sandler wants to see a new with-profits model with many new features including:

(1) each year the insurer should disclose to customers the current redemption value, the proceeds on death, the projected maturity value and the value of the unsmoothed asset value;
(2) the smoothing account inherent in the with-profits concept must be neutral over the long term (and so cannot build up an inherited estate of undistributed assets as now);
(3) there should be no shareholder participation in with-profits payouts (currently it is common for insurers marketing with-profits plans to pay 10 per cent of payouts to shareholders);
(4) there should be standard rules for the calculation of charges so they are consistent across products and providers.

It is clear that if the Sandler recommendations are accepted by the Government new investment plans based on underlying with-profits principles will be much more transparent than those available today. However, the impact of the Sandler recommendations on with-profits pension plans will be less obvious as those that are available today as 'stakeholder' pensions are already more transparent, with the whole of the profits earned by the fund being payable to policyholders (with no 10 per cent cut to shareholders) and having a simple charging structure of no more than 1 per cent a year.

8.7 GUARANTEED EQUITY FUNDS

Guaranteed equity funds, sometimes called 'structured products', are designed to provide planholders with the benefits of equity investments, but without the associated risk of loss of capital. Typically these funds, using financial instruments such as derivatives, guarantee a minimum return of capital together with a proportion of the growth in a recognised index, for example the FT-SE 100 Index over a specified period. (The FT-SE 100 Index reflects the total collective value of the top 100 companies in the UK stock market, not including the dividends paid by these companies to shareholders.) Because a minimum return of capital is guaranteed, the potential for equity growth is limited.

Growth in these funds is usually based on two elements:

(1) the level of guarantee; and
(2) the gearing mechanism.

The level of guarantee limits the loss in the value of the pension units to which the planholder is exposed in any specified period; for example the guarantee is typically 97–100 per cent of capital.

The gearing mechanisms represent the growth in the FT-SE index over a period, for example, three months, one year, three years (known as set dates). At the end of the period the unit price is adjusted by a percentage (known as the gearing). Gearings are higher where the planholder is prepared to accept some loss of capital, for example under a 97 per cent guarantee. Where the planholder requires a 100 per cent capital guarantee the gearings are lower.

Investment growth as measured by the gearings is calculated on the set dates and is 'locked in' to the planholder's fund. Planholders are not generally permitted to switch out of these funds during the set dates without incurring a surrender penalty.

8.8 COMPARISONS OF UNIT-LINKED FUNDS

The most important factor determining the value for money which a unit-linked planholder receives is the performance of the investment fund to which his plan is linked. How is the investor to assess the likely future performance of different life companies' investment funds?

Performance league tables are not by themselves the answer. The fact that one fund has performed particularly well over a period in the past – especially a short period – is no assurance that it will perform well in the period which matters to the new planholder, which is the future. Past performance over that period may have been the result of special circumstances which will not be relevant in the future.

The best solution is to look for the features which are likely to result in consistent long-term performance. No one can guarantee future performance, but certain features can point to the likelihood of consistent long-term performance, or act as a warning that future performance is likely to be volatile. The following checklist may be helpful:

(1) Does the fund have the benefit of a regular cash inflow?
(2) Has the fund a consistent long-term performance record?
(3) How long has the fund been in existence?
(4) What is the size of the fund?
(5) How has the fund coped with market upheavals?
(6) Is the fund broadly based or is it a specialised fund?
(7) How have the company's other funds performed?
(8) Does the fund have continuity of investment management?
(9) Does the name of the fund reflect its composition?

The significance of these factors is analysed in detail below.

8.8.1 Assured regular cash inflow

Investment managers often state that nothing assists them more than the knowledge that there is a regular cash inflow, and nothing can harm investment performance more than a sudden drying-up of funds or, worse still, a sudden need to liquidate investments to meet cash requirements of investors wishing to take out their money. A regular cash inflow makes it easy for an investment manager to change the weighting of investments in the fund without bearing the heavy costs of selling some shares in order to buy others. A sudden outflow can involve not merely the expense and the difficulty of selling shares on a falling market, but can force a fund to change its unit valuation from an 'offer price' to a 'bid price', which may in the most exceptional circumstances reduce the unit price by 6 or 7 per cent overnight. So a fund which shows up well in a short-term league table might still be highly vulnerable if it does not have a source of regular cash inflow.

8.8.2 Assessing a fund's future prospects

When assessing the future prospects of a fund which has shown up well in a past performance league table, the following other factors should be taken into account:

(1) If the table is for a relatively short term, check up on the fund's performance over other periods, particularly long-term periods. It is not uncommon for funds which are in the 'Top Ten' of this year's one-year performance tables to figure in the 'Bottom Ten' of next year's tables. What matters to a planholder is consistent, long-term performance.

(2) How long has the fund been in existence? Many new funds have shown very good performance in their first year or two, only to lapse into disappointing performance in later years.

(3) Is the fund still a small fund? As there are a large number of small funds in existence, often with specialised investment policies, there are frequently a number of small funds near the top of the yearly league tables. The following year there may still be a number of small funds among the leaders, but they are likely to be different small funds. Any successful fund with a regular cash flow will soon become a large fund – and the real test is the ability to show consistent long-term performance.

(4) A fund should be judged in bad conditions as well as good. For example, how did the fund cope with the contrast between the bull markets in the late 1990s and difficult equity markets during the last three years.

(5) Does the fund have a broadly based investment policy or is it a specialist fund? Specialist funds (invested in one type of share or one country) often lead the short-term league tables because that type of share is in fashion during that year or that country's stock market has a good run for a year. These funds frequently fall sharply the following year; for example, over the last ten years there have been a number of specialist funds such as technology funds in the top ten performance tables in one year but many of those same funds also appear in the bottom ten tables in other years.

(6) Where one fund of a life company or unit trust group shows up well in a performance table, how did the other funds managed by the same company or group perform over that period? Some life companies and unit trust groups have anything up to 40 different funds, so that a few of their funds are generally in the upper levels of the league table in any one period, even if most of their funds do not perform well – but of course no one knows in advance which of their funds will perform well.

(7) Does the fund manager describe each fund in terms of relative risk (eg cautious, balanced or adventurous)?

(8) Pension scheme trustees now have to specify their policy over ethical investments. The regulations also require trustees to disclose their policy on the exercise of voting rights relating to the shares they hold.

8.8.3 Assessing property funds' performance

In assessing the performance of property funds these additional factors should be considered:

(1) Is the fund large enough to include a broad spread of properties? Some small funds may achieve very good performance for a year or two when invested in only two or three properties, including one 'special situation' property which gives the fund a non-repeatable boost to performance. However, it can be vulnerable to a fall if there is a change in the marketability of that particular property (eg a change in business conditions in that area, perhaps because one large firm closes down).

(2) Is the fund invested directly in property or in shares of property companies? Shares of property companies tend to be volatile, as exemplified by the October 1987 crash, whereas direct investment in property has a more stable history.

8.8.4 Continuity of investment management

Good past performance is not necessarily even a pointer to the future if the investment management has changed hands. Some smaller funds have changed hands on a number of occasions, and may well be sold on again in the future.

8.8.5 The fund's name and composition

A property fund investor would probably expect the fund to consist of shops, offices, industrial units and cash. However, small 'property' funds could consist of a large amount of cash and only a few properties. A 'managed' fund might comprise a mixed portfolio of equities, properties, gilt edged securities and deposits or it might be largely concentrated in one sector in which case 'managed' might really mean 'managed equity'.

8.8.6 Market benchmarks

The volatility of a fund's performance is important as well as its absolute performance. Standard deviation measures the average deviation of a series of returns relative to their mean. When a benchmarked fund has a wide range of returns it has a high standard deviation, indicating that there is a greater potential for volatility. If returns are normally distributed, then approximately two-thirds of returns would occur within plus or minus one standard deviation from the mean.

9

SMALL SELF-ADMINISTERED SCHEMES AND INSURANCE COMPANY HYBRID SCHEMES

9.1 INTRODUCTION

Small self-administered schemes are similar to insured schemes in that the emerging benefits which may be enjoyed by the members are exactly the same, being governed by the same legislation and to a large extent the same Inland Revenue practice. In a self-administered scheme, however, the trustees, either directly or indirectly, are responsible for managing the scheme's investments and administration. This contrasts with an insured scheme where the trustees pay contributions to an insurance company which manages the scheme and is responsible for investing the contributions.

Under a small self-administered scheme the directors of a company are the scheme's sole or principal members and also normally act as a scheme's trustees. They are then able to exert a considerable degree of control over the fund's investments and the level of benefits provided. A small self-administered scheme is defined as a self-administered scheme with less than 12 members.

A scheme is regarded as self-administered if some or all of the income and other assets are invested otherwise than in insurance policies. Scheme assets, of small amounts, held in a current account (whether interest-bearing or not) with a bank or building society for these purposes are not treated as an investment 'otherwise than in insurance policies'.

A small self-administered scheme may not earmark particular investments for particular members, although the calculation of the amount of a member's benefits may be notionally linked to the value of specific investments. The trust provisions will ensure that the member's entitlement to benefits is against the funds of the trust as a whole.

9.1.1 **Self-investment**

The main attraction of self-administered schemes to directors is the scope to exercise wide investment powers available to the company through *self-investment* rather than *self-administration*.

Self-investment in areas which would assist the employer in its operations can be achieved through:

(1) loans to the company and/or its subsidiaries;
(2) the purchase of property from the company (but not from its directors or connected persons);
(3) investment in the company's own shares.

The above areas are considered in more depth later in this chapter.

9.2 GUIDELINES FOR SCHEME INVESTMENTS

The Inland Revenue was concerned about some aspects of potential abuse and issued guidance on the approval of small self-administered schemes in February 1979 in the form of Memorandum 58. The Inland Revenue's major concern related to the problems which could arise if the potential beneficiaries under the trust decided to wind up the trust and distribute the assets amongst themselves. Under a normal pension scheme this would be a practical impossibility because there would be so many members and potential beneficiaries; under a small insured scheme the insurance company could be expected to prevent this, but under a small self-administered scheme providing benefits for possibly only one person the enforced termination of the trust by all potential beneficiaries is a real possibility.

The Retirement Benefit Schemes (Restriction on Discretion to Approve) Small Self-Administered Schemes Regulations 1991, which were made on 15 July 1991 and came into force on 5 August 1991, limit the Inland Revenue's discretion relating to the approval of small self-administered schemes and specify certain requirements for the approval of a small self-administered scheme. Chapter 20 of the latest Inland Revenue Practice Notes (reproduced in Appendix 3) amplifies the effects of the regulations.

The Social Security Act 1990 also introduced restrictions on self-investment by self-administered pension schemes to not more than 5 per cent of the value of pension fund assets through the Occupational Pension Schemes (Investment of Scheme Resources) Regulations 1992. However, these restrictions are relaxed under small self-administered schemes provided that the following conditions are met:

(1) that all scheme members are trustees of the scheme (this is not as unwieldy as it seems because these schemes are generally only set up for a small group of people, normally the company directors), and the scheme requires the written consent of all members to any self-investment;

(2) that the trust deed requires trustees' decisions on investment policy to be unanimous;

(3) that all members are party to investment decisions.

Most small self-administered schemes are exempt from the Department of Work and Pensions (DWP) Regulations as they are in a position to ensure compliance.

9.2.1 Company loans

The scope for a small self-administered scheme to make available loans to assist the company represents a valuable and flexible facility. The lenders, however, (normally the directors as trustees of the scheme) should ensure that the employer has the ability to repay the loan. The following conditions apply:

(1) The loan should not exceed 50 per cent of the scheme's total assets (in the first two years 25 per cent of the total assets excluding transfers received from other schemes). The 'total assets' of the scheme exclude scheme funds which support the benefits of retired members, widows, widowers and dependants where annuity purchase has been deferred.

(2) There should not be a regular pattern of lending back to the company part of successive employers' contributions.

(3) The loan should be on commercial terms at a realistic rate of interest: the Inland Revenue specifies a rate of 3 per cent per annum above Clearing Bank Base Rate (unless the borrower can show in writing that he could have obtained a loan at less than this rate from another lender on otherwise similar terms). Interest must be charged and paid. The loan agreement should state the terms of the loan including the circumstances when the borrower would be in breach of the conditions of the agreement.

(4) The loan must be used for a genuine commercial purpose, for example to purchase capital equipment or another specific capital requirement. Loans made solely to keep an ailing business afloat or to employers who are technically insolvent may lead to the withdrawal of approval of the scheme.

(5) Loans, being generally required on an unsecured basis, are normally made short term. If the loan to the employer is to be on a long-term basis, the trustees may wish to take security, for example a charge on

company assets, such as property owned by the employer. In any event the loan should be subject to a written agreement under which repayment can be legally enforced.

(6) The loan must be for a fixed term as agreed between the parties to the loan agreement and it is not acceptable for the term to be longer than necessary. It may be possible to roll over these loans into a fresh loan agreement for a further period (but not more than twice) provided the interest is paid to date.

(7) From 1 October 2002 there is no requirement for the borrowing company to deduct tax from interest paid on the loan.

(8) Loans to scheme members or any other members with a contingent interest (eg relatives) are prohibited as is the sale, purchase or lease of any assets from or to scheme members or anyone connected with a scheme member.

It is expected that further restrictions on loans to companies will be introduced following restrictions on loanbacks from insured pension arrangements (see 9.7 below). These are likely to include requirements for trustees to examine the accounts of the company before advancing loans.

9.2.2 Commercial and residential property

If the trustees are considering buying commercial property from the sponsoring employer, the Inland Revenue will normally want to be satisfied that:

(1) The trustees of the self-administered scheme buy the property at current market value, supported by an independent surveyor's valuation.

(2) The rental income should give a reasonable yield – currently 8 to 10 per cent per annum, again supported by the advice of an independent surveyor.

(3) With regard to residential property, investments in residential property for use by, or leasing to, a director or shareholder or to the employer will not be approved unless the property is occupied by an arm's length employee (such as a caretaker).

(4) Investment in residential property may also be acceptable if it is occupied by someone unrelated to the members of the scheme (or to a person connected with a scheme member) in connection with his or her occupation of business premises (eg a shop with a flat above it) where those premises are held by trustees of the scheme as an asset.

Investment by trustees in holiday property is not regarded as consistent with approval.

Other factors which the trustees will have to consider are:

(1) The concentration of scheme investments in property may result in liquidity problems should funds be needed to provide benefits on death or on transfer to another scheme. However, the need to sell a property to provide a member with retirement benefits is now not so essential as it was in the past as the trustees may pay an income out of the fund, deferring the purchase of an annuity until the member's 75th birthday.
(2) There should be adequate funds elsewhere so that the property would not have to be sold at an inopportune time to provide death benefits.
(3) The trustees of the self-administered scheme will normally have the powers in the trust deed to effect a short-term commercial mortgage to finance the initial purchase of a property which may well prove attractive because:
    (a) the company contributions to the scheme to enable the trustees to purchase the property and pay off the loan will attract tax relief;
    (b) rental income paid by the employer to the trustees can be offset as an expense for the purposes of corporation tax;
    (c) rental income from the property accumulates tax free in the self-administered scheme; and
    (d) when the property is sold by the self-administered scheme trustees they do not have to pay capital gains tax on the sale.

9.2.3 Company shares

Although the trustees of a small self-administered scheme may invest in shares of the sponsoring employer, this is not common. The practice has been that most private companies operated by shareholding directors do not declare dividends or pay minimal dividends on ordinary shareholdings. This can cause problems when the trustees of a small self-administered scheme wish to acquire such shares because the Inland Revenue will want to be satisfied that the holding will represent a reasonable investment in terms of expected annual dividends whereas normally the directors will not wish to declare substantial dividends.

In considering the purchase of company shares, the trustees will have had to have ensured that:

(1) advance clearance has been obtained from the Inspector of Taxes of whether the transaction gives rise to an assessment for income tax under ICTA 1988, s 703;
(2) there is a genuine commercial reason for the share transaction and it is not an exercise in tax avoidance;
(3) the shareholding in the company is taken into account when looking at the overall degree of self-investment, including loans;

(4) the shares have been professionally valued;

(5) the value of the shareholdings in the company is reasonable in relation to the overall value of the pension fund. In practice, this means that the Inland Revenue may object if it is proposed that more than, say, 25 per cent of the pension fund is invested in company shares, although it may be prepared to agree a higher proportion if a sound case is put up;

(6) investments in the company shares should not exceed 30 per cent of the company's issued share capital; and

(7) shares in the company will have to be realised when the members retire and this may be difficult simply because shares in private companies tend not to be marketable.

9.2.4 Unlisted company shares

If scheme trustees acquire shares in an unlisted trading company (a company not listed on a recognised stock exchange within the meaning of ICTA 1988, s 841) they may be able to control or convert what would otherwise be taxable trading profits into a dividend which, being investment income, is exempt from tax in their hands. To limit tax avoidance in this area the trustees of a small self-administered scheme are prohibited from investing in shares in any unlisted company which:

(1) carry more than 30 per cent of the voting rights in the company; or

(2) entitle the holder of the shares to more than 30 per cent of any dividends disclosed by the company.

Shares in unlisted public limited companies, and in companies listed on the Alternative Investment Market (AIM), are subject to the above restrictions.

9.2.5 Notification of transactions

The Regulations require automatic notification of any transactions between the scheme and a 'connected person'. This is normally taken to include the principal employer, another employer which participates in the scheme, a company associated with the principal employer or participating employer because it is a subsidiary or it shares a common trade, shareholdings or directorships and scheme members, the member's spouse, relative or the relative's spouse. This information has to be furnished to the Inland Revenue within 90 days from the date of the transaction; failure to do so could result in a penalty.

9.2.6 Conventional investments

These include:

(1) quoted shares or stocks listed on a recognised stock exchange;
(2) gilt-edged stocks (eg UK Government loan stocks);
(3) bank and building society deposits;
(4) insurance policies (subject to possible restrictions on second-hand policies (usually endowment policies)); and
(5) unit trusts and open-ended investment companies.

9.2.7 Investments in works of art, valuable chattels, etc

Investments in such 'pride in possession' assets such as antiques, works of art, rare books, gold bullion, jewellery, etc are not permitted.

9.2.8 Borrowings

It is not uncommon for a scheme to borrow money to help finance the purchase of investment. Borrowings are limited to three times the amount of the employer's ordinary annual contributions to the scheme and three times the annual contributions paid by scheme members in the year of assessment ending immediately before the time of borrowing (excluding any additional voluntary contributions) plus 45 per cent of the market value of the existing scheme investments.

'Ordinary annual contributions' means the smaller of:

(1) the annual average of the contributions paid by the employer in the three scheme accounting periods preceding the date on which the ordinary annual contribution is to be determined (or, where the scheme has been established for less than three years, the total amount paid to the scheme by the employer divided by the number of years since the scheme was established (a part year counting as one); and
(2) the amount of the annual contribution which has been advised by an actuary in writing within three years of the date on which the ordinary annual contribution is determined, and is necessary to secure the benefits payable under the scheme.

9.2.9 Provision of information

In addition to the general requirement under small self-administered schemes that trustees provide actuarial valuations every three years at least, schemes now have to volunteer other items of information relating to investments in the areas outlined above (using the statutory forms) together with an undertaking that the transaction does not infringe current Inland Revenue requirements.

9.3 OTHER INLAND REVENUE REQUIREMENTS

9.3.1 Pensioneer trustee

The Regulations require that all small self-administered schemes appoint a 'pensioneer trustee'. If this is not done the scheme will not be approved or existing approval will be withdrawn.

If the scheme ceases to have a pensioneer trustee the Inland Revenue must be notified in writing within 30 days and a replacement pensioneer trustee must be appointed within 60 days. Also, the Inland Revenue has to be given written notification of the name of the new pensioneer trustee within 30 days of appointment.

The main functions of the pensioneer trustee are to prevent the premature winding-up of the scheme other than in accordance with the approved terms for winding-up in the scheme rules and to undertake to notify the Inland Revenue of wrongdoing or any transaction undertaken by the scheme which, in his opinion, is likely to infringe requirements for approval.

A pensioneer trustee is an individual or body widely involved with occupational pension schemes and known to the Inland Revenue who approve the appointment. It is generally accepted that the pensioneer trustee is jointly and severally liable for the trust's administration with the other trustees, although some pensioneer trustees have sought to limit their responsibilities to the primary function above.

In its Update 69 on small self-administered schemes, the Inland Revenue extended the role and responsibilities of the pensioneer trustee. A new undertaking has to be completed by the pensioneer trustee seeking approval by the Inland Revenue. The Update states that, in accordance with the normal requirements of trust law, the pensioneer trustee must be a co-signatory to all scheme accounts and the registered owner of all scheme assets along with the other scheme trustees.

9.3.2 Investment strategy

Full details of the funding assumptions and the investment strategy must be submitted when Inland Revenue approval of the scheme is sought.

In addition to the initial actuarial report the Inland Revenue requires subsequent actuarial reports every three years containing details of investments.

9.3.3 Inland Revenue scrutiny

As the Inland Revenue scrutinises the investment strategy adopted by the trustees of a small self-administered scheme to ensure that it is suitable, the trustees must satisfy themselves that the main purpose of the scheme is the provision of retirement benefits, rather than the avoidance of tax, and that any substantial investment in a particular area is appropriate to the benefits being provided for the members: in particular if all members are close to retirement, then purchasing a property may be regarded as inappropriate because of the possible problems in selling the investment to provide pensions.

9.3.4 Death-in-service benefits

If the death benefit formula provided under the scheme exceeds the value of the member's share in the scheme's assets, then the balance of any death-in-service benefits promised must be insured with a life office.

9.3.5 Purchase of pensions and income drawdown

The Inland Revenue announced in May 1994 (Memorandum No 119) that small self-administered scheme rules may permit the purchase of an annuity to be deferred for retiring members until they reach age 75. During this period (potentially 25 years) the member's pension may be paid directly from the scheme assets.

The scheme actuary must provide the Inland Revenue with a certificate, initially and thereafter at triennial reviews, comparing the pension being paid direct from the scheme's resources with an annuity on the same terms that could be secured on the open market. The actuary must explain any divergence of more than 10 per cent.

At the end of the period – if the scheme assets have not been exhausted – the trustees must purchase an annuity. This will be an important decision for the trustees as investment conditions may vary considerably during this period. However, unless inflation proofing is at the fixed rate of 3 per cent per annum the trustees may retain the right to pay any increases in pension in line with movements in the RPI directly to the pensioner out of the plan assets. The decision on when to purchase an annuity rests with the trustees.

As an alternative to the above method of deferring the outright purchase of an annuity, scheme trustees may now adopt the procedures available under personal pension schemes (explained in Chapter 19). This method also enables the trustees to defer annuity purchase until the member's 75th birthday, paying an income which lies between 35 and 100 per cent of the annuity which could have been purchased for the member based on annuity tables published by the Government Actuary. As with personal pensions, the income must be reviewed every three years and adjusted if necessary in accordance with annuity rates at that time. Under this method the decision on when to purchase an annuity rests with the member.

However, the treatment of death benefits is different: whereas under personal pensions the fund can be paid as a lump sum subject to a 35 per cent tax charge, under a small self-administered scheme the member is treated as if he or she had retired on the day before death. The death benefit becomes the guaranteed period under the notional annuity (usually five years) minus the income payments already paid out. This method of 'drawdown' or 'income withdrawal' is not so attractive as under personal pensions.

9.3.6 Provision of information to the Inland Revenue

The Inland Revenue must be notified by scheme administrators of specified transactions on relevant Inland Revenue forms (see Appendix 3) covering the following:

(1) loans to employer or an associated employer;
(2) acquisition or disposal of land including buildings;
(3) acquisition or disposal of shares in the employer, associated employers or unlisted companies;
(4) borrowing of money;
(5) purchase or sale from or to an employer;
(6) commutation for serious ill health.

These transactions must be reported to the Inland Revenue within a period of 90 days from the date of acquisition or at the date when the scheme is submitted to the Inland Revenue if this is later.

In the case of the last item above, a scheme may permit a member who is in exceptional circumstances of ill health to commute the whole of his or her pension. Members of small self-administered schemes, in the majority of cases, will be controlling directors in which case the *prior* approval of the Inland Revenue to the commutation is required. The scheme administrator must give the Inland Revenue 14 days' notice and supply copies of medical reports. The Inland Revenue is then obliged to say before the end of the 14 days whether the proposal is acceptable.

9.3.7 Self-assessment for tax

Trustees of small self-administered schemes have been within the scope of self-assessment from 6 April 1996.

9.3.8 Funding

The maximum funding bases for insured executive pension plans and small self-administered schemes were closely aligned with effect from 11 March 2003 when the latter became subject to the funding basis introduced for executive pension plans on 4 March 2002. The new basis applies immediately to all new small self-administered schemes and to existing schemes from the next funding reassessment.

9.3.9 Transfers to and from small self-administered schemes

The prior written consent of IR SPSS had to be obtained before making any transfer payment of any kind to or from a small self-administered scheme before 19 December 2002.

From the 20 December 2002 it is only necessary to obtain IR SPSS agreement where:

(1) the scheme has applied for approval but approval has not yet been given; or
(2) the transfers are in relation to the reorganisation of the employer's pension arrangements or following mergers, takeover or change of ownership; or
(3) the transfers relate to overseas schemes; or
(4) the value is £250,000 or more, or when added to any other transfer payments made to or from the same scheme for the member in the previous 364 days is £250,000 or more.

Where a transfer is being made to a small self-administered scheme, the scheme making the transfer payment must obtain certain confirmation from the pensioneer trustee of the receiving small self-administered scheme before making the transfer. The pensioneer trustee must confirm in writing that the transfer is to go ahead and that the payment is to be made directly into a small self-administered scheme bank account, providing payee details of which the pensioneer trustee is a mandatory co-signatory.

9.4 COST OF SETTING UP AND RUNNING A SMALL SELF-ADMINISTERED SCHEME

The costs involved in a small self-administered scheme vary considerably depending on the services given. The services required in order to establish and run a small self-administered scheme include:

(1) **Documentation and Inland Revenue negotiations.** These include drafting the definitive deed and rules, and preparing announcements to members setting out benefits under the scheme. The documents then have to be submitted to the Inland Revenue for approval and from time to time the employer will require advice in connection with the interpretation of the scheme rules and Inland Revenue practice.

(2) **Actuarial services.** These involve an initial actuarial report and triennial actuarial reports. From time to time, interim actuarial reports may be required, for example on company takeovers or if a claim is made on the scheme trustees, for instance on a member's death or early retirement.

(3) **Pensioneer trusteeship.** See 9.3.1 above.

(4) **Accounting and financial management.** This includes keeping records of assets and payments in and out of the scheme and how they are allocated between members; it includes, for example:
    (a) reconciling bank statements;
    (b) preparing audited annual accounts;
    (c) completing annual tax returns;
    (d) settling tax liabilities;
    (e) reclaiming any tax;
    (f) collecting dividends, interest and rental income.

(5) **Payment of benefits.** This includes the payment of death benefits to beneficiaries, the purchase of annuities for scheme members and their dependants and the payment and acceptance of transfers from other approved pension schemes.

The cost of obtaining all these services varies enormously from specialist to specialist and depends on the method of charging fees which can be either on a time cost basis or as a percentage of the assets under management, or even a combination of the two. The amount of work involved in setting up a small self-administered scheme tends to be the same whether £10,000 or £100,000 is being invested.

These costs usually relate solely to the day-to-day administration. They do not take into account the cost of managing the assets, such as the legal costs involved in purchasing property, the stockbroking costs incurred in managing an investment portfolio and the costs of seeking and obtaining Inland Revenue approval to the types of investment covered in this chapter such as loans and investment in shares in the employer.

9.5 KEY ADVANTAGES AND DISADVANTAGES OF SMALL SELF-ADMINISTERED SCHEMES

The potential advantages include:

(1) The scope to assist company finances through self-investment in own company assets, particularly commercial premises used by the business.
(2) Loans to the company of up to 50 per cent of the fund (or 25 per cent during the first two years of the scheme's establishment). This requirement is also normally satisfied by policy loans available under executive pension plans offered by insurance companies – see below.
(3) The opportunity to achieve a high investment return where the directors have an interest or expertise in a particular investment sector.
(4) If the fund is large, the cost may be cheaper than under insured arrangements.
(5) The personal satisfaction of direct personal control over investment selection and administration of the scheme.
(6) The ability to defer purchase of a pension (see 9.3.5 above).
(7) The ability to allocate scheme assets across a number of members, so avoiding or mitigating the effects of a surplus.

Disadvantages of self-administered schemes include:

(1) The cost of appointing outside specialists to provide actuarial reports, legal advice and pensioneer trustee services.
(2) The cost in terms of executive time required to manage investments and carry out trustee responsibilities.
(3) Most directors of small family companies are not likely to be expert in long-term investment; they do not have the time, ability and resources to research markets in depth in order to maximise gains and minimise losses.
(4) The possible loss of control if company assets, such as properties, are switched to form part of a small self-administered plan. In particular a property which has been purchased by the small self-administered scheme from the company cannot then be put up as security for loans to the company as it no longer forms part of a company's asset base.
(5) A small self-administered scheme is a common trust fund which means that the assets are held for the benefit of all the members (in practice, a small number of directors) as a whole. This contrasts with executive pension plans where assets are earmarked for each individual member.

Under a common trust fund, in the event of a claim being made by a beneficiary, for example on the death of a member, the beneficiary is entitled to a proportion of the assets of the common trust fund, say one-third. The trustees then have to realise one-third of the fund in order to meet their liabilities to the beneficiary. This could cause problems for the trustees if the deceased member, when alive, had invested what he regarded as 'his share' of the fund in an area of investment which had shown poor returns, as the remaining two members of the scheme could have to subsidise the deceased member from other investments of the fund which had performed better.

The inability to earmark assets under common trust funds is a problem which has come to the fore over the past few years as more insurance companies have been prepared to set up and administer small self-administered schemes where a portion of the assets are invested in insurance policies. These policies are, by their very nature, taken out by the trustees in respect of individual scheme members but they represent merely an investment vehicle on the trustees' part. The proceeds of the policy are not earmarked for individual members.

This contrasts with a straightforward executive pension plan, which is not a common trust fund, and where the proceeds of each separate policy are indisputably earmarked for the member concerned.

9.6 PROPERTY PURCHASE

Many small self-administered schemes are set up with a view to purchasing property (although the scheme may not purchase a property from the director(s)). The property may already be owned by the company, or it may be one which the director or the company is considering purchasing, and from which the company will operate. The following tables set out the pros and cons of the methods of property purchase.

Table 9.1 Property purchase by the director

Pros	Cons
(1) The property is separate from the company and can be sold independently.	(1) Additional life assurance is required by the lender as collateral.
(2) The property does not have to be sold at retirement and could generate rental income which supplements any pension received.	(2) The director may have given personal guarantees to his company creditors so that the property is not necessarily free from creditors.

Table 9.1 Property purchase by the director *(cont.)*

Pros	Cons
(3) When the property is sold by the director there is a potential CGT liability but this should be substantially mitigated by the indexation allowance (for inflation up to April 1998).	(3) When obtaining a loan to buy the property it is unlikely that the director will be able to obtain a 100% mortgage so that he may have to put up additional security such as his own private residence: this may be unacceptable, or may conflict with personal guarantees given to other lenders.
(4) The increasing value of the property could be used as collateral security for further ventures of a personal or corporate nature.	(4) If a full market rent is received from his company he is not entitled to business retirement relief. A proportion of the business retirement relief is given if the rent received is less than the full market rent.
(5) If the director does not charge the company rent for the use of his property he is entitled to business retirement relief usually from age 50 onwards.	(5) The director may be unable to obtain a personal long-term interest-only loan.
(6) If the director uses the tax-free cash emerging from his pension plan to repay the capital he effectively obtains tax relief on the capital repayment.	(6) Other directors may be unhappy about the property being owned by one director.
(7) IHT relief for business property may be available.	

Table 9.2 Property purchase by the company

Pros	Cons
(1) It is the most natural place for the property to be held and the property can be used for future expansion.	(1) The company will probably be unable to obtain a loan on a long-term interest-only basis. It is likely to be of a fairly short term with capital repayments every year.

Table 9.2 Property purchase by the company *(cont.)*

Pros	Cons
(2) The company rather than an individual director is much more likely to be able to obtain a loan if a substantial amount is involved.	(2) When the property is sold there is a potential corporation tax liability on the gain and when the director sells his shares he has a potential CGT liability. It may be possible to avoid this double tax charge if the company is sold as a whole, rather than individual elements of it.
(3) The company although paying interest and capital on the loan does not have to pay rent.	(3) Although life assurance is not necessary as collateral security, it is advisable.
(4) Collateral life assurance is not necessarily needed. The death of one of the directors would not necessarily affect the loan (unless the deceased was a keyman in the company).	
(5) IHT relief for business property may be available.	
(6) The method is simple.	

Table 9.3 Property purchase by the SSAS

Pros	Cons
(1) When the property is sold by the fund to provide the director with his retirement benefits there is no CGT to pay.	(1) The scheme is a common trust fund and the individual members lose their personal investment choice; see above.
(2) The capital growth of the property does not increase the value of the director's shares for CGT and IHT purposes.	(2) Death, ill health, leaving service and early retirement could involve the scheme's trustees in having to sell the property, or obtain a loan at an inopportune time.
(3) If there are younger directors in the scheme the property could effectively remain in the fund when older directors retire. There is no need to sell the property if the share of the fund which belongs to the retiring director can be met from other scheme assets.	(3) The proposed property investment may not be a suitable investment for a scheme as it would not satisfy Revenue rules.

Table 9.3 Property purchase by the SSAS *(cont.)*

Pros	Cons
(4) The rent paid by the company to the trustees of the fund reduces corporation tax liability.	(4) The property could not be used as collateral for future loans to the company.
(5) The property is free from creditors (provided there has been no attempt to defraud creditors)	(5) The company would have to pay a commercial rent to the scheme.
	(6) As an actuarial valuation of the fund is required every three years this requires a valuation of the property, an added cost.
	(7) If the scheme borrows to purchase the property, it is faced with high capital repayments so as to keep the term of the loan to a minimum: interest payable on the loan by the trustees does not rank for tax relief – the scheme does not pay tax.

9.6.1 Property purchase – summary

Some companies make the mistake of setting up a small self-administered scheme to purchase a property, while the real aim should be to purchase the property on the most commercial and cost-effective terms to the company, with the pension fund as a secondary objective.

Example 9.1

The company is considering purchasing a property which will cost £200,000. Whilst it is feasible that a small self-administered scheme could be used to purchase the property, in practice this may be an unacceptable option as the cost of financing the project would be too expensive for the following reasons:

(1) The annual contribution to the scheme would be around £50,000.

(2) The maximum loan which the scheme's trustees could obtain would be £150,000 (three times the regular annual contribution, averaged over the previous three years in line with Inland Revenue practice).

(3) The trustees now have £200,000 to purchase the property, assuming the lender is prepared to lend 75% of the valuation of the property. However in the case of an existing scheme, the facility to borrow an additional amount equal to 45% of scheme assets will assist the purchase.

(4) The company directors may have to increase their salaries and/or bonuses from the company to justify regular contributions to a scheme of £50,000, affecting the directors' personal tax liability and the company's NIC liability.

(5) The company will have to pay a commercial rent to the scheme for the use of the property, say, £18,000 per annum.

(6) Even with corporation tax relief on the annual contribution of £50,000 and rent of £18,000, and on the cost of the directors' remuneration, the total cost commitment may well be beyond the company's resources.

An alternative method would be to regard the purchase of the property and the setting up of a pension scheme as two completely separate free-standing objectives. The property purchase would be financed by the directors or by the company on a long-term basis which would reduce the strain on cash flow and a pension plan could be set up at modest levels. If, for various reasons, the company were unable to pay contributions to the pension plan this would not prejudice mortgage payments in respect of the property purchase and if the property had to be sold at an inopportune time it would not undermine the pension benefits of the directors and their beneficiaries.

9.7 INSURANCE-BASED HYBRID SCHEMES

Insured executive pension plans are often adapted to provide some or all of the features of a small self-administered scheme. This is done quite simply by:

(1) Including the executive pension plan policy within a fully fledged small self-administered scheme on the basis set out above. The fund's balance is invested by the trustees in other areas. The insurance company then carries out either limited administration of the scheme or provides a full service including preparation of documents, negotiations with the Inland Revenue, accounting services, actuarial services and acting as pensioneer trustee. The Inland Revenue and DWP regulations summarised above also apply to these schemes.

(2) Offering a loan facility alongside its executive pension plan on the basis that this normally satisfies the requirements of most directors of small family companies. However, this type of arrangement does *not* constitute a small self-administered scheme. Under this method the insurance company lends to the employer an amount currently not exceeding one-half of the pension fund, taking as security the pension policy itself. A loan made within two years of setting up the pension plan may not, however, exceed 25 per cent of the fund value, excluding the value of transfer payments included in the fund. The loan to the employing company must be for a genuine commercial purpose and interest is payable at a commercial rate (3 per cent above the current base rate of a particular clearing bank).

   The loan must be repaid 12 months before the member's retiring age (or if the member leaves the company, or dies, or the company becomes insolvent). Failure by the borrowing company to repay the loan may result in the reduction of the member's benefits – and in particular of the tax-free cash sum available at retirement.

The member must give his consent to the policy being used by the trustees as security, but in practice the member is a controlling director of the company directly involved in using the money borrowed from the insurance company for a commercial purpose.

On 26 August 1999 the Inland Revenue announced new restrictions on insured loanback arrangements, set out in new practice notes (see Appendix 2). The following is a brief summary of the changes:

(1) Normally the duration of the loan is expected to be no more than five years and for some purposes, for example where the loan is for stock-in-trade, a duration of one year would be more appropriate.
(2) The duration of the loan may not exceed two years unless level capital repayments are made at least every six months.
(3) Before the trustees grant the pensions policies as security for the loan, they must undertake a credit check on the borrower (the employer) ideally containing a rating on the borrower.
(4) The securing of an 'injudicious' loan on the insured policies may lead to loss of approval of the scheme.
(5) A certificate PS 8 (also reprinted in Appendix 2) signed by the employer and the trustees of the scheme must be sent to the Inland Revenue within 90 days of making the loan.
(6) If the insurer forecloses on the loan, and therefore reduces the policies by the amount of the outstanding loan, the scheme trustees have right of action against the employer. This could result in the scheme being regarded as a small self-administered scheme rather than a simple insured scheme.

In practice, loans on the above basis are not considered practicable.

9.8 PROHIBITION ON TRANSACTIONS – SSASs AND NON-APPROVED SCHEMES

Transactions of any description between any tax approved scheme and any non-approved scheme are prohibited. This applies in respect of any transactions between:

(1) tax approved schemes and non-approved schemes of the same employer; and
(2) tax approved schemes of one employer and non-approved schemes of another employer, whether or not there is any connection between the employers or the schemes.

Examples of prohibited transactions are:

(1) **Transfers.** Transfers may not be made between tax approved schemes and non-approved schemes (see Chapter 5 for descriptions of non-approved schemes).

(2) **Loans.** Loans from small self-administered schemes to members are prohibited. A loan from the trustees of a small self-administered scheme to the trustees of a non-approved scheme set up for the benefit of the member would also be prohibited (being an example of a 'back-to-back loan' which has had long-standing prohibition).

(3) **Selling assets.** The trustees of small self-administered schemes may not sell assets directly or indirectly to members or connected persons of the small self-administered scheme. An indirect sale of small self-administered scheme assets could occur by the setting up of a non-approved scheme for the small self-administered scheme member and the trustees of the small self-administered scheme selling assets to the trustees of the non-approved scheme.

(4) **Joint investments.** The trustees of a small self-administered scheme may invest in a particular asset with other parties (such as a property investment by a syndicate) provided the other parties do not include members of the small self-administered scheme or connected persons. A joint investment with the member of the small self-administered scheme could occur by setting up a non-approved scheme for the member of the small self-administered scheme and the trustees of the non-approved scheme entering into the joint investment behalf of the member.

9.9 PENSIONS SIMPLIFICATION

The new tax regime proposed in the Inland Revenue's consultation document, 'Simplifying the taxation of pensions: increasing choice and flexibility for all', will extend to small self-administered schemes and will include rules setting:

(1) limits on the holding of shares in the sponsoring employer's company so that the current 5 per cent requirement for larger occupational schemes would apply to all;

(2) limits on loans to employers;

(3) limits on loans to scheme members.

These limits will apply to new investments with transitional rules over existing scheme assets.

10

TOPPING-UP GROUP SCHEMES

Most directors or senior executives have some form of retirement provision but very few enjoy benefits in line with the absolute maximum levels permitted by the Inland Revenue. This chapter identifies the ways in which existing benefits can be topped up either by the member or with the help of his employer or a combination of the two.

The methods of increasing benefits depends to a large extent on the type of scheme from which the member's main benefits will emerge from and the date on which he joined it as this determines whether he is classed as a pre-1987 member, a 1987–89 member or a post-1989 member. The introduction of stakeholder pension schemes from 6 April 2001 gave further options for increasing benefits.

The Inland Revenue's consultation document, 'Simplifying the taxation of pensions: increasing choice and flexibility for all', will have a significant impact on the ways in which members top up their scheme benefits. It will also ease the burden on scheme administrators who have to ensure that the benefits emerging from the various top-up pension arrangements at retirement comply with Inland Revenue limits. Under the new proposed tax regime the options will be easier for investors to understand and for schemes to administer.

10.1 GROUP SCHEMES

Many group schemes provide benefits related to final salary (although defined contribution schemes are now the norm for new entrants, except in the public sector). For directors and senior executives this is likely to be at least one-sixtieth of final salary for each year of service as a scheme member: in the event of death a widow's or widower's death-in-retirement pension is payable and, in the event of death in service, there will probably be a lump sum payable of between twice and four times salary together with a spouse's death-in-service pension of one-half of the prospective personal pension. When in payment, the pension is likely to remain level or increase at a rate linked to increases in the Retail Prices

Index (RPI) with a maximum of 5 per cent per annum compound although the Government has recently proposed an easing of the maximum rate from 5 per cent to 2.5 per cent a year. Retirement age is usually at age 65, although in recent years age 60 has become common. The following comparison table shows the benefits which a director who enters a scheme aged 35, earning £50,000 per annum, is likely to receive under a typical group pension scheme compared with the maximum levels permitted.

Table 10.1

Benefit	Typical group scheme	Maximum benefits
Member's pension	$30/_{60}$ × £50,000 = £25,000 pa	$2/_3$ of £50,000 = £33,333 pa
Pension increases at	3% to 5%	In line with Retail Prices Index
Widow's pension	50% of member's pension = £12,500	$2/_3$ of member's pension = £22,222 pa
Lump sum death benefit	2 × £50,000 = £100,000	4 × £50,000 = £200,000

The difference between actual benefits received under a typical group scheme and the maximum benefits approvable are even greater than those set out above. Maximum benefits can be paid from age 60 rather than 65, total remuneration may be pensioned including such items as bonuses, commissions, director's fees, and the taxable element of fringe benefits: a typical group scheme limits pensionable salary to basic salary only and excludes fluctuating items. Thus there is usually plenty of scope for topping-up the benefits of a director or executive even if he is a post-1989 member and might be affected by the earnings ceiling of £99,000 (in 2003/04).

10.2 ADDITIONAL VOLUNTARY CONTRIBUTIONS (AVCs)

The Inland Revenue allows contributions by members of up to 15 per cent of their total remuneration. If the member is already paying normal contributions to the scheme of, say, 5 per cent, he may increase this by a further 10 per cent. Since 26 October 1987, scheme members have a choice between investing AVCs through either:

(1) their employer's scheme (scheme AVCs or 'in house' AVCs); or
(2) free-standing AVCs.

The choice of investment vehicle for voluntary contributions is wide, including insurance contracts, building society and bank accounts and unit trusts. AVCs started after 8 April 1987 are not permitted to generate directly a lump sum but only pension.

(1) **Scheme AVCs.** The whole of the member's additional contributions are deductible from his pay before tax, thus giving relief from income tax at the highest rate (known as the net pay system).

(2) **Free-standing AVCs.** This is a contract which is completely separate from any employer sponsored scheme, to which a scheme member can pay AVCs. Tax relief is not given through the net pay system. Instead the individual obtains basic rate tax relief at source and claims any higher rate relief through his tax assessment. (For further details see 10.9 below.)

(3) **Added years.** Public sector schemes often allow 'added years of service' to be purchased but very few private schemes adopt this approach since it requires a commitment on the part of the employer to underwrite salary inflation. For example, a voluntary contribution of 5 per cent of salary might secure three or four years' additional pensionable service for a young member. If, however, his salary increases substantially later in life, the pension fund would have to meet the additional liabilities which have not been matched by the voluntary contributions paid by the member. From the member's point of view, this would be very attractive but is unsatisfactory to the employer.

10.3 AUGMENTATION UNDER THE GROUP SCHEME

In the past, it was common for companies which pensioned their staff through defined benefit schemes to use those schemes to augment the entitlement of certain individuals and groups. Accordingly, senior executives may be awarded a pension of, say, $\frac{1}{40}$ of final salary for each year of service from a scheme under which the standard formula is $\frac{1}{60}$.

The provision of augmented benefits in this way is decreasing for the following reasons:

(1) the trend away from defined benefit schemes towards defined contribution schemes;

(2) the growing insistence on the application of corporate governance good practice; and

(3) scrutiny and potential objections from scheme trustees and shareholders of the company.

The loss of confidentiality inherent in this method of augmentation means that it is much more likely that the following method, which involves setting up a separate arrangement, will be more suitable.

10.4 TOPPING-UP THROUGH EXECUTIVE PENSION PLANS

The Inland Revenue permits categories of employees to have (effectively) two normal retirement dates: a director or executive could, for example, be a member of a group pension scheme with a normal retirement age of 65 when the majority of employees will retire, and also be a member of an executive pension plan arranged specially for him with a retirement age of 60 if this age is the best estimate of his date of retirement. For the purpose of deciding the maximum approvable benefits under the executive pension plan there must be taken into account the benefits payable under the main scheme on retirement at the supplementary scheme age, ie the benefits on early retirement.

When setting up a pension plan to top up group scheme benefits, it is important to consider the member's status, ie pre-1987, 1987–89 or post-1989.

By combining an executive pension plan with a group pension scheme sufficient funds can be accumulated to provide:

(1) a full two-thirds pension at 60 rather than at 65;
(2) increases in dependants' benefits;
(3) increases in pensions in line with increases in the cost of living;
(4) increases in the tax-free lump sum up to the maximum permitted.

Further features of adopting the executive pension plan route are:

(1) improved rights in the event of leaving service – if the director or executive leaves service, his benefits (often in the form of an individual policy) can be transferred to his new employer (and even if it is not transferred, they continue to benefit from future growth);
(2) improved death-in-service protection;
(3) the use of dynamised final remuneration (as explained in 4.8);
(4) improved benefits on early retirement;
(5) the director has greater control over the investment medium in which his contributions are invested and greater privacy over his retirement provisions;
(6) items which are not normally pensionable (eg bonus, commission) are more easily handled under an executive pension plan;
(7) the employer may use it for discretionary payments in respect of certain directors from time to time, and as a benefit when recruiting executives who do not wish to join a group salary-related scheme.

The following example shows the extent to which a director could top up his benefits.

Example 10.1

A is a member of a group pension scheme which provides him with two-thirds of his final salary as a pension from the age of 65, having joined the scheme when he was 25, and is now aged 38. Current salary is £50,000. The scope for investment in an executive pension plan may be calculated as follows:

Prospective pension at age 65 based on current basic salary	$= \frac{2}{3} \times £50,000$
	$= £33,333$ pa
Early retirement at age 60	$= \frac{35}{60} \times £50,000 \times 0.7*$
	$= £20,416$ pa
Salary required to support this pension if he were entitled to maximum benefits at age 60	$= £20,416 \div \frac{2}{3}$
	$= £30,624$
Non-pensioned basic salary	$= £50,000 - £30,624$
	$= £19,376$
Add other items averaged over three years, eg bonus, taxable element of fringe benefits, say,	£2,000
Total non-pensioned remuneration	£21,376

*Early retirement actuarial factor to bring forward group scheme pension from age 65 to 60.

The approximate initial contribution which could be paid to an executive pension plan in this example to provide a maximum member's pension is around £8,741 (increasing in future in line with salary increases).

No allowance has been made for increasing any widow's pension or making provision for post-retirement increases in the group scheme pension.

10.5 SALARY SACRIFICE

If a director's benefits are to be topped-up by means of a separate executive pension plan, which requires approval by the Inland Revenue in the usual way, the employer must contribute towards the costs. If the employer is unwilling to bear any additional expenditure, the employer's contribution can be made by the director giving up part of his salary voluntarily – a practice known as 'salary sacrifice'. Because the employer is paying a lower salary to the director, it has the funds to contribute to an executive pension plan. Amounts sacrificed in this way must be documented usually in the form of an exchange of letters, for example:

Dear Mr X,

This is to inform you that with effect from 1 October your salary will be reduced from £50,000 pa to £46,000 pa.

Yours sincerely,

For the Company . . . . Date . . . .

I agree to this reduction in salary.

Signed . . . . Date . . . .

Director

It is essential that the letter makes no reference to the application of the forgone amount to pension contributions and that it is exchanged before the reduction in salary commences. Failure to observe these rules almost certainly results in the treatment of the sacrifice as ineffective by the local Inspector of Taxes.

Details of the amount of salary sacrifice should be sent by the employer direct to the Schedule E tax district where the amount is £5,000 or over. The Schedule E tax district decides whether the sacrifice is an effective reduction of the employee's remuneration assessable to income tax.

If the director is considering paying personal contributions in addition to salary sacrifice the Inland Revenue requires that the employer's contribution is not a derisory proportion of the total, and normally wishes to see 10 per cent of the total contribution paid by the employer.

The effect of salary sacrifice is that the director never receives the sacrificed salary so that he therefore cannot pay tax or national insurance contributions (NICs) on it. The company obtains tax relief whether it pays a level of salary to the director or a lower level of salary plus a pension contribution. The director's salary must, however, be reduced for all purposes including his pensionable salary on which his pension benefits are calculated.

The following example shows how contributions may be paid:

Example 10.2

		Total contribution £
Salary	£50,000	
Salary sacrifice	£ 4,000	4,000 from employer
Revised salary	£46,000	

Personal contribution of, say, 15%	£ 6,900	6,900 from employee
		10,900

The employer will contribute £10,900 and deduct the member's share of £6,900 from his salary under a net PAY arrangement.

If, however, the company intends recouping the member's share in monthly instalments over a period of 12 months, then it is effectively giving him an interest-free loan on a reducing basis which might be in breach of the Companies Act 1985, s 330 if the member is a director of a public company or of a company in a group which includes a public company. If there is any likelihood of such a breach then the employer should recoup the member's share in one lump.

10.6 DIVIDEND WAIVER

The principle of dividend waiver is that the shareholder (who will be a working director or employee of the company) renounces in advance his entitlement to any dividend that may be declared in respect of his holdings so that he never becomes entitled to the dividend. The waiver should take the form of a unilateral deed under seal executed by the shareholder only. The waiver should be executed before payment in the case of an interim dividend and before declaration in the case of a final dividend. The waiver must relate only to dividends payable within 12 months of execution and there must be no connection between the dividend waiver and the provision of pension benefits.

10.7 BONUS SACRIFICE

Some employees are entitled to a bonus or commission which is calculated when the employer's accounts have been certified. For income tax purposes the bonus or commission is treated as accruing during the period to which it relates, for example by reference to annual, quarterly or monthly accounts. A bonus or commission sacrifice which is made after the end of the relative period is regarded by the Inland Revenue as retrospective and therefore as ineffective. The Inland Revenue takes the view that the employee's entitlement is fixed at the end of the relative accounting period. When that point is reached the employee cannot sacrifice any part of his bonus or commission even though the exact amount may not be quantified until a later date.

However, the Inland Revenue is prepared to accept a reduction which is agreed sufficiently long before the year end so that the reduced annual sum is not less than the remuneration which has already accrued at the former rate. Ultimately, however, the question of whether a sacrifice is effective is a matter for the local Inspector of Taxes.

10.8 EFFECT OF INCOME SACRIFICE ON NICs

To the extent that an individual sacrifices income (whether salary, bonus, commission, etc) there is a saving in the employer's NICs.

Since 6 October 1985 national insurance contributions have been payable by employers on all earnings (prior to that time they were limited to the upper earnings level. There is a limit on earnings on which an employee pays NIC although an erosion of the limit took effect on 6 April 2003 with the introduction of a 1 per cent surcharge for employees, directors and the self-employed with earnings above the upper earnings limit (£30,940 a year in 2003/04).

Example 10.3

- An executive earning above the upper earnings limit sacrifices a bonus of £10,000.
- The employer saves £1,280 in NICs.
- Employer's contributions to pension plan can be between £10,000 and £11,280.
- Net income sacrificed by executive £6,000 (assuming a 40% taxpayer).
- NIC saving by executive £100.

Example 10.4

- The employer is prepared to spend £10,000 including NICs.
- If the executive opts to receive a bonus he obtains £8,865 gross, £5,230 net (assuming a 40% taxpayer) and after 1% NIC saving on £8,865.
- If the executive sacrifices his bonus the company invests £10,000 in a pension plan.

10.9 FREE-STANDING AVCs

From 6 April 1988, the Social Security Act 1986 required employers to offer members of their occupational schemes the facility to pay additional voluntary contributions (AVCs) to top up their benefits, although many schemes had provided such facilities for years and had encouraged scheme members to take advantage of the tax efficiency of AVC arrangements.

From 26 October 1987, a different type of AVC arrangement became available, known as a 'free-standing AVC' (FSAVC). This type of pension contract was introduced by F(No 2)A 1987 and has the following characteristics:

(1) It must be used to provide income in retirement only, not tax-free lump sums. This restriction also applies to scheme AVCs which started after 7 April 1987.

(2) Contributions are subject to the normal limits applying under occupational schemes approved under ICTA 1988, ss 590–612 (see Appendix 4). There are two main restrictions:
   (a) The maximum contributions that may be paid by an individual amount to 15 per cent of his remuneration (including any personal contributions which his employer may require him to pay under an occupational scheme or under a separate executive pension plan).
   (b) Benefits will also be subject to the normal limits applying under occupational schemes approved under ICTA 1988 (see Chapter 4), but broadly there is a maximum pension on retirement from all sources of two-thirds of final remuneration.

(3) The FSAVC scheme is completely separate from the employer's occupational scheme although there is liaison between the trustees of the employer's occupational scheme and the pension provider of the AVC, when benefits become payable, for example on retirement. The trustees of the employer's scheme inform the pension provider of the maximum benefits permitted under Inland Revenue rules, and the amount being provided under the employer's scheme. The balance may be provided by the FSAVC scheme. If there is a surplus when benefits become payable it has to be returned to the members minus a tax charge (see below).

(4) Prior to 6 April 1987 the Inland Revenue required AVCs to be paid for at least five years, or to retirement if earlier, in order to attract tax relief. From 6 April 1987 members have been permitted to vary the amount and timing of AVCs, making these arrangements even more flexible.

(5) They may be arranged through an extended number of pension providers which includes insurance companies, banks, building societies and unit trusts.

(6) Because contributions are paid directly by the individual to the pension provider, tax relief is not obtained in the same manner as tax relief on contributions to an occupational pension scheme or executive pension plan where the 'net pay arrangement' normally operates. Instead, the individual pays contributions net of basic rate

tax: for example an individual wishing to pay £100 per month to an FSAVC contract therefore has to pay only £78 per month net to the pension provider who reclaims the tax deducted, ie £22 per month from the Inland Revenue, and credits the additional £22 per month to the contract (this example assumes basic rate tax relief of 22 per cent). Any higher rate tax relief is obtained by application to the Inland Revenue, ie through the individual's tax return.

Leading scheme procedures

The Inland Revenue has issued revised FSAVC Guidance Notes which confirm leading scheme administration requirements. These have now been enacted in the form of regulations.

A member of an occupational scheme may contribute to an in-house AVC, an FSAVC, or both at the same time (within the overall contribution limit). Furthermore he may have contributed to more than one FSAVC during his employment (but contributions may not be made to more than one such FSAVC in any one financial year).

The leading scheme is defined as:

(1) the last FSAVC, where the member has not made any contributions to an in-house AVC;
(2) the employer's scheme, if any in-house AVC contributions have been made.

The Administrator of the leading scheme is required to instruct the various FSAVC schemes involved (if applicable) as to what benefits should be paid, including any surplus amounts payable as cash arising from over-provision.

In order to determine whether or not maximum benefits have been exceeded, the employer's scheme must certify the maximum member's pension payable from all approved occupational/statutory schemes in respect of the member's service with the employer. For this purpose the employer's scheme may use the best definition of final remuneration allowed by the Inland Revenue, or the definition upon which the employer's scheme benefits are calculated (which may be more restrictive than Inland Revenue rules, for example the definition of final remuneration may be basic salary only).

If the total pension benefits from the main scheme and FSAVCs taken together exceed maximum benefits certified by the employer's scheme, then the member may choose either to:

(1) take the whole of the surplus fund as a cash sum subject to tax; or
(2) to maximise pension benefits in accordance with Inland Revenue rules, hence only taking a cash refund if a surplus still exists.

10.9.1 Over-provision

If the combination of benefits under the main occupational scheme and the FSAVC provides excessive benefits the main scheme benefits are not reduced but the surplus arises under the FSAVC. The scheme administrator of the FSAVC must deduct tax at 32 per cent of the surplus fund if the individual is a basic rate taxpayer. Assuming a surplus of £1,000, tax is deducted of £320 with £680 payable to the member. This amount, £680, is treated as income which has suffered basic rate tax (taken to be 22 per cent). The net amount received by the individual of £680 has a grossed up equivalent of £871.79 but there is no further liability to tax in the case of a basic rate taxpayer. Even if the individual is not liable to tax the amount paid by the scheme administrator cannot be recovered. If the individual is a higher rate taxpayer, further tax at 18 per cent is payable on the grossed up amount, in this case £156.92 further liability. In the case of a higher rate taxpayer, therefore, there is total tax to pay of £476.92, representing an effective tax rate of approximately 48 per cent on the surplus of £1,000. Any surplus arising on death is also taxed at 32 per cent.

10.9.2 Estimating benefits

An individual wishing to pay AVCs will wish to ascertain how much could be contributed to the FSAVC to top up the overall benefits to the Inland Revenue maximum. An indication of the scope for AVCs can be provided by the main scheme trustees or by the pension provider which runs the FSAVC. An individual wishing to pay contributions of £2,400 per annum or more must provide the FSAVC provider with information relating to his main scheme and previous retained benefits. The pension provider then tests the possibility of over-provision, known as a 'headroom test'. If this is likely the pension provider informs the intending contributor of the reduced level of contributions which should be paid to ensure that overall benefits do not exceed Inland Revenue limits. If contributions, however, are less than £2,400 per annum the FSAVC provider does not have to carry out an initial check (but will do so should the contributions exceed £2,400 per annum in the future).

Although a disadvantage of the FSAVC scheme is the inability to take any of the emerging benefits in the form of a tax-free lump sum, in practice this problem may be overcome by looking at the combined benefits emerging from the FSAVC scheme and the individual's other pension arrangements. To the extent that an individual takes a tax-free lump sum from any pension scheme, his pension is bound to be lower: in practice, many pensioners reinvest any lump sum in other areas to provide additional income in order to maintain a reasonable standard of living. If, however, an individual is deterred from paying contributions to an FSAVC scheme because it does not provide a tax-free lump sum, he should investigate the rules of his main occupational scheme. Although it might provide a cash lump sum of, say, only $\frac{3}{80}$ of his final salary for each year of service, the rules often contain powers of augmentation allowing the trustees to increase the tax-free lump sum (and other benefits) up to the maximum permitted by the Inland Revenue (not available under statutory schemes). The individual, therefore, could take increased cash from his occupational scheme leaving a lower income from that scheme which would be topped up by the pension emerging from his FSAVC scheme.

Example 10.5

Company pension scheme provides:

- a pension of £6,666 pa ($\frac{20}{60}$ of pensionable salary of £20,000); or
- a cash lump sum of £15,000 ($\frac{3}{80}$ of pensionable salary for each year of pensionable service, ie $\frac{60}{80}$ plus a reduced pension of around £5,416 pa).

The Inland Revenue allows tax-free cash to be calculated using the greater of $\frac{3}{80}$ of pensionable salary for each year of pensionable service or 2.25 × the pension before commutation. Both methods would produce the same result. If the member contributes to an FSAVC scheme which produces an additional pension of £1,000 pa, this can be taken into account in the calculation. The member could then take £17,250 under the main company scheme as a cash lump sum (2.25 × £7,666, plus a reduced pension of £5,229 pa together with the FSAVC pension of £1,000 pa).

10.9.3 Transitional arrangements

The F(No 2)A 1987 introduced changes affecting AVCs. Only new AVC arrangements entered into after 7 April 1987, including contributions to FSAVC schemes, are affected by the 'no commutation rule'. The following (which is an extract from Memorandum 87 published by the Inland Revenue on the subject) will not be affected:

(1) An arrangement whereby a contractual obligation was entered into before 8 April 1987, even if the first contribution had not been paid until after that date.
(2) Continuation of an arrangement following the re-organisation of an employer's pension arrangements, or the restructuring or sale of part or all of the employer's business.
(3) A change in the amount or timing of AVCs; examples are an increase in the percentage of salary being paid or a change from a monthly to annual payment basis.
(4) A break in contributions, provided that on recommencement the AVCs are paid to the original arrangement or to another arrangement which is part of the employer's scheme.

(5) A change in investment medium for the AVCs (eg a switch from an insurance contract to a building society deposit) provided that the new investments are held under an AVC arrangement first entered into before 8 April 1987.

10.9.4 Recent improvements in AVCs

In July 1999, the Inland Revenue announced greater flexibility for in-house and free-standing AVCs. Benefits under these arrangements no longer have to be taken at the same time as the main scheme benefits. This facility will be readily available under FSAVCs. However, because in-house AVCs form part of the main scheme, the separation of the AVC fund from the rest of the benefits will depend on the scheme's administration systems and the willingness of the scheme trustees to offer the facility.

The recent improvements also extend to allowing 'income drawdown' (also known as 'income withdrawal') under AVCs and FSAVCs rather than the straightforward purchase of an annuity. This concept is described in Chapter 19 in relation to personal pensions.

Where benefits under AVCs and FSAVCs are taken before the main scheme benefits, income drawdown must be used. This is of dubious benefit because income drawdown is a complex procedure under personal pensions, often applying only when the accumulated fund is at least £100,000. Under income drawdown arrangements, the fund is not converted into an annuity. Instead, an income is withdrawn from the fund, subject to Inland Revenue rules, with annuity purchase deferred until age 75. In the meantime, the fund has to be invested in a manner which gives a sufficient return to ensure that income can be maintained or even increased in later years while not exposing the pensioner to unnecessary risk. Under personal pensions, the risk is borne by the individual member: under an AVC, the scheme trustees will bear some responsibility for the ongoing investment management of the drawdown fund but will seek to limit their liabilities insofar as their overall trustee duties and responsibilities allow.

10.10 TIERED SCHEMES AND MATCHING ARRANGEMENTS

Some schemes allow choice over levels of accrual rate (under defined benefits schemes) or over levels of contribution (under defined contribution schemes).

For example, a defined benefit scheme provides a pension of one-sixtieth of final salary for each year of service, with members paying contractual contributions of 5 per cent per year. The tiered arrangements allow, say, members to opt for a higher rate of pension accrual of one-fiftieth of final salary for each year of service but with members' contributions at 6 per cent per year. The member who opts for the increased pension will also obtain an employer subsidy because the additional benefit (one-fiftieth minus one-sixtieth) of final salary will not be met purely by the increased member's contribution of 1 per cent. The balance of the cost will be met by the employer.

Under a defined contribution scheme the employer may pay, for example, 6 per cent of pay with members paying 4 per cent of pay, giving a total of 10 per cent. Under a matching arrangement the employer may offer to match every 1 per cent of additional contribution paid by the member, on a one-for-one basis (or more): if, say, the member increases contributions to 6 per cent the employer will increase contributions to 8 per cent, giving a total contribution of 14 per cent.

Under tiered or matching arrangements the member increases the rate of *contractual* contributions, up to retirement: the member does not pay additional *voluntary* contributions. Taking advantage of tiered or matching arrangements is almost certainly likely to be better than paying AVCs or FSAVCs.

10.11 STAKEHOLDER PENSION SCHEMES

Executives (but not directors) earning less than £30,000 in 2000/01 and 2001/02 may contribute up to £3,600 to a stakeholder pension as well as up to 15 per cent of their total remuneration to an occupational pension scheme. The stakeholder pension will not count towards the maximum benefits permitted under the occupational pension scheme. The £30,000 limit is the net pay after superannuation that appears on the employee's form P60 (or payslip or form P45) from the employer. The form P60 excludes form P11D benefits (the taxable element of fringe benefits such as a company car). For the purposes of the form P60 'superannuation' means contributions to occupational pension schemes such as contractual contributions and in-house AVCs but not free-standing AVCs.

Contributing to a stakeholder pension may be a better option than contributing AVCs, both in-house and free standing, because up to one-quarter of the stakeholder pension may be taken as a tax-free lump sum from age 50, whereas AVC benefits must be taken in pension form only (except where contributions started before April 1987).

10.12 PENSIONS SIMPLIFICATION

It will be seen from this chapter that topping up group scheme benefits (both in the private and public sectors) with individual pension arrangements like AVCs, FSAVCs and personal pensions is complicated for the following reasons.

(1) The need for knowledge of the intricacies of Inland Revenue rules and practice relating to different tax regimes.

(2) The need to perform a 'headroom test' to establish the extent to which an individual can top up benefits.

(3) Having to comply with complex eligibility rules, for example controlling directors are not permitted to have an FSAVC or a personal pension and scheme members with P60 earnings of less than £30,000 may use a personal pension rather than an AVC or an FSAVC as long as they do not pay more than £3,600 a year.

(4) The marrying of defined benefits (the basis for many group schemes) with money purchase principles (the basis for FSAVCs, personal pensions and AVCs except 'added years').

(5) Historical inconsistencies, for example, pre-1987 AVCs and FSAVCs can generate a fund at retirement of which one-quarter can be taken as a tax-free lump sum whereas post-1987 plans must be taken in the form of pension only.

(6) The need to monitor Inland Revenue limits when paying out benefits on retirement.

Under the new tax regime starting on 6 April 2005 the means of topping up group schemes will be greatly simplified. The previous tax regimes will be replaced by a new regime in which there will be an annual limit on contributions of £200,000. (For defined benefit schemes 'contribution' will be assessed in relation to an increase in the notional value of the member's benefits, on a basis prescribed by the Inland Revenue.) There will also be an overall lifetime fund limit of £1.4 million (in 2002 terms) of which one-quarter may be taken as a tax-free lump sum.

Individuals who are members of pension schemes, defined benefit or defined contribution, will be able to top up those schemes with individual person pensions if they wish. It is likely that new FSAVCs will cease to be marketed by providers as these contracts make no provision for a tax-free lump sum. It is possible that providers of existing FSAVCs may be able to alter their provisions in order to allow a tax-free lump sum, or as an alternative may offer policyholders a new personal pension in substitution.

Pension schemes are currently obliged to offer members the opportunity to pay AVCs although the Government has stated that it will introduce regulations making this optional in future in order to reduce the burdens on employers and their schemes. In time, therefore, AVCs and FSAVCs will cease to exist.

11

STATE BENEFITS

11.1 INTRODUCTION

The State Pension forms the main pillar of pension provision for most people in the UK. It is made of the following components:

(1) the basic State Pension – the main benefit;
(2) many people also receive or will benefit from the State Second Pension (S2P) which started in April 2002, or the scheme that it replaced, the State Earnings Related Scheme (SERPS) which started in 1978;
(3) the predecessor of SERPS, the State Graduated Scheme;
(4) the Pension Credit, which starts in 2003, which is a means-tested top-up pension for pensioners with low earnings and savings.

11.2 STATE PENSION AGE

The State Pension age is currently 65 for men and 60 for women.

In 1993, the Government announced that the State Pension age for men and women would be equalised at age 65. This will be phased in for women over a ten-year period commencing April 2010.

The phasing in will operate as follows:

(1) the State Pension age for women born during or before March 1950 will remain at 60;
(2) the State Pension age for women born during or after April 1955 will be 65;
(3) the State Pension age for women born in the period April 1950 to March 1955 will be on a transitional basis.

For example:

Date of birth	Pension age
6 April to 5 May 1950	60 years 1 month
6 October to 5 November 1950	60 years 7 months
6 April to 5 May 1951	61 years 1 month
6 October to 5 November 1951	61 years 7 months
6 April to 5 May 1952	62 years 1 month
6 October to 5 November 1952	62 years 7 months
6 April to 5 May 1953	63 years 1 month
6 October to 5 November 1953	63 years 7 months
6 April to 5 May 1954	64 years 1 month
6 October to 5 November 1954	64 years 7 months

For dates of birth between those shown the retirement age will be on a corresponding basis. Thus, a woman born on 9 July 1953 would have a retirement date of 9 November 2016 (ie 63 years 4 months).

In June 2003, the Government published its response to consultation on the Green Paper published in December 2002, 'Simplicity, security and choice: working and saving for retirement, action on occupational pensions'. In its response the Government confirmed that it is committed to leaving the State Pension age at 65.

11.3 THE BASIC STATE PENSION

In the tax year 2003/04 the basic State Pension is £77.45 a week for a single person and £123.80 for a married couple. To obtain the maximum pension men and women need to build up sufficient 'qualifying years' which are years in which they have paid national insurance contributions (NICs), or are treated as having paid NICs. To obtain the full basic State Pension employed and self-employed individuals must have paid or been credited with full NICs for at least 90 per cent of their working lives.

The working life for a man is 49 years. For a woman the working life is 44 years if her State Pension age is 60; 49 if her State Pension age is 65; and interpolated years for women retiring between 60 and 65.

NICs can be credited where people claim unemployment benefit, maternity and sickness benefits.

Individuals earning below the lower earnings limit (£77 a week in 2003/04) do not pay NICs and are not entitled to the basic State Pension. However, individuals earning between £77 a week and the primary threshold for NICs (£89 a week in 2003/04) qualify for the basic State Pension though they do not pay NICs.

The basic State Pension currently increases in payment each April in line with increases in the Retail Prices Index (RPI). Although the pension is increased in line with the RPI it loses its value in relation to increases in national average earnings so that over time the basic State Pension will fall significantly as a proportion of national average earnings. Currently, the basic State Pension represents around 17 per cent of national average earnings but if earnings outstrip prices by 1.5 per cent over the next 20 years the basic State Pension will represent only 11 per cent of national average earnings. The need for additional pension benefits like the State Second Pension (SP2) and Pension Credit is obvious, preferably topped up with private provision.

Example 11.1

The following figures show pensions illustrations for men at various ages. Contributions start at £100 a month and increase every year in line with inflation, assumed to be at 2.5% a year. The pension is payable at age 65, increases in payment at 2.5% a year compound, and in the event of the death of the annuitant is followed by a one-half spouse's pension. The fund is used to buy pension only, with no tax-free lump sum payable. The weekly pension is, in today's terms, as follows:

Age on 5 April 2003	Weekly pension
55	£17
45	£40
35	£71
25	£115

The above figures are taken from www.pensioncalculator.org.uk produced jointly by the Association of British Insurers and the Financial Services Authority.

The pensions illustrated above are for men: the figures for women are very similar owing to the configuration used – a pension which reduces by one-half on the death of the first annuitant. Illustrations of pensions without contingent dependant's pensions will be lower for women. The pension fund is assumed to grow at 7% a year and the annual management charge on the fund is 1% a year.

The illustration system used in the above website allows for other optional illustrations:

(1) with and without a dependant's pension;
(2) with and without a pension increasing in payment;
(3) the effect of delaying the pension start date;
(4) the effect of increasing contributions;
(5) the impact of existing contributions;
(6) the effect of state benefits;

(7) calculating the contribution for a given pension at retirement (rather than showing the pension at retirement for a fixed contribution, as in the above figures);

(8) different pension start dates.

11.4 THE STATE GRADUATED SCHEME

The State Graduated Scheme lasted from 1961 to 1975 and provided an additional earnings-related pension on top of the basic State Pension. The maximum pension under this scheme is currently around £8 a week for a man and £7 a week for a woman.

Many contributors were contracted out of this scheme as their employers provided them with pensions that matched the graduated pension or provided superior benefits.

11.5 THE STATE EARNINGS RELATED PENSION SCHEME (SERPS)

Following extensive consultation between the Government and the pensions industry culminating in the Social Security Act 1975 the State Earnings Related Pension Scheme (SERPS) started in 1978. It provided an earnings-related pension in addition to the basic State Pension for employed people, but not the self-employed:

(1) Originally a person who reached State Pension age before 6 April 1999 was entitled to a pension of 1.25 per cent of revalued earnings within the upper earnings band for each year between 1978 and 1999, giving a maximum pension of 25 per cent of upper band earnings, revalued in line with earnings thereafter.

(2) People who reached State Pension age in 1999/2000 or later were originally entitled to a pension of the average of their best 20 years' revalued upper band earnings.

Various changes were made to SERPS over the years to cut pension entitlement and reduce costs. Following the Social Security Act 1986, the SERPS pension was reduced from 25 per cent to 20 per cent of revalued lifetime earnings in the upper earnings band rather than the best 20 years' earnings.

Further reductions in SERPS were made in the Pensions Act 1995:

(1) When SERPS was set up the pension was based on the individual's total earnings up to the upper earnings level. These earnings were

then revalued in line with increases in national average earnings then reduced by the *lower earnings limit in force at State Pension age* with the final SERPS pensions being calculated on the final figure.

(2) From 6 April 2000 the basis changed: the individual's earnings in each tax year are reduced by the *lower earnings level in that tax year* and the resulting figure is revalued in line with increases in national average earnings to State Pension age. The effect is to reduce SERPS by around 5 per cent.

11.6 THE STATE SECOND PENSION (S2P)

The State Second Pension (S2P) replaced SERPS from 6 April 2002, as a result of the Child Support, Pensions and Social Security Act 1999. The main purpose of S2P is to ensure that low earners and non-earners, such as carers, will have a supplementary pension in addition to the basic State Pension and to improve the pensions of low and moderate earners. S2P continued the earnings-related nature of SERPS by providing benefits at least equal to SERPS in its initial phase. However, S2P will become a flat-rate scheme in the future: this was originally planned for 2006 or 2007 although an implementation date appears now to have been dropped.

11.6.1 Phase 1 of S2P

In phase 1 there are three different accrual rates for different bands of earnings, based around a new threshold called the lower earnings threshold (LET) which is increased each year in line with earnings:

(1) People earning below the LET (£11,200 in 2003/04) are treated as if they earned the full amount of the LET. This includes people such as non-earners and carers who will earn a pension to supplement the basic State Pension for the first time.

(2) For earnings up to the LET, S2P accrues at double the rate of SERPS accrual on earnings between the LET limit (£4,004 in 2003/04) and the LET.

(3) The rate of accrual between the LET and £25,600 will be one-half of the SERPS accrual rate, amounting to 10 per cent accrual for those reaching State Pension age after 5 April 2009.

(4) For earnings between £25,600 and the upper earnings limit (£30,940 in 2003/04) the rate of accrual is the same as SERPS accrual, ie 20 per cent for those reaching State Pension age after 5 April 2009.

11.6.2 Phase 2 of S2P

S2P will move to a flat rate in phase 2. The likely basis will be for the accrual for earnings above the LET to disappear for individuals up to an upper age limit, possibly age 45. For those aged over 45, earnings-related accrual will continue as in phase 1. The move to a flat rate will encourage people with earnings above the LET to contract out: the contracted-out terms should be favourable as they will continue to be earnings related in phase 2.

11.7 DEATH BENEFITS – BEREAVEMENT

The Welfare Reform and Pensions Act 1999 brought about equal treatment for widows and widowers, with effect from 9 April 2001. The benefits payable on bereavement are as follows (subject to the deceased spouse having had a satisfactory record of NICs):

(1) a tax-free **bereavement payment** of £2,000 payable on the death of the spouse provided at the time of death the deceased spouse was not entitled to basic State Pension, or the surviving spouse was under State Pension age;

(2) a **widowed parent's allowance** (taxable) if the survivor is entitled to child benefit or is expecting her late husband's baby;

(3) a **bereavement allowance** (taxable) for 52 weeks after the death of the spouse provided the surviving spouse is aged at least 45 at the date of death and is not entitled to a widowed parent's allowance.

Bereavement benefits cease on remarriage or co-habitation.

11.8 DEATH BENEFITS – WIDOW'S AND WIDOWER'S PENSIONS

All eligible widows and widowers are entitled to the bereavement payment above but if they are under age 45 and have no dependent children there are no further benefits payable. A widow over State Pension age but less than age 65 when her husband dies can receive either a widow's pension until age 65 or a basic State Pension of the same amount. From age 65 the State Pension is payable (again subject to her husband having a satisfactory National Insurance Record). There is no equivalent widower's pension. Widows and widowers can inherit all or part of their late spouse's S2P and SERPS. Other means-tested benefits may be payable.

11.9 INHERITED SERPS

Before 6 April 2000 a widow (not a widower) could inherit up to 100 per cent of her deceased husband's SERPS pension. The Government's intention was to cut this to 50 per cent from that date but after a political row about poor communication from the Department of Social Security to the public about this change the originally planned reduction to 50 per cent has been deferred until 6 October 2010. If the husband or wife is due to reach State Pension age after 6 October 2002 but before 6 October 2010, on their death the maximum inherited pension is between 90 per cent and 60 per cent of their SERPS. If the husband or wife is due to reach State Pension age on or after 6 October 2010 the maximum inherited pension is 50 per cent of their SERPS.

11.10 STATE PENSION CREDIT AND MINIMUM INCOME GUARANTEE

The State Pension credit started in October 2003 and replaced the minimum income guarantee (MIG) which started in April 1999 as a means of income support for those who had little or no income above the basic State Pension. The MIG had a number of adverse features: it was not available to people with capital over £12,000, any income received by the pensioner above the basic State Pension, for example from investments, reduced the MIG on a £1 for £1 basis, and the form-filling needed to make a claim was complicated with the result that many people eligible for the MIG did not claim it.

The State Pension credit is made up of the guarantee credit and the savings credit. The guarantee works in a similar way to the MIG, aiming to provide a minimum level of income for those aged 60 and over. Between 2010 and 2020 the starting age will rise when State Pension ages for men and women are equalised at age 65. The minimum income is around £100 a week for a single person and £154 a week for a married couple.

The savings credit is payable from age 65 and is therefore not in line with the guarantee credit. The credit provides 60p for every £1 of income above the basic State Pension up to the guarantee credit ceiling and withdraws 40p for every £1 of income thereafter. Using 2003 figures, the thresholds above which no savings credit is paid will be £135 a week for a single person and £200 a week for a married couple.

Example 11.2

1. A single pensioner with no private income and only the basic State Pension of £77 a week could claim a guarantee credit of £23 taking the total up to £100 a week
2. A single pensioner with a basic State Pension of £77 a week and a private pension of £15 a week, giving a total income of £92 a week, could claim a guarantee credit of £8 taking the income to £100 and a savings credit of £9 (60% of the private pension of £15 a week).
3. A married couple with a State Pension of £133 a week and a private income of £57 a week, giving a total of £190 a week, would not be entitled to any guarantee credit. However, they would be entitled to a savings credit of £4.20 [(60% of £154 – £123) minus (40% of £190 – £154)]. Thus their total income would be £194.20 a week.

11.11 MEANS TESTING

The means test for both the guarantee and savings credits will not be so intrusive as the test for the MIG. The first £6,000 of capital will be ignored and for capital above £6,000 the Department for Work and Pensions will assume a notional rate of income from capital at around 10 per cent so, for example, £18,000 of capital will be assumed to generate £1,200 of income. This income of £1,200 will reduce the entitlement to guarantee credit by £1,200 a year but would qualify for savings credit of £720.

In practice the ceiling for capital will be around £36,000 for a single person entitled to only the basic State Pension and around £46,000 for a married couple.

Means-tested benefits are an increasingly significant part of pensioner incomes.

11.12 STATE PENSION SCHEME CONTRIBUTIONS

Pensions are paid by levying NICs on the working population on a 'pay as you go basis'. The employer's contributions may be set against profits for corporation tax purposes but employee contributions are not tax deductible. (NICs are collected through the PAYE system.)

NIC rates incorporate other national insurance benefits such as short-term sickness, National Health and redundancy payments. They do not therefore represent the actual cost of State Pensions alone.

Table 11.1 sets out contracted-in and contracted-out NICs payable by employers and employees in 2003/04.

Table 11.1

| Tax year | Employer | | | Employee | |
| | Contracted out | | | | |
	COSR (%)	COMP (%)	Contracted in (%)	Contracted out (%)	Contracted in (%)
6.4.03–5.4.04					
Earnings per week					
£0–£89.00	nil	nil	nil	nil	nil
£89.01–£595	9.3	11.8	12.8	9.4	11.0
above £595	9.3	11.8	12.8	1.0	1.0

Note:
'COSR' means contracted-out salary related and 'COMP' means contracted-out money purchase.

11.13 UPPER AND LOWER EARNINGS LIMITS

The ceiling on earnings for national insurance purposes (mentioned in 11.3 above) is known as the upper earnings limit (UEL). The lower earnings limit (LEL) corresponds roughly with the flat rate pension for a single person while the UEL is around seven times the LEL: both limits are adjusted in April each year. Table 11.2 sets out upper and lower earnings limits for 1981/82 to 2003/04 inclusive.

Table 11.2

Earnings limits

Tax year	Lower earnings limit £ pa(a)	Upper earnings limit £ pa(a)
1981/82	1,404	10,400
1982/83	1,534	11,440
1983/84	1,690	12,220
1984/85	1,768	13,000
1985/86	1,846	13,780
1986/87	1,976	14,820
1987/88	2,028	15,340
1988/89	2,132	15,860
1989/90	2,236	16,900
1990/91	2,392	18,200
1991/92	2,704	20,280
1992/93	2,808	21,060
1993/94	2,912	21,840
1994/95	2,964	22,360
1995/96	3,260	22,880
1996/97	3,430	23,660

Table 11.2 *(cont.)*

1997/98	3,224	24,180
1998/99	3,328	25,220
1999/2000	3,432	26,000
2000/01	3,484	27,820
2001/02	3,744	29,900
2002/03	3,900	30,420
2003/04	4,004	30,940

Note:
(a)   52 times the weekly amount

11.14 INCREASES DURING PAYMENT

The amount of SERPS/S2P benefit is increased each year by the state (along with the basic State Pension) in line with increases in the RPI.

11.15 DEFERRED PENSION

If an individual, on reaching pensionable age, is still in regular employment (see above) or defers claiming the State Pension, additional pension benefits will accrue at a rate of 7.5 per cent for each full year deferred. The rate of increase for those who reach State Pension age in 2010 or later will be 10.4 per cent for each full year deferred.

The maximum period of deferment is currently five years to age 70 (males), 65 (females), and no further NICs are payable by the individual during this period (although employers' Class 1 contributions continue for as long as the employment continues with no upper age limit). The maximum additional pension which may be earned over a full five years' deferment is approximately 37 per cent. However, from 2010 there will be no limit on the period of deferment.

If any social security benefits (except attendance allowance, mobility or benefit for a child) are received, or an unemployability supplement is paid with a disablement pension in any week, no additional pension will accrue for that week.

Any additional pension earned by deferment may also be inherited by a widow(er) on the individual's death.

11.16 SUMMARY OF STATE PENSIONS

Table 11.3

Basic Old Age Pensions

From	Single person £ per annum	Married couple £ per annum
23 November 1981	1,539.20	2,462.20
22 November 1982	1,708.20	2,732.60
21 November 1983	1,770.60	2,834.00
26 November 1984	1,861.60	2,979.60
25 November 1985	1,991.60	3,187.60
28 July 1986	2,012.40	3,221.40
6 April 1987	2,054.00	3,289.00
6 April 1988	2,139.80	3,426.80
6 April 1989	2,267.20	3,629.60
6 April 1990	2,438.80	3,905.20
6 April 1991	2,704.00	4,329.00
6 April 1992	2,815.80	4,508.40
6 April 1993	2,917.20	4,669.60
6 April 1994	2,995.20	4,789.20
6 April 1995	3,060.20	4,893.20
6 April 1996	3,179.80	5,083.00
6 April 1997	3,247.40	5,189.60
6 April 1998	3,364.40	5,376.80
6 April 1999	3,471.00	5,548.40
6 April 2000	3,510.00	5,610.80
6 April 2001	3,770.00	6,026.80
6 April 2002	3,926.00	6,276.40
6 April 2003	4,027.40	6,437.60

Table 11.4 shows the single person's pension and Table 11.5 shows the married couple's pension, both as a percentage of salary.

Note that SERPS/S2P is not included in Tables 11.4 and 11.5. It is very difficult for individuals to calculate their own SERPS/S2P pension with accuracy, especially if they have been contracted out for part of their working life. The best course of action is to contact the Pensions Service for a pensions forecast (see 11.17 below). S2P will have a greater impact on pensioners who have had low to moderate earnings during their working lives.

Table 11.4

			Salary			
£8,000	£9,000	£10,000	£15,000	£20,000	£25,000	£40,000
50.3	44.7	40.3	26.8	20.1	16.1	10.1

Table 11.5

			Salary			
£8,000	£9,000	£10,000	£15,000	£20,000	£25,000	£40,000
80.4	71.5	64.4	42.9	32.2	25.6	16.1

11.17 THE PENSIONS SERVICE

In general, the calculation of state benefits is a complicated exercise especially as so many conditions attach to the benefits. In practice, the benefits themselves will probably be inadequate so that the need to top up state benefits through private provision, for example by membership of an occupational scheme or through a personal pension scheme, is of paramount importance, particularly in relation to widow(er)s' benefits.

The Pensions Service publishes a number of leaflets describing state benefits and these are essential reading for anyone who wishes to comprehend fully all the conditions which apply. The principal leaflets are *A Guide to State Pensions*, ref NP46, *A Guide to Your Pension Options*, ref PM1, *State Pensions – Your Guide*, ref PM2 and *Pensions for Women – Your Guide*, ref PM6.

In addition, the Department for Work and Pensions (DWP) has produced some easy to understand explanatory pages on its website at www.thepensionservice.gov.uk. The Pensions Service also publishes a series of manuals on pensions for the self-employed and stakeholder pensions.

To obtain an estimate of state benefits, an individual should send a completed form BR19, 'State Pension Forecast' to Retirement Pension Forecasting, Whitley Road, Newcastle-upon-Tyne NE98 1BA (the form is available from DWP offices).

11.18 CONTRACTING OUT

This chapter has concentrated mainly on benefits provided under SERPS/S2P. The next chapter looks at how it is possible to contract out of S2P.

12

CONTRACTING OUT OF THE STATE SCHEMES

12.1 INTRODUCTION TO CONTRACTING OUT

Contracting out of the State Second Pension (S2P) may be achieved either through membership of an occupational scheme set up by the employer or by taking out a personal pension scheme. However contracting out through a personal pension scheme was not possible before 1 July 1988.

Since 6 April 1978, it has been possible for occupational schemes to contract out. This can be achieved on either a defined benefit or money purchase basis; the latter was not available before 6 April 1988. Many of the schemes which had been in existence prior to 1978 provided worthwhile benefits so that in 1978 they required only fine-tuning to enable them to meet the original conditions for contracting out.

12.2 CONTRACTING OUT ON A DEFINED BENEFIT BASIS

If a defined benefit/final salary scheme provides a certain level of benefits it can be used to contract out. The detailed rules that apply have changed over the years as the State Earnings Related Pension Scheme (SERPS) changed when it was replaced by S2P.

12.2.1 Original requirements for contracting out of SERPS

To contract out of SERPS the scheme had to satisfy two tests:

(1) A quality test which required a final salary pension of $\frac{1}{80}$ of final salary ('salary' could be basic salary only) for each year of service in the scheme from April 1978 or $\frac{1}{100}$ of final salary if 'salary' was defined as total PAYE earnings. A widow's pension also had to be provided.

(2)   A quantity test which required an underlying 'guaranteed minimum pension' (GMP) which overall had to match the pension that the member would have accrued in SERPS had he not been in the contracted-out scheme. The scheme also had to provide a widow's GMP (WGMP) and a widower's GMP since 1988. The GMP/WGMP has to be identifiable in the scheme because it has to be increased broadly in line with inflation as measured by the Retail Prices Index (RPI). GMPs stopped accruing after 5 April 1997.

12.2.2 Current requirements for contracting out

From 6 April 1997 GMPs no longer had to accrue but those that had built up to 5 April 1997 remained. A new test was introduced, known as the Reference Scheme Test. It requires the scheme to provide a pension at age 65, or earlier, of at least $\frac{1}{80}$ of 90 per cent of earnings in the middle band of earnings, for each year of pensionable service from 6 April 1997. The Reference Scheme Test must be satisfied by at least 90 per cent of eligible members.

A widow's/widower's pension of 50 per cent of the member's pension must also be provided.

Pensions must increase in line with Limited Price Indexation.

The changes were introduced to simplify the administration of contracted-out schemes (although the need to hold records of GMPs for members who joined before April 1997 increased the administration).

As with contracted-out money purchase schemes (COMPS) and appropriate personal pensions (APPs), the state will top up the contracted-out scheme pension with the difference between S2P and SERPS.

Contracted-out rebates in national insurance contributions

The current rebate for schemes contracted out of S2P on a defined benefit/final salary basis is 5.1 per cent of upper band earnings (split 1.6 per cent to the employee and 3.5 per cent to the employer). This rebate applies for the five-year period 2002 to 2007.

12.3 CONTRACTED-OUT MONEY PURCHASE SCHEMES (COMPs)

Up to 5 April 1997, occupational money purchase schemes could be contracted out if the employer guaranteed to pay contributions equal to the flat rate contracted-out national insurance contribution (NIC) rebate to the scheme. The benefits based on these contributions are known as 'protected rights'. Contributions could be paid above the flat rate rebate and these contributions would secure benefits above the protected rights level.

Since 1997 a number of changes have been made to the basis of contracting out under these schemes. From April 1997 to April 1999 the rebate was paid in two parts: a flat rate rebate of 3.1 per cent of upper band earnings (split 1.6 per cent to the employee and 1.5 per cent to the employer) in the form of lower NICs. In addition an age-related contributions was paid to the scheme by the Department of Social Security. There was an upper limit to the age-related portion of 9 per cent of middle band earnings

From April 1999 to April 2002 the rebate was reduced: the flat rate rebate was reduced to 2.2 per cent (split 1.6 per cent to the employee and 0.6 per cent to the employer). The age-related portion was also reduced, but the upper limit remained at 9 per cent.

From April 2002 the level of rebates changed again with the start of the S2P. The age-related rebates for the five-year period 2002 to 2007 are higher than previously, with the maximum rebates increasing from 9 per cent to 10.5 per cent.

However, these rebates are lower than those payable to APPs (see 12.5). Under a COMP, a scheme member is only partially contracted out, to the extent of SERPS, with the state paying a benefit to members at retirement equal to the difference between SERPS and S2P. Under an APP the rebate reflects the full S2P given up through contracting out.

Table 12.1

Tax year	Employee (%)	Employer (%)
1993/94 to 1996/97	1.80	3.00
1997/98 to 1998/99	1.60	1.50
1999/2000 to 2001/02	1.60	0.60
2002/03 to 2003/04	1.60	1.00

In addition, from 6 April 1997, a further age-related rebate is payable by IR NICO, as follows:

Table 12.2 COMPS age-related rebates (percentage of upper band earnings) from 6 April 2003

Age last birthday on 5 April	
20	2.8
30	3.4
40	4.2
50	7.9
51	9.1
52 to 63	10.5

12.4 CONTRACTED-OUT MIXED BENEFIT SCHEMES (COMBs)

With effect from April 1997, contracted-out salary related schemes (COSRs) were allowed to retain GMP liabilities built up to that date and to contract out on a money purchase basis after that date. The scheme could therefore run two contracted-out sections, one on a salary-related basis and the other on a money purchase basis.

12.5 APPROPRIATE PERSONAL PENSIONS (APPs)

Employees may contract out of S2P through an appropriate personal pension provided that they are not already contracted out through an occupational scheme. An APP includes a stakeholder pension (merely a personal pension with restrictions on charges, and flexible access conditions). When contracting out through an APP, employees and employers pay full-rate NICs.

Following the end of the tax year, the IR NICO rebates part of these contributions directly into the APP. Tax relief at basic rate on the employee's share of the rebate is also paid. These payments into the APP provide 'protected rights' benefits as under COMPs.

Since April 1997, rebates have been age-related and in April 1999 were increased to allow for a reduction in the investment yield assumed to be earned in the APP.

12.5.1 Review of contracting-out terms for appropriate personal pensions

A new set of rebates came into force from 6 April 2002 with the start of S2P. The rebates are set at three levels corresponding to the three bands of earnings on which S2P is calculated. The rebates quoted are usually those that apply to the upper band of earnings.

Example figures are as follows for 2003/04:

Age on 5 April	On earnings between £25,601 and £30,940 (upper band earnings)
20	4.4%
30	4.8%
40	5.3%
50	8.9%
51	10.0%
52 to 63	10.5%

The rebates that apply to earnings between £4,004 and £11,200 are double those above while the rebates that apply to earnings between £11,201 and £25,600 are one-half of those above.

The employee's share of the rebate is 1.6 per cent. This is the net amount after tax relief at 22 per cent. The gross amount before tax relief is 2.05 per cent so the tax relief is 0.45 per cent, which should be added to the rebates in the table above.

Employees who earn less than the Lower Earnings Threshold (£11,200 in 2003/04) will receive a top up S2P pension from the state as well as receiving a rebate in NICs if they contract out.

Example 12.1

A person with part-time earnings of £9,000 a year would receive a rebate based on earnings of £4,996 (£9,000 – £4,004) plus an additional S2P pension from the state based on notional earnings of £2,200 (£11,200-£9,000). If he is aged 30 the rebate will be:

40% accrual band (£9,000 – £4,004) @ 9.6%	=	£479.62
Tax relief (£9,000 – £4,004) @1.6%/0.78 × 22%	=	£22.55
Total rebate	=	£502.17

A person aged 51 with earnings of £30,000 in 2003/04 contracts out of S2P with an appropriate personal pension. The rebate is as follows:

40% accrual band (£4,004 to £11,200) @20%	=	£1,439.20
10% accrual band (£11,201 to £25,600) @5%	=	£ 719.95
20% accrual band (£25,601 to £30,000) @10%	=	£ 439.90
Tax relief (£30,000 – £4,004) @1.6%/0.78 × 22%	=	£ 117.32
Total rebate	=	£2,716.37

12.6 CONTRACTING OUT – TRENDS

On 1 July 1988, individuals were allowed to effect a personal pension scheme and contract out. Any person acting before 6 April 1989 was allowed to contract out retrospectively from 6 April 1987.

The rebate was originally a flat-rate rebate, ie it was not age- or sex-related, and as a result favoured the young. However, in order to reduce the numbers of people ceasing to contract out and opting back into SERPS, the Government introduced age-related rebates from 1997/98. The payment of an additional incentive of 1 per cent to personal pensions for persons aged 30 and over from 1993/94 to 1996/97 was a step in that direction.

On 6 April 1988, employers were allowed to contract out through occupational schemes which provided benefits on a money-purchase basis. Prior to that time employers could contract out only if the scheme provided benefits on a defined benefit basis, as described above.

However, the new terms that apply to APPs from 2002/03 are generally regarded as an improvement on the previous terms. Nevertheless some pension providers are encouraging existing policyholders to contract back into S2P for the future, arguing that with the recent falls in annuity rates, and the uncertain investment climate, the contracting-out terms are not sufficient to warrant taking the gamble that a private pension will match the certainty of a State Second Pension.

Managers of occupational schemes that are contracted out, either on a defined benefit or money purchase basis, are also concerned at the inadequacy of the national insurance rebates. However, in many cases, they would not be able to reverse their contracting-out decision without significant upheaval to their schemes and this is a factor in maintaining the current position.

Contracting out of S2P may become more popular when, and if, it changes from an earnings-related scheme to a flat-rate pension around 2006 or 2007, the dates that were once mooted.

The number of new individuals contracting out through personal pensions has levelled off as the terms become less attractive. However, the new terms that apply to APPs for 2002/03 and subsequent years are an improvement on the previous terms.

12.7 MECHANICS OF CONTRACTING OUT THROUGH APPROPRIATE PERSONAL PENSION SCHEMES (INCLUDING STAKEHOLDER SCHEMES)

The individual, having examined the options open to him, decides he wishes to contract out. The process which follows this decision is as follows:

(1) The individual and the pension provider complete a joint notice which is sent to the IR NICO. The employer continues to deduct NICs at the contracted-in rate. The employer need not necessarily be aware of the employee's decision. Individuals wishing to contract out through personal pension schemes are either in non-pensionable employment or are members of a contracted-in occupational pension scheme.

(2) At the end of the tax year the IR NICO pays the contracted-out rebate directly into the personal pension scheme.

(3) An indication of the rebates for APPs is given in 12.5.1 above.

12.8 CHARACTERISTICS OF APPROPRIATE PERSONAL PENSIONS

The contributions paid by the IR NICO constitute 'protected rights', and are separated from any other contributions paid by the employee and/or employer, and are subject to the following conditions:

(1) Protected rights may be used to provide a pension only in retirement, from state pensionable age (currently 65 men, 60 women), there being no provision for early retirement.

(2) It is not be possible to take protected rights in the form of a cash lump sum.

(3) As a move towards a reduction in sex discrimination, protected rights must buy annuities on a unisex basis. This means that there must be no discrimination between males and females (in practice, this means a downward movement in annuity rates for men). Unisex rates, however, do not have to be used in respect of annuities purchased in the event of the death of the member whilst in service before state pensionable age.

(4) A change in legislation in 1989, to allow members to take protected rights benefits from age 60 under a COMP scheme to prevent sex-discrimination in favour of females, was followed by a similar change to personal pensions with effect from April 1996.

(5) For benefits arising from rebates before 5 April 1997 the annuity must be increased by the lower of the increase in the RPI and 3 per

cent per annum. This also applies to any widow(er)'s annuity. The basis changed for benefits arising from rebates in respect of 1997/98 and beyond; the annuity must be increased by the lower of the increase in RPI and 5 per cent a year.

(6) Protected rights do not have to provide a guaranteed minimum pension. If at State Pensionable age protected rights purchase benefits lower than what SERPS/S2P would have provided if the individual had not been contracted out, the state will not make up the shortfall. However, any excess benefits the individual.

(7) An open-market option must be available at retirement.

An individual may have a series of personal pension schemes but only one of these schemes may accept the contracted-out rebate.

An election to contract out for a particular tax year must be made by 5 April of that year.

12.9 CONTRACTING BACK INTO SERPS

Persons approaching the pivotal ages when contracting out ceases to be attractive should consider informing the IR NICO that they no longer wish to be contracted out. This is done by sending a completed form APP 2 'Cancellation Notice' to the IR NICO. A member of a COMP scheme has to approach his pension scheme trustees to find out his options, which might include switching into a 'not contracted-out' category of membership whilst remaining in the scheme.

The managers of these schemes will usually contact scheme members and/or their financial advisers at the pivotal ages. These ages will depend on the managers' assumptions about future investment growth rates and mortality. Individuals also need to consider their own attitudes to risk.

13

EXECUTIVE PENSIONS AND INHERITANCE TAX PLANNING

13.1 INTRODUCTION

Lump sums on death payable under retirement benefit schemes approved under ICTA 1988, ss 590–612 (see Appendix 4), retirement annuity contracts approved under ICTA 1988, ss 619–627 (ICTA 1970, s 226: see Appendix 4) and personal pension schemes approved under ICTA 1988, ss 630–655 (see Appendix 4), are largely free of inheritance tax (IHT). The methods of inheritance tax planning through retirement annuity contracts and personal pension schemes are set out in Chapter 14. This chapter deals with the use of executive pension plans in assisting a director in passing on his company to future generations without saddling his family with inheritance tax liabilities.

The FA 1989 lessened the effectiveness of executive pension plans for inheritance tax planning in the case of directors who are categorised as 'post-1989 members' because of the cap on earnings.

In general terms a director should try to make provision for his spouse through the inter-spouse exemptions: all life-time gifts and property left by one spouse to the other on death are exempt from inheritance tax (although there is a restriction if the donor spouse is domiciled in the United Kingdom but the donee spouse is not).

In order to make provision for future generations, however, it is advisable to use death benefits arising from an executive pension plan. The rules of a pension scheme which has been designed specifically for controlling directors and key executives will contain a list of persons to whom the lump sum benefit may be paid such as the director's spouse, children, dependants and other individuals whom he has nominated. The rule will give the trustees power to pay to such one or more of the persons specified as they may in their discretion choose. Ideally the rules should also allow the trustees to pay monies to a separate trust (outside the trust governing the executive pension plan) for the benefit of the deceased's children: the trust could also provide for sums to be lent to the widow(er) for immediate needs.

Since the trustees exercise their discretion on who will receive the benefit after the director's death, it cannot form part of his freely disposable estate for inheritance tax purposes, and the pension plan is exempt from the normal charging provisions relating to discretionary trusts because it comes within IHTA 1984, s 58(1)(d).

Directors will normally indicate their preferences to the trustees in advance of their death by completing a nomination form or expression of wish letter, although these will not bind the trustees, who may decide to disregard their wishes.

As the trustees are often fellow directors (eg wife or husband) or the limited company itself the directors may be reasonably happy that their wishes will be complied with and by this simple device they can pass to their children and grandchildren considerable sums which will escape inheritance tax altogether.

If at the time of death a member was using an income drawdown facility (see 13.2.1 below), the lump sum and annuity payable will be governed by the income drawdown rules.

13.2 DEFERRING RETIREMENT

A director who defers his retirement may have benefits paid in the event of his subsequent death on either of the following bases:

(1) the usual death in service benefit of a lump sum equal to four times final remuneration (subject to the earnings cap of £99,000 in 2003/04 for post-1989 members) together with a refund of his own personal contributions plus growth; or
(2) the benefits based on the assumption that he had retired on the day before his death, ie a lump sum payment equal to five years' pension payments, which is the usual guarantee period attached to pensions.

Although in both situations the payment will be free of inheritance tax, where the guarantee under the pension itself is more than five years, the guarantee payments as they fall due must be paid to the deceased's estate – it is not possible to commute them.

In addition, a widow(er)'s pension can also be paid in either circumstance which would of course be free of inheritance tax.

13.2.1 Income drawdown

Whilst choosing to defer their retirement a director, with the trustees' agreement, may take a tax-free lump sum and withdraw an income from the fund, within certain limits set by the Government Actuaries' Department (GAD), until they reach age 75. In the event of death during the period when income is being withdrawn, a lump sum may be available if the member had selected an income calculation basis with a five-year guarantee period or less at outset. In these circumstances a lump sum is payable if he dies within the guarantee period. The lump sum is as follows:

(1) the balance of the payments to the end of the guarantee period assuming an income of the maximum GAD rate calculated at commencement of the withdrawals; plus

(2) the difference between the maximum GAD rate calculated at commencement and what the member has actually withdrawn.

Any remaining fund must be used to provide survivors' pensions in accordance with the normal rules.

The death benefits of income drawdown facilities under occupational pension schemes are generally less favourable than under personal pension schemes.

13.2.2 Phased retirement

A director may transfer his benefits which have accumulated under the executive pension plan to a personal pension scheme (subject to the trustees of the executive pension plan providing a certificate to the effect that it is not 'overfunded' (ie that the fund would provide benefits which do not exceed Inland Revenue limits)).

The subsequent payment of benefits, on retirement, or on death, would then be subject to personal pension scheme rules; more flexibility might be provided on retirement because under the personal pension scheme benefits may be taken in stages up to age 75 at which point the remaining fund must be used to provide a pension. On death, however, the benefits under the personal pension scheme may not be so advantageous for controlling directors or high earners as they would have been under the executive pension plan; on death only one-quarter of the fund under the personal pension scheme may be paid in the form of a lump sum (unless there is no widow(er)) whereas under the executive pension scheme, as stated above, it is generally possible to pay a larger lump sum. Thus, although the personal pension scheme, through the use of 'phased retirement' options, can provide flexibility in retirement benefits, its facility to provide lump sums free of inheritance tax are less advantageous for controlling directors or high earners.

Also, it is by no means certain that such a transfer into a personal pension scheme, even if written in trust, would necessarily provide inheritance tax-free benefits on death. In the event of death within two years of the transfer, it is highly unlikely that death benefits would escape inheritance tax.

Under a personal pension scheme an income may also be withdrawn from the fund, within certain limits, with the purchase of an annuity being deferred until age 75 at the latest. On death during the period when income is being withdrawn the fund may be paid to the deceased's dependants subject to a 35 per cent tax charge. This will be free of inheritance tax provided that the scheme is subject to a suitable trust. (Income withdrawal schemes are covered in detail in Chapter 19.)

13.3 PERSONAL CONTRIBUTIONS

As the object of the exercise is to pass as much capital to the next generation free of inheritance tax, basis (1) under 13.2 above is normally the most favourable. In fact, a director who is setting up an executive pension plan should, where there is a need, ensure that part of the contributions are paid in the form of personal contributions from his own salary to maximise death in service benefits. If he already has an executive pension plan in existence where the contributions are paid wholly by the employer, then, if necessary, he should take a larger salary from the company enabling him to pay personal contributions and reduce the employer's contributions appropriately. The following example and table show the effect of paying personal contributions.

Example 13.1

Current position
(1) Director's remuneration = £50,000
Company's contribution to executive pension plan = £10,000 pa
Company's total expenditure in remuneration and pensions = £60,000 pa
Maximum lump sum death in service benefit which can be provided under the plan = £200,000 (4 × £50,000).

Alternative position
(2) Director's revised remuneration = £58,823
Director's personal contribution under PAYE = £8,823 (15% of £58,823)
Company's contribution to executive pension plan = £1,177 pa
Company's total expenditure in remuneration and pensions = £60,000 pa
Maximum lump sum death in service benefit which can be provided under the plan = £235,292 (4 × £58,823) *and* £8,823, plus growth, for each year of payment.

Notes:

(1) The director's remuneration has been increased by 17.65%, a factor that can be applied to any level of remuneration.

(2) Any increase in remuneration increases national insurance contributions. In this example the extra contributions would be 11.90% of £8,823, ie £1,050 which is not included in the company's total expenditure above.

(3) Where the director is a post-1989 member the lump sum will be restricted to four times capped remuneration, so the above method of increasing the lump sum through the use of personal contributions is of even greater value (although the personal contribution will also be restricted to 15% of capped remuneration).

Table 13.1

A member of an executive pension plan has an initial salary of £10,000 pa, which increases by 4% pa. He pays personal contributions of 15% of salary. The lump sum that could be paid free of inheritance tax on death in service is shown below, assuming pension fund growth of 6% pa after charges. The member is not subject to the cap on earnings applicable to post-1989 members.

At the end of:	4 × salary death in service benefit £	Increasing additional cover £	Total permissible cover £
5 years	48,660	9,660	58,320
10 years	59,200	24,690	83,890
15 years	72,030	47,350	119,380
20 years	87,640	80,770	168,410
25 years	106,630	129,260	235,890

13.4 RESTRICTIONS ON 20 PER CENT DIRECTORS

In March 1979, the Inland Revenue, through Memorandum No 59, limited the ability of a 20 per cent director to ensure that monies could be paid to succeeding generations free of capital transfer tax, the forerunner of inheritance tax. If he is still in service at the age of 75, then in the event of his subsequent death the lump sum payable must be made either to the legal personal representatives, or to the surviving spouse, or in the absence of any surviving spouse, to the legal personal representatives.

If, however, the member had retired and died during the first five years following his retirement, and there was a five-year guarantee attaching to his pension, then the value of the outstanding pension instalments may be paid to the trustees who can then pay them at their discretion to the usual range of beneficiaries.

13.5 OPTIONS AT RETIREMENT

On reaching normal retirement date, it is possible to:

(1) take all the benefits, ie cash and pension;
(2) defer all the benefits and continue working; or
(3) take the tax-free lump sum, but defer the pension benefits (provided that the director is not classed as a post-1989 member);
(4) take the tax-free lump sum, and an income from the fund until the member reaches age 75, then an annuity.

From an inheritance tax point of view, however, taking cash and deferring pension is not to be recommended as this effectively triggers the director's retirement for the purposes of determining future benefits. In the event of his subsequent death while still working with the company, he will be regarded as having retired on the day before he died.

Example 13.2

Salary at date of death £90,000.

Maximum pension is £60,000 per annum or a reduced pension of around £45,000 per annum plus a tax-free cash sum of £101,250.

(1) If tax-free cash of £101,250 has been taken the maximum death benefit will be 5 × the reduced pension of £45,000 per annum, ie £225,000.

(2) If all benefits have been deferred the maximum death benefit will be calculated on the normal death in service basis, ie 4 × salary, ie £360,000.

The difference between the two bases is magnified where the length of time between the taking of tax-free cash and death is increased.

13.6 CONTINUATION FACILITIES

Term assurance is the usual means of providing death in service benefits under executive pension plans. However, if the director takes his benefits on retirement, or if he leaves service, death in service benefits will usually cease. Most executive pension plans offer an option to the director to convert the term assurance into an ordinary life assurance policy, for example a whole of life policy in his own name, without the need to produce medical evidence. The whole of life policy will be a personal contract where contributions are paid by the director himself at the rate applicable to his age when he effects the contract. Thus, a director can convert term assurance to permanent insurance. These policies can be written in trust and can provide a way of mitigating inheritance tax liability for the rest of his life. If he takes his pension from his pension plan the cost of the whole of life policy may be met from the pension payments.

13.7 SUMMARY

Executive pension plans have not always been used to provide pensions. Directors of family-owned companies who had no intention of retiring but required a means of passing on their companies to succeeding generations have used executive pension plans to provide death benefits, free of inheritance tax. This, in turn, gave dependants the capital to continue to run the companies and/or to pay inheritance tax on other assets passing on death.

If the director did not retire from the business and take any retirement benefits from the executive pension plan a benefit could be paid to the director's dependants on death. The director would be in a position to defer taking pension benefits either because he was continuing to work and draw an income from the company in the form of salary or dividends and/or had other resources on which to live. However, although many executive pension plans (and small self-administered pension plans) are in existence today for this purpose this method of tax planning has become less useful in recent years. Directors who fall into the category of 'post-1989 members' have to take retirement benefits by age 75 so these plans cannot be used to provide death benefits beyond that date.

The Inland Revenue's and Treasury's consultation document, 'Simplifying the taxation of pensions: increasing choice and flexibility for all', will curtail the use of pension plans as tax planning tools in the manner described above. The following words in the consultation document are clear: 'These new rules reflect the fact that pensions get favourable tax treatment so that they can establish income in retirement. This is why it will not be possible to pay any capital sums past age 75, the age by which pension savings must be used to deliver retirement income. They also signal that pension tax relief is not provided to encourage estate planning.'

Nevertheless it will be possible to provide the following death benefits:

Before 'vesting' (ie taking) pension savings the reformed tax rules will allow:

(1) unlimited tax-free lump sums except for the recovery charge; and/or
(2) taxable income benefits for dependants.

The recovery charge will be one-third of any lump sum exceeding the lifetime limit (£1.4 million in 2002 terms): the remainder of the excess after tax will be taxed as income giving an effective tax charge of 60 per cent.

The lump sum on death will not be subject to the current limit of four times remuneration at the date of death.

For scheme members who die after starting to receive scheme benefits the simplified tax rules will allow:

(1) up to age 75, lump sums taxable at 35 per cent of no more than the value of the vested funds used to provide the pension income less the sum of pension payments paid before death; and

(2) taxable income benefits for dependants.

13.7.1 Pensions simplification: review of existing arrangements

The new pensions tax regime, to take effect from 6 April 2005, will affect not only new schemes but all existing pension arrangements. Directors will have to assess the likely impact of the new legislation especially where executive pension plans have been used mainly as devices for tax planning, closely linked to the future existence of their businesses.

14

PERSONAL PENSIONS, STAKEHOLDER PENSIONS AND RETIREMENT ANNUITIES

14.1 BACKGROUND

Traditionally, retirement annuities were the means by which the self-employed provided for retirement. The term 'self-employed retirement annuity' (the common generic title for these contracts) is misleading as it suggests that eligibility was confined to one group; in fact people in non-pensionable employment may have taken out these contracts although the vast majority were self-employed.

On 1 July 1988 there was a considerable development in the legislation surrounding retirement annuities and their successors, personal pension schemes. From that date personal pension schemes, introduced by F(No 2)A 1987 and now incorporated in ICTA 1988, Chapter IV, came into force and no new retirement annuities (governed by ICTA 1970, ss 226–228, now incorporated in ICTA 1988, Chapter III) were available from that date.

Personal pension schemes are similar to retirement annuities but there are important differences, notably the facility to use the former to contract out of the earnings-related part of the State Pension scheme (see Chapter 12).

Retirement annuities taken out before 1 July 1988 may continue beyond that date, and may be concurrent with personal pension schemes. In order to distinguish between the two contracts a 'retirement annuity' denotes an ICTA 1988, ss 618–629 contract (see Appendix 4) and a 'personal pension scheme' denotes an ICTA 1988, ss 630–655 contract (see Appendix 4).

Because many people contribute to both types of contract, and the interaction of the two can be significant, both types are described in this chapter.

The next significant date was 6 April 2001, when stakeholder pension schemes became available. These are a form of personal pension scheme subject to regulations relating to the maximum charge that may be taken by providers (1 per cent a year), to access (mainly to assist low to medium earners to contribute for retirement) and to flexibility (allowing contributors to stop and restart payments without penalty). Stakeholder schemes with their low charges have become a benchmark against which other personal pension schemes are compared.

On 6 April 2001, a number of changes were made affecting personal pensions generally, including the stakeholder variant. These changes are contained in the Welfare Reform and Pensions Act 1999, the Finance Act 2000, numerous regulations and over one hundred pages of Inland Revenue Guidance Notes. The main headings are as follows, with more detail given later in this chapter.

(1) **Eligibility.** Contributions may be paid to a personal pension of up to £3,600 a year without the need for 'net relevant earnings'. This extends the use of personal pensions to new groups including carers, minors, students, and the unemployed and enables, for example, grandparents to start a pension for grandchildren and an individual with earnings to start a pension for a spouse who has no earnings.

(2) **The self-employed.** Contributions for the self-employed, previously paid before tax relief, are now paid on the same basis as for employed people, net of basic rate tax.

(3) **Waiver of contribution.** Tax relief is not given on the cost of waiver of contribution on new plans.

(4) **Pensions life cover.** The ability to obtain tax relief on life cover linked to pensions was significantly curtailed.

(5) **Clustering.** The practice of splitting personal pension plans into identical segments (typically 100 or 1,000) to allow the taking of retirement benefits in stages is no longer necessary. New plans allow this flexibility without the need for clustering.

(6) **Carry forward and carry back.** Carry forward of unused tax relief was abolished and carry back is now only allowed into the previous tax year (previously carry back for two years was permitted in some circumstances).

Overall, the changes, while opening up personal pensions (including stakeholder pensions) to a greater number of people, brought about greater complexity. Retirement annuities and personal pensions set up before 6 April 2001 still exist and will continue for many years. As with occupational pension schemes, much of the complexity arises as a result of the continuation of legislation and practice that applies to previous generations of plan.

14.1.1 Future simplification

On 6 April 2005, assuming that the Government's radical plans for the simplification of pensions become law, all existing retirement annuities and personal pension schemes will become subject to the new tax regime, in particular the lifetime limit (tax-favoured) (£1.4 million in 2002 terms) on retirement and death benefits, and the annual limit on inflow into the individual's fund of £200,000. These limits will have a much more significant effect for high earners in occupational schemes. Individuals paying large contributions into retirement annuities and personal pensions will also be affected by the lifetime limit. There will be transitional arrangements for those who have already built up large funds close to or over the lifetime limit on 6 April 2005. Overall, personal pension schemes will fit well within the new pensions tax rules.

14.1.2 How personal pension schemes and retirement annuities work

Under the terms of a personal pension scheme which is effected between the individual and the pension provider (which can be an insurance company, friendly society, bank, building society, investment company or unit trust company), the individual pays contributions in order to secure benefits in the form of pension and a tax-free lump sum. The contributions may be payable:

(1) annually on a level basis, or with provision for increases each year;
(2) monthly, but with provision for increases to be made; or
(3) as single contributions.

Personal pension schemes often have the facility to convert from a monthly to an annual basis, and vice versa, and also to take additional single contributions from time to time.

If the personal pension scheme is used for contracting out of the State Second Pension (S2P) contributions are also paid by the National Insurance Contributions Office (NICO). Personal pension schemes may also take contributions from an employer: the employer's contributions are treated as a deductible business expense like an employer's contributions to an approved retirement benefits scheme.

The contributions, excluding any paid by the NICO, are subject to maximum limits arising from the legislation (set out below).

Retirement annuities, the forerunners of personal pension schemes, work in a similar way except that they cannot be used to contract out of S2P. They do not receive contributions from the NICO, and nor can they accept contributions from an employer, or any third party.

14.1.3 Comparison of personal pension schemes and retirement annuities

Although full information on the differences between retirement annuity contracts and personal pension schemes is given throughout this chapter, a brief comparison of the major differences is set out in the following table.

Table 14.1

	Retirement annuity	*Personal pension scheme*
Benefit ages	Between 60 and 75	Between 50 and 75
Basis of calculating tax-free cash	3 × the annuity remaining after cash has been taken	25% of fund used to provide the member's pension[1]
Facility to carry back contributions	Yes	Yes
Facility to carry forward unused relief	Yes	No[4]
Ancillary benefits eg life assurance, waiver of contribution	Yes	Yes[5]
Ability to contract-out	No	Yes
Cash limit	£150,000[6] (unless effected before 17 March 1987)	None
Tax relief on contributions at source	No	Yes
Ability to accept employer's contributions	No	Yes
Facility to accept transfers from other schemes	No[2]	Yes
Facility to pay transfer to other schemes	Yes	Yes
Ability to write in trust	Yes	Yes
Open market option available	Yes	Yes
Income withdrawal[3]	No	Yes

Notes:
(1) Any part of the fund which consists of 'Protected Rights' will have to be excluded for this purpose when the scheme was taken out after 27 July 1989. In the case of a scheme taken out before 27 July 1989 although Protected Rights do not have to be excluded, any part of the fund which is used to buy a widow(er)'s annuity may have to be excluded. This means that, in practice, around 20 per cent of the total fund may be taken in cash. Under the new tax regime, however, the cash limit will be 25% of the fund.
(2) Except other retirement annuities.
(3) For details of income withdrawal see Chapter 19.
(4) There is no tax relief on contributions for waiver of contribution benefit linked to personal pension schemes set up on or after 6 April 2001. The position of ongoing tax relief on contributions to schemes set up before 6 April 2001 is not clear: it may end under the new tax regime.
(5) The facility to carry back under the new pension tax regime will not be available. The facility to carry forward contributions under retirement annuities will also cease.
(6) The £150,000 cash limit applies to each retirement annuity policy.
(7) The minimum benefit age will be set at age 55 in 2010: this restriction will also apply to existing schemes with pension ages below age 55 including those in specialised occupations.

14.1.4 Benefits

Income in retirement

The sole purpose of the personal pension scheme is to provide an annuity in retirement commencing at any time between the ages of 50 and 75 (currently) but an annuity can be drawn regardless of whether the individual is working. Indeed it is possible to stagger the benefits over that period. For personal pensions that started before 6 April 2001, that was achieved by either having a series of separate schemes or one scheme within which there were a number of arrangements which provide for the benefits to be paid at intervals. For personal pensions starting after 5 April 2001, parts of the plan may be cashed in separately without the need to have separate schemes or arrangements.

The facility to take benefits under a personal pension scheme from age 50 compared with age 60 under a retirement annuity was a welcome improvement, although in practice it is unlikely to be seen as a sufficient reason for stopping contributions to a retirement annuity in favour of a personal pension scheme. Most planholders will not have had the opportunity of building up sufficient funds to provide a worthwhile income at age 50. In any case, the minimum pension age will increase to age 55 from 2010.

Lump sums

Generally, up to one-quarter of the fund accumulated in a personal pension scheme may be taken as a tax-free lump sum. The retirement annuity legislation restricts the maximum tax-free lump sum to three times the remaining pension after the cash has been taken. Although more complicated than the personal pension scheme legislation this method may provide more tax-free cash, depending on the level of annuity rates.

These options are very valuable as they give the member the flexibility of having more tax-free money in his hands, but if he is more interested in income he can use the tax-free cash to buy a purchased life annuity (ICTA 1988, s 656) which is taxed only on the interest content.

Assuming a retirement fund of £100,000 the amounts which could be taken in the form of a tax-free cash sum are as follows:

Table 14.2 Comparison of PPP and RAC tax-free cash (Fund value £100,000)

| | Age | Personal pension scheme | Retirement annuity | |
			Yield 3.15%	5%
Men	60	£25,000	£15,231	£17,958
	65	£25,000	£17,245	£19,855
	70	£25,000	£19,747	£22,196
	75	£25,000	£23,630	£25,921
Women	60	£25,000	£14,139	£16,944
	65	£25,000	£15,812	£18,507
	70	£25,000	£18,035	£20,616
	75	£25,000	£21,126	£23,588

Notes:
(1) Under the retirement annuity the tax-free cash increases as age increases, and differs according to sex. When annuity rates were higher the cash sum under retirement annuities was higher than under personal pension schemes. However, in recent years, as annuity rates have fallen, the cash sums under retirement annuities have also fallen, so that personal pension schemes now give a higher proportion of tax-free cash sum.
(2) Under a retirement annuity, the Inland Revenue allows the tax-free lump sum to be calculated as though the most favourable annuity basis (ie annually in arrears without guarantee) had been selected. After the lump sum has been taken, the balance of the fund can be used to provide an annuity on a different basis, normally payable quarterly or monthly in advance, guaranteed for five years.
(3) If an open market option is exercised under a retirement annuity and transferred to a personal pension scheme, tax-free cash will be 25 per cent of the fund.

For personal pension schemes that commenced after 5 April 2001, the fund can be taken in stages to provide an annuity. In these cases the lump sum at each stage is one-third of the fund used to buy the annuity. This equates to one-quarter of the entire fund value cashed in.

Example 14.1

A fund of £100,000 built up under a personal pension scheme might provide an income payable in monthly instalments throughout the life of a man aged 65, guaranteed for five years, of £6,625 per annum, but subject to tax at, say, 22 per cent, leaving a net income of £5,168 per annum.

Alternatively the fund could be taken in the form of a tax-free lump sum of, say, £25,000 plus a reduced income of £4,969 gross, netting down to £3,876: the cash of £25,000 could be used to buy a purchased life annuity. Part of the annuity is regarded as a return of the purchase price – known as the capital content – and is not subject to tax: the balance is interest and is subject to tax.

The cash lump sum of £25,000 could be used to buy a purchased life annuity of, say, £1,663. Of this, £253 is interest and would be taxed (leaving a net income of £1,607 for a basic rate taxpayer).

The combination of the two net annuities is £5,483, an increase of £315 over the income obtained if the whole fund is used to buy an annuity. This demonstrates the benefit of taking advantage of the tax-free lump sum even if income is a priority.

14.1.5 Open market option

The treatment of open market options is different for retirement annuities and personal pensions.

Retirement annuities usually permit an 'open market option' where the accumulated fund can be transferred, when the benefits are being cashed, to another insurance company. The policyholder takes advantage of the open market option if another insurance company offers annuity rates better than those of the original insurance company. Money passes from insurer to insurer (not through the policyholder). Sometimes the policyholder incurs a penalty if the money is transferred to another insurance company.

Under retirement annuities, when the open market option is exercised, the new insurance company issues a 'substituted contract' to provide the pension *and* the tax-free lump sum. Thus the whole fund is transferred from the first insurance company to the second with both cash and pension paid by the second. There is no objection, however, to a transfer of only part of the value of the planholder's benefit under the contract. In that event, both the original and the substituted contracts must limit the tax-free lump sum by reference to the pensions payable under the respective contracts.

Since 1 July 1988, it has not been possible to take out new retirement annuities, including substituted contracts. This means that if an open market option is exercised money must be transferred from the retirement annuity either to another retirement annuity (which must have been effected before 1 July 1988) or to a personal pension scheme and subject to its rules which include a limitation on the tax-free cash to 25 per cent of the fund used to provide the member's pension. In recent years, however, this has not caused hardship because low annuity rates have often meant that the tax-free cash under the retirement annuity would be less than 25 per cent of the fund (see Table 14.2 above) and is the current position as at July 2003.

Personal pension schemes arranged through banks, building societies and unit trusts are not allowed to provide pension benefits on retirement directly; the underlying funds after tax-free cash has been paid have to be transferred to an insurance company which then provides the annuity.

Personal pension schemes arranged through insurance companies have to offer the right to a transfer as a condition of approval.

14.1.6 Types of pension available

On taking the benefits from the personal pension scheme or retirement annuity, the member normally has various options including the facility to take a reduced pension on his own life, which will continue, in the event of his death, to the spouse. For example, £100,000 would, at the time of writing, purchase the following types of annuity on the open market for a man aged 65. These annuities are not necessarily at the top of the market as annuity rates change frequently. (Further comments on this topic are given in Chapter 19.)

Table 14.3

Type of Annuity	Amount per annum
Single life annuity payable annually in arrears	£6,949
Single life annuity payable monthly in advance	£6,688
Single life annuity payable monthly in advance but for a minimum of five years	£6,625
Single life annuity payable monthly in advance but for a minimum of ten years	£6,441

Table 14.3 *(cont.)*

Single life annuity payable quarterly in advance for a minimum of five years, increasing each year by 3% pa compound	£4,885
Joint life annuity, (not increasing) during the lives of the man and his wife, aged 62, payable quarterly in advance	£5,110

14.1.7 Death before taking benefits

The amounts payable vary widely between different contracts but the choices include:

(1) no return of contributions (rare);
(2) return of contributions without interest (old contracts);
(3) return of contributions with interest at around 4 per cent (old contracts);
(4) return of the accumulated fund.

Example 14.2

Return on death after various periods of years, where the annual contribution is £1,000

	10 years £	*After* *20 years* £	*30 years* £
No return of contributions	–	–	–
Return of contributions without interest	10,000	20,000	30,000
Return of contributions with interest at 4% pa compound	12,006	29,778	56,084
Return of accumulated fund, assuming unit growth of 7% pa after charges	13,800	40,995	94,460

14.1.8 Life cover

Personal pension schemes allow life assurance to be provided through an authorised insurance company. The advantage of paying contributions to a policy approved under this section as opposed to an ordinary life assurance policy of a similar class is that the contributions for the former are fully deductible from earnings for income tax purposes.

Before 6 April 2001, life assurance contracts were provided under ICTA 1988, s 637 (see Appendix 4). Since 6 April 2001, s 637 contracts can only be taken out if there is also a personal pension plan in place to provide retirement benefits that started before 6 April 2001, and has an option in the plan to include life assurance. The maximum contribution for s 637 contracts is 5 per cent of net relevant earnings.

For personal pension plans that started after 5 April 2001, life cover is still available but contributions are restricted to 10 per cent of relevant pension contributions. 'Relevant pension contributions' are contributions to pension plans that the member started after 5 April 2001.

The relief in 2003/04 is at 22 per cent of the contribution so that the net outlay would be only 78 per cent of the contribution payable for a basic rate income tax payer (or lower rate or non-taxpayer). For higher rate tax-payers, higher rate relief will be reclaimed through their self-assessment tax return.

It is possible to assign life cover with the result that these policies have been used to provide collateral security where the individual is borrowing money; they are also used for partnership assurance.

Life assurance may also be provided under the retirement annuity legislation (ICTA 1988, s 621(1)(b) (see Appendix 4)) provided that the policy was effected before 1 July 1988. These policies may also be assigned.

The changes introduced from 6 April 2001 mean that stand-alone life cover is no longer an option, and that the amount of life cover that can be arranged is much smaller than before (because the cost of the life cover must fall within 10 per cent of pension contributions). Pensions life cover associated with pension plans set up after 5 April 2001 is rare.

The treatment of life cover and contributions for the life cover is not yet clear under the Inland Revenue's proposals for simplification.

14.2 PERSONAL PENSION SCHEMES IN MORE DETAIL

The relevant legislation is ICTA 1988, Chapter IV, ss 630–655 (see Appendix 4). Under a personal pension scheme various types of benefit may be provided within the scheme rather than by means of separately approved contracts as applies to retirement annuity contracts under ICTA 1988, ss 620–621 (see Appendix 4). In this way a personal pension scheme is rather similar to an approved retirement benefit scheme. The benefits that may be provided within the scheme are as follows:

(1) An annuity must be payable by an authorised insurance company chosen by the member (currently). The annuity may commence between the ages of 50 and 75. Earlier commencement than age 50 is possible in the event of permanent incapacity or where earlier retirement ages are agreed for special occupations. Under the Government's proposals for pensions tax simplification the earliest pension age will be increased from age 50 to 55 in 2010: this will also apply to existing plans with pension ages below age 55 including those with much earlier pension ages that apply to specialised

occupations. These proposals, currently under consultation, are expected to become law in April 2005. The member may use an income withdrawal facility and defer the purchase of the annuity until no later than age 75. Until the purchase of the annuity the member may draw varying amounts of income from the fund. (For details of income withdrawal see Chapter 19.)

(2) A lump sum may be provided for the member provided it is payable when the annuity is first payable (it is not possible to provide for a lump sum alone). It must not exceed one-quarter of the value of the retirement benefits provided for the member. If the member uses the income withdrawal facility, the lump sum must be taken at the start of the income withdrawal period. There will also be changes to the methods of income withdrawal in April 2005.

(3) A dependant's annuity may be provided for the surviving spouse or dependants if pension provision is being made for the member.

(4) Life assurance may be provided by an authorised insurance company on the death of the individual before he attains the age of 75. (This is the same as the benefit allowed under ICTA 1988, s 621(1)(b) for retirement annuities set up before 1 July 1988.)

14.2.1 Existing retirement annuities

The relevant legislation is found in ICTA 1988, ss 618–629: an extract from the legislation is contained in Appendix 4.

It has not been possible to take out a retirement annuity approved under the above legislation since 30 June 1988, but contracts already in existence at that time may continue in force and will be able to accept subsequent increases in contributions (provided that the contract is sufficiently flexible). Contracts taken out from 1 July 1988 will be personal pension schemes approved under ICTA 1988, ss 630–655 (see Appendix 4).

Three types of benefit can be provided within the retirement annuity legislation:

(1) A retirement annuity approved under s 620, having for its main object the provision of an annuity in old age, but with provision for commutation of part of the annuity for a lump sum. Contracts effected on or after 17 March 1987 must limit the lump sum to £150,000. (This £150,000 limit may be raised by Treasury Order.) The annuity may commence between the ages of 60 and 75. However, earlier commencement is possible in the event of permanent incapacity or where earlier retirement ages are agreed for special occupations.

(2) A dependant's annuity approved under s 621(1)(a). This is a contract which provides an annuity for the individual's spouse or any one or more dependants of the individual.

(3) Life assurance approved under s 621(1)(b). This is a contract the *sole object* of which is the provision of a lump sum on death of the individual before he attains the age of 75. The lump sum can be paid in instalments to provide income for dependants.

14.2.2 Earnings and eligibility

Prior to 6 April 2001, contributions to personal pensions were based on age and relevant earnings (see 14.2.6 below).

14.2.3 Changes from 6 April 2001

From 6 April 2001, individuals do not have to have relevant earnings to contribute to a personal pension. Anyone can pay up to £3,600 in a tax year to a personal pension provided:

(1) they are resident and ordinarily resident in the United Kingdom;
(2) they are not members of an occupational pension scheme or they are in an occupational pension scheme but they do not earn more than £30,000 a year and are not a controlling director.

However, higher contributions may be paid depending on age and relevant earnings as described in 14.2.6 below.

This change does not apply to retirement annuity contracts where relevant earnings are still needed in order to make contributions.

14.2.4 Pensions for new groups

The changes referred to in 14.2.3 above have opened up personal pensions to many more individuals including children, wives, husbands, the unemployed, students and carers. The changes allow, for example, grandparents to start pensions for their grandchildren and an individual to start a pension for a spouse who has no earned income.

14.2.5 Concurrent membership of occupational pension schemes

From 6 April 2001, members of occupational pension schemes may contribute to personal pension plans at the same time provided:

(1) they earned less than £30,000 in any one of the preceding five tax years – the earliest tax year that may be used is 2001/02;
(2) they are not controlling directors; and
(3) they do not contribute more than £3,600 in each tax year.

This is known as 'concurrency' and applies to occupational pension schemes that provide retirement benefits (which includes pension and lump sums, or lump sums only). These concurrency rules do not apply to retirement annuity contracts.

Members of occupational schemes that provide lump sum life assurance benefits on death before age 75, or some lower age, and/or an annuity to the surviving spouse or dependant, may pay contributions to personal pension schemes. Contributions are not restricted to £3,600 in any one tax year but may be based on age and net relevant earnings (subject to satisfactory evidence of earnings).

14.2.6 Relevant earnings

For the purpose of a personal pension scheme 'relevant earnings' is defined in s 623(2) and means:

(1) Emoluments chargeable under Schedule E from an office or employment held by the individual. This includes benefits in kind and emoluments from an employment which are paid in accordance with a profit-related pay scheme, but excludes anything arising from the acquisition or disposal of shares or an interest in shares or from a right to acquire shares (share option schemes) and anything in respect of which tax is chargeable by virtue of s 148 ('golden handshakes').
(2) Income from property which is attached to or forms part of the emoluments of any such office or employment held by the individual.
(3) Income which is chargeable under Schedule A, Schedule B or Schedule D and is immediately derived by the individual from the carrying on or exercise by him of his trade, profession or vocation either as an individual, or, in the case of a partnership, as a partner personally acting therein. In practice income under Schedules A and B is investment income and does not constitute relevant earnings.
(4) Income treated as earned income by virtue of ICTA 1988, s 529 (patent rights).
(5) Earnings from certain commercial lettings of furnished holiday accommodation, although assessed to tax under Schedule D Case IV, are treated as a trade for the purposes of s 623(2) and regarded as relevant earnings.

'Relevant earnings' do not include:

(1) Any remuneration as director of a company whose income consists solely or mainly of investment income if the individual, either alone or together with any other persons who are or have been at any time directors of the company, controls the company.

(2) Any remuneration from a company in which the individual
  (a) was a controlling director in the year of assessment or has been a controlling director of the company at any time in the ten years immediately preceding that year of assessment, and
  (b) is in receipt of benefits under a superannuation scheme of the company or where benefits have been transferred from that superannuation scheme into a personal pension scheme.

These exclusions prevent a controlling director of a company pensioning his service through an occupational pension scheme, retiring and taking his benefits and then continuing to receive an income from that company which is pensioned by means of a personal pension scheme.

However, for the purposes of an existing retirement annuity, relevant earnings can include share options and 'golden handshake' payments from non-pensionable employment and the pensioning of earnings of a director who is already in receipt of a pension from that company.

If, however, the scheme provides in addition to life asssurance benefits a widow's or dependant's pension this would render the occupation pensionable for *retirement annuity purposes* (unless extra statutory concession A38 applies).

The following points are also relevant for the purposes of both personal pension schemes and retirement annuities:

(1) A scheme does not have to be insured, or even funded at all. A formal promise to an employee of a pension to be paid when he reaches pension age, with no previous provision made for it, is a sponsored superannuation scheme (although it may be regarded as an unapproved pension scheme – see Chapter 5).
(2) Membership of an overseas scheme which is not approved in the United Kingdom is regarded as pensionable employment for the purposes of the retirement annuity legislation, but does not preclude membership of a personal pension scheme.
(3) Where an employee is covered by a permanent health insurance (PHI) arrangement providing only for the continuation of what in effect is long-term sick pay up to State Pension age, or if earlier, the normal retirement date of the employee (the employee remaining in the service of the employer until the date when the PHI contract ceases to provide benefits), such an arrangement will not be regarded as pensionable employment.
(4) Membership of the State Pension scheme is not regarded as pensionable employment.

The relevant earnings for an employee or director taxed under Schedule E would be his actual earnings during the fiscal year beginning on 6 April and ending on 5 April, but for a self-employed individual relevant earnings for the year of assessment will be based on the earnings in his accounting year which ends in the fiscal year.

14.2.7 Net relevant earnings

The contributions which an individual may pay to retirement annuity contracts or to personal pensions where contibutions are above £3,600 in each tax year are calculated with reference to net relevant earnings (see ICTA 1988, ss 646(b) and 623 in Appendix 4).

Net relevant earnings means the amount of relevant earnings less business expenses including any deductions in respect of losses or capital allowances.

Personal charges such as alimony, charitable covenants and non-business interest do not reduce net relevant earnings.

14.2.8 Allowable maximum

In arriving at an individual's net relevant earnings for the purposes of a personal pension scheme, any amount in excess of the allowable maximum is ignored.

Table 14.4

The allowable maximum amounts of net relevant earnings are:

Tax year	Amount
1988/89	none
1989/90	£60,000
1990/91	£64,800
1991/92	£71,400
1992/93	£75,000
1993/94	£75,000
1994/95	£76,800
1995/96	£78,600
1996/97	£82,200
1997/98	£84,000
1998/99	£87,600
1999/00	£90,600
2000/01	£91,800
2001/02	£95,400
2002/03	£97,200
2003/04	£99,000

There is no allowable maximum for the purposes of a retirement annuity contract.

14.2.9 Associated employments

For the purposes of a personal pension scheme, if an individual has earnings from two or more employments which are associated and both are non-pensionable the earnings are aggregated for the purposes of assessing net relevant earnings and the earnings cap (see (1) and (2) in Example 14.3 below).

If one of the associated employments is pensioned through an occupational pension scheme or executive pension plan the earnings from the second employment on which contributions may be based is restricted to the excess of the earnings cap over the pensionable earnings (see (3) in Example 14.3 below).

However if an individual has two sources of earnings, one from employment which is pensioned and the other from self-employment, then the pensionable earnings may be disregarded (see (4) in Example 14.3 below).

Example 14.3

(1) Two jobs – neither pensioned	
Earnings from Job A	£70,000
Earnings from Job B	£50,000
Total non-pensionable earnings	£120,000
Capped NRE from Job A plus Job B	£99,000
(2) Two jobs – Job A fully pensioned through a personal pension scheme and Job B unpensioned	
Earnings from Job A	£70,000
Earnings from Job B	£50,000
Total non-pensionable earnings	£120,000
Capped NRE from Job B (ie £99,000, less £70,000 already pensioned)	£29,000
(3) Two jobs – Job A pensioned through an occupational pension scheme and Job B non-pensionable	
Earnings from Job A	£70,000
Earnings from Job B	£50,000
Total non-pensionable earnings	£50,000
Capped NRE from Job B (ie £50,000 restricted to £99,000 less pensionable earnings)	£29,000

(4) Two jobs – Job A pensioned through an occupational scheme, Job B self-employed	
Earnings from Job A	£70,000
Self-employed earnings	£50,000
NRE from self-employment (£50,000 is not restricted by pensionable earnings)	£50,000

Personal pension scheme and retirement annuity contributions themselves, although requiring to be deducted in order to arrive at total income for tax purposes, are not deductible for the purposes of arriving at net relevant earnings (NRE).

The NRE in the year of assessment in which the annuity commences, or in which a personal pension scheme providing a lump sum on death terminates, are the earnings for the whole of the year.

14.2.10 Summary of calculation

Those in non-pensionable employment (taxed under Schedule E) normally have no deductions to make from their relevant earnings. Their gross earnings from their employment are their net relevant earnings and all deductions (such as tax, national insurance contributions, alimony, covenants and interest) whether or not allowable for tax are ignored.

In the case of an approved personal pension scheme any employer's contributions are not regarded as emoluments of the employment chargeable to Schedule E income tax.

The self-employed (taxed under Schedule D) have to make the following deductions from their gross profits in order to arrive at their net relevant earnings:

(1) all expenses incurred in earning the profits, such as rent, rates, business interest, employee's salaries, etc;
(2) losses, whether
  (a) incurred in the current tax year, or
  (b) incurred in a previous tax year and carried forward to set against profits in the current tax year under ICTA 1988, s 385(1), or
  (c) incurred in a previous tax year, relieved against other income under s 380, and not yet deducted from net relevant earnings;
(3) capital allowances.

Personal mortgage interest and covenants to charity can be ignored. All self-employed individuals are now taxed on the 'current year' basis.

14.2.11 Capital allowances, Business Expansion Schemes and Venture Capital Trusts

Only capital allowances relating to the trade reduce net relevant earnings. Investments in Business Expansion Schemes (prior to 31 December 1993 when the scheme ended) and Enterprise Zones are personal investments and do not reduce NRE. Similarly, subscriptions to Venture Capital Trusts are not treated as reducing NRE.

14.2.12 Interest

Interest payable on money borrowed to buy into a partnership or buy shares in a close company is statutorily deductible, but it does not reduce NRE because it is money laid out for a personal purpose. The principle appears to be that interest on money borrowed for the purpose of running the business, which is deductible on normal accounting principles as an expense and not prohibited under ICTA 1988, s 74, reduces NRE while interest paid on money borrowed for personal purposes which is specifically allowable under ICTA 1988, Part IX does not reduce NRE.

This gives some scope for tax planning because a partnership, for instance, could provide extra finance for work in progress either by the partners applying to increase their business overdraft or by an individual partner borrowing money in a personal capacity to buy into (or increase his share in) the partnership. The money would be available for the partnership's business purposes either way but interest on the first loan would reduce the NRE of the partners concerned, while that on the second would not.

14.2.13 Basis Years (s 646B ICTA 1988)

When a member wishes to pay 'higher level contributions', ie contributions above the earnings threshold (currently £3,600) the member must nominate a basis year for his net relevant earnings (s 646B ICTA 1988), and produce evidence of those earnings. The basis year does not need to be a year when the individual was a member of a personal pension scheme but it must not be a year in which the member was in pensionable employment for the whole of the tax year. The basis year can be the current year or any of the previous five tax years. The net relevant earnings in the basis year can be used to justify contributions in the basis year itself and in the following five tax years (see Example 15.2 in Chapter 15). For high earners the net relevant amount is the smaller of the evidenced earnings in the basis year and the earnings cap in the year in which the contribution is paid.

14.2.14 Cessation of earnings (s 646D ICTA 1988)

This complicated section of ICTA 1988 allows the member to pay higher level contributions (ie contributions above the earnings threshold) to his scheme for up to five years immediately following the tax year in which the member ceased to have a source of relevant earnings (see Example 15.3 in Chapter 15).

14.2.15 Maximum contributions (as a percentage of net relevant earnings)

The contributions which may be made from the tax year 1996/97 onwards to a personal pension scheme are:

(1)   *Monetary limit*

Age on 6 April	*Maximum contribution*	*1996/97* £	*1997/98* £	*1998/99* £	*1999/ 2000* £
Up to 35	17.5%	14,385	14,700	15,330	15,855
36 to 45	20.0%	16,440	16,800	17,520	18,120
46 to 50	25.0%	20,550	21,000	21,900	22,650
51 to 55	30.0%	24,660	25,200	26,280	27,180
56 to 60	35.0%	28,770	29,400	30,600	31,710
61 to 74	40.0%	32,880	33,600	35,040	36,240

Monetary limit

Age on 6 April	*Maximum contribution*	*2000/01* £	*2001/02* £	*2002/03* £	*2003/04* £
Up to 35	17.5%	16,065	16,695	17,010	17,325
36 to 45	20.0%	18,360	19,080	19,440	19,800
46 to 50	25.0%	22,950	23,850	24,300	24,750
51 to 55	30.0%	27,540	28,620	29,160	29,700
56 to 60	35.0%	32,130	33,390	34,020	34,650
61 to 74	40.0%	36,720	38,160	38,880	39,600

(2) For personal pension schemes that started before 6 April 2001 with an option to add life assurance, or life assurance contracts that started before 6 April 2001, up to 5 per cent of NRE for life assurance/ dependants' pension contracts are included in the maximum contributions above, as is the cost of waiver of contribution benefit.

(3) For life assurance contracts that started after 6 April 2001, the maximum contribution that may be paid for life assurance is 10 per cent of all relevant pension contributions. Relevant pension contributions

are contributions to provide pension benefits under pension plans that started after 6 April 2001. Life assurance contributions are included in the maximum contributions above.

(4) Where a personal pension scheme is used for contracting-out purposes, the minimum contributions made by the NICO are payable in addition to the maximum contributions above.

(5) The maximum contributions for retirement annuity contracts, are:

Age on 6 April	Maximum contributions
Up to 50	17.5%
51 to 55	20.0%
56 to 60	22.5%
61 to 74	27.5%

Note: All the above figures are inclusive of any contributions for life assurance and waiver of contribution benefit.

14.2.16 Interaction of contributions to personal pension schemes and retirement annuities

Many people who contribute to existing retirement annuities also wish to take advantage of the higher contribution limits available under personal pension schemes. However, special conditions apply in these circumstances.

The maximum amount that may be paid to a personal pension scheme includes any contributions being paid to a retirement annuity contract; if the latter is to continue this may mean that no contributions can be paid to the personal pension scheme.

Example 14.4

An individual aged 53 has NRE of £80,000. He currently contributes 20% to a retirement annuity contract, ie £16,000.

He wishes to top up through a personal pension scheme in 2003/04 where the maximum contribution is £29,700 (30% of £99,000).

As £16,000 is already paid to the retirement annuity he has scope to pay £13,700 to the personal pension scheme.

Example 14.5

An individual aged 43 has NRE of £120,000. He currently contributes 17.5% to a retirement annuity contract, ie £21,000.

He is unable to top up with a personal pension scheme as the maximum contribution to a personal pension scheme is £19,800 (20% of £99,000), which is less than his contribution to the retirement annuity contract.

Further examples showing the scope for contributions to a personal pension, if the maximum contributions are being paid to a retirement annuity, are contained in Table 14.5.

14.2.17 Over-funding

The personal pension scheme must make provision, under ICTA 1988, s 640 (see Appendix 4), to ensure that the member's and any employer's contributions to the arrangement, in aggregate, do not exceed the permitted maximum. Any excess must be repaid to the contributor, as appropriate.

Excess contributions to retirement annuity contracts are not expressly prohibited under ICTA 1988 but insurers will not knowingly accept excess contributions from policyholders.

14.2.18 Tax relief – pension relief at source

Under retirement annuities, contributions are paid gross and tax relief is given later. In the case of an employee this is normally done by an adjustment to his tax coding.

Since 6 April 2001, contributions made to personal pension schemes by employed and self-employed persons are paid net of basic rate tax. The scheme administrator has to accept the net payment in the same way as if no deduction had been made and recovers the amount withheld from the Inland Revenue. If the individual is a higher rate taxpayer the difference between the actual rate of tax and the basic rate of tax may be reclaimed later when the individual completes his self-assessment tax return and normally results in an adjustment to the individual's tax coding. This system is known as 'PRAS' or 'pension relief at source'.

The method of granting higher-rate tax relief for contributions made to a personal pension/stakeholder scheme on or after 6 April 2001 is different to that used for contributions paid before that date. Under the old method a contribution paid by an individual to a personal pension scheme was deducted or set off against any NRE for the year of assessment in which the contribution is made. Since April 2001, higher rate relief is given through an increase in the basic rate tax band. This means that higher rate relief is given against the individual's income regardless of whether it is investment income or earned income.

This system gives a cash-flow advantage over the system used under retirement annuity contracts. Even when the employed individual's earnings

Table 14.5 Tax year 2003/04 Scope for contributions to personal pensions (if maximum paid to retirement annuity contract)

NRE	Ages											
	35 or less		36–45		46–50		51–55		56–60		61–74	
	RAC	PP	RAC	PP	RAC	PP	RAC	PP	RAC	PP	RAC	PP
Up to £99,000	17.5%	Nil	17.5%	2.5%	17.5%	7.5%	20%	10%	22.5%	12.5%	27.5%	12.5%
£100,000	£17,500	Nil	£17,500	£2,300	£17,500	£7,250	£20,000	£9,700	£22,500	£12,150	£27,500	£12,100
£110,000	£19,250	Nil	£19,250	£550	£19,250	£5,500	£22,000	£7,700	£24,750	£9,900	£30,250	£9,350
£120,000	£21,000	Nil	£21,000	Nil	£21,000	£3,750	£24,000	£5,700	£27,000	£7,650	£33,000	£6,600
Earnings above which PP contributions are Nil	£0		£113,142		£141,428		£148,500		£154,000		£144,000	

Notes:
(1) If NRE is £154,000 or higher then it can be seen that if maximum retirement annuity contributions (RACs) have been paid, there is *no* scope for a personal pension (PP) contribution *regardless of age.*
(2) If an RAC is paid at a level lower than the maximum, then a PP can be used to top up (but only to PP maximum).

would not be chargeable to tax because they are low, or have been reduced for tax purposes by personal allowances, contributions are still paid net of basic rate tax. The basic rate of tax is 22 per cent (in 2003/04) even though the first £1,960 of income is taxed at 10 per cent.

Income for the purposes of calculating personal allowances is income after deduction of the contribution, so that the net income (after tax relief) is looked at when arriving at the abatement of the higher personal allowances applicable to those aged over 65 or over 75 (on the £1 for every £2 basis) when it exceeds the statutory level (£18,300 for 2003/04).

However, an Inland Revenue Extra Statutory Concession A102 enables a personal pension/stakeholder contribution made from 6 April 2001 to reduce an individual's income for the purposes only of determining the level of age related personal allowance and married couple's allowance. A person up to the age of 75 can normally pay a contribution of up to £3,600 gross each year to a personal pension or stakeholder scheme provided he is resident and ordinarily resident in the United Kingdom. Before 6 April 2001, the person would have needed to have NRE to support the contribution.

14.2.19 Tax relief on contributions by third parties (excluding employers)

A third party may pay a contribution to a personal pension on behalf of a member, for example a parent for a child. Contributions are paid net of basic rate tax as if the member had paid the contribution personally, and so the member's liability to tax counts rather than the tax liability of the third party. However, if the member has a liability to higher rate tax the member will be able to claim higher rate tax relief.

Example 14.6

(1) A husband pays £2,808 to a personal pension plan for his wife who has a small earned income and is a basic rate taxpayer. If the husband is a higher rate taxpayer he may not claim higher rate relief on the contribution. In effect, the husband has made a gift of £2,808 to his wife.

(2) A wife has received an inheritance part of which she uses to pay a contribution to a personal pension for her husband who is in non-pensionable employment. Her husband is a higher rate taxpayer and so he will be able to claim higher rate relief on the contribution paid by his wife.

14.2.20 **Carry forward/carry back facilities**

It is possible for eligible persons to take advantage of two valuable facilities to maximise pension contributions and obtain the best possible taxation advantages on those contributions. The facilities are generally referred to as 'carry forward of unused relief' and 'carry back provisions'. From the 2001/02 tax year, carry forward has been abolished for personal pension schemes. Carry forward is still available for retirement annuity contributions.

Carry forward of unused relief: retirement annuity contracts only

(1) This facility enables a planholder to pay a higher contribution than normally available for the current year in order to catch up for missed contributions from the previous six years.

(2) Tax relief is, however, available against the current year, *having no effect on tax paid in past years*, and is therefore calculated according to current tax rates. It is important to note that tax relief is only available up to the level of tax payable on earned income for the current year. Thus there is no tax relief available upon payments in excess of the level of taxable earnings, and the sum of the contributions for the current year and previous years may not exceed the net relevant earnings in the current year even though taxable earned income will be lower than net relevant earnings as a result of personal allowances. However, tax relief is at the highest rates, reflecting any investment income and income from pensionable employment.

(3) If the individual pays more than the year's normal maximum contribution in order to take advantage of this facility, then his local tax inspector automatically refers back over the previous six years in order to discover any unused relief which can be carried forward to absorb the excess contribution. Unused relief is only carried forward from previous years after the maximum contribution has been paid for the current year.

Carry back provisions: retirement annuities and personal pension schemes

(1) A contribution (or part of a contribution) may be carried back to the tax year preceding the year of payment, regardless of the date of assessment and regardless of whether or not there are relevant earnings in the year in which the contribution is paid. A contribution to a personal pension cannot be carried back more than one year. However, with retirement annuity contracts if there were no net relevant earnings in the preceding tax year then the contributions may

be carried back one further year. However, contributions may never be carried back more than two years.

(2) Carrying back a contribution in this way means that it will be treated for tax purposes exactly as if it had been paid in the year to which it is carried back and the maximum contribution is based on the limits for that year, ie the normal maximum for that year plus any unused relief from the six previous years (retirement annuities only).

Thus a contribution paid in 2003/04 and carried back to 2002/03 would, for tax relief purposes, be allowed against the 2002/03 tax bill (subject to the limits applicable to 2002/03). If this was a retirement annuity contract this contribution could include an amount relating to missed contributions carried forward from 1996/97.

Mechanics of carry back

In order to carry back a contribution to the previous tax year, the following procedures must be followed:

(1) The contribution must be received by the pension provider before 6 April in the *current* tax year for retirement annuity contracts and on or before 31 January in any year of assessment for personal pensions.

(2) An election must normally be made in writing to the Inspector of Taxes before 31 July following the tax year in which the contributions were made for retirement annuity contracts. With personal pensions the election has to be made to the scheme administrator before or at the same time as the contribution is made.

(3) An election for carry back may be made in the middle of a tax year. Normally, the Inland Revenue treats all methods of payment (annual, monthly or single) alike for tax relief purposes. Under a personal pension scheme an election to carry back has to be accompanied by a completed Inland Revenue form PP43 (NEW) or by letter, fax, or a form issued by the scheme, or when the scheme permits, electronically or by telephone.

It is important to be aware that the Inland Revenue adheres very strictly to these rules.

14.2.21 Administrative requirements

In April 2001, the Inland Revenue published new Guidance Notes on personal pension schemes, incorporating the new regulations. These include the administrative requirements which have to be met by the individual and by the pension provider. The individual when applying to the pension provider has to provide details of his name and address, national insurance number, the Inspector of Taxes office dealing with his affairs and its reference number for him, whether he is employed or self-employed and details of any other retirement annuity contracts or personal pension schemes to which contributions are being paid by the individual or by his employer.

The individual also has to provide evidence to the pension provider of his earnings if the individual is not resident in the United Kingdom or if contributions to all personal pensions and retirement annuity contracts exceed £3,600 in each tax year. The administrator of the personal pension scheme also has to obtain fresh evidence if the individual wishes to increase his contributions.

14.3 SPECIFIC BENEFITS UNDER PERSONAL PENSION SCHEMES AND RETIREMENT ANNUITY CONTRACTS

14.3.1 Death benefits

Death benefits are largely assimilated with ordinary life assurance policies, in that they can be written in trust using similar procedures and with similar inheritance tax consequences, except that they are treated more favourably.

Where the contract also provides for a pension, this remains under the control of the policyholder and he will continue to decide when and how to take his pension (within the limits imposed by the legislation) and in unit-linked contracts, for example, whether to switch or change the combination of investment funds at his disposal. The pension in payment and the tax-free cash sum are still required by law to be personal to the policyholder and cannot be assigned.

Personal pensions are often set up under deed poll and follow model rules published by the Inland Revenue. Death benefits will fall outside the member's estate and the scheme administrator (normally the insurer) will have the responsibility of deciding who should benefit from the proceeds of the policy. The member will usually have nominated an individual, although the scheme administrator will not be obliged to pay the proceeds to the nominee.

14.3.2 Flexible trusts

It is possible to write death benefits emerging from personal pension schemes and retirement annuity contracts in a form of flexible trust which provides for:

(1) **an immediate beneficiary** to whom it is intended benefits should go on death immediately after setting up the trust; and

(2) **a class of potential beneficiaries** with a power of appointment under which the death benefit may be appointed to any potential beneficiary, in addition to or to the exclusion of the current immediate beneficiary.

The power of appointment (revocable or irrevocable) is exercised by the policyholder during his life or by the trustees within 79 years from the commencement of the trust, although the appointment has to be made within two years of death to avoid inheritance tax liability.

The policyholder's lifetime power of appointment is subject to the exception that appointments back to the planholder himself must be made by at least two trustees (of whom the planholder may be one).

It is desirable to have a second trustee in addition to the policyholder himself so that the death benefit can be paid to the surviving trustee without waiting for probate.

14.3.3 Inheritance tax implications

Regular contributions

Under personal pension schemes and retirement annuity contracts, regular contributions on which tax relief is obtained are ignored for inheritance tax (IHT) purposes. The principle is that they are paid primarily to provide the planholder with a personal benefit (his pension) and that the death benefit, which has been gifted to the trust beneficiaries, is incidental. Additional contributions paid from time to time, for example to pick up unused relief, or putting an existing contract in trust, are treated differently.

Under ICTA 1988, s 621 (see Appendix 4) regular contributions for life assurance contracts and the life assurance benefit within a personal pension scheme are not ignored because by definition they are not paid to provide a personal benefit, but to provide the in-trust death benefit, but in virtually every case they are exempt as normal expenditure out of income.

Proceeds on death

Payment is made on death to the trustees who use the money in accordance with the trust provisions. Normally they pass the money to the immediate beneficiary under the trust chosen by the planholder. Since the money is paid to the trustees and not to the deceased's estate, there is no inheritance tax liability.

Discretionary trusts

Provided the trust has been drawn up correctly and, in effect, is the same as the type of trust used for retirement benefit schemes approved under ICTA 1988, ss 590–612 (see Appendix 4), the normal rules for discretionary trusts do not apply, ie there are no exit charges or ten-year periodic charges, as it falls within IHTA 1984, s 58(1)(d). Also, there is no 'interest in possession' so there is no charge to inheritance tax should there be any change in the destination of the death benefits away from the person nominated by the member during his lifetime, provided this occurs within two years of death.

Interest in possession trusts

Under this type of trust the chosen beneficiary or beneficiaries have an immediate entitlement to any income produced by the trust. This means that for IHT purposes the beneficiary is treated as owning the capital and it is included in his estate. In an interest in possession trust every appointment of a potential beneficiary to immediate entitlement involves the reduction (or disappearance) of the entitlement of the current immediate beneficiary. For example, if A alone is entitled to the benefits and B and C are appointed in addition, then A, B and C are each entitled to a one-third interest and the interest of A, who was previously entitled to the whole benefit, has been reduced by two-thirds. If B and C had been appointed to the whole interest to the exclusion of A, his interest would have disappeared altogether.

On each such occasion, the value of the policy is treated as passing for inheritance tax purposes as a potentially exempt transfer to the extent that the current immediate beneficiary's entitlement is reduced. The tax is calculated on the personal 'meter' of the beneficiary from whom the benefit was switched but it is payable by the trustees. There will be no IHT to pay if the beneficiary losing his interest survives for seven years.

On lifetime appointments, the value switched is the market value of the death benefit and this is usually too small to attract inheritance tax. The value is only significant in the exceptional case where the planholder is in such poor health that a benefit payable on his death is imminent enough to make it attractive to a notional buyer of the policy.

If appointments are made in the two years after the planholder's death, the value switched is the actual death benefit paid, and in that case there may well be inheritance tax payable, unless the appointment is to the planholder's spouse, which would be exempt.

Children's pensions

Pensions for children can be paid (ie gifted) for by a third party (parent, grandparent, aunt, uncle, godparent and so on).

When a third party contributes to a pension for a child, each contribution will be a transfer of value for IHT purposes. The amount of transfers is the contribution(s) net of basic rate tax, as the basic rate tax is being reclaimed by the provider, on behalf of the child.

The transfer of value will be a potentially exempt transfer unless it is covered by an available exemption, for example normal expenditure out of income (most likely if contributions are paid by the third party every year) or the £3,000 annual exemption. This latter exemption could be particularly useful where the normal expenditure exemption cannot be used since the maximum annual contribution for any one child is £2,808 (with the child's pension contribution being grossed up to allow for basic rate tax relief to £3,600). For IHT purposes, it is the loss to the estate of the third party, which is the transfer of value, and the loss to the estate will be the contribution of £2,808.

Protected rights

Some personal pension schemes have discretionary trust provisions contained in the rules of the scheme. Other personal pension schemes will allow individual trusts to be declared in respect of the death benefit, as with retirement annuities described above. If the personal pension scheme is used to contract out, the protected rights, which cannot be assigned, can still be subject to discretionary disposal provisions in accordance with the rules, with nominated beneficiaries.

14.3.4 Putting existing policies in trust

Declaring a trust of an existing retirement annuity policy or personal pension is also in principle a gift for IHT purposes. The value transferred is the market value of the death benefit unless the immediate beneficiary is the planholder's spouse, in which case the transfer is exempt because it is between spouses.

Non-regular contributions to a personal pension scheme, or to a retirement annuity contract, for example an additional contribution in respect of unused relief carried forward from previous years, are treated in the same way.

In practice, however, such transfers are likely to be treated as negligible unless the planholder dies from natural causes within two years of making the declaration of trust. In these cases, the Capital Taxes Office (CTO) of the Inland Revenue may treat the market value at the time of the transfer as a transfer made at the time of the declaration with IHT being payable at death rates. On the other hand, if the declaration had not been made, the entire fund value (not its market value at the date of the declaration) would have fallen into the estate on death and been chargeable at the death rates. So while it is sometimes difficult to say whether a declaration is liable to precipitate a charge to IHT and at what level, as a general rule planholders have something to gain by declaring trusts of their policies and little or nothing to lose.

Retirement annuity contracts, including life assurance contracts under s 621 and personal pension schemes, should be written in trust. If they are not written in trust then the planholder is missing out on an obvious way of passing monies to beneficiaries free of IHT, and the pension provider cannot pay out the proceeds until probate has been granted. It is essential, therefore, when considering retirement planning, to ensure that the pension provider can offer a suitable trust and should any existing policies not be written in trust to put them into trust.

Deferring benefits

From age 50 (or age 60 in the case of a retirement annuity) a policyholder may elect to take retirement benefits. Where the policyholder does not take benefits at the specified age and has still not done so when he dies, the CTO may consider that the failure to take retirement benefits before death gives rise to a charge to IHT. This may arise where there is prima facie evidence that the policyholder's intention was to increase the estate of someone else – ie the beneficiaries of the death benefit. The CTO will look closely at arrangements where the policyholder became aware that he was suffering from a terminal illness or was uninsurable and at that time or after that time the policyholder took out a new policy and:

(1) assigned the death benefit on trust;
(2) assigned on trust the death benefit of an existing policy;
(3) paid further contributions to a single premium policy or increased contributions to a regular premium policy where the death benefit had been previously assigned on trust; or
(4) deferred the date for taking retirement benefits.

A claim by the CTO is unlikely to be pursued where the policyholder survived for two or more years after making these arrangements, or where the death benefit was paid to the policyholder's spouse and/or dependants.

14.3.5 Disability benefits

The past few years saw an increase in the number of life offices offering different types of disability cover. Most offer a waiver of premium benefit while a few offer disability incomes and incapacity pensions. However, the legislative changes that took effect from 6 April 2001 will halt this trend.

Waiver of premium – plans set up before 6 April 2001

Retirement annuity contracts and personal pension plans set up before 6 April 2001 may allow the planholder to opt for waiver of premium benefit. The benefit protects the planholder's commitment to pay pension contributions during sickness or disability at modest cost. Tax relief is given on the cost of waiver in the same way as for the main pension benefit. Where waiver of premium benefit is not in force on 5 April 2001 it may still be possible for the planholder to elect for this benefit later, if the contract terms allow.

The benefit is usually only available to those under age 55 and normally ceases at age 60 or 65. There is usually a deferment period of three to six months during which disability has to exist before the waiver of premium benefit comes into operation.

The cost of waiver must fall within the pension contribution limits set out in 14.2.15 above.

Waiver of premium – plans set up after 5 April 2001

For plans set up after 5 April 2001, tax relief is not permitted on the cost of waiver of premium. However, some insurers offer this benefit, packaged alongside the personal pension. The benefit may be a long-term insurance contract similar to that on pre-6 April 2001 plans or it may be a general insurance contract. The latter will be a short-term contract, reviewable on an annual basis covering pension contributions if the individual is unable to work through sickness or disability and may be extended to include redundancy cover for a limited period, typically 12 months.

14.3.6 Tax treatment of pensions

Pensions payable under retirement annuity contracts and personal pension schemes to:

(1) the planholder;
(2) the planholder's dependant under the continuation of a joint life pension;
(3) the planholder's dependant under a nomination;

are taxed as earned income. (The only situation in which the above pensions are taxed as investment income is where the contributions under a retirement annuity contract from which the pension arises were not all completely relieved for tax.)

Retirement annuities are taxed under Schedule D of the Taxes Acts, for both employees and the self-employed. In practice this means that the annuities are paid net of basic rate tax with any additional tax being payable by the annuitant to the Inland Revenue. Any excess tax deducted from the annuity will be refunded by the Inland Revenue.

Personal pensions are taxed under Schedule E for both employees and the self-employed. Usually the first one or two annuity payments are taxed at an emergency rate, with subsequent payments taxed at the correct rate, as confirmed by the Inland Revenue to the pension provider.

Where a planholder dies during the period for which his pension is guaranteed (normally five years), the remaining guaranteed instalments (the right to which will have passed under the planholder's will) are taxed as investment income.

14.3.7 Overseas aspects

The overseas aspects of retirement annuities and personal pension schemes can be split into two parts: the first relates to foreign earnings and whether they constitute relevant earnings and so support contributions; the second is the effect on the payment of a pension to a planholder living abroad at the time.

Member abroad with net relevant earnings

A person who is resident outside the United Kingdom is still eligible to contribute to a personal pension plan during a tax year in which he has net relevant earnings. He may contribute up to the higher of £3,600 and the appropriate percentage of his net relevant earnings, according to age at the start of the tax year.

Member abroad with no net relevant earnings

A person who is resident outside the United Kingdom and has no net relevant earnings in a tax year is still eligible to contribute in that tax year if one of the following applies:

(1) at some time in the tax year he is resident and ordinarily resident in the United Kingdom; or
(2) at some time in the five tax years preceding the tax year in question he has been resident and ordinarily resident in the United Kingdom

and was resident and ordinarily resident in the United Kingdom when he started the personal pension; or

(3) he is a Crown servant serving abroad, or the spouse of a Crown servant serving abroad.

Provided that person is not accruing benefits under an occupational pension scheme, he may contribute up to the higher of £3,600 and the relevant percentage of net relevant earnings from a chosen basis year (the basis year meaning the current tax year or any one of the previous five tax years). These contributions may continue for a maximum of five tax years.

Foreign earnings deduction

Individuals qualifying for the 100 per cent foreign earnings deduction which applies to certain employees working outside the United Kingdom (seafarers only from 17 March 1998) are still eligible to contribute to a personal pension plan for any year in which they have relevant earnings chargeable to UK income tax.

Contributions are limited to the higher of £3,600 and the relevant percentage of net relevant earnings in a basis year.

An individual receiving foreign emoluments may contribute to a personal pension even if they are a member of an overseas scheme that corresponds to a UK tax-approved scheme. Contributions are limited to £3,600.

Where a UK resident takes a job abroad with a foreign employer which involves him in actually living abroad, as opposed to a job with a UK employer which usually involves spending long periods abroad, then he usually becomes non-resident for tax purposes. In that case, his foreign earnings are outside the UK tax net altogether, there is no question of their being liable to UK tax and, as a result, he is not eligible for a contribution in respect of those earnings to a retirement annuity or to a personal pension scheme.

Payment of pensions

Pensions payable from a UK source, including the pension emerging from a retirement annuity and from a personal pension scheme, are in principle liable to UK tax regardless of the residence of the pensioner.

In practice the position is governed by the double tax agreement, if any, in operation between the United Kingdom and the pensioner's country of residence. Most modern double-tax agreements provide that private pensions (as opposed to ones paid by the Government to former civil servants) are liable to tax in the country of residence and therefore not in the country of origin.

Where this situation applies, the life office can obtain permission from the Inland Revenue to pay the pension gross. A lump sum which may be tax free when paid to a UK resident may not enjoy the same favourable treatment in the country of residence.

If permission has not been obtained to pay a gross pension, the pension provider will adopt its normal procedure which applies to UK residents and deduct tax at basic rate from the instalments of pension.

14.4 SPECIALISED OCCUPATIONS

The Inland Revenue currently permits a pension age lower than age 50 under personal pension schemes (PP) and 60 under retirement annuity contracts (RAC) in the case of occupations where early retirement is customary. The following is the list of early retirement ages which have been agreed by the Inland Revenue.

Table 14.6

Profession or occupation	Maximum retirement age
Air Pilots (RAC)	55*
Athletes (appearance and prize money only) (PP)	35
Badminton Players	35
Boxers	35
Brass Instrumentalists (RAC)	55*
Cricketers	40
Croupiers (RAC)	50*
Cyclists (Professional)	35
Dancers	35
Distant Water Trawlermen (RAC)	55*
Divers (Saturation, Deep Sea and Free Swimming)	40
Firemen (Part-Time) (RAC)	55*
Footballers	35
Golfers (tournament earnings)	40
Ice Hockey Players (PP)	35
Inshore Fishermen (RAC)	55*
Jockeys	
– Flat Racing	45
– National Hunt	35
Members of the Reserve Forces (PP)	45
Models (PP)	35
Moneybroker Dealers (excluding Directors and Managers responsible for dealers) (RAC)	50
Moneybroker Dealers (Directors and Managers responsible for dealers) (RAC)	55*
Motorcross Motorcycle Riders	40
Motorcycle Riders (Motorcross or Road Racing)	40

Table 14.6 *(cont.)*

Motor Racing Drivers	40
Newscasters (ITV) (RAC)	50
Nurses, Physiotherapists, Midwives or Health Visitors who are females (RAC)	55*
Off-shore Riggers (RAC)	50
Psychiatrists (who are also maximum part-time specialists employed within the National Health Service solely in the treatment of the mentally disordered) (RAC)	55*
Tennis Players (including Real Tennis)	35
Royal Naval Reservists (RAC)	50
Rugby League Players	35
Rugby League Referees (RAC)	50
Rugby Union Players (PP)	35
Singers	55*
Skiers (Downhill)	30
Snooker/Billiards Players	40
Speedway Riders	40
Squash Players	35
Table Tennis Players	35
Tennis Players	35
Territorial Army Members (RAC)	50
Trapeze Artists	40
Wrestlers	35

Note: Under personal pension schemes there is provision to take benefits between ages 50 and 75 so that individuals falling within those professions or occupations, and marked with an asterisk, may prefer a personal pension scheme if they wish to have access to benefits earlier than age 55.

From time to time new occupations and professions are added to the list, usually as a result of representations made by a trade body or professional association.

An individual falling into one of the above categories has the option of paying contributions into a personal pension scheme which will provide for benefits to commence at the earlier pension age shown above: he is entitled to defer the benefits in the usual way.

The earlier pension ages are intended to benefit individuals who fall into one of the specialised occupations. If the individual's job changes to one which would not fall into one of the above categories, he should stop paying contributions to the original contract and divert future contributions to a separate personal pension scheme which will specify the normal range of pension ages, 50 to 75.

An individual who falls into one of the above occupations but was not aware of the earlier pension ages, or where they have been reduced since he effected his original contract, may nevertheless take benefits at the earlier pension age provided that he can show that his occupation fell into one of the above categories at the time he took out the contract.

Although the earlier pension ages may appear to be attractive to an individual whose occupation is such that his earning capacity will drop considerably after an early age, this does not necessarily mean that his retirement income will be adequate because the period of time during which he is contributing will be short, whereas the period during which he will be receiving an income will be long.

The Government's proposals for pensions tax simplification, to come into force from 6 April 2005, will have a significant impact on those who have taken advantage of the low pension ages set out above. The December 2002 consultation document, 'Simplifying the taxation of pensions: increasing choice and flexibility for all', states: 'So, as part of the reform of tax rules for pensions, the Government intends to set the minimum age at which tax privileged pension benefits can be drawn – the minimum benefit age is at 55 in 2010. This measure is intended to encourage people to work and to save for their retirement for longer. By giving people notice of the change, younger working people will have time to rearrange their plans if they need to do so.'

14.5 BENEFIT LEVELS

This chapter, so far, has dealt with technical matters such as eligibility, the meaning of 'net relevant earnings' and how to obtain tax relief in the current year and previous years, but it is important not to lose sight of the principal purpose of retirement annuities and personal pension schemes, namely to provide a worthwhile income in retirement.

In practice, the only way of doing this within the legislation is to contribute the maximum tax-relievable contributions allowed. Many people, however, do not contribute anything like the maximum contributions because they are not aware of the effect that inflation will have on their current pension planning.

Table 14.7 below shows the benefits emerging from a typical personal pension scheme at age 60 based on contributions starting at 10 per cent of income:

(1) but not increasing in line with increases in income; and
(2) continuing at that level in line with salary increases.

The table is based on an initial income level of £10,000 per annum, and assumes that income increases by 4 per cent per annum to age 60, and that fund growth amounts to 7 per cent per annum before charges.

Table 14.7

Man aged	Projected income at age 60	Projected level pension produced by £1,000 pa investment contribution			
		Level		Indexed at 4% pa	
24	£41,039	£7,160	(17.4%)	£12,600	(30.7%)
29	£33,731	£5,220	(15.5%)	£8,670	(25.7%)
34	£27,724	£3,700	(13.3%)	£5,720	(20.6%)
39	£22,787	£2,550	(11.2%)	£3,650	(16.0%)
44	£18,729	£1,670	(8.9%)	£2,210	(11.8%)
49	£15,394	£997	(6.5%)	£1,200	(7.8%)
54	£12,653	£475	(3.8%)	£524	(4.1%)

The table clearly demonstrates the importance of keeping pension provision under regular review and of planning for retirement many years before the event – in fact, it may be rather daunting to some people. The above figures, however, could be increased by 75 per cent if maximum contributions were made (or even doubled for a man over age 45).

The most important figures in the above table are not the projected incomes on retirement and the projected pensions emerging from the pension plan, but the relationship between the two, for example, the individual aged 39 retiring at age 60 will receive an income from his personal pension of either 11.2 or 16 per cent of his final income depending upon whether or not he has increased contributions throughout the previous 20 years.

Table 14.8 below shows the pension emerging from a personal pension scheme as a *percentage* of final income in retirement. Income at retirement and the benefits under a personal pension scheme may appear extremely high in relation to today's earnings (figures are not shown) but in relation to final earnings, they may well be a very small percentage. The pension is based on contributions of 10 per cent of income throughout (ie an increasing contribution) on the same assumptions as the previous table.

Table 14.8

Age	Men		Women	
	Pension age 60	Pension age 65	Pension age 60	Pension age 65
24	30.7%	41.3%	29.2%	38.5%
29	25.7%	34.6%	24.3%	32.4%
34	20.6%	28.8%	19.5%	26.8%
39	16.0%	23.3%	15.1%	21.6%
44	11.8%	18.1%	11.2%	16.9%
49	7.8%	13.3%	7.4%	12.4%
54	4.1%	8.9%	3.9%	8.2%

The purpose of this table is to show what a future pension will be *worth* rather than showing the pension as a sterling amount.

The pensions are level: pensions increasing at 5 per cent per annum compound would be approximately 60 per cent of the percentage pensions illustrated.

Example 14.7

A man aged 39 paying contributions of 10% of his income throughout could expect to receive an income of 16% of his income at age 60.

If he requires 50% of his income to live on, the contribution level required, as a percentage of his income, is as follows:

$$\frac{50.0\%}{16.0\%} \times 10 = 31.25\%$$

This exceeds the permitted amount for an individual aged 39 (20%) and demonstrates the need to start pension planning at an earlier age.

14.6 OTHER SCHEMES FOR PARTNERS

14.6.1 Retired partners' annuities

A partner who has made no provision for income through the retirement annuity or personal pension scheme legislation may nevertheless receive a pension from his firm on retirement.

Such a pension, because of old age or ill health, is normally treated as a charge for basic and higher rates of tax on the earned income of the paying partners under ICTA 1988, s 683(1) although it cannot be deducted from the investment income except to the extent that the pension exceeds the allowable limits under ICTA 1988, s 628.

In order for the pension to be regarded as earned income at the hands of the recipient, under the provision of s 628, it must be within the allowable limits, ie not more than 50 per cent of the average profits of the retiring partner for the best three out of the last seven years prior to his retirement during which he had devoted substantially the whole of his time to acting as a partner.

The payment must be in accordance with the partnership agreement or a supplementary agreement. The firm may make increases in the pension paid to a former partner in order that it may keep pace with inflation, as measured by the retail prices index for the December preceding the year of assessment for which the revised pension is to be paid compared with the December in the year of assessment in which he ceased to be a member of the partnership. It is permissible for the pension to continue for a widow or dependant.

Payments made by continuing partners to a retired partner do not reduce the net relevant earnings of the former.

There are several disadvantages in relying on a pension from the firm:

(1) The pension is usually limited to a period of, say, ten years simply because the continuing partners are unlikely to commit themselves to continue paying a pension for the life of a retired partner or even the life of his dependant.
(2) If several of the retiring partners leave the firm either on death or on retirement, the pension liability could be too great a burden on the continuing partners which might result in the dissolution of the partnership or a reduction in the pension paid to the retired partners. In fact it may be difficult for the firm to enter into mergers with other firms which might otherwise be desirable or it may prevent new partners from joining the firm.
(3) The continuation of the pension paid to the retired partner will depend on the continued success of the firm over which the retired partner has no control.

14.7 SELF-INVESTED PERSONAL PENSIONS (SIPPs)

Prior to the introduction of personal pension schemes on 1 July 1988, a few insurance companies had introduced a variation on the retirement annuity contract whereby contributions were paid by a number of partners to the insurance company which would issue a policy to the partners as policyholders in an approved retirement annuity contract. The insurance company was the beneficial owner of the investments. The partners had an influence on the investment of the policies in a similar way to a self-managed or personalised life assurance mini-bond to the extent that the insurance company was prepared to take account of the preferences for investment as expressed by the policyholders. The partners could invest only in approved investments for the retirement annuity fund, but these could include, for example, approved quoted investments or, more commonly, the premises occupied by the partnership.

The main attraction of these schemes was the possibility of transferring property owned by the partnership into the retirement annuity or using the funds built up to purchase a property from which the partnership would operate.

Under the personal pension scheme legislation this is no longer possible. Inland Revenue practice on 'self-investment' is now much more restricted and was originally contained in their 'Memorandum 101', dated October 1989. This has now been superseded by The Personal Pension Schemes (Restriction on Discretion to Approve) (Permitted Investments) Regulations 2001. The following is an extract from Part 11 of the Personal Pension Scheme Guidance Notes, IR 76 (2000), relating to SIPPs:

CHOICE OF INVESTMENTS

11.8   There is a wide range of investments available to SIPPs. The investments are governed by The Investment Regulations (SI 2001/117). A list of permitted and prohibited investments is at Appendix 24 and Appendix 25 respectively. Such restrictions are necessary because, for example, of the requirement of section 633 for the scheme to have the sole purpose of providing benefits for retirement. The member cannot receive any benefits from the scheme other than in the prescribed forms.

SOLE PURPOSE

11.9   The sole purpose of a SIPP should always be a consideration in relation to any potential investment. However certain investments are of particular concern in relation to this.

- If any land or property is to be acquired by a SIPP which is directly adjacent to any land or property owned by the member, or any person connected with the member, the *scheme administrator* must be satisfied that no additional benefit could be gained by the member or connected person as a result of the SIPP's investment. Further, the property owned by the SIPP in such circumstances must remain separate from the adjacent property owned by a member or connected person. This is obviously also a concern where an existing property is split, with one part being purchased by the member and the other part being purchased by the SIPP.

- A SIPP may purchase a leisure property i.e. a property principally designed to offer a leisure service or charge for the use of recreational facilities. Such properties include golf courses, leisure centres and bowling alleys. The principal sole purpose concern in relation to these premises is that the member or connected persons do not use the facilities, other than at a commercial rate.

CONNECTED TRANSACTIONS

11.10   Given the 'sole purpose' test mentioned in paragraphs 11.8 and 11.9, it follows that investment transactions should be on a proper commercial basis. If non-commercial terms were to apply, there is a risk that the *personal pension scheme* is being used for tax reasons not in accordance with the 'sole purpose'. As a way of reducing the risk of non-commercial transactions taking place, SIPPs may not enter into transactions with a member or person connected with a member, except where permitted by the Regulations (see paragraphs 11.14 and 11.16).

11.11   For the purposes of SIPP investments a person is connected with a member if that person falls within the definition of 'connected persons' in section 839, which is reproduced in full in Appendix 9.

It should be noted that the exception in section 839(4) has no relevance in this context as it relates solely to transactions between partners (but see paragraph 11.16). It is, however, relevant that a close company that is controlled by a member, either alone or with others, is, by virtue of section 839(6) and sections 416(2) and (3), a connected person in relation to that member.

11.12   *Scheme administrators* need not consider whether a transaction is a connected one if it relates to a pooled fund. For this purpose, pooled funds are funds

- which are genuinely open to any member of the public,
- which are clearly described in the provider's literature and disclosure documents as being standard funds open to all,
- where the investment management is undertaken by the provider with no direction or influence by members, and
- where a common value is applied across the membership with no segregation or linking of particular assets or particular members.

11.13   The acquisition by the scheme of a member's commercial property or portfolio of stocks and shares is prohibited, as is the acquisition by the member of any of the scheme's assets. All transactions in UK or overseas securities should take place through an Inland Revenue recognised stock exchange. Recognised stock exchanges are as defined in section 841. To find out whether a particular exchange is listed you may call our Helpline (0115 974 1777) or access the Inland Revenue website (www.inlandrevenue.gov.uk/fid/rse.htm) to obtain a list.

COMMERCIAL PROPERTY

11.14   SIPPs may invest in commercial property including land. As an exception to the rule whereby schemes may not normally enter into transactions with a member or person connected with a member, there will be no objection to a SIPP acquiring a commercial property on the open market, which is then leased for the purposes of a trade or profession to the business of the member or company connected with the member. The *scheme administrator* should ensure that the lease is on commercial terms and that the rent payable is supported by an independent professional valuation.

Holding of Unlisted Shares in Property Management Companies

11.15   It is a common feature with property purchase that communal areas and facilities are owned and/or managed by a private limited company set up and run specifically and solely for this purpose. When a related property is purchased it is a requirement that each purchaser also acquires a share in the relevant service company. The acquisition of such a share by a SIPP is not considered to be the acquisition of an investment in its own right. Such a share acquisition is ancillary to the acquisition of the related property investment. The holding of such a share does not bear the normal characteristics of an investment e.g. it does not have the potential to produce any income, dividend or capital growth.

Transactions Between Connected Arrangements

11.16   Transactions between *arrangement*s where the members are connected by virtue of being in the same partnership or company are prohibited except in the following circumstances, involving the joint ownership of a commercial property (being the business premises) between two or more SIPP *arrangement*s. These exceptions are

- where the member of a SIPP purchasing a share of a commercial property is, or becomes within a reasonable time after the acquisition, a partner in or director of the business, or
- at such other time, for example on the death or retirement of a scheme member, or on a member leaving the business,

then the share of the property held under that member's *arrangement*(s) may be sold, on commercial terms, to any other SIPP *arrangement*(s) which hold an interest in that property.

Where a transaction is made between *arrangement*s where the members are connected, as with any property transaction, the *scheme administrator* should ensure that

- the lease is granted on normal commercial terms,
- the amount of rent payable is at a commercial rate, and
- the amount of rent is supported by a commercial valuation.

Such transactions can take place between members connected through the same business, even if the members are otherwise connected (by marriage or as relatives).

Residential Element of Commercial Property

11.17   The inclusion in a commercial property of

- a caretaker's flat,
- a residential part of a property occupied by an employee as part of their employment or,
- a flat held on a long term leasehold by an unconnected party,

would not preclude the property being held as a scheme investment. Any such residential accommodation must be an integral or associated part of the commercial property.

11.18   Commercial property with a residential aspect, such as hotels, guest houses and nursing homes, is not a prohibited investment. It would not however be permissible for the member or any connected person to use the facilities other than at a commercial rate.

11.19   The intention to convert a residential property to commercial use, or indeed even the existence of planning permission for such a conversion, is not sufficient reason to allow the purchase of that residential property by a SIPP.

JOINT INVESTMENTS

11.20   SIPPs may enter into an agreement whereby an asset of the scheme is jointly owned with another party. Such an investment may be made with an unconnected third party or one or more other SIPPs or trustees of a small self-administered scheme, regardless of any connection between the members. Joint ownership with a connected person is not, however, permitted. In the case of joint ownership by SIPPs, whose members are connected, no transactions may take place between those SIPPs except as outlined in paragraph 11.16.

Joint ownership of an asset between a SIPP and an unconnected person would not confer a degree of connection between the parties. Therefore any future transaction between the parties involving the asset would not be prohibited.

3 YEAR RULE FOR CEASING TO BE CONNECTED

11.21   No asset may be acquired if the member or a connected person has held it within the previous 3 years. Similarly any asset sold by the scheme must not be sold to the member or a connected person within 3 years of its sale by the scheme. Otherwise the transaction would be regarded as an indirect sale to the member.

TRANSFER TO A SIPP

11.22   The 3 year restriction on acquiring an asset previously held by a member or connected person would not apply in relation to the transfer of an asset from a small self-administered scheme to a SIPP, or a SIPP to SIPP transfer. Likewise another pension scheme is not deemed to be a connected person for the purposes of making a transfer. Other than in these circumstances any investment becoming an asset of a SIPP, either through transfer or *conversion* (see part 23), must comply with the SIPP investment restrictions.

LENDING BY A SCHEME

11.23   SIPPs may not make loans to any party.

BORROWING BY THE SCHEME

11.24   SIPPs may borrow money for specific purposes and within specific limits. Borrowing may only be undertaken for the purpose of purchasing an interest in a commercial property or for the development of such a property, except as described in paragraph 11.29. Any borrowing must be made at a commercial rate.

Limit of Borrowing for SIPPs

11.25   The amount of any borrowing by a SIPP *arrangement* must not exceed

- 75 per cent of the purchase price (including legal and other incidental costs), or the appropriate share of the purchase price, of the commercial property, or
- 75 per cent of the cost, or the appropriate share of the cost, of any development of a commercial property held by the SIPP *arrangement*.

11.26   If a SIPP enters into a joint investment with one or more other SIPPs, one overall loan may be taken. The amount borrowed should be proportionally allocated between the SIPPs and is subject to the 75% borrowing limit for each one.

Security Used for Borrowing and Repayment of Loan

11.27   The borrowing may be secured on the property or on any other asset of the scheme. However, there is a link between the borrowing and the commercial property in that, if the property is subsequently sold, any outstanding amount of the loan must also be repaid on completion of the sale of the property. No borrowing may be secured by a personal guarantee or through a life assurance contract.

Replacement Borrowing

11.28   An original borrowing arrangement may be substituted with a replacement loan, not exceeding the outstanding amount of the original loan.

Incidental Borrowing

11.29   SIPPs may also borrow money to pay the VAT liability arising from the purchase or development of a commercial property. The duration of such a loan must not exceed the shorter of

- 12 weeks after the date on which the purchase or development of the property is completed, or
- the period starting from the date on which the purchase or development of the property is completed and ending on the date on which the amount of the liability to VAT is refunded to the purchaser.

INVESTMENT RESTRICTIONS IN INCOME WITHDRAWAL

11.30   No new investment in commercial land or property is permissible if the member has reached the later of

- the *pension date* in relation to the *arrangement*(s) from which the purchase is to be made, or
- age 65.

11.31   A scheme may not enter into any borrowing arrangement or take any further instalments under any previously agreed serialised borrowing arrangement, after the *pension date* of the member, in relation to the *arrangement*(s) for which the borrowing is made.

OTHER INVESTMENT RESTRICTIONS

11.32   The development, improvement or modification of any land or property held as an investment of a SIPP must be paid for from the *arrangement* concerned and must be carried out by an unconnected party. The maintenance of a property under the usual terms of a lease would be excluded from this restriction.

INVESTMENTS BY PERSONAL PENSION SCHEMES THAT ARE NOT SIPPs

11.33   There are two notable differences for the investments that are allowable for *personal pension scheme arrangement*s that are not SIPPs. The differences are that

- loans may be made, except to a member or person connected with a member, and
- there is no specific limit on the amount of borrowing they may have, except that it should not overstretch the resources of the member's fund, given the need to provide a pension at some point before age 75.

REPORTING INVESTMENT TRANSACTIONS TO THE INLAND REVENUE

11.34   The Personal Pension Schemes (Information Powers) Regulations 2000 (SI 2000/2316) give the Inland Revenue wide powers to request details of scheme transactions. However, in practice, details of only selected acquisitions will be required. The transactions that will need to be reported will be property acquisitions or sales plus any scheme borrowing. Providers will be notified when, and in what form they should submit this information to the Inland Revenue.

TRANSITIONAL ARRANGEMENTS

11.35   The following provisions apply in relation to investment transactions which took place prior to 6 April 2001.

11.36   Investment transactions made up to and including 5 April 2001, which are in accordance with guidelines existing prior to 6 April 2001, may stand and continue unchanged for the future. Such transactions include

- borrowing of more than 75% of the purchase price or development cost of commercial property held as a SIPP asset, and
- borrowing related to assets other than commercial property.

11.37   Other investments made before 6 April 2001 that may stand are

- leasing of a commercial property to the business of a person connected with the member, provided that it is in accordance with the scheme provisions and
- the lending of money which has taken place prior to 14 March 2001, provided it is
  - in accordance with scheme provisions, and
  - not to the member or a person connected with the member.

11.38   All investment transactions entered into on or after 6 April 2001 must comply with The Investment Regulations (SI 2001/117).

Appendix 24

PERMITTED INVESTMENTS FOR SIPPs

- Stocks and shares listed or dealt in on any Inland Revenue recognised stock exchange (including the AIM), including:
  - equities
  - fixed interest securities issued by governments or other bodies
  - debenture stock and other loan stock
  - warrants (for equities)
  - permanent interest bearing shares
  - convertible securities
- Shares received by a SIPP as a contribution to the scheme in accordance with paragraph 4.32.
- Futures and options, relating to stocks and shares traded on a recognised futures exchange
- Authorised unit trusts resident in the UK and authorised under Financial Services Act (FSA)
- Tax exempt unauthorised unit trusts that do not hold residential property
- Investment trusts:
  Stocks and shares in investment trusts purchased and held through investment trust savings schemes or investment plans operated by persons:
  - resident in the UK and authorised for that purpose under FSA
  - resident outside the UK but subject to regulation for that purpose in terms of the FSA
- UK based open ended investment companies (OEICs) or FSA recognised EEA member state equivalents (investments limited to stocks and shares or related warrants)
- Insurance company managed funds and unit-linked funds, investment policies or unit linked funds of a UK insurance company or an insurance company within the EEC authorised under Article 6 of the First Life Insurance Directive 79/267/EEC
- Endowment policies traded by a FSA regulated person (TEPs)
- Deposit accounts held with any UK based deposit taker (as defined in section 481(2) in any currency
- Commercial property (including land whether development land, farmland or forestry) in or outside the UK including
  - hotels and motels
  - guest houses
  - nursing homes
  - public houses
- Borrowing to finance the purchase or development of a commercial property. Or to pay for VAT liability arising from the purchase or development of any such property
- Undertaking for Collective Investment in Transferable Securities (UCITS) that is either a recognised scheme or a designated scheme within the meaning of section 86 or 87 of the Financial Services Act 1986.
- Ground rents

- Depositary Interests (including CREST Depositary Interests)
- Individual Pension Accounts (IPAs)

Appendix 25

PROHIBITED INVESTMENTS FOR SIPPs INCLUDE

- Premium bonds
- Loans to any party
- Milk quotas
- Fishing quotas
- Residential property (except as an element of commercial property as specified in 11.17 of Part 11)
- Gold bullion
- Shares traded on OFEX
- Unlisted shares (except in a site maintenance company, for the necessary extent needed to purchase a commercial property (see 11.15) and those received as contributions in accordance with paragraph 4.32).
- Personal chattels (e.g. paintings, antiques, fine wine and jewellery)
- Borrowing other than that specified in 11.25,11.28 or 11.29 of Part 11

When personal pension schemes first started in July 1988 new providers such as banks, building societies and unit trusts were permitted to offer them, not just insurance companies. The above extracts from the Inland Revenue's Guidance Notes show the extended choice available to individuals by allowing all providers to offer members the facility to decide exactly how their fund can be invested. In effect the member can take advantage of a 'portfolio management' type service if this is offered by the pension provider.

The scheme may borrow to purchase a commercial property. Originally there was no restriction on the amount but the extract from the Guidance Notes above (paragraph 11.25) shows that this flexibility has now been restricted by limiting scheme borrowings to 75 per cent of the purchase price.

It will be seen that loans and other transactions with scheme members and their associates are banned. Loans to the employer/company and unsecured loans generally are not permitted. Although investment in commercial property is allowed and the property may be used in connection with the member's (or his associate's) business, because of the prohibition on transactions with the member it will not be possible for the member to transfer to his personal pension scheme an *existing property* owned by his business. If a property is bought on the open market by the personal pension scheme and then leased back to the member's business the terms of the lease and the level of rent must be on commercial terms.

219

As with small self-administered schemes run by small limited companies, investments in residential property or 'pride in possession' assets is not permitted.

The above Guidance Notes also prohibit any associated loans from a third party, for example a bank, where the return on the member's personal pension scheme fund would be affected. Under similar arrangements operated within the retirement annuity legislation it was not uncommon for a loan to be granted to a member on condition that a switch was made from his investment fund into another fund where the future return was linked in some way to the rate of interest charged on the loan. This is prohibited under personal pension schemes offering these facilities.

The income withdrawal facility (see Chapter 19) allowing members of personal pension schemes to defer the purchase of an annuity until no later than age 75, drawing income from the fund, in the meantime, is also available under self invested personal pensions. The Inland Revenue's proposals for pensions tax simplification will affect income withdrawal facilities although their impact, due to come into effect on 6 April 2005, is not yet clear.

14.8 DEFERRED ANNUITY PURCHASE

Legislation now allows those with personal pension schemes to take 25 per cent as a lump sum at any time from age 50 and defer the purchase of an annuity to a later date, up to age 75. Until the actual purchase of the annuity, the planholder can draw down varying amounts of income subject to certain limits. This option has become increasingly popular as annuity rates have fallen in recent years, although the improved flexibility has resulted in greater complexity. This is covered in Chapter 19. Under the Inland Revenue's simplification changes to come into effect on 6 April 2005 there will be no requirement to buy an annuity at age 75.

14.9 BANKRUPTCY

Retirement annuities and personal pensions are treated differently for the purposes of bankruptcy.

On a member becoming bankrupt under the 1986 Insolvency Act, control of the assets passes to the Trustee in Bankruptcy, who will be either the Official Receiver or a licensed insolvency practitioner. What this effectively means is that the Trustee in Bankruptcy can make any financial decisions that the bankrupt could have made prior to being made bankrupt (eg the sale of a house).

Where the bankruptcy occurred before 29 May 2000, the date when certain provisions of the Welfare Reform and Pensions Act 1999 came into force, the Trustee in Bankruptcy has the same powers in relation to the personal pension as the bankrupt did. Therefore, when the bankrupt reaches age 50 (or an earlier retirement age if in a special occupation), the Trustee in Bankruptcy can access any benefits from a personal pension (excluding the protected rights). It is not true that placing a personal pension in trust can avoid this situation, as a trust only relates to death benefits.

Before reaching age 50 (or an earlier retirement age if in a special occupation), the Trustee in Bankruptcy cannot access any of the benefits whatsoever.

In the event of death before retirement, any lump sum death benefits which are subject to a trust must be distributed by the trustees under the trust rules. The Trustee in Bankruptcy cannot claim these benefits. In certain circumstances the Trustee in Bankruptcy can apply to the court for an order to set aside the trust, for example if it was set up within two years of the person being declared bankrupt. In this case the plan would pass to the Trustee in Bankruptcy as if there had been no trust.

Any personal pension which has passed to the Trustee in Bankruptcy is not automatically returned following discharge. Unless the personal pension is specifically reassigned by the Trustee in Bankruptcy, the position remains as described above.

If an individual who is or has been bankrupt continues or restarts contributions under the pension plan he or she had when he or she went bankrupt, it is possible the Trustee in Bankruptcy's rights to the bankrupt's pension may extend to any pension 'purchased' by the new contributions. Therefore, any bankrupt who wants to restart pension contributions should do so under a new plan, having obtained permission from the Trustee in Bankruptcy to do this.

Where the bankruptcy occurred after 29 May 2000, the Welfare Reform and Pensions Act 1999 protects personal pensions against Trustees in Bankruptcy. For bankruptcy petitions presented to the court on or after that date, personal pensions have protection against Trustees in Bankruptcy who cannot, for example, compel the individual to take his pension benefits. The Trustee in Bankruptcy may be able to obtain an income payments order against a pension which is in payment or against any tax-free cash sum that is taken before the individual is discharged from bankruptcy. Where excessive contributions to the pension plan have been paid, the Trustee in Bankruptcy may apply to the court for an excessive contributions order to have the contributions repaid.

The vesting powers in the Trustee in Bankruptcy under a personal pension is based on the judgment in a court case, *Re Landau*. Whilst this case was about a retirement annuity contract, the principle that the Trustee in Bankruptcy can claim the retirement benefits without an Income Payments Order from the court also extends to personal pensions. However, the legal position on personal pensions will not be certain until it is clarified by the courts.

The powers of a Trustee in Bankruptcy apply equally to retirement annuity contracts, but the minimum age for taking retirement benefits from these contracts is age 60 (unless in a special occuption, or where benefits are transferred to a personal pension plan). Any decision to invoke these powers is for the Trustee in Bankruptcy and may vary from case to case.

Any lump sum benefit payable on death is paid to the Trustee in Bankruptcy, unless it is held in trust. However, the Trustee in Bankruptcy could still apply to the court for an order to set aside the trust, although the court's decision would depend upon a number of factors including the length of time the plan has been in trust.

14.10 PENSIONS SIMPLIFICATION

Although the Inland Revenue's proposals for pensions tax simplification are radical their impact will be felt more by occupational pension schemes than personal pension schemes and retirement annuities. The introduction of a lifetime limit of £1.4 million (in 2002 terms) will affect individuals who have been in a position to pay large conributions over the years. For the majority of pension investors, however, the lifetime limit is unlikely to be restrictive. Nevertheless the new proposals will affect the following areas in a manner not yet known as details have not yet been published or resolved:

(1) **Retirement annuities**: currently these are paid on a gross basis with tax relief claimed through the Inspector of Taxes. Under the new proposals tax relief will be given at source, as applies under personal pensions. It is unlikely that existing retirement annuities will be easily converted.

(2) **Waiver of contribution and life assurance benefits**: tax relief is given on these ancilliary benefits under retirement annuities and personal pension schemes taken out before 6 April 2001 or after 6

April 2001 if there is an option under the policy to add these bene-fits later. The treatment of waiver of contribution benefit is not clear. It is also unclear how the lifetime limit will apply to death benefits including those insured with a pensions term assurance policy.

15

TAX PLANNING HINTS
THROUGH PENSIONS

This chapter contains brief notes on ways of using pension schemes in order to achieve not only retirement income for the member and his family, but also a means of overall tax planning.However, tax planning as a reason for investing in pensions has generally become less important as tax rates have reduced. Nevertheless, people with high earnings and access to capital will wish to take advantage of the opportunities available during the period leading up to the date when pensions are simplified (expected to be 6 April 2005). After that date the scope for pension planning for high earners will reduce.

The first part of this chapter deals with executive pension plans and the second half with personal pension schemes, including stakeholder pensions, and existing retirement annuity contracts. It is suggested, however, that the whole of the chapter is read by both the company director and the self-employed person, because they may well change status throughout their careers. Indeed, it is not uncommon for persons to have income from limited companies and also from sole proprietorships or partnerships, in which case executive pension plans, personal pension schemes and retirement annuity contracts may be used concurrently.

15.1 EXECUTIVE PENSION PLANS: PLANNING HINTS

(1) Ensure that employers' contributions are paid by the end of the accounting period otherwise tax relief will be lost – there is no provision for carrying back pension contributions to a previous year.
(2) Pension contributions can create, or augment, a trading loss which can be carried back one year or carried forward indefinitely.
(3) A trading loss (possibly caused by payment of a pension contribution) can be set against chargeable gains in the same year or in the previous year or carried forward indefinitely.
(4) Special, one-off contributions can be paid to purchase past service benefits. Tax relief will be given on the special contribution in the

year in which it is paid unless it amounts to more than £500,000 in which case it may be spread (see Chapter 7).

(5) Any personal contributions paid by the director (not exceeding 15 per cent of remuneration) are relieved in the fiscal year in which they are paid (not the company's accounting year). Thus any personal contributions should be paid by 5 April in any year. Since 6 April 1987 it has been possible to vary the amount and timing of any additional voluntary contributions.

(6) Apart from specialised occupations the earliest normal retirement date that you may specify under an executive pension plan is age 60. This, therefore, is normally the best possible date to choose even if you are considering working beyond this date. Having chosen age 60, you may still defer the benefits if you continue working. A normal retirement date of age 60 is the earliest date at which you are entitled to take maximum benefits from your pension plan, ie a pension of two-thirds of your final salary, part of which you may exchange for a maximum tax-free lump sum of up to 1.5 times your final salary.

If you are classed as a pre-1987 member and choose a normal retirement date of 65, but subsequently decided to retire at, for example, age 63, you will not be entitled to maximum benefits even though you may well have completed 20 years' service by age 63. You will be treated as going on early retirement with resulting limitations on your maximum benefits.

The only exception to this recommendation is that if you can only complete 20 years' service with the company by, say, age 63 and are proposing to fund for maximum benefits, then you should choose a normal retirement date of 63.

(7) Although you cannot choose a normal retirement date before age 60, it is still possible to take substantial benefits from age 50 onwards on early retirement from the company.

If you are classed as a 'post-1989 member' of an executive pension plan you will be entitled to a pension of two-thirds of your final (capped) remuneration from age 50 onwards if you have completed 20 years' service by that date, so that if funds are available, an executive pension plan could provide maximum benefits from an early age. However, advance funding by the employer is not permitted in these circumstances; contributions may only be paid into the executive pension plan to provide the maximum benefits at age 60 but in the event of immediate early retirement at age 50 the short-fall may be provided by means of a one-off contribution into the plan at that time or in the case of a large group occupational scheme the required amount to provide the maximum pension could be drawn from the fund.

(8) As maximum benefits are related to 'final remuneration' which is usually based on the average of the best three or more consecutive

years' remuneration ending not earlier than ten years before retirement (whether normal retirement or early retirement), ensure that you pay yourself remuneration at higher levels for at least three consecutive years in the period. These three consecutive years do not necessarily have to be the *last* three, for example they may be the levels of remuneration in the 12, 11 and ten years prior to retirement increased in line with the ten Retail Prices Index (RPI), up to retirement.

(9) If you are classed as a pre-1987 member for an executive pension plan, it is possible to fund purely for the tax-free lump sum of 1.5 times final remuneration if you can complete 20 years' service: on reaching normal retirement date (ideally age 60 for the reasons set out above) the whole of the pension fund can be taken in the form of a tax-free lump sum but you can continue working for the company. There is no necessity to retire, but you cannot receive any further lump sum retirement benefits, and any death benefits will have to be calculated as if you had retired before your death. Pre-1987 membership is particularly valuable because it is possible to fund for a two-thirds pension over ten years rather than 20 years under post-1987 membership.

(10) A pension contribution will attract tax relief as well as savings in national insurance contributions (NICs) following the increase in the latter by 1 per cent in April 2003, and the removal of the upper earnings limit for employees' contributions.

Example 15.1

Current situation

Employee draws remuneration of £40,000

Alternative

Employee draws reduced remuneration of £36,000

Company pays £4,000 to an executive pension plan.

Personal tax saving	=	£1,600	(40% of £4,000)
Personal NIC saving	=	£40	(1% of £4,000)
Company's NIC saving	=	£512	(12.8% of £4,000)
		£2,152	

Thus £4,000 is invested at a net cost of £1,848 (£4,000 – £2,152 saving).

It is also possible for the employer's NIC saving to be invested too, especially where the employee has influence over the company.

(11) Because of the effect of compound interest, it is the early years' pension contributions which generate most of the pension fund as the following examples show, so that provided profits permit, it is preferable to pay contributions in the early years rather than waiting until retirement approaches:
   (a) A director pays contributions of £3,000 per annum for ten years between ages 40 and 50 and builds up a fund of £66,400 at age 60, assuming 7 per cent growth before charges.
   (b) Another director pays contributions of £1,500 per annum between the ages of 40 and 60 and builds up a fund of £52,300 assuming 7 per cent growth before charges.

(12) Where pension fund contributions are paid out of company profits, which lie between £300,000 and £1,500,000, tax relief is obtained at marginal rates. The rates of corporation tax for 2003/04 have been set at the following levels:

Over £1,500,000	30%
Small companies' rate £50,001 to £300,000	19%
Marginal rate	32.5%

(13) If you own a property, for example, a commercial property which is used by your company, resist the temptation to transfer it to a self-administered pension fund which you may set up. Apart from incurring a possible capital gains tax (CGT) charge on the disposal of the asset, and conveyancing costs and stamp duty, you will be converting a capital asset over which you have personal control into earned income. When the trustees of the self-administered scheme sell the property it will be paid to you largely in the form of earned income with only a proportion of the total pension fund assets being paid to you in the form of tax-free cash. In practice, it is now only possible to transfer a personally owned property to a self-administered pension fund via a third party which must hold it for three years.

From 6 April 2005, when the new Inland Revenue proposals on tax simplification are expected to come into force, there will be a lifetime limit on pension funds, initially £1.4 million (in 2002 terms). This will apply to all pension fund assets including property investments in small self-administered schemes, and self-invested personal pensions. Personal ownership of assets such as properties is likely to be an important aspect of financial planning alongside approved pension plans which should not exceed the lifetime limit and incur a recovery tax charge.

(14) You may consider taking dividends from your company, rather than salary, avoiding NICs. The disadvantages in taking this course of action are:
   (a) by not taking salary, your pension contributions will be limited to £3,600 a year and you will only be eligible for a personal pension

although the use of 'basis years' – see Example 15.2 below – may allow contributions of more than £3,600 for five years;

(b) State Second Pension (S2P) may be lost, although provided salary is taken alongside dividends, S2P will be protected (the minimum salary should be more than the lower earnings level of £4,004 in 2003/04);

(c) the payment of a dividend by the company may form a base for valuing the company and this may have an adverse effect on future inheritance tax.

The following table shows a comparison of effective tax rates using a £10,000 slice of profits to provide benefits for a director. In the case of the last column the figures show, for simplicity, that one-half of the £10,000 available profits are paid into an executive pension plan.

Table 15.1

	Salary	Dividend (Corp Tax at 19%)	Dividend (Corp Tax at 32.75%)	Salary plus Executive Pension Plan
Company outlay	£10,000	£10,000	£10,000	£10,000
Salary	(£8,865)	–	–	(£4,433)
NIC	(£1,135)	–	–	(£567)
Executive pension plan	–	–	–	(£5,000)
Taxable profits	Nil	£10,000	£10,000	Nil
Corporation tax	Nil	(£1,900)	(£3,275)	Nil
Dividend	Nil	(£8,100)	(£6,725)	–
Gross dividend including tax credit (100/90 of dividend)	–	£9,000	£7,472	–
Director's income (gross)	£8,865	£9,000	£7,472	£4,433
Income tax at, say, 40%*	(£3,546)	(£2,925)	(£2,428)	(£1,773)
Balance of income tax	–	(£2,025)	(£1,681)	–
Company's NIC	(£1,135)	Nil	Nil	(£567)
Personal NIC 1%	(£89)			(£44)
Tax and NIC	£4,770	£3,925	£4,956	£2,384
Effective 'tax' rate	47.70%	39.25%	49.56%	23.84%

*Higher rate income tax on dividends is at 32.5%

(15) Under s 646B ICTA1988 an individual may base contributions to a personal pension plan on net relevant earnings in the tax year in which the contribution is paid or in any of the previous five tax years (see Example 15.2 below). The effect of this is that the earnings of one tax year can justify contributions for up to six tax years.

This facility could be of use to a controlling director (who is not subject to Inland Revenue practice as set out in *IR35*) to draw a high salary for one tax year and then take remuneration from the company in the form of dividends for the next five tax years with salary at a low level equal to the threshold for NICs. However, this strategy is likely to be short-lived in view of the pensions simplification proposals (see Chapter 1 and below) that are expected to take effect from April 2005.

(16) If you are classed as a pre-1987 member or a 1987–89 member you may, on retirement, opt to be treated as a post-1989 member. Although you would be subject to the post-1989 rules relating to the earnings cap, years of service required to achieve maximum benefits and lump sum restrictions, you may still be better off, especially if you are proposing to retire early from age 50 onwards.

15.2 PERSONAL PENSION SCHEMES AND RETIREMENT ANNUITY CONTRACTS: PLANNING HINTS

Contributions do not have to be paid by the end of your accounting period in order to attract tax relief; contributions are relieved in the tax year in which they are paid, or the previous tax year if carried back.

In the case of retirement annuity contracts, where contributions have not been paid in previous years, you can carry forward the unused reliefs for up to six years, and by using the carry back facility you can effectively carry forward unused relief for seven years.

By taking advantage of the ability to carry forward unused relief from previous years you can reduce current tax liability substantially through retirement annuity contracts. For example, you may carry forward unused relief from previous years when you were paying tax at lower rates to the current year when you may be paying tax at higher rates.

Although you may have retired having sold your business, there may still be scope for paying personal pension scheme contributions and carrying them back one year to a period when you were in business, in order to obtain a tax refund.

If on reaching retirement you have sources of capital and/or income, you should exhaust these before drawing on your pension benefits simply because the pension fund receives preferential tax treatment and will usually grow faster than your other investments. Take advantage of the 'arrangements' or 'contracts' within a personal pension scheme (typically there would be 100 or 1,000 of them within a scheme) to phase your retirement benefits in stages between the ages of 50 and 75.

To the extent that you defer your benefits, you are deferring an increasing capital sum which, in the event of your death, can be returned to a wide range of beneficiaries free of inheritance tax (provided the policy is written under a suitable trust).

If you are considering increasing contributions an existing retirement annuity may give a higher proportion of the fund in the form of a tax-free lump sum (see Chapter 14). However, the retirement annuity has to be sufficiently flexible to take increases in contributions.

The life assurance benefits under the retirement annuity and personal pension scheme legislation can provide substantial amounts free of inheritance tax, provided the policy is written under a suitable trust. The contributions attract tax relief up to the highest rate on earned income. This type of policy can be used to provide life cover for your family and also business associates, for example, co-partners. From 6 April 2005, assuming that the Inland Revenue's proposals on tax simplification are enacted, any life assurance policies arranged within the current pensions legislation will have to be aggregated with any other death benefits and tested against the lifetime limit (£1.4 million in 2002 terms), with a recovery tax charge being imposed on any lump sum above this limit.

If you are already paying maximum contributions for yourself and you employ your spouse, you should set up an executive pension plan for your spouse: the contributions that you may pay to an approved pension scheme of that nature are generally much higher than the contributions that you could pay to your own personal pension scheme or retirement annuity contract (see Chapter 14). Typically these plans are set up for working wives. If your wife works in your business, you can pay her a salary which will be a deductible expense provided, of course, that her employment can be justified.

If your P60 earnings are less than £30,000 and you are not a controlling director you should consider investing up to £3,600 into a personal pension. The pension will not count towards your maximum benefits permitted by the Inland Revenue under any occupational pension scheme.

You may wish to spread your assets throughout your family by gifting up to £2,808 (which will be grossed up to £3,600 to allow for basic rate tax) into a personal pension for other family members such as your spouse, children or grandchildren.

On taking a tax-free lump sum from a pension scheme you could invest £2,808 of it into a personal pension which itself will be able to provide a further tax-free lump sum and an annuity by age 75.

With a personal pension it is possible to pay contributions in relation to a 'basis year', which may be the current tax year or any of the previous five years (provided there were net relevant earnings in those years).

Example 15.2

Assuming the following pattern of net relevant earnings:

1997/98	£53,000
1998/99	£55,000
1999/00	£41,000
2000/01	£45,000
2001/02	£50,000
2002/03	£48,000
2003/04	£50,000.

then a contribution can be made in 2003/04 based on £50,000 or on the earnings in any of the previous five years. The year 1997/98 cannot be used as it is more than five years from 2003/04. If funds are available 1998/99 could be used as the basis year when earnings were higher.

Where an individual has a tax year in which he stops receiving net relevant earnings different rules apply. Contributions in the cessation year may be based on the net relevant earnings for the nominated basis year. The same nominated basis year's net relevant earnings may continue to be used for the next five years or until an earlier tax year in which the individual has net relevant earnings again or the individual becomes a member of an occupational pension scheme.

Example 15.3

Assuming the following pattern of net relevant earnings:

1997/98	£53,000
1998/99	£37,000
1999/00	£41,000
2000/01	£45,000
2001/02	£50,000
6 April 2002 to March 2003	£25,000
2003/04 to 2007/08	No earnings

then a contribution in the cessation year 2002/03 may use the net relevant earnings for the nominated basis year. The same nominated basis year's net relevant earnings may continue to be used for the next five tax years or until an earlier tax year in which the individual has net relevant earnings again or the individual becomes a member of an occupational pension scheme. The 'nominated' basis year could be 1997/98, which would maximise scope for contributions, this being the year with the highest net relevant earnings. This year can be used for contributions in the next five years, from 2003/04 to 2007/08. From 2007/08 contributions can be paid, but only up to the 'earnings threshold' currently £3,600.

15.3 PENSIONS SIMPLIFICATION

Tax planning arrangements made now should take account of the new pensions regime that will come into force from 6 April 2005, in particular the lifetime pension fund limit (tax-favoured) of £1.4 million (in 2002 terms) and the maximum annual inflow of £200,000 in a year.

Individuals whose current pension funds are close to but below £1.4 million, or over £1.4 million, should consider maximising their pension contributions before 6 April 2005 using the current pension fund rules if that would be beneficial. They will be able to register the value of their pension funds at 6 April 2005 with the Inland Revenue within three years of that date: the new tax regime will permit those pension funds to be honoured even though they exceed the new lifetime limit. The values as at 6 April 2005 will be increased thereafter in line with price increases.

16

LEAVING SERVICE BENEFITS

16.1 PRESERVATION OF BENEFITS

Much of the publicity relating to pension schemes over the past few years has related to the treatment of members who change their jobs. Until 1975, many pension schemes provided nothing for the job mover whether he was dismissed for misconduct, was made redundant or left of his own accord.

The Social Security Act 1973 altered the benefits of early leavers considerably with effect from 6 April 1975. Schemes had to provide benefits at or after normal retirement age for scheme members who attained age 26 and who left service having completed five years of scheme membership. The Social Security Act 1985 removed the age 26 qualification. The Social Security Act 1986 reduced the service qualification to two years from 6 April 1988 and provided for 5 per cent revaluation of that part of the early leaver's preserved pension (from a final salary scheme) which related to service after 1 January 1985 in respect of early leavers after 1 January 1986.

The Social Security Act 1990 extended this requirement to revalue preserved pensions in respect of *all* service for leavers after 1 January 1991.

In June 2003, in its response to industry consultation on its Green Paper published in December 2002, 'Simplicity, security and choice: working and saving for retirement', the Government set out its action plan for a number of measures relating to pensions (see Chapter 20). One of these actions is that it intends to extend the benefits available to early leavers. Employees who have been scheme members for at least three months but who leave during a vesting period must be offered the choice of a refund of their personal contributions, less tax, or a cash equivalent transfer value which they must transfer out of their scheme to another occupational scheme, or personal pension or stakeholder pension of the member's choice. The cash equivalent transfer value will include the value of the employer's contribution.

The options normally available to the employee are set out below, although some of the options may not be granted either as a result of the preservation requirements under the Act or because the employer's pension scheme does not provide some of the options.

(1) A deferred pension (sometimes known as preserved, paid up or frozen pensions) may be provided, payable when the member reaches normal retirement age, although early and late retirement options will be permitted.

(2) A deferred annuity may be purchased from an insurance company which issues s 32 annuities, sometimes called 'buy-out plans'.

(3) The assignment of an employee's individual 'earmarked' pension policy to the scheme of a new employer.

(4) A cash transfer of the member's rights under the original scheme to the new employer's pension scheme but not via the member.

(5) A cash transfer of the member's rights under the original scheme to a personal pension scheme.

(6) A refund to the employee of his contributions to the pension scheme.

(7) The assignment by the trustees of the original scheme of an employee's individual pension policy to the employee personally, subject to the provisions of the original scheme. It may be possible for the policy to be written in trust, thereby enabling the proceeds to be paid without attracting a charge to inheritance tax.

(8) Again, in the case of an individual policy scheme, the policy may continue to be held by the trustees and will participate in any future growth. If the original trust deed allows, it may be possible for separate trustees to be appointed to hold the leaver's individual policy.

The members' options may be constrained by contracting-out requirements, for example if a receiving money purchase scheme is not contracted out it cannot receive any part of a transfer value representing any guaranteed minimum pension (GMP). If the money purchase scheme is contracted out any GMP liability being transferred is converted into protected rights.

16.2 DEFERRED PENSIONS

A deferred pension is generally limited to a proportion of the employee's total final remuneration at the date of leaving his employment. For pre-1987 members and 1987–89 members the maximum proportion under Inland Revenue limits is two-thirds of the fraction obtained by taking the number of actual years of service under the number of potential service which the employee could have achieved at normal retirement age.

Example 16.1

An employee aged 45 who is a pre-1987 member leaves the service of a company having completed 20 years' service. His salary on leaving is £22,000. He was a member of a scheme providing a pension of $\frac{1}{60}$ of his final salary for each year of service at age 65. His deferred pension payable from age 65 will be £7,333, ie $\frac{20}{60}$ of £22,000, subject to statutory revaluation which is generally 5 per cent (see below). His maximum deferred pension is:

$$\text{Total remuneration} \times \frac{\text{Actual service to date of leaving}}{\text{Potential service to age 65}} \times \frac{2}{3} = \text{Deferred pension}$$

The deferred pension must be revalued in line with the cost of living between the date of leaving and normal retirement age, subject to a maximum of 5 per cent per annum. Assuming the deferred pension of £7,333 is revalued at 5 per cent per annum it will amount to £19,456 per annum at age 65.

For post-1989 members the maximum proportion is one-thirtieth of total remuneration for each year of service to the date of leaving, subject to an overall limit of two-thirds of salary.

Example 16.2

An employee aged 45 who is a post-1989 member leaves the service of a company having completed 15 years' service. His salary is £30,000. He was a member of a scheme providing a pension of $\frac{1}{60}$ of his final salary for each year of service at age 65. The deferred pension from age 65 will be £7,500 per annum, ie $\frac{15}{60}$ of £30,000, subject to statutory revaluation. His maximum deferred pension is:

Total remuneration × actual service to date of leaving × $\frac{1}{30}$.

Again, this maximum pension must currently be increased in line with the cost of living between the date of leaving and normal retirement date.

Defined benefit company pension schemes which are contracted out of the earnings-related part of the state scheme must protect against inflation the guaranteed minimum pension (the proportion of the deferred pension which would have been provided by the state if the employee had not been contracted out) which will have accrued up to 5 April 1997.

Part of the pension may be exchanged for a lump sum on reaching normal retirement date. The maximum lump sum is calculated on the same basis as for early retirement (see Chapter 4).

In the case of a former employee dying before reaching normal retirement age, the scheme may provide benefits for a widow or dependants, in which case maximum benefits are calculated as on death in service.

16.3 PROBLEMS OF THE EARLY LEAVER

16.3.1 Frozen pensions

For a long time anyone who left their job – and their final salary scheme – before reaching pension age lost out on their pension benefits because their pension was frozen at the date of leaving (except to the limited extent of revaluation of the GMP under a contracted-out scheme).

The Social Security Act 1985 provided protection for the early leaver:

(1) The proportion of a deferred pension which relates to pensionable service with the employer from 1 January 1985 must be revalued in line with increases in the RPI over the term to retirement, up to a maximum of 5 per cent a year. This resulted in little immediate improvement in early leavers' benefits in the short term as no account was taken in respect of service with the employer before January 1985. This revaluation applied to the preserved pension above any GMP which was already subject to its own revaluation.

(2) The Social Security Act 1990 extended revaluation requirements so that the revaluation of benefits above any GMP must apply to all service for any scheme member leaving the employer's service on or after 1 January 1991.

The following example shows the effect of the Social Security Acts in providing for revaluation at 2.5 per cent per annum. It assumes that an individual has four jobs, each providing a pension of one-eightieth of final salary for each year of service. Without revaluation the combined total pensions would be £9,893 per annum, around 60 per cent of the pension which would have been payable had the employee remained in the first job for 40 years, ie $^{40}/_{80}$ of £32,434 = £16,217 per annum. With revaluation, the pension is increased by around one-third.

Example 16.3

	Age on leaving	Salary on leaving		Frozen pension entitlement	Pensions revalued at 2.5% pa
Job 1	35	£10,000	$^{10}/_{80}$	= £1,250	£2,622
Job 2	45	£14,802	$^{10}/_{80}$	= £1,850	£3,031
Job 3	55	£21,911	$^{10}/_{80}$	= £2,739	£3,506
Job 4	65	£32,434	$^{10}/_{80}$	= £4,054	£4,054
				£9,893	£13,213

Note: It has been assumed that salary increases at 4.0% per annum and that the whole of the deferred pension is revalued at 2.5% per annum.

The Pensions Act 1995 brought in further changes, including the abolition of GMPs for service after 5 April 1997. From that time, schemes had to provide pensions broadly equivalent to or better than those specified by a new reference test. If a transfer is made to a personal pension any GMP is converted into protected rights and cannot be used to provide any tax-free cash sum at retirement.

16.4 SECTION 32 ANNUITY

Rather than providing deferred benefits under the scheme as above, the trustees may purchase from an insurance company chosen by the member a deferred annuity in the name of an employee. FA 1981, s 32 (now ICTA 1988, s 591(g)) enabled such annuities to be purchased: this may be an attractive option to pension scheme trustees and those leaving or thinking of leaving an employer.

The maximum pension and the maximum tax-free cash lump sum permitted by the Inland Revenue will be endorsed on the policy issued by the insurer. These benefits may be increased between the date on which the transfer is made into the s 32 annuity policy and retirement in line with increases in the retail prices index subject to a maximum of 5 per cent per annum. The projected benefits payable under such a policy should be carefully examined and compared with the alternative deferred pension.

A s 32 policy effected without the consent of the member and following the provision of the required actuarial certification under The Occupational Pension Schemes (Preservation of Benefit) Regulations 1991 has to contain an option allowing the member to surrender or assign the policy in exchange for another s 32 policy, for example of the member's own choice, a personal pension scheme or an occupational pension scheme.

The s 32 annuity itself may include an open-market option and power to surrender the policy and transfer it to a new scheme including a personal pension scheme. The GMP within the s 32 policy may also be transferred to a new scheme.

Benefits (pension *and* tax-free cash lump sum) may be taken from age 50 onwards, but not later than age 75, regardless of whether or not the policyholder has retired or is continuing to work. These benefits may include the GMP element.

On death, before taking benefits, the policy may provide for a lump sum to be paid equal to four times remuneration on leaving the previous scheme, up to the date of death.

If a transfer is made to a s 32 plan, benefits relating to service after 5 April 1997 in a contracted-out final salary scheme will be in the same form, including the facility to take part of the benefits as a tax-free lump sum but without any guarantee as to the amount.

16.5 PERSONAL PENSION PLANS

An individual leaving his employer's scheme also has the option of transferring his benefits into a personal pension plan.

This new option may be more flexible than the s 32 annuity described above because the transferred benefits will be subject to the personal pension legislation allowing ongoing contributions to be paid by the member if he has net relevant earnings and also any subsequent transfer payments. Since 6 April 2001, it has been possible to pay contributions of up to £3,600 a year into a personal pension even if there are no relevant earnings. If the individual was a member of a contracted-out defined benefit scheme the transfer will include a guaranteed minimum pension (GMP). On transferring into the personal pension there will no longer be any need for the guarantee to continue, but 'protected rights' will have to be provided instead. Protected rights benefits may be paid after the member reaches the age of 60, although the non-protected rights benefits may be paid in stages between the ages of 50 and 75 regardless of whether or not the policyholder has retired or is continuing to work.

On death before taking benefits, one-quarter of the plan's value may be paid as a lump sum with the balance being paid as a widow(er)'s pension. If there is no dependant, the whole amount may be paid as a lump sum.

However, before benefits may be transferred to a personal pension scheme the administrator of the employer's scheme must provide certificates as required in Inland Revenue regulations, as follows:

Certificate for 'regulated individuals'

This certificate is required only if the transfer is being made to a personal pension plan set up for an individual who has either:

(1) been a controlling director at any time in the ten years before the transfer date; or
(2) is over age 45 and has received remuneration greater than the 'earnings cap' applicable at the transfer date in any of the six years before the transfer date (£99,000 in 2003/04).

The administrator of the employer's scheme cannot provide the certificate if the transfer value is greater than the figure calculated in accordance with the requirements of Part III of the Personal Pension Schemes (Transfer Payments) Regulations 2001.

A cash sum certificate

The requirement for this certificate also applies to regulated individuals, as defined above, at the transfer date. The certificate must state the maximum cash lump sum payable under the transferring scheme at normal retirement date based on salary and service at the date of leaving.

The maximum cash sum that may be paid from a personal pension scheme arising from the transfer payment is the lesser of 25 per cent of the accumulated fund (excluding any 'protected rights' if the personal pension plan was effected on or after 27 July 1989) or the certified cash amount increased in line with increases in the Cost of Living Index between the date of transfer and the date benefits are taken under the personal pension scheme.

For persons who are not controlling directors or high earners there may be opportunities to transfer into a personal pension scheme in order to increase the amount of cash lump sum at retirement.

Where a transfer is made from a scheme where retirement benefits are restricted to a non-commutable pension only, for example a Free Standing Additional Voluntary Contribution Plan, a NIL certificate is required.

16.5.1 Assignment of an individual policy under an executive pension plan

Where benefits are secured by an individual earmarked policy, it is possible for that policy to be transferred, without surrendering it, to a compatible scheme of a new employer. When a policy is assigned in this way, the surrender penalties often associated with the following option may be avoided.

16.5.2 Transfer values

When an employee leaves one employment to take up another employment, his benefits under the original pension scheme may be transferred to the new pension scheme (if it meets standards laid down by the DWP and Inland Revenue) provided the new employer scheme is willing and able to accept a transfer value. Alternatively the trustees may pay the transfer value to an insurance company of the employee's choice to buy a s 32 annuity or to a personal pension scheme as described above, or to a combination of both. However, it is not possible for the transfer value to be paid direct to the individual.

16.5.3 Right to a transfer value

With effect from 6 April 1997, the provisions of the Pensions Act 1995 extend the right to request a transfer value to employees who left an employer's pension scheme before 1 January 1986. Before 6 April 1997, only those employees who left their employer's scheme after 1 January 1986 have a right in law to a transfer value payment, although in fact most schemes will pay a transfer value to an approved scheme.

The Pensions Act also requires final salary schemes to guarantee transfer values for three months, and reduces the period within which the transfer value must be paid by the trustees to six months. Failure to comply with these provisions of the Pensions Act may result in the imposition of monetary penalties on the trustees and/or administrators by the Occupational Pensions Regulatory Authority (Opra).

At the time of writing (June 2003), trustees are permitted by Opra to delay issuing a statement of entitlement to a transfer value to a scheme member if the delay is necessary to protect the interests of the remaining scheme members. Before trustees decide to delay providing a quotation of a transfer value Opra expects them to have obtained the advice of the scheme actuary, considered taking legal advice and looked closely at the funding position of the scheme.

16.5.4 Calculation of transfer values

A transfer value is the current cost of providing the benefits to which the employee was entitled under his former scheme and is based on the value of the benefits on the date the transfer value is requested. The transfer value must take into account any statutory increases that apply to the benefits if they were to continue to be preserved within the scheme. Discretionary pension increases are likely to be treated differently. In the current investment climate (June 2003) the trustees of final salary schemes may wish to consider whether an existing practice of providing discretionary pension increases, for example above inflation, can be sustained.

In calculating transfer value, trustees must have regard to a Guidance Note published by the Institute of Actuaries (reference GN11) which ensures that members of defined benefit schemes exercising a right to a transfer value can be assured that it reflects the reasonable expectation of benefits otherwise available on withdrawal and ensures that incoming and outgoing transfers are dealt with consistently. The assumptions used in the calculations, however, may be overridden by the transfer regulations which affect regulated individuals, as described above.

Transfer values are a constant source of difficulty as the amount which is transferred from one scheme to another depends on various assumptions, for example:

(1) whether the former scheme provides benefits on a final salary or money purchase basis;
(2) whether the deferred pension otherwise available in the former scheme will be increased between the date of leaving and retirement;
(3) if a transferred payment is regarded by the receiving scheme as purchasing an additional number of years' service (added years), it is usually found that the purchased years will be less than the years of service actually obtained by the employee in the former pension scheme.

The major boost to improved transferability was provided by the liberalising provisions of the Social Security Act 1985.

16.5.5 Transfer Club

The Transfer Club provides special terms for employees of certain schemes, mainly in the public service. There is a standard actuarial basis used to calculate the transfer values being paid out of the scheme, and the benefits granted on transfer values paid into the scheme. This ensures that employees moving between member organisations lose less on transferring: in some cases, pensionable service is deemed to continue without a break.

16.6 REFUNDS OF MEMBERS' CONTRIBUTIONS

Currently, no refund can normally be made if the employee has completed two years' membership of a pension scheme (although the Government has stated that the period will be reduced to three months). The 1991 Regulations on preservation removed the option to take a refund of pre-April 1975 contributions as part of short-service benefits. This option had previously been available to early leavers whose pensionable service ended on or after 28 February 1991. Regulations permit trustees to buy out benefits for leavers who have completed between two and five years' membership.

Any refund may include interest on the contributions. If a refund of contributions is made to a former employee (except in the event of his death), the administrator of the scheme has to account to the Inland

Revenue for tax at the rate of 20 per cent on the contributions (including any interest) repaid to the member.

16.7 WHICH SCHEMES MAY PERMIT A TRANSFER VALUE?

Table 16.1

Previous scheme	New scheme					
	PPP	Occ MP	Occ FS	R Ann	FSAVCs	s 32
Personal pension plan (PPP)	✓	✓	✓	✗	✓	✗
Occupational-money purchase (Occ Mp)	✓	✓	✓	✗	✗	✓
Occupational-final salary (Occ FS)	✓	✓	✓	✗	✗	✓
Retirement annuity[1] (R Ann)	✓	✓	✓	✓	✗	✗
Free-standing additional voluntary contributions (FSAVCs)	✓	✓	✓	✗	✓	✓
Section 32[2]	✓	✓	✓	✗	✗	✓

Notes:
(1) A transfer may only be taken from a retirement annuity by endorsing the policy accordingly.
(2) A transfer from a s 32 is only allowed if the previous scheme rules permit. Transfers out of s 32s established before October 1983 are not permitted.

16.8 EFFECTS OF THE SOCIAL SECURITY ACT 1990

The Social Security Act 1990 made a number of significant changes to occupational pension schemes, including:

(1) Early leavers are entitled to revaluation of all of their deferred pensions, including the portion which accrued before 1 January 1985.
(2) Self-investment by pension schemes is limited to 5 per cent of the scheme assets (see Chapter 9).
(3) A number of measures were introduced to help the individual member: the setting up of a 'Pensions Ombudsman', the development of the role of the Occupational Pensions Advisory Service (OPAS) in providing a conciliation service between scheme members and scheme trustees, and the establishment of a register of occupational

and personal pension schemes to provide a tracing service for scheme members.

16.8.1 Deferred pensions

Prior to the Social Security Act 1990, the preserved pension of an early leaver from a defined benefit occupational scheme was subject to limited revaluation: the amount of preserved pension accruing in respect of pensionable service from 1 January 1985 would be subject to increases at the lesser of increase in the RPI and 5 per cent per annum. The Social Security Act 1990 extended the compulsory revaluation of the preserved pension in respect of pensionable service accrued up to 31 December 1984 from 1 January 1991.

16.9 GOLDEN HANDSHAKES

Following the issue of a Statement of Practice by the Inland Revenue in October 1991, care must be taken to distinguish between *ex gratia* payments on retirement (or death) and 'golden handshakes' made under s 148 as described below.

If there is an 'arrangement' to make an *ex gratia* payment to a director or employee, and the recipient is not a member of a tax approved scheme of the employer, the payment may receive tax approval from the Inland Revenue and be treated as a relevant benefit. If these conditions are not met, then the payment may be treated as emerging from an unapproved pension scheme.

16.9.1 Application of the 'golden handshake' legislation

Section 148 only applies to payments 'not otherwise chargeable to tax'. Consequently, a payment made under the terms of a contract of service or in respect of services (past, present or future) will be taxable as an emolument under the normal Schedule E rules. It is still, therefore, as important as it was before FA 1981 to ensure that the documentation of the golden handshake is carefully worded so as to avoid reference to past services.

Statutory redundancy payments are taxed under the golden handshake provisions rather than the provisions of Schedule E by ICTA 1988, s 572. The Inland Revenue has also agreed that non-statutory redundancy payments will be taxed in the same way provided there is a 'genuine' redundancy. The Inland Revenue will be satisfied that the redundancy is genuine if:

(1) the payment is only made on account of redundancy as defined in the Employment Protection (Consolidation) Act 1980, s 81;

(2) the employee has been in continuous service for at least two years;

(3) the payments are not made to selected employees only; and

(4) the payments are not excessively large in relation to the employee's earnings and length of service.

On the other hand, certain payments which are not taxable under Schedule E are also exempted from the charge in s 187. The main examples of these payments are:

(1) payments made on the employee's death or on the termination of his employment on account of injury or disability;

(2) considerations for certain restrictive covenants;

(3) payments made under certain approved pension schemes in the United Kingdom and abroad; and

(4) certain payments made by Royal Warrant or Order in Council to members of the forces.

The amount of the redundancy payment which is exempt from taxes in the hands of the employee is £30,000.

16.9.2 Close companies

Two problems arise in connection with golden handshakes made to directors who are shareholders of close companies or to members of their families:

(1) the non-tax deductibility of the payment from the company's point of view; and

(2) the possibility of the payment being treated as a distribution.

Unlike contributions to an exempt approved scheme, golden handshake payments will only be allowed as a deduction for the purposes of Schedule D if it is allowed by the Inspector in accordance with the normal 'wholly and exclusively' rule. It may be that in normal 'arm's length' cases that payment will not be allowed because, for example, the payment is made in conjunction with a cessation of trade or winding-up. In the case of a close company, however, it must be very likely that the payment will be disallowed as being a payment made for the personal benefit of the director or his family.

Potentially more serious, however, is the possibility of the payment being treated as a distribution under ICTA 1988, s 209. It seems that in cases where the distributor holds nearly 100 per cent of the share capital it will very likely be treated as a distribution.

On the other hand there is a good chance of the question of a distribution not being raised if:

(1) the individual has put in genuine service of the quality and length that would have recommended him for a severance payment were he an arm's length employee;
(2) the shareholding is modest (say around 5 per cent); and
(3) the amount involved is modest (up to £25,000).

Where, as will be common, the case falls between these two extremes, all that can be said is that the payment should not be made while the recipient is still a controlling shareholder and that if de-control is possible, the higher the former shareholding and the more recently de-control took place, the more likely it is that the inspector will treat it as a distribution.

16.9.3 Pensioning 'golden handshakes'

If the employment from which the golden handshake is payable is already pensionable, the payment may not be included in remuneration for the purposes of providing additional retirement benefits through augmentation or voluntary contributions by the employee.

If the employment was not pensionable, the individual will be entitled to contribute to a personal pension scheme. However, the golden handshake payment must be excluded from earnings for this purpose. No such restriction applies if the individual has a retirement annuity contract (which must have been in existence on 29 July 1988); in these circumstances the taxable element golden handshake payment may be included in the definition of 'net relevant earnings'.

16.10 'HANCOCKS'

A Hancock annuity is now little more than a way of describing the outright purchase of an immediate or deferred annuity for an employee at the time of or after his retirement, or for the widow(er) or dependant of a deceased employee.

The name is derived from the case of *Hancock v General Reversionary and Investment Co Ltd* (1918) TTC 358 which established that the payment by an employer to purchase an annuity for an employee on his retirement is an allowable expense in the year in which it is paid and is not regarded as additional remuneration to the employee.

The only aspect in which the *Hancock* precedent may provide a better position than the legislation now provides is that it will not require relief on the payment to be spread forward if it is more than the employer's ordinary annual contribution (see Chapter 6). In such cases, it is understood that the Inland Revenue will direct that the scheme be approved as an exempt approved scheme if it feels that the relief should be spread forward, so the advantage is more apparent than real.

The Hancock procedure is now the only method of providing a pension for an employee or director who has attained age 75. Since FA 1989, it has not been possible to accumulate funds within an approved pension scheme and provide benefits after age 75, and under personal pension schemes and retirement annuities benefits must be taken by age 75.

16.11 TRANSFERS FROM OCCUPATIONAL SCHEMES AFTER RETIREMENT

An individual is allowed to transfer on or after normal retirement date provided that:

(1) the benefits have already come into payment;
(2) the scheme rules permit the transfer to take place;
(3) either the individual left pensionable service prior to normal retirement date or remains in employment at the date of transfer.

This applies to members of all of the various tax regimes.

17

PENSION SHARING ON DIVORCE OR ANNULMENT

17.1 BACKGROUND

Before 1996, there could be no division of pension benefits between a divorcing couple. The only option then available to them was to offset the value of the pension against other matrimonial assets. The usual example of this practice was that the ex-wife kept the house and the husband kept the pension.

From July 1996, it has been possible for pension benefits to be 'earmarked' (as an alternative to offsetting). This means the court can order that, when the benefits eventually come into payment, some or all are paid to the former spouse and any remainder (only) goes to the pensioner. This does not, however, create a clean break. Generally it also means that the former spouse loses their entitlement if they remarry or if the person whose benefits are earmarked dies before those benefits come into payment. The holder of the pension plan can decide when to retire and, therefore, when the divorced spouse is to receive a benefit through earmarking. In theory, the holder of a personal pension plan could delay vesting benefits until age 75 by which time the divorced spouse may have remarried or died.

17.2 INTRODUCTION OF PENSION SHARING

From 1 December 2000, the law allows couples who start divorce proceedings (or apply for their marriage to be annulled) to split or 'share' their pension benefits. However, the sharing option is not available:

(1) to those who started divorce/nullity proceedings before 1 December 2000, because the legislation does not have retrospective effect;
(2) where the couple apply for a legal separation only, regardless of the date of their application.

Where pension sharing is a possibility, it won't be compulsory. This means that the divorcing couple will still be able to offset and/or earmark instead.

17.2.1 Person responsible for complying with the pension sharing requirements

The legislation puts responsibility for providing relevant information and implementing any consequent share on:

(1) the trustees of an occupational scheme;
(2) the trustees or managers of a personal pension scheme;
(3) the insurer of any individually owned policies;
(4) the provider of annuities, or pensions, in payment.

They are known as 'the person(s) responsible' for the pension arrangement in question.

17.2.2 Gathering information before a share

As soon as a couple decide to start divorce proceedings, they are entitled to certain basic information about each other's pension benefits. The particular information that has to be provided about any pension arrangement, including any valuation of the benefits, is set out in regulations, as are the fairly tight deadlines by which the information must be disclosed.

17.2.3 Shareable benefits

The share will be based on the cash equivalent transfer value (CETV) of all the shareable pension benefits under the arrangement in question. These include guaranteed minimum pensions, protected rights and any pension or annuity in payment. Essentially, the only benefits which cannot be shared are:

(1) those which do not have any possible surrender value, ie life cover, waiver of contribution, etc;
(2) equivalent pension benefits (EPBs) accrued in an occupational scheme, as a result of contracting out of the State Graduated Scheme that became defunct in 1975, but only if EPBs are the sole benefits provided;
(3) benefits which are already the subject of an earmarking order; and
(4) the basic State Pension (SERPS/S2P benefits are shareable).

17.2.4 Calculation of the share

England, Wales and Northern Ireland

The CETV is calculated in the same way as it would be in 'normal' circumstances. For example, in relation to a member of an occupational scheme it is calculated as if the member were exercising a statutory right to transfer on leaving pensionable service. Where there is no such statutory right, regulations provide for actuarial calculation of the CETV for pension sharing purposes. This includes calculation of the CETV of a pension in payment (because it is this value that will be shared, not the pension itself). In that particular case, account may also be taken of the pensioner's state of health and possibly that of any contingent beneficiary.

Scotland

Under Scottish matrimonial law, the pension rights which the court can take into account as a matrimonial asset are restricted to those rights attributable to the period of the marriage. This means that the court can take account of only that fraction of the CETV (calculated as at the date the divorcing couple separated) which reflects the period of the marriage as a fraction of the period of scheme membership (to the date of separation).

17.2.5 Awarding the share

In England, Wales and Northern Ireland the share can be made only by an order of the court that specifies the percentage (up to 100 per cent) of the CETV that must be used to provide benefits for the former spouse. In Scotland, the share may be made by court order or, more likely, by a 'qualifying agreement' between the divorcing couple; in either case, the former spouse may be granted a specified percentage *or* a specified amount (not exceeding 100 per cent of the final CETV).

Regardless of where in the United Kingdom the divorce or annulment is granted, the final CETV that is required to be shared is calculated on a day (decided by the person responsible for the arrangement) that falls in the implementation period.

17.2.6 The implementation period

A pension sharing order or Scottish qualifying agreement is effective on the latest of:

(1) the date stated in the order/agreement; and

(2) the date the person responsible for the arrangement is in receipt of the last of all the relevant matrimonial documents and any other information they need.

The share must be implemented within four months of the effective date of the pension sharing order or qualifying agreement.

The amount finally awarded to the former spouse is known as their 'pension credit'. In relation to the person whose benefits have been reduced, the same amount is described as their 'pension debit'.

17.3 THE PENSION CREDIT

The person responsible for the arrangement must settle their liability for a pension credit, within the implementation period, either:

(1) by an internal transfer – in other words, by providing pension credit benefits for the former spouse in the same arrangement as that from which the pension credit is derived, *if* the person responsible for the arrangement is able and willing to offer the option and *if* the former spouse chooses it; or
(2) by making an external transfer – in other words, by paying the pension credit to another qualifying arrangement, as described below, that is chosen by the former spouse.

The former spouse has the stututory right to an external transfer, regardless of whether or not an internal transfer is an option.

17.3.1 Qualifying arrangements

In relation to approved schemes and contracts, a qualifying arrangement is:

(1) an approved personal pension scheme of which the person entitled to the pension credit is or becomes a member; or
(2) an approved occupational pension scheme of which the person entitled to the pension credit is a member; or
(3) an appropriate annuity contract or insurance policy; or
(4) an appropriate immediate annuity; or
(5) certain overseas arrangements.

Also, a qualifying arrangement must be able and willing to accept the pension credit. This means, for instance, that a transfer of guaranteed minimum pension (GMP) or protected rights value can be made only to a contracted-out arrangement that will provide 'safeguarded rights' benefits (which broadly correspond with protected rights benefits) for the person entitled to the pension credit. In June 2003, the Government announced that it would introduce changes to the law on safeguarded rights on divorce. To simplify the treatment of pensions on divorce it will abolish safeguarded rights in order to provide greater flexibility in implementing a pensions share for the former spouse and the pension scheme. It will also align normal benefit age as the earliest age from which a pension share may be payable from all private pension arrangements. This could be a restriction for an ex-spouse who currently could draw a pension credit from a personal pension or stakeholder scheme from age 50. The 'alignment' of normal benefit age is likely to mean that benefits will be linked to the definition of 'normal benefit age 'under an occupational scheme, ie ages 60 to 70.

17.3.2 Pension credit and Inland Revenue limits

In relation to a person awarded a pension credit:

(1) The benefits arising in the form of a pension are generally without limit, although restrictions will apply to the cash payable (so, for instance, the pension credit cash payable under a personal pension scheme is limited to 25 per cent of the pension credit fund).

(2) The pension credit benefits, whether paid as a pension and/or cash, are not taken into account in any calculation of maximum contributions or benefits, which means, for example, that:
   (a) if a member of an occupational scheme was entitled to a maximum pension of £15,000 per annum; and
   (b) if the pension credit awarded to his former wife is the equivalent of £4,000 per annum pension; and
   (c) if the former wife is a member of an occupational pension scheme in her own right that will provide her with a maximum pension related to the employment of £15,000 per annum,
   then the former wife may be provided with a total pension of £15,000 + £4,000 = £19,000 per annum in total.

17.3.3 Other arrangements

The following cannot accept pension credit transfers:

(1) retirement annuity contracts;
(2) buy-out contracts already held by the person entitled to a pension credit in relation to own right benefits.

The pension credit arising from a retirement annuity contract will have to be transferred into an occupational or personal pension scheme. The credit arising from a buy-out contract will have to be transferred into another buy-out contract, a personal pension scheme or occupational scheme.

17.4 THE PENSION DEBIT

The creation of a pension debit has the consequences described below.

17.4.1 All arrangements

Where appropriate, each and every:

(1) shareable benefit under a final salary scheme, including GMP; and
(2) element of a money purchase scheme fund, including any protected rights element,

must be reduced by an amount that is equal to the percentage specified in the pension sharing order (or, in a Scottish case, the percentage of the CETV represented by the specified amount).

17.4.2 Retirement annuity contracts, personal pensions and simplified defined contribution schemes

Under a retirement annuity contract, personal pension (individual or group) or a simplified defined contribution scheme, the pension debit reduces the fund that is available to provide the debited person with benefits. However, there is no added restriction on future contributions nor the benefits provided, so the same contribution and benefit limits apply after the share as did before.

17.4.3 Occupational pension schemes

Under an occupational pension scheme (of whatever type – group scheme, small self-administered scheme, etc and whether defined benefit or defined contribution, excluding only simplified defined contribution), the debited pension must still be taken into account in determining the benefits payable to the member, unless advantage can be taken of the administrative easement. Broadly speaking, the administrative easement applies to members, other than controlling directors, with earnings of no more than 25 per cent of the earnings cap. Where the easement does not apply, the debited pension is known as a 'negative deferred pension' and will have to be deducted:

(1) from the ultimate pension payable to the member under a final salary scheme;
(2) in calculating the maximum allowable pension payable under a money purchase scheme; and
(3) in calculating the maximum tax-free cash lump sum payable under either.

By way of example, this means that:

(1) if before the share the member was entitled to a maximum pension of £15,000 per annum; and

(2) if the pension credit awarded to his wife is the equivalent £4,000 per annum pension;

then the member's maximum pension is permanently reduced to £15,000–£4,000 = £11,000 per annum.

17.4.4 Deferred annuity contracts

Under a deferred annuity contract (such as a buy-out policy) any limits on the pension or lump sum benefit must be reduced appropriately to take account of the pension debit.

17.4.5 Pensions in payment

In relation to a pension in payment, the reduced pension payable may be reconfigured to take account of the pensioner's changed circumstances, provided Inland Revenue limits that take the pension debit into account are not exceeded.

17.5 PENSION SHARING COSTS

The legislation allows the person responsible for the pension arrangement to recover the 'reasonable administrative expenses' incurred in connection with pension sharing.

17.6 ADVICE ISSUES

Clearly, pension sharing adds another layer of complexity to pensions and pensions advice. As well as the divorcing couple, the family lawyer will need expert pensions advice and scheme trustees and employers will need help to understand the implications.

Former spouses will need advice on what to do with the pension credit awarded to them. If they choose (or must make) an external transfer, they will need help to decide on the most suitable arrangement to transfer to. Also, if the internal transfer option is available to them, they will need help in deciding whether this will provide better benefits than those that could be secured by an external transfer. This could also be an occasion for the person who has not previously made any pension provision of their own to realise the importance of doing so.

As for the person whose benefits have been debited, they should, of course, be reconsidering their reduced pension provision, with a view to topping it up so far as is possible. This will certainly call for advice.

The perception, however, is that family lawyers won't necessarily see pension sharing as an alternative to the more tried and tested route of off-setting other matrimonial assets against the pension. Generally, it is still considered preferable for one party to have a whole pension and the other to have, say, a whole house, especially when children are involved, rather than for the couple to each have a fractional share of each asset. It is therefore the case that pension-sharing orders may not be appropriate in all cases.

18

VARIOUS ASPECTS OF EXECUTIVE PENSION PLANS

18.1 INVESTMENT COMPANIES

An investment company is a company the income of which would be treated as investment income for tax purposes if it were the income of an individual. A company which is treated for tax purposes as an investment company cannot set up a pension plan and obtain approval under the Inland Revenue's discretionary power under ICTA 1988, s 591 (see Appendix 4) if the membership includes 20 per cent directors or controlling directors of that employer or directors who while not owning 20 per cent of the shares themselves, or being controlling directors, are members of a family together controlling more than 50 per cent of the shares.

Controlling directors of investment companies are prohibited from contributing to personal pension schemes other than up to £3,600 a year. The only other route (see Chapter 14) is through a scheme approved under ICTA 1988, s 590 (see Appendix 4) which requires the Inland Revenue to approve a scheme if it meets the more stringent conditions of that section. Very few directors would be happy with the benefits which may be provided under that section, and very few life offices are prepared to write s 590 schemes.

The only benefits which can be provided under s 590 are a pension of $\frac{1}{60}$ of final remuneration for each year of service (part of which may be exchanged for a lump sum which does not exceed $\frac{3}{80}$ of final remuneration for each year of service) and a widow's pension which does not exceed two-thirds of a member's pension and is payable only on death in retirement. There is no sliding scale of accelerated accrual, and no death in service benefits are allowed, including a refund of any contributions made by a member. Remuneration which can be pensioned under s 590 is limited, as the Schedule E income which a director can receive from an investment company is usually very low.

There is no Inland Revenue objection to the provision of retirement benefits for employees and non-controlling directors of investment companies.

18.2 SERVICE COMPANIES

Professional firms sometimes establish service companies to provide clerical staff, accommodation and administrative services for the firm, the directors of the company usually being partners in a practice. The question then arises over the possibility of providing the partner who is also a director of the service company with additional pension benefits through an executive pension plan in respect of his Schedule E earnings as a director.

While in principle this is acceptable, the Inland Revenue is not prepared to approve schemes for such directors where the benefits are geared to a level of remuneration exceeding the amount allowed by the local Inspector as a trading expense of the company. The local Inspector will, in turn, generally take the view that the duties which the director performs for the company are minimal and so the remuneration allowable as a trading expense of the company will be correspondingly very small – as his other profit earning activities are in his capacity as partner of a firm. It will be seen that, in most cases, the amount of additional pension which can be provided for a partner/director will be insignificant, although there may of course be exceptions, where the facts of the case warrant them; for example, it may be possible to show as a matter of fact that the main duties of, say, a staff partner related properly to the service company and should be remunerated from the service company.

Once again, there is nothing to prevent service companies from providing pension benefits in the usual way for its employees.

18.3 SPECIAL OCCUPATIONS – RETIREMENT DATES

There are a number of occupations where a reasonable case may be made out for a normal retirement date earlier than the normal range of 60 to 70. Because of the particular characteristics of the occupation, it may be possible for certain jobholders to agree with the Inland Revenue a retirement date in the range 50 to 55, for example airline pilots, advertising executives, money dealers and trawlermen.

However, an earlier normal retirement date is not automatic simply because the individual follows one of these occupations (as is the case with the special occupations for which early retirement dates can be chosen under retirement annuity contracts and personal pension schemes – see Chapter 14) and a case has to be put to the Inland Revenue for each executive pension plan detailing the exact nature of the work.

If the Inland Revenue accepts that a normal retirement date of 50 to 55 is appropriate in a particular case, it will normally insist that benefits have to be taken at normal retirement date and cannot be deferred if the individual works beyond the retirement date, whether in the same or another occupation.

18.4 RETIREMENT DATES BELOW AGE 50

There are also a number of occupations which cannot be continued much beyond the mid-30s and for these the Inland Revenue may agree to much earlier normal retirement dates – even as low as 35. The occupations to which this applies are usually limited to professional sportsmen and women, for example:

(1) professional footballers (normal retirement date 35);
(2) professional tennis players (normal retirement date 35);
(3) professional motor-racing drivers (normal retirement date 40).

If an early retirement date is chosen, severe restrictions will be placed on the benefits, in particular:

(1) the pension is limited to $\frac{1}{60}$ of final salary for each year of service;
(2) the cash lump sum is limited to $\frac{3}{80}$ of final salary for each year of service;
(3) no early retirement is allowed, except through incapacity;
(4) late retirement is restricted to five years, for example a footballer still playing in his forties must receive his benefits from the pension plan at age 40;
(5) if the member takes on some other occupation with the same employer, for example a footballer becoming a coach or manager, he must still take his benefits at his normal retirement date.

In its consultation document, 'Simplifying the taxation of pensions: increasing choice and flexibility for all', the Inland Revenue announced proposals to extend the minimum benefit age to 55 from 2010. This applies to existing arrangements and to sports people. The likely date for this proposal to become law is 6 April 2005.

18.5 INTERNATIONAL ASPECTS OF EXECUTIVE PENSION PLANS

18.5.1 Pensions simplification

The impact of the Government's tax simplification proposals on overseas issues as set out below (see 18.5.3 to 18.5.7) is not yet known. Until this is clarified the position is as follows:

(1) The basic rule is that if an employee is effectively chargeable to UK tax under Schedule E Case I or II, then the employer can provide executive pension plans benefits for him.

(2) The benefits of a tax-approved executive pension plan are available to employees who are resident, but not necessarily domiciled, in the United Kingdom, for example the Swiss-domiciled manager of the UK-based agency of a US corporation.

(3) The only exception to the above rule is the provision by a *UK resident employer* of executive pension plan benefits for an employee who is both resident and domiciled outside the United Kingdom, for example the Spanish sales manager of a UK-based company, who is a Spanish national and lives in Spain ordinarily.

18.5.2 Definitions

(1) 'United Kingdom' means England, Scotland, Wales and Northern Ireland – it does not include the Channel Islands, the Isle of Man or the Republic of Ireland.

(2) Domicile refers to the country which is a person's natural home, and for most people would be their country of birth.

(3) Residence for tax purposes is determined by a number of criteria such as the length of time spent in the country during a fiscal year.

(4) Foreign emoluments describes remuneration paid by an employer who is not *resident* in the United Kingdom to an employee who is not domiciled in the United Kingdom. If a UK resident receives foreign emoluments, he will be assessable to tax under Schedule E on their full amount.

(5) An overseas employer is one who is not resident in the United Kingdom for tax purposes and whose trading profits are, if at all, assessable to UK tax only to the extent that they arise from a branch or agency in this country.

18.5.3 Overseas employer with UK-resident employees

The Inland Revenue will tax-approve an executive pension plan established by an overseas employer conditional upon:

(1) the appointment of a UK-resident person as an 'administrator' of the pension plan, who will be responsible for ensuring that Inland Revenue requirements are met. It is usual for the trustee of the executive pension plan to act as the administrator;

(2) an undertaking to exclude from the pension plan UK-domiciled employees who qualify for full income tax relief on account of the length of time spent overseas.

In establishing an executive pension plan, the overseas employer should give critical consideration to whether it is the most suitable vehicle for the particular employee.

(1) For employees who are both UK-resident and UK-domiciled, there is no alternative to a UK tax-approved pension plan.

(2) For employees who are not UK-domiciled, much will depend on how long they will be resident in the United Kingdom. For highly mobile employees who are unlikely to remain in the United Kingdom sufficiently long to build up a significant benefit, clearly the executive pension plan is not satisfactory as a retirement savings medium.

Other aspects which may affect an overseas employer's consideration of whether to provide retirement benefits through a UK tax-approved pension plan are:

(1) Concern about the obligations, liabilities and expense involved in establishing a UK pension plan, especially where the overseas employer is unfamiliar with UK pensions legislation, and where the business connection is either in its early stages or not intended to be long-term in nature.

(2) The overseas employer may be able to obtain relief in respect of its contributions to the pension plan from its home tax authorities, so that relief will be confined to its UK profits, if any.

(3) The overseas employer may be subject to restrictions which prevent it contracting with a UK insurer or remitting contributions to the United Kingdom. Also the inconvenience of having to comply with accounting requirements under domestic legislation (eg in the United States) covering pensions provisions for employees of overseas subsidiaries may deter overseas employers from establishing UK pension plans.

18.5.4 Offshore plans

Overseas employers with multi-national representation often prefer to adopt a global strategy in relation to retirement provision for overseas employees. They may accordingly establish an offshore plan in a tax-efficient area, such as the Bahamas, or else include their overseas employees in parallel plans to those established for the corporation's home-based employees. The advantages of this strategy are:

(1) uniform benefits can be provided for all employees regardless of where they are stationed at any time;

(2) the problem of having to comply with local national legislation on retirement provision and social security can be mitigated;

(3) for employees who have a series of overseas posts, it avoids the accumulation of pension funds in different countries each subject to different jurisdiction and regulation.

The disadvantages are:

(1) Tax relief may not be available on either the employer's contributions or the fund. Conversely, the employee may be taxed on the employer's contribution paid for his benefits.
(2) Depending on the employee's country of residence at retirement,
    (a) the pension benefit may be subject to double taxation;
    (b) the pension may be secured in an unsatisfactory currency;
    (c) the emerging benefit may be completely inappropriate. In many countries lump sum benefits on retirement are the norm; elsewhere there are generous State Pension benefits giving rise to the problem of over-provision, although the current world-wide tendency is either to reduce these benefits and/or to fund pension liabilities.

18.5.5 Corresponding approval

If it can be shown to the Inland Revenue's satisfaction that a pension plan established offshore for an employee receiving foreign emoluments 'corresponds' to a UK-approved scheme, then tax relief will be permitted both on the employee's contributions and in respect of the employers' contributions to the plan. This means that the benefit structure of the offshore pension plan must be similar to the structure of a pension plan approved under ICTA 1988, s 591. The Inland Revenue is concerned to prevent the encashment of benefits by an employee on leaving service, or in other circumstances before retirement, and may require an undertaking from the plan administrator in that regard.

Employees applying for corresponding approval relief after 23 February 1995 must satisfy additional Inland Revenue requirements in relation to residence of the scheme, etc.

18.5.6 Section 615 plans (known previously as section 218 plans)

A half-way house to a full offshore pension plan, which is operated by some UK-based multi-national corporations for employees who are resident overseas, is a plan established under ICTA 1988, s 615. A s 615 plan enjoys exemption from UK taxation on its investment income and emerging benefits but is otherwise a much less flexible pensions vehicle than a genuine offshore plan established outside the United Kingdom.

18.5.7 Overseas resident employees

With the agreement of the Inland Revenue an employee who is resident abroad – perhaps in a succession of different countries and with different employers – may be included as a member of a UK tax-approved scheme for an aggregate period of up to ten years, subject to the following conditions:

(1) written confirmation of a definite expectation that the employee will eventually either be employed in the United Kingdom by an employer participating in the scheme, or retire in the United Kingdom;
(2) the overseas employer must reimburse the relevant UK employer for the cost of contributions to the scheme;
(3) scheme benefits should be calculated in relation to a level of remuneration appropriate to similar employment in the United Kingdom;
(4) transfers to the UK scheme from overseas arrangements, simultaneously providing benefits in respect of the overseas service, are not permitted;
(5) the period of service abroad should not exceed ten years.

18.6 PENSIONERS RESIDENT ABROAD

The questions that arise when a pensioner is resident abroad generally relate to the payment of the cash sum and the pension from the UK scheme. As far as the cash payment is concerned, problems will only arise if there are exchange controls in force at the time of retirement (there are none at present) in which case the Bank of England's permission will be needed to effect the transfer abroad. There is no problem about paying pensions abroad but their taxation needs greater consideration. The position is that, as a general rule, all pensions must be paid from the United Kingdom under deduction of Schedule E tax under the PAYE system. There is no general exemption for pensioners resident abroad even where they have worked abroad, but exemption can be granted if the last ten years' service in respect of which the pension is paid was abroad or half the total service and at least ten out of the last 20 years' service was abroad. Alternatively, exemption may be due under a double-taxation agreement (DTA) under which the pension is taxed in the country of residence – such DTAs exist with most of the major countries in the West to which pensioners are likely to go, but not the local tax havens – the Channel Islands and the Isle of Man. Where a DTA applies, the Financial Intermediaries and Claims Office is able to authorise gross payments at source.

18.7 OVERSEAS TRANSFERS

It may be possible to transfer benefits from a UK pension arrangement to an overseas arrangement, or vice versa. In general, such transfers can only be made with the prior agreement of the UK Inland Revenue, and considerable information may be needed, depending on the circumstances. There may also be tax implications for the individual, and requirements set by the overseas authorities.

The UK Inland Revenue is particularly concerned to ensure that transfers to and from overseas are made only in circumstances where a person is or has been genuinely resident and working abroad. Agreement to a transfer from overseas is therefore usually only given if the member has been employed in the overseas employment to which the proposed transfer relates for at least two years.

Similarly, a transfer can only be made to an overseas arrangement in the individual's country of residence and confirmation is needed that the person has no intention of returning to the United Kingdom and understands that the transfer is permanent.

Before approving the transfer payment, the Inland Revenue requires copies of the receiving scheme's constitutional documentation (the trust deed and rules equivalent) and confirmation of the benefits to be provided by the scheme in respect of the transfer value.

Reciprocal arrangements exist for transfers between the United Kingdom and the Isle of Man, the Channel Islands and the Republic of Ireland, which qualify or set aside some of the requirements for transfers to and from overseas. There are also special arrangements for transfers to the pension scheme for staff of the European Communities.

19

RETIREMENT OPTIONS – INVESTMENT CONSIDERATIONS

It is not the purpose of this chapter to deal with generalised aspects of retirement, but solely with some of the investment considerations which arise when benefits are paid under pension plans.

The options available at retirement have already been discussed in previous chapters – they differ according to whether benefits are paid from an executive pension plan, retirement annuity or personal pension scheme. Investment considerations, however, are similar for both:

(1) Should the benefits be taken wholly in the form of a pension annuity?
(2) Or should the maximum tax-free lump sum be taken with a reduced pension annuity?
(3) What type of annuity should be taken, level, escalating, single life or joint life?

An indication of the different types of annuity purchased by a fund of £100,000 at age 60 is given in Chapter 14 (and is repeated below), as is the effect of using tax-free cash emerging from a pension plan to buy a purchased life annuity which is taxed only on the interest portion.

Another consideration is whether to take advantage of the facility to draw an income from the pension fund, deferring the purchase of an annuity until later, age 75 at the latest.

19.1 TYPES OF PENSION AVAILABLE

On taking the benefits from a personal pension scheme or a retirement annuity, the policyholder normally has various options including the facility to take a reduced pension on his own life but which continues in the event of his death to the spouse. For example, £100,000 would purchase the following types of annuity on the open market for a man aged 65. These annuities, based on an investment yield of 3.15 per cent, are not necessarily at the top of the market as annuity rates change frequently.

Table 19.1

Type of annuity	Amount per annum
Single life annuity payable annually in arrears	£6,949
Single life annuity payable monthly in advance	£6,688
Single life annuity payable monthly in advance but for a minimum of five years	£6,625
Single life annuity payable monthly in advance but for a minimum of ten years	£6,441
Single life annuity payable quarterly in advance for a minimum of five years, increasing each year by 3% compound	£4,885
Joint life level annuity (not increasing), during the lives of the man and his wife, aged 62, payable quarterly in advance	£5,110

19.2 PURCHASED LIFE ANNUITIES

As an example, a fund of £100,000 built up under a personal pension scheme would provide an income payable in monthly instalments in advance throughout the life of a man aged 65, guaranteed for five years, of £6,625 per annum, but subject to tax as earned income at, say, 22 per cent leaving a net income of £5,168 per annum.

Alternatively, the fund could be taken in the form of a tax-free lump sum of £25,000 plus a reduced income of £4,969 (gross), £3,876 (net); the cash of £25,000 could be used to buy a purchased life annuity of £1,663 of which £253 is interest and would be taxable as unearned income. The net income would be £1,607. The combination of the two net annuities amounts to £5,483, an increase of £315 per annum.

A further alternative is sometimes available under personal pension schemes and retirement annuities – the option to take a unit-linked annuity. The planholder may choose a pension which varies with the value of the units, in for example, a managed fund, a property fund, an equity fund, a gilt edged fund, a fixed interest deposit fund, and overseas funds.

The pension is expressed as the value of a fixed number of units determined at the time that benefits start to be drawn and depending upon the planholder's age and upon mortality experience at the time. When each pension payment falls due, the amount of pension is calculated by applying the bid price of the units on the due date to the fixed number of units calculated at the commencement of the pension. The value of the units, and hence the pension, rises to the full extent of the income plus the capital growth of the fund (after charges) in any year so that the pension's growth potential is maximised. The initial pension, however, starts off at a much lower amount than the level pension. If a unit price goes down, so does the pension.

Table 19.2 shows the history of a unit-linked pension for a man aged 65 secured by a fund of £1,000 commencing on 1 May 1981 and shows subsequent payments compared with level and escalating pensions. The pensions are linked to accumulation units in the pension managed and the pension property funds.

Table 19.2

Date	Unit-linked (annuity) (£ pa)		Sterling annuity (£ pa)	
	Pension managed fund	Pension property fund	Level	Escalating at 5%
1 May 1981	61.18	61.18	152.22	112.39
1982	68.36	69.93	152.22	118.01
1983	89.56	73.69	152.22	123.91
1984	104.23	80.92	152.22	130.11
1985	123.37	88.37	152.22	136.61
1986	159.13	93.83	152.22	143.44
1987	188.88	104.43	152.22	150.61
1988	189.29	127.00	152.22	158.14
1989	220.64	156.99	152.22	166.05
1990	228.33	172.08	152.22	174.35
1991	254.42	157.19	152.22	183.07
1992	277.37	152.19	152.22	192.23
1993	321.52	151.62	152.22	201.84
1994	379.13	194.37	152.22	211.93
1995	379.55	209.10	152.22	222.52
1996	466.45	220.71	152.22	233.65
1997	496.45	247.13	152.22	245.33
1998	604.24	287.60	152.22	257.60
1999	661.06	319.46	152.22	270.48
2000	723.50	366.51	152.22	284.00
2001	710.85	404.67	152.22	298.20
2002	666.25	438.32	152.22	313.11
2003	561.55	477.44	152.22	328.77

Notes:
1. If the unit price goes down, so will the pension.
2. Pensions will be payable for life, quarterly in advance, guaranteed for at least five years even if death occurs.

In deciding what type of annuity the planholder should take he will have to consider the following factors:

(1) Is he in poor health, in which case would it be better to opt for a higher-level pension rather than a lower escalating or unit-linked pension? It may be possible to obtain an 'impaired life' annuity from an insurer which specialises in people in poor health.

(2) Is there a history of longevity in the family, in which case might he opt for the lower escalating pension?

(3) If he opts for the unit-linked pension and it drops in value, will he have other income to fall back on?

(4) Does his wife have an income in her own right – if not should he perhaps opt for a joint life last survivor pension?

(5) If he opts for a lower escalating or unit linked pension, how long will it take to overtake the level pension in real terms? It is interesting to compare the level and 5 per cent escalating pensions starting at £152.22 and £112.39 respectively. It takes six to seven years for the escalating annuity to match the level annuity (£158.14 compared with £152.22). During these years an amount accumulates by having a higher annuity. This amount gradually reduces as the escalating pension is paid. However, it is not until 13 years that the excess built up in the first six to seven years is exhausted. This makes no allowance for the notional investment of the excess funds in the first six/seven years.

(6) It can be seen from the figures in Table 19.1 that the difference in an annuity with a five-year guarantee compared with an annuity with no guarantee is only £63 per annum (cf £6,625 and £6,688). Similarly, the difference in an annuity with a ten-year guarantee is only £247 per annum (cf £6,441 and £6,688). It may be worthwhile taking this reduction in view of the benefit payable should death occur during the guaranteed period.

19.3 PHASED RETIREMENT

Personal pension plans can provide for benefits to be taken in stages, in line with income needs in retirement. Before 6 April 2001, to achieve this, many personal pension plans (and retirement annuities) were subdivided into mini-policies or segments. Since 6 April 2001, personal pensions do not need to be sub-divided in this way but can be cashed in, in part, to give the required level of phasing.

(Since 6 April 2001, if part of the plan is encashed, the cash lump sum is calculated as one-third of the fund used to buy the annuity: this equates to one-quarter of the fund value.)

On 'retirement' the planholder may cash in some of the plan to provide a cash lump sum and an annuity, always maintaining the statutory requirement that only one-quarter of the fund is surrendered and may be taken as a cash lump sum. Further parts can be surrendered subsequently.

This facility enables the planholder to avoid taking more of the pension fund as is necessary in relation to his overall financial position at the time. Any remaining fund must be taken by age 75.

Phased retirement is very useful for planholders who are taxpayers and whose personal circumstances do not require them to use the tax-free lump sum for a capital purpose. Instead they may use it to provide income.

The cash lump sums may be used to provide income to top up the annuities taken. For example say the planholder aged 65 paying tax at 40 per cent requires a net income from the personal pension fund of £20,000 per annum. This could be provided by cashing in sufficient fund value to provide a tax-free lump sum of £17,707 plus an annuity of around £3,822 per annum gross, £2,293 per annum net after tax at 40 per cent, giving a total net amount of £20,000.

In the second year if the planholder requires a further net income of £20,000 more fund could be encashed to provide a further tax-free lump sum of £15,600 plus an annuity of £3,512 per annum gross, £2,107 per annum net, which with the original annuity of £2,293 gives £20,000.

Deferring the purchase of annuities introduces the risk that the fund will not grow at a sufficient rate to ensure that the total income, both before and after age 75, will exceed that payable if the fund is fully used to buy an annuity at the outset. However, the purchase of annuities each year should be helpful in providing a spread of different annuities bought in different economic conditions. This should be particularly advantageous if annuity rates are low now.

On death before age 75 the fund may be returned to the member's beneficiaries and if the plan is arranged under a suitable trust the death benefits may be paid free of inheritance tax (IHT) and these death benefits arise in respect of any segments of the plan which have not been surrendered.

19.4 INCOME WITHDRAWAL OPTION

Personal pension plans and occupational schemes (provided the scheme rules permit) give planholders greater flexibility at retirement. Rather than having to purchase an annuity, the planholder may draw an income from the fund from age 50 onwards, and defer purchasing an annuity up until age 75. The income withdrawn must be within limits set by the Inland Revenue. The pension fund remains invested, benefiting from any future investment growth. These arrangements are usually called income drawdown schemes or pension fund withdrawal schemes.

They are sometimes advertised as 'pensions unlocking schemes' which promote the so-called attractions of obtaining access to 'your pension fund' without sufficient warnings about the risks involved.

19.4.1 Personal pension plans

The maximum income that may be withdrawn is 100 per cent of the notional annuity that the planholder could obtain using rates published by the Government Actuary (known as the 'GAD rate'). These rates vary according to the yield on 15-year gilt-edged securities. As economic circumstances change, so too do the notional annuities. However, once income starts to be drawn from the fund the maximum and minimum amounts are fixed, but subject to adjustments every three years. The minimum income which may be withdrawn is 35 per cent of the maximum income. The amounts withdrawn during the year can fluctuate, provided that the total amount withdrawn is between the 35–100 per cent limits.

If the planholder dies while withdrawing income from the fund, the remainder of the fund is returned to the deceased's estate, or to the scheme's trustees, minus a tax charge of 35 per cent. Alternatively the dependant may normally continue to draw an income from the fund until such time as the deceased would have reached age 75, or the survivor reaches age 75, whichever is the earlier, or may purchase an annuity.

If the planholder wishes to take a tax-free cash sum Inland Revenue rules require income to be withdrawn from the fund at the same time. Usually the tax-free cash sum is a key requirement and this drives the amount of income which is withdrawn. For example, take a client who has a personal pension fund valued at £300,000 on retirement which would provide a tax-free cash sum of £75,000 and £225,000 to buy an annuity, or to generate income withdrawals.

The planholder needs a tax-free cash sum now of only £30,000, for example to pay off the remainder of a mortgage or start up a small business. The planholder would like to take only the tax-free cash sum of £30,000 and no income, having sufficient resources elsewhere to satisfy income needs. However, Inland Revenue rules do not permit this, so the minimum income has to be taken from the fund.

The fund which needs to be used is only £120,000 – the minimum needed to give a tax-free lump sum of £30,000. The remainder of £90,000 will fund the income at between £8,370 per annum (the approximate maximum amount) and £2,929 per annum (the minimum amount assuming that the maximum notional annuity is £8,370 per annum for a male aged around 65).

The balance of the total fund of £300,000 (£180,000) can remain invested to provide further tax-free cash and annuity, or income at a later stage.

Since 6 April 2001, an individual no longer needs net relevant earnings to contribute up to £3,600 each year to a personal pension plan. If the individual does not want the income, it could be reinvested in another personal pension. If the individual has net relevant earnings, contributions above £3,600 a year may be possible.

19.4.2 Occupational pensions

The rules for occupational pension scheme drawdown are similar to those for personal pensions. However, normal benefit tests must be applied when withdrawals from the fund start and when the annuity is purchased. The benefit tests must be based on the annuity basis selected by the member, however, the member may change this basis when actually purchasing an annuity.

The death benefits are different to those under personal pensions. A tax-free lump sum on death is only available if the member elected for a five-year guarantee (or less) when starting drawdown and then dies during the guarantee period. The lump sum is made up as follows:

(1) the balance of payments due to the end of the guarantee period assuming an income of the maximum GAD rate that applied when withdrawals started; plus
(2) the difference between the maximum GAD rate calculated when withdrawal started and the actual income the member has withdrawn.

Any fund remaining after a lump sum has been paid must be used to buy an annuity in accordance with the normal rules. If a surplus arises then normal rules will apply.

Not all occupational schemes are able to offer the income drawdown facility. Those that can include this in their rules are:

(1) money purchase schemes (defined contribution) provided they are not contracted out;
(2) schemes that include both a defined contribution element and defined benefit element, but only for the defined contribution element provided it is not contracted out;
(3) AVC schemes and FSAVCs; and
(4) s 32 plans (excluding contracted-out benefits).

19.4.3 Annuities or income drawdown?

Annuities involve the insurer in an insurance risk: the insurance company will pay an annuity which is guaranteed, for life, regardless of how long the annuitant lives for. If the annuitant dies shortly after buying the annuity, the annuity instalments paid are likely to be less than the purchase price of the annuity. However, some annuitants live for many years and annuities provide a form of insurance against longevity. The insurance company makes a profit from those who die in the early years, but makes losses in respect of those who survive into a very old age.

Many planholders do not like to think of the insurance company keeping the balance of 'their fund' if they die shortly after buying the annuity: they would like to retain the pension fund which they have built up over the years when they were investing contributions. The income withdrawal option is likely to appeal to these people although there are risks.

19.4.4 Risks of income withdrawal

Many people approaching retirement and pensioners are likely to have a cautious attitude to investment. However, the planholder who decides not to buy an annuity is turning down the opportunity to invest in a pooled environment. Instead, the planholder has to bear the investment risk personally. The pension fund has to accumulate at a sufficient rate to ensure that when the annuity is finally purchased, the amount of the annuity is at least equal to what it would have been if an annuity had been purchased at the outset. The rate of return on the investment increases with age. The following table indicates the real rate of return needed at various ages and also demonstrates the subsidy inherent in annuities. Note that these figures do not take into account the effects of charges, and the underlying mortality assumes standard insurance industry experience of annuitants.

Table 19.3

Client age	Additional growth required over and above interest rates (no charges) (%)
50	0.19
55	0.36
60	0.70
65	1.41
66	1.60
67	1.83
68	2.08
69	2.36
70	2.67
71	3.02
72	3.40
73	3.83
74	4.30

In order to obtain real rates of retirement at the above levels, plan-holders need to hold a proportion of their pension fund in equity-type investments. As age increases this proportion becomes greater, and attitude to risk would have to be speculative to contemplate a real rate of return above 3 per cent. In practice, even a seasoned speculative pensioner would be unlikely to defer purchasing an annuity beyond age 70.

Income withdrawal facilities have increased awareness of the investment options open to people approaching retirement and to pensioners. Because annuity rates are linked to the returns on gilt-edged securities, there may be a case for investing all or part of the investment funds in gilts. However, in practice this is not feasible for individuals because they are unlikely to find an individual gilt which matches their requirements and in any case they will not know in advance when they will want to buy an annuity.

Table 19.4 compares the various options according to annual changes in interest rates and annual growth in the Financial Times All Share Index. The grid indicates by black squares the situations in which the conventional annuity is likely to be the best option.

Withdrawing income from the fund is likely to be better than a conventional annuity assuming there is FTSE growth combined with low increases in interest rates (and hence annuity rates) or even reductions in FTSE at the same time as more significant increases in interest: the grid indicates this by diamonds.

Withdrawing income from a fund which is invested in gilts will protect the planholder against changes in interest rates. However, this protection is reduced if there is FTSE growth; the grid indicates this by triangles.

The light squares indicate that withdrawing income from the fund while investing in a 'guaranteed fund' would be better than buying a conventional annuity provided that there is high FTSE growth and falling interest rates. The 'guaranteed fund' used in this example would invest in gilts with the dividends being invested in options linked to FTSE. Again this fund would give protection against changes in interest rates but requires high levels of FTSE growth to be effective. Other types of guaranteed funds exist in the marketplace, but in practice provide similar results.

Table 19.5 sets out the common requirements of potential pensioners and the options usually available under personal pensions (although the individual's investment profile will have a significant bearing in the options).

Table 19.4 – Some investment options

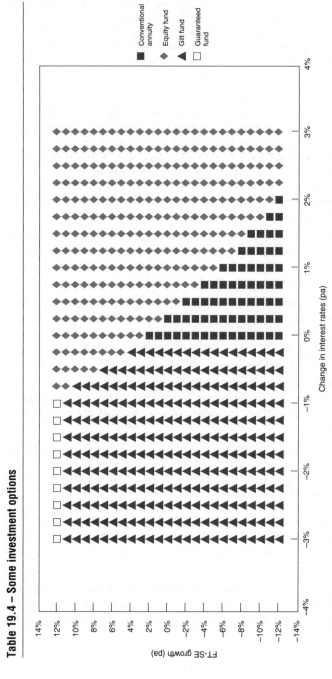

The figures compare an immediate annuity with an annuity purchased after three years under income withdrawal. A dividend yield of 3% pa is assumed. Interest rates are 3.75% at commencement. Figures are based on a man aged 60, taking withdrawals annually in arrears. All annuity rates are typical (as at June 2003). Fund charges assumed for annuity deferral are 3% initial and 1% pa ongoing.

Table 19.5

Requirements	Options	Favoured route
1. Maximum cash lump sum plus maximum income	Annuity or income withdrawal	Annuity
2. Maximum cash lump sum plus minimum (or variable) income	Income withdrawal	Income withdrawal
3. Income only	Annuity, phased annuities or phased income withdrawals	Phased annuities

Notes:
(1) The table ignores the effect of death benefits. These could be provided through the remainder of the annuity instalments if a pension is bought on a guaranteed basis, through an annuity continuing to a dependant if a joint life pension is bought, or through the return of the pension fund, minus a 35 per cent tax charge, if the income withdrawal option is used.
(2) Where death benefits are of prime importance, the favoured route would be to defer taking all benefits, so that on death the whole fund would be returned, without a 35 per cent tax charge.
(3) Under requirement 2 above it may be possible to use a combination of unit-linked annuities on a joint life basis in order to minimise the income taken. However, this would not provide the planholder with the ability to vary that income.
(4) Unit-linked annuities and with-profits annuities may provide greater flexibility for those approaching retirement who already have guaranteed income in their portfolios.

19.5 INCREASING CURRENT INCOME

Generally, planholders should not take tax-free lump sums from pension funds unless they are obliged to do so (eg under some occupational pension schemes) or unless there is a definite need for the lump sum.

Withdrawing the lump sum to reinvest it in other investment areas is very unlikely to be financially attractive because the gross investment return within the pension fund will be replaced by a taxed investment return elsewhere. However, where other lump sums are available the following investment areas may be appropriate.

Individuals investing to increase current income will normally be looking at a range of 'money' investments including bank deposits, building societies and fixed interest securities such as gilts. Of these investments, deposit accounts of any kind, whether bank, building society or national savings, are rarely appropriate because the level of income is variable, unpredictable, and the capital base generating the income is

Table 19.6 Income withdrawal/drawdown comparison between occupational schemes, AVC schemes and personal pension schemes

Occupational schemes	AVC and FSAVC schemes	Personal pension schemes
Available for: • Non-contracted out insured or self-invested money purchase schemes • SSAS which provides only money purchase benefits • EPP • Section 32 contracts	• Group AVC • FSAVC	• Any personal pension scheme
Tax-free cash Based on length of service and final remuneration with a maximum of 2.25 times the initial rate of pension before commutation. Where scheme rules directly link amount of pension and tax-free cash, maximum cash is based on amount of income withdrawal *actually* drawn. May therefore be less.	Not normally available except for pre-8 April 1987 arrangements – but see calculation of income withdrawal amount below.	Up to 25% of non-protected rights fund in arrangement may be taken. If benefits are from transfer from occupational scheme, tax-free cash may be restricted to less than 25% of the fund.
Death during income withdrawal period: (a) Lump sums • If five-year guarantee selected at commencement of income withdrawal, balance of instalments payable between	(a) Lump sums • Return of contributions plus interest (or return of fund where secured by unit-linked policy).	(a) Lump sums • Payable subject to 35% tax charge. • Lump sum may be paid as a survivor's

Table 19.6 *(cont.)*

Occupational schemes	AVC and FSAVC schemes	Personal pension schemes
date of death and end of guarantee period may be paid based on 100% of GAD annuity at commencement of income withdrawal; *plus* Any difference between 100% of income withdrawal and amount of income withdrawal taken can be paid.		fund* – if a fund is nominated by the member or chosen by the scheme administrator; *or* • If no survivor's fund is nominated by the member or chosen by the scheme administrator, lump sum may be paid under the discretionary powers in the rules.
Example Five-year guarantee; 100% income withdrawal = £10,000 pa. Member takes £4,000 pa and dies after three years. Lump sum available on death: 2 × £10,000 = £20,000 3 × £6,000 = £18,000 Total £38,000 If annuity purchased in guarantee period, any guarantee on annuity is reduced by time elapsed since income withdrawal began.		*Survivor's fund needs to be chosen for survivor to have choice of lump sum, income withdrawal or annuity. If no survivor's fund chosen, only a lump sum can be paid.

275

Table 19.6 *(cont.)*

Occupational schemes	AVC and FSAVC schemes	Personal pension schemes
(b) Survivors' pensions benefits • Any remaining member's fund after provision of lump sum benefits can be used to provide survivors' pensions subject to Inland Revenue limits. • Any surplus dealt with under normal surplus rules for occupational schemes. • Must be aggregated with survivor's own right pension to determine Inland Revenue limits. • Survivor can elect for income withdrawal – annuity must be taken on earlier of survivor attaining 75 and date member would have attained 75.	(b) Survivors' pensions benefits • As for occupational schemes	(b) Survivors' pensions benefits • Only payable if a survivor's fund has been norminated by member or scheme administrator; survivor may then choose: – income withdrawal or – an annuity. • Can take lump sum within two years of member's death if income withdrawal taken. • If survivor under 60, can choose to defer annuity to start at age 60 but cannot then take income withdrawal or lump sum.

Notes:
(1) SSAS = small self-administered scheme; EPP = executive pension plan. Both are used for directors and key executives of companies.
(2) GAD = Government Actuary's Department.

fixed. Such investments should be regarded as a store for uninvested cash which may be required at short notice; in other words, as an alternative current account.

Fixed interest securities such as gilts do have a role for investors seeking income because the income flow is predictable and guaranteed. Once again, it might be unwise for an investor to put more than a small percentage of his investment in such an area since guarantees, contrary to popular belief, still represent an investment risk. Investments giving a guaranteed income as such should only be used as a major part of the portfolio if the need for income is very short term.

Individuals seeking a long-term rising income with capital appreciation should consider investing a reasonable portion of their lump sum in asset-backed investments such as unit trusts and insurance bonds, specifically those which invest in companies with good dividend records. Personal equity plans (PEPs) in existence on 5 April 1999 may continue, but further investments into them are not permitted. Any income and capital gains from PEPs will still be tax-free (although the PEP plan manager will only be able to reclaim the tax credit associated with UK dividends until April 2004).

The date 6 April 1999 marked the launch of a new, tax-free savings scheme known as an individual savings account (ISA) which replaced PEPs and tax exempt special savings accounts (TESSAs). Like PEPs, any income or capital growth from ISAs is free of personal taxes and ideally the first tranche of long-term capital should be invested in an ISA up to the current maximum. ISA managers can reclaim the tax credit on UK dividends until April 2004.

In the past, higher rate taxpayers were less interested in receiving investment income and would be more interested in achieving capital growth in order to make use of the CGT exemptions. If a higher rate taxpayer invested in a spread of low yielding unit trusts, there was a reasonable chance that even in the short term one or more of the funds would show a gain, hence giving the investor scope for profit taking within the CGT exemptions. As the top rate of tax on both income and capital is 40 per cent, higher rate taxpayers are unlikely to distort their investment decisions by trying to reduce income and increase their returns through capital growth.

Taking withdrawals from insurance bonds is also a popular way to supplement income in a tax efficient way. Insurance bonds have the further advantage that they have a wider spread of underlying investments than unit trusts, which enable the investor to have some exposure to property or take advantage of the managed fund concept.

To summarise: for individuals who are seeking income, then income producing ISAs, unit trusts and insurance bonds provide a very high quality secure source of income. Income can be received on regular dates throughout the year.

19.6 PRODUCING INCOME IN THE FUTURE

Most planholders who are already taking benefits from pension plans are less likely to require income in the future, but they may wish to provide income for succeeding generations. If this was the case, a broad spread of equities should protect the real value of an investment, while providing a reasonable income, and should form a part of the investment portfolio of any prudent investor.

19.7 GUARANTEED OPTIONS ON RETIREMENT

Scheme members approaching retirement with pension arrangements set up in the 1970s and early 1980s should consider the retirement options available. These arrangements may provide for annuities to be purchased on guaranteed annuity rates set at a time when annuity rates were higher than today. Some arrangements set up in the form of deferred annuities may provide favourable terms for converting part of the annuity into a cash sum. Both of these options may be better than exercising an 'open market option' and transferring the fund to another provider, even one which offers high annuity rates today.

19.8 PENSION MATURITIES – OPEN MARKET OPTIONS

Insurance companies must disclose the options available to policyholders who are considering retirement benefits under a pension plan (personal pensions including a stakeholder scheme, free standing additional voluntary contribution schemes and retirement annuities, and s 32/buy-out plans where there is an open market option in the contract terms). Companies have to explain the open market facilities and that policyholders may be able to improve their pension income by shopping around. The explanation must cover:

(1) the member's choice to buy an annuity from the current provider or from a different annuity provider;
(2) the reasons why the individual might want to use a different provider;
(3) the possibility of buying a higher income from another annuity provider;

(4) how to go about making use of the option, for example seeking independent advice.

A reminder of the right to shop around must be sent at least six weeks prior to the retirement date together with an estimate of the final value of the retirement fund.

These disclosure rules also apply to income drawdown arrangements and to plans where annuities are being phased over a period.

The Government intends to extend the requirement to inform policy-holders about open market options to members of defined contribution schemes.

19.9 EQUITY RELEASE PLANS

The saying 'capital rich, income poor' is more relevant today to retired people than for many years. On paper, many retired people are worth more, sitting in properties whose values have increased considerably and which could be used to provide a much-needed capital sum or income through an equity release plan. These plans allow access to some or all of the equity tied up in a property without the owner having to move house or having to demonstrate the means to repay a loan generated from that equity out of income.

Many retired people might find the simplest way of raising capital would be to sell their existing house, taking advantage of the current upward trend in prices and 'trade down' – buy a smaller house leaving a capital profit.

The problem is that some retired people may not be able to achieve all this without having to move away from their neighbourhood, perhaps to a different part of the country where they have no friends or associations. They will also have to bear the costs of selling their current home and buying a new one, like estate agents' fees, legal costs and stamp duty. For many retired people the process of selling up, finding a new home and building new relationships in a new town are too much to contemplate.

The alternative is an equity release plan that enables the homeowner to stay put but to release some of the profit that has built up over the years.

Some of the old home income plans or equity release plans involved borrowing money at variable interest rates which increased over time and which caused severe problems to the elderly planholders. Other variants to these plans involved the investment of the amount borrowed in a plan (an investment bond) where the investment returns reduced rather than increased, again causing cash-flow problems to the planholders.

There are now two main forms of equity release:

(1) reversion plans that involve the home owner selling a share in his property; and

(2) cash release or roll-up plans which require the owner to take out a loan secured on the property.

A mortgage is advanced against the security of domestic property. No capital or interest payments are required until a specified event occurs: the member (or the surviving member in joint cases) dies, the property is sold and another property is bought, for example the member goes into a nursing home, or the member wishes to end the plan voluntarily. The maximum amount that can be borrowed depends on the age of the applicant.

If the value of the house falls such that the proceeds of the sale on death are insufficient to pay off the mortgage a 'no negative equity' guarantee might come into play and makes good the difference. This means that the estate will never be left with a debt relating to the plan. Any growth in the value of the property (after repayment of the capital and interest) belongs to the planholder or the estate.

Equity release plans involve the individual, or couple, selling their property to the insurer which in turn pays a monthly annuity income based on part or all of the value of the property and provides a secure lifetime lease on the property. The initial annuity income is calculated allowing for the value of the property and the current age or ages of the applicants. Income in subsequent years can vary in line with the value of properties.

Another feature of equity release allows the planholder to retain a share in the value of the property, for example, to provide an inheritance for children or grandchildren. Planholders may also find a modest cash lump sum would be useful to top up their regular income. A facility can be arranged to allow the planholder to draw cash: the cash is provided by means of a loan secured against the planholder's interest in the eventual proceeds of the sale of the property. Interest on the loan is automatically deducted from the monthly income, whilst the capital value is repaid out of the property retention thereby reducing the remaining equity when the property is eventually sold.

19.10 PENSIONS SIMPLIFICATION

19.10.1 Limited period annuities

In its consultation document, 'Simplifying the taxation of pensions; increasing choice and flexibility for all', the Inland Revenue/Treasury proposes 'limited period annuities'. This would allow an individual to use part of the accumulated fund to buy an annuity for a fixed period, say, for three or five years. This facility might be useful to someone who is uncertain of their future beyond the short term, for example they may have a need to top up a reduced income from part-time employment. At the end of the period the annuitant could use the remainder of the fund with any growth to buy another limited period annuity or a lifetime annuity. This could be an alternative to income drawdown. If the annuitant dies before age 75 while receiving annuity income from a limited period annuity the remaining fund will be subject to tax at 35 per cent, as would apply under drawdown. When the initial fixed annuity is bought the individual might be in good health but when the second and/or subsequent annuity is bought the health of the individual might have deteriorated such that he may then be able to obtain the benefit of impaired life annuity rates.

19.10.2 Value protected annuities

This kind of annuity would make a residual payment on the death of the annuitant before age 75 equal to the difference between the amount paid out to buy the annuity and the stream of payments made under the annuity up to the date of death. Where an annuitant dies before age 75 a 35 per cent tax charge will apply to the residual fund.

Example 19.1

An individual uses his retirement fund of £100,000 at age 60 to buy a value protected value annuity of £9,000 a year. He dies after receiving four annual payments of £9,000. The maximum lump sum that can be paid is £41,600 calculated as follows:

Amount paid for annuity	£100,000
Annuity payments made	36,000
Residual fund	64,000
Tax at 35%	22,400
Lump sum death benefit	41,600

Alternatively the member's income can be established with an income guarantee for a minimum period – a conventional annuity. This would mean the annuity would be paid for the balance of the guarantee period in the event of death during that period. The guarantee period may not exceed ten years.

If an individual elects for a value protected value annuity initially it is not possible to switch to a guaranteed, conventional annuity.

Under the Inland Revenue's proposals for pensions simplification income will be payable in the following forms:

(1) **Secured benefits**: these are benefits a pension scheme or pension provider promises to pay for the member's life, for example pension payments from an occupational pension scheme or annuity payments from an insurer.

(2) **Unsecured benefits**: these benefits are similar to those payable under an income drawdown arrangement. There is no guarantee that they will be paid for life (because the fund from which the income is being withdrawn could be depleted and ultimately exhausted through poor investment performance and/or high withdrawals). There will be a number of conditions relating to unsecured benefits:

    (a) the minimum income must be at least £1 a year;
    (b) the maximum income will be based on the annuity that could be bought on the open market with the unsecured fund;
    (c) the maximum income must be reviewed at least every five years, or annually after age 75.

It will not be necessary to buy an annuity at age 75 as applies today under income drawdown arrangements. Instead income may continue to be drawn from the fund after age 75. However, no lump sum benefit may be payable where the member dies after age 75.

20

THE FUTURE

20.1 THE GREEN PAPER AND OTHER DEVELOPMENTS

In December 2002, the Department for Work and Pensions (DWP) published a Green Paper, 'Simplicity, security and choice: working and saving for retirement', in which it set out its proposals to simplify occupational and private pensions saving and make flexible retirement easier. This Green Paper was published at the same time as the consultation document from the Treasury and Inland Revenue which contained their radical proposals to simplify the pension tax rules. The reaction from many in the pensions industry was disappointment that the DWP Green Paper contained little that was new, although this reaction may have been because there were few immediate proposals for change. It also contrasted with the far-reaching nature of the Inland Revenue's proposals for tax changes to pensions. The proposals relating to simplification of the pensions tax rules are covered in Chapter 1.

The Green Paper responded to most of the proposals recommended by Alan Pickering in his independent report published in July 2002, 'A Simpler Way to Better Pensions', but generally it called for more consultation on the issues rather than making firm statements that changes will be made and taking immediate action. However, a new independent commission is being set up to report regularly to the DWP on the level of pension provision being achieved through voluntary pensions saving and to consider whether compulsory private saving should be introduced.

In June 2003, the Government issued its response to the consultation on the December 2002 Green Paper with another document entitled 'Working and saving for retirement: action on occupational pensions'. The following paragraphs summarise the response and set out the action that the Government states it will address. It is expected that most of the proposals will become law on 6 April 2005.

20.1.1 State Pension age

The Government is committed to leaving the State Pension age at age 65.

20.1.2 New influential bodies following on the Green Paper

A new Pensions Commission is being set up, chaired by Adair Turner. Its remit is to monitor and keep under review the private pension and long-term savings system, including if there is a case for additional compulsion. The Pensions Commission will publish an interim report in summer 2004; its first full report will be published in summer 2005.

An Employer Task Force is also being set up, chaired by Sir Peter Davis. The aim of this body is to increase and extend the employer's role in occupational and personal pension provision and to disseminate best practice. It will report to the Secretary of State for Work and Pensions within 18 months on the employer's role in pension provision.

20.1.3 Protection for defined benefit schemes

Pensions Protection Fund

The Government will introduce a new compensation scheme to guarantee members a specified minimum level of pension when the sponsoring employer becomes insolvent.

(1) It will be run by a statutory body.
(2) It will protect members of private sector defined benefit schemes where employers become insolvent with unfunded liabilities in the scheme.
(3) The Pensions Protection Fund will pay a maximum of 100 per cent of pensions in payment and 90 per cent of benefits for those who are still working. The final salary used to calculate any entitlement paid by the Pensions Protection Fund will be capped between £40,000 and £60,000 (subject to the views of the Employer Task Force and others).
(4) There will be a higher risk-based premium paid by schemes that are underfunded.
(5) Well-funded defined benefit schemes will pay a lower flat-rate levy.

This is likely to be a controversial area when details are announced. Well-run and well-funded schemes will object to having to subsidise poorly-run and underfunded schemes. The impact on the Fund of a large claim could be crippling. Some employers considering switching from a defined benefit scheme to a defined contribution scheme may decide that the cost of the Fund is another hurdle that they could avoid. The Government will not be the ultimate guarantor of the Fund.

Solvent employers of underfunded defined benefit schemes

The Government will now require solvent employers who wind up their defined benefit occupational pension scheme to meet their liabilities with a full buy-out of the rights of members. However, scheme trustees can agree a lower amount if a full buy-out would put the company itself at risk. Once laid, the regulations shall apply to schemes that begin to wind up on or after 11 June 2003. The regulations will be laid in summer 2003.

In addition, employers will only be able to take surpluses out of a defined benefit scheme if the scheme can meet its pension promise in full (ie it can fully buy-out benefits).

Statutory priority order

The statutory priority order sets out how assets of a scheme will be applied to meeting liabilities – currently, pensioners rank higher than non-pensioners and non-pensioners rank equally. Pensioners will still come first but changes will be made so that:

(1) members who contributed the longest will be protected the most; and
(2) priority will be given to non-pensioners over indexation of pensions in payment.

Draft regulations will be consulted on in summer 2003 and are expected to come into force in autumn 2003.

Scheme specific funding

Scheme specific funding will be introduced for defined benefit schemes instead of the prescriptive minimum funding requirement (MFR). The framework for this will be:

(1) statement of funding principles;
(2) full actuarial valuation of the scheme every three years;
(3) schedule of contributions;
(4) as a last resort, trustees will have powers to freeze or wind up the scheme if there are funding concerns;
(5) trustees will regularly need to send information to scheme members on the funding position of the scheme;
(6) clarification of the scheme actuary's duty of care to scheme members.

20.1.4 New type of pensions regulation and a new Pensions Regulator

The Government will introduce a new system of private pension regulation with a new Pensions Regulator to build on the foundations of Opra. The new regulator will be more risk-focused and proactive than Opra has been to date. The intention is that the FSA and new regulator will complement one another.

The Government recognises that pensions legislation needs to be restructured and simplified. In addition it will give the new Pensions Regulator the power to issue codes of practice (this will reduce the need to set out detail in regulations). This would mean that only breaches of legislation would be sanctionable: the Codes would represent the Regulator's view of the law.

20.1.5 Better informed and better trained trustees

Legislation will require trustees to be familiar with or have knowledge of their responsibilities. The codes of practice will state what is expected of trustees.

20.1.6 Extending TUPE protection to private sector

On private sector business transfers where there are existing pension arrangements, the Government envisages obliging the new employer to match employee contributions to a stakeholder scheme up to a level of 6 per cent.

20.1.7 Early leavers

Where employees, who have been scheme members for at least three months, leave during a vesting period they must be offered a choice of a refund of their own contributions (less tax) or a cash equivalent transfer value which they must transfer out to another occupational scheme or personal/stakeholder scheme of their choice. Schemes will still be able to have vesting periods of up to two years.

(This differs from the Green Paper, which proposed *immediate* vesting and compulsory *de minimis* transfers.)

20.1.8 Employers must consult before they change pension arrangements

The Government plans to issue a consultation document during summer 2003 on the implementation of the EU Information and Consultation Directive.

20.1.9 Limited Price Indexation

The Government has decided to reduce the cap on mandatory indexation of pensions in payment down to 2.5 per cent (from 5 per cent). This change will not affect pensions already in payment or any existing accrued rights. Price inflation is currently running at around 2.5 per cent. The lower indexation benefit should result in a reduced cost to the employer.

20.1.10 Amendment to the section 67 requirements

Section 67 of the Pensions Act restricts the ability of occupational pension schemes to change any member's accrued rights without the member's consent. The Government has altered its proposals for simplification and schemes will be able to make rules changes if:

(1) there is power in the scheme rules to make the change;
(2) the change does not involve converting defined benefit rights to defined contribution rights;
(3) the trustees approve the changes;
(4) the total actuarial value of the member's accrued rights is maintained;
(5) pensions already in payment are not reduced; and
(6) members are consulted before a change is made.

20.1.11 Member-nominated trustees

The minimum requirements will be in legislation backed by guidance from the new Pensions Regulator.

20.1.12 AVC facility

Occupational schemes will not need to offer an AVC facility. Instead they will be able to choose whether or not they want to do this. This is new and will be seen by employers as a useful means of simplifying scheme administration. (Scheme members, excluding those who are directors, with P60 earnings of less than £30,000 now have the facility to invest up to £3,600 a year into a stakeholder pension scheme.)

20.1.13 Contracting out

The Government intends to:

(1) simplify the procedures for contracting out of the State Second Pension (S2P);

(2) continue to explore options on simplifying administration of guaranteed minimum pensions (GMPs) and the anti-franking legislation;

(3) relax *some* restrictions on tax-free cash being taken from contracted-out rights;

(4) relax *some* restrictions on contracted-out rights being paid at the same time as other benefits;

(5) increase the trivial commutation level;

(6) not require member consent to commutation of equivalent pensions benefits (pre-1975 contracted-out rights) where that is the only benefit;

(7) allow commutation on serious ill health for contracted-out rights under personal pension schemes (this was not mentioned in the December 2002 Green Paper);

(8) allow contracted-out mixed benefit schemes to remain.

20.1.14 Other simplifications

These are as follows:

(1) to rationalise the rules on how occupational schemes communicate with members;

(2) to streamline internal dispute resolution rules;

(3) to clarify the jurisdiction of the Pensions Ombudsman so maladministration clearly falls within his remit;

(4) to simplify treatment of pensions on divorce (abolish safeguarded rights and align normal benefit age).

20.1.15 Information to members

Information requirements are as follows:

(1) to require all defined benefit schemes to issue annual benefit statements to their members showing the amount of pension already built up as well as the likely amount they will receive when they retire (most do this already);

(2) within the next five years, the Government hopes to be sending State Pension forecasts automatically to everyone of working age;

(3) to encourage further voluntary combined (State and private) pension forecasts to members on a regular basis: if the Government does not achieve sufficient coverage on combined pension forecasting it will then think about making it compulsory;

(4) continue to develop a web-based retirement planning tool so people can see their total projected pension income from both State and private sources;

(5) pilot a scheme to evaluate the effectiveness of different forms of pensions information and advice in the workplace. If the pilot is successful then legislation will compel employers to provide access to pensions information and advice.

20.1.16 Age discrimination

The timetable is as follows:

(1) In summer 2003 there will be consultation on the options for implementing age discrimination legislation.

(2) Legislation will be laid in late 2004.

(3) In late 2006, the legislation will come into force.

20.1.17 Retirement age

(1) By 2010 the earliest pension age from which a pension may be taken will have been increased from age 50 to age 55.

(2) The normal pension age in public service schemes will be increased to age 65 for new staff by the end of 2006 with transitional arrangements for existing staff.

20.1.18 Reforming incapacity benefits

Pilot schemes to help recipients of incapacity benefits return to work will start in late October 2003, with further tranche schemes in April 2004.

20.1.19 Issues dropped or deferred

Compulsory membership

The Government has decided not to allow employers to make compulsory membership of their occupational pension scheme a condition of employment for all new members. However, the Pensions Regulator could give general guidance that employers should ordinarily include employees unless they actively opt out (some employers already do this).

Changes to survivors' benefits

No changes are proposed despite the Pickering recommendations that employers should be able to simplify their schemes by dropping the need to provide survivors' benefits. Survivors' benefits will still be required.

20.1.20 The Government's agenda on other relevant topics

Tax simplification and annuity reform

(1) Further details on the Inland Revenue's radical plans to reform taxation of pensions will be published in autumn 2003.
(2) The Inland Revenue have confirmed that 6 April 2005 is the implementation date for reforms to the taxation of pension schemes including flexible retirement.
(3) The National Association of Pension Funds (NAPF) is helping the Inland Revenue come up with a solution on cross-subsidy between unconnected employers in a multi-employer scheme.

Sandler products

In summer 2003, details of the revised sales regime and product specifications for simplified investment products will be finalised.

20.1.21 The European Dimension

The UK pensions scene is increasingly affected by what happens in the rest of the European Union (EU). Pension scheme administrators of multinational companies have often complained that they have to run separate pension schemes in the European countries in which they employ staff. Local rules about taxation, regulation and social security have meant that it is very difficult to operate one large pension scheme across the EU. Although this is still a long way off, recent EU developments will help to bring about the 'pan-European pension scheme'. The European Commission has been working on a Pensions Directive for a long time, the most recent being published in October 2000. In May 2003, the Council of Finance Ministers agreed the Directive approved by the European Parliament in March 2003 and as a result the Directive has been adopted. Member states have two years to implement its provisions.

The key effects will be seen in four areas:

Prudential supervision of schemes to protect members

(1) The scheme must be registered with the regulator.
(2) Pension fund assets should be separated from the employer.
(3) There should be competent trustees.
(4) Information should be disclosed to scheme members and beneficiaries including target benefits on retirement, details of the funding position, investment options and management costs, and the annual report and accounts.

Minimum funding requirements

(1) An annual assessment of the scheme's ability to meet its liabilities is required although triennial valuations backed up with an annual statement will be permitted.
(2) Although this will affect defined benefit schemes, defined contribution schemes that provide enhanced benefits, for example on ill health retirement, will also be affected.
(3) Schemes should normally be fully funded. Although schemes in the domestic country will be allowed to fall below a fully-funded position for limited periods there must be a scheme-specific plan to revert to a fully-funded position. The scheme must be fully funded if it is to be used for cross-border purposes.
(4) If a scheme guarantees the payment of benefits, for example annuities, it must hold assets above its expected liabilities as a contingency, which could increase scheme costs.
(5) The regulator will have wide powers (wider than Opra's current powers and probably more in line with what the new UK regulator will have if the UK Government's proposals set out in the December 2002 Green Paper come into effect). These powers include access to scheme annual reports and actuarial valuations and assumptions.

Investment rules

To ensure that Member States have access to a single market the Directive will limit investment restrictions that individual states may impose. Member States must permit schemes to invest:

(1) at least 70 per cent in equity investments (although a lower amount will be allowed if a scheme provides benefits with a long-term interest guarantee, for example in Germany);
(2) at least 30 per cent of the assets covering funding requirements in non-matching currencies;
(3) in venture capital projects.

Despite these conditions the Directive permits Member States to impose more stringent conditions if they are prudently justified.

Investment by the pension fund in the employer is limited to 5 per cent.

Where a scheme is used for cross-border purposes a Member State may require that no more than 30 per cent of the assets may be invested in equities that are not traded on a regulated market in respect of scheme members resident within the borders of that Member State. This restriction only applies where the Member State places similar restrictions on its own domestic schemes.

Cross-border rules

Member States will be required to allow employers to contribute to schemes established in another Member State. Schemes must also be allowed to offer membership to individuals in another Member State. If scheme membership is offered to people in another Member State the scheme trustees must notify their own regulator, which in turn must notify the regulator of that other Member State. The scheme can only operate when the regulator of the other Member State has informed the domestic regulator of the rules and regulations relating to the occupational scheme under which the scheme must operate. The elements of this process are all subject to timescales during which the various parties must act.

Pan-European schemes

Although the Directive sets out a framework for pan-European schemes they are unlikely to come about until taxes and social security systems are harmonised. For example, the UK does not offer the same tax relief on pension contributions made to pension schemes in other Member States as it does to contributions to UK schemes. However, a number of cases from different Member States awaiting judgment by the European Court of Justice may help to clarify matters.

20.1.22 Civil partnership registration

In June 2003 the Department of Trade and Industry (DTI) published a consultation document proposing setting up a civil partnership registration scheme through which same-sex couples in England and Wales would be able to gain legal recognition for their partnerships. The scheme would be for adult same-sex couples who are not in an existing registered partnership or marriage and are not closely related. Couples would have new legal status as 'registered civil partners' and would acquire a package of rights and responsibilities.

Rights and responsibilities during the relationship might include:

(1) joint treatment of income-related benefits;
(2) joint State Pension benefits;
(3) ability to gain parental responsibility for each other's children.

Rights and responsibilities on dissolution might include:

(1) fair arrangements for property division;
(2) residence arrangements;
(3) appropriate contact with children.

Rights and responsibilities following the death of one partner might include:

(1) right to register the death of a partner;
(2) right to claim a survivor pension;
(3) eligibility for bereavement benefits;
(4) compensation for fatal accidents or criminal injuries;
(5) recognition under inheritance and intestacy rules;
(6) tenancy succession rights.

The impact on pension schemes will include additional costs, administration such as changes to scheme rules and business processes and communication with scheme members. However, the changes will not come as a surprise to employers, scheme administrators and trustees as case law in recent years has given an indication of the sorts of changes proposed in this consultation document.

20.1.23 Proposals to outlaw age discrimination

In July 2003, the DTI published a consultation document on proposals to outlaw age discrimination in the workplace by October 2006.

The Government is consulting on how the UK should implement the EU Employment Directive that prohibits age discrimination in employment and vocational training. The document 'Age Matters' seeks views on a range of specific policy aims including:

(1) the abolition of employers' mandatory retirement ages (dismissal at a given age) unless employers can objectively justify them;
(2) the possibility of a default retirement age of 70, at which employers could retire employees;
(3) proposed legitimate aims which employers, exceptionally, could use to help justify the retention of a small number of age-related practices; and
(4) changes to the legislation regarding unfair dismissal and redundancy.

APPENDIX 1
GLOSSARY OF TERMS

This glossary provides an explanation of expressions commonly used by pension scheme practitioners

Accrual rate   The fraction of earnings for each year of service which forms the basis of pension entitlement in a final salary or average salary scheme (eg 'one-sixtieth' for each year of pensionable service).

Accrued benefits   The benefits in respect of service up to a specific date calculated in relation to current earnings or projected final earnings. Sometimes known as accrued rights.

Actuarial certificate   A certificate given by an actuary, especially a certificate in respect of the solvency test required for contracted-out schemes.

Actuarial valuation   An investigation into whether a pension scheme has sufficient assets to meet its liabilities. The investigation is usually to assess the degree of solvency of the scheme, the funding level and to recommend a contribution rate.

Added years   This is a method of increasing a member's benefits where additional periods of pensionable service are provided, especially when a transfer payment has been made from a previous scheme. Sometimes members have the option of paying additional voluntary contributions in order to purchase added years, for example an additional three-sixtieths of final remuneration.

Additional component   The state earnings related pension above the *basic component.*

Additional voluntary contributions (AVCs)   Contributions over and above a member's normal contributions (if any), which a member may pay in order to secure additional benefits.

Administrator   The person notified to the Inland Revenue as being responsible for the management of the pension scheme. Often the trustee or employer.

AEI   Average Earnings Index.

Annuity   A regular guaranteed income, usually payable for life by an insurance company in return for a lump sum investment.

Anti-franking   The requirement that bans setting statutory increases in guaranteed minimum pension against other scheme benefits rather than adding the increase to the member's benefits.

Appropriate Personal Pension   A personal pension which is used to contract out of SERPS and which receives only the national insurance rebate, together with basic rate tax relief.

Bridging pension   A pension which bridges the gap between early retirement and normal retirement when the state pension becomes payable.

Buy back terms   An expression used to describe the payment of a *state scheme premium* to the DSS when a scheme ceases to be contracted out and to reinstate all or part of an individual's SERPS benefits.

Buy out plans   The purchase by pension scheme trustees of an insurance policy (a s 32 annuity) in the name of the beneficiary who gives up his entitlement to benefits under the scheme on leaving service.

CAT Standards   Minimum standards relating to charges, access and terms. Stakeholder pension schemes are subject to CAT standards.

Chapter I Scheme   A scheme approved under Chapter I of Part XIV, ICTA 1988. Defined benefit schemes, SSAS, executive pension plans and FSAVC schemes are approved under Chapter I. Defined contribution schemes may be approved under Chapter I or Chapter IV.

Chapter IV Scheme   A scheme approved under Chapter IV of Part XIV, ICTA 1988. Personal pension schemes are approved under this part of the law. Defined contribution occupational schemes can be approved under Chapter IV or under Chapter I.

COMBS   The abbreviation for a contracted-out mixed benefit scheme, an occupational pension scheme which has separate defined benefit and money purchase sections and which contracts out on both bases.

COMP   The abbreviation for a contracted-out money purchase scheme.

COSRS   The abbreviation given to an occupational pension scheme which is contracted out on a salary-related basis.

Concurrency   Membership of an occupational pension scheme and a personal pension scheme (including a stakeholder pension scheme) for the same period of employment.

Continuation option   Where a member leaves a pension scheme which also provided life assurance benefits, the insurance company underwriting those benefits may grant the facility to continue cover under a life assurance policy, without having to provide evidence of health. There is normally a time limit of one month after leaving the scheme for the facility to be taken up.

Contract out   Where an occupational pension scheme is used to provide its members with a level of benefits replacing part of the earnings related state scheme benefits that they *would* have enjoyed had they not been members of a contracted-out scheme. Contributions to the state scheme in respect of employees who are contracted out are lower than for employees who are not contracted out.

Contracting-out certificate The certificate issued by the Contributions Agency (an executive office of the Inland Revenue which administers the national insurance contributions system) to a scheme which meets the conditions for contracting out.

Contributions equivalent premium (CEP) A type of state scheme premium which may be paid when a member leaves an occupational pension scheme after a short period of contracted out employment. The state scheme then takes over the obligation to provide the member with his **guaranteed minimum pension**.

Controlled funding A type of funding commonly used in connection with insured final earnings schemes, where the contributions are assessed to the liabilities of the pension scheme as a whole rather than for individual members.

Decision tree A tool, in the form of algorithms, to help a potential investor decide whether to join a stakeholder pension scheme.

Deductive amount A reduction in pension or pensionable earnings in order to achieve a degree of integration with the state scheme.

Deposit administration A type of insurance policy where contributions, after expense charges, are accumulated and to which interest and/or bonuses are added. The interest usually reflects prevailing interest rates or building society lending rates.

Director Special rules apply to persons classed as directors (normally of private limited companies). A 20 per cent director is one who either on his own or with one or more associates beneficially owns or is able to control directly or indirectly or through other companies 20 per cent or more of the ordinary share capital of the company.

Discretionary scheme A scheme where employees to be included are selected by the employer on a purely discretionary basis. The discretion normally extends to benefits and contributions for each member.

Dynamisation The index linking of earnings for determining *final remuneration* for the purpose of Inland Revenue limits. The term is sometimes also used to describe escalation or indexation.

Earmarking An order of the court under a divorce settlement directing pension scheme trustees or managers to pay part, or all, of the member's benefits to the divorced party at the time they become available to the member.

Earnings cap The maximum amount of earnings that may be pensioned, and in respect of which a member may make personal contributions under an occupational scheme, currently £99,000 (2001/02). Also, the maximum earnings in respect of which contributions may be paid to a personal pension scheme in 2003/04.

Earnings threshold The maximum amount that can be paid to a personal pension scheme approved under Chapter IV, ICTA 1988 without the need for net relevant earnings: curently £3,600.

Equivalent pension benefit (EPB)   The benefit which must be provided for an employee who was contracted out of the former graduated pension scheme during the period 6 April 1961 and 5 April 1975 (sometimes known as the Boyd-Carpenter scheme).

Executive pension plan   A scheme for selected directors or employees.

Exempt approved scheme   An approved scheme established under an irrevocable trust and thus enjoying the tax relief specified in the Finance Acts.

Expression of wish   Where a member makes a nomination indicating his wishes for the destination of death benefits to the trustees of the scheme. They are not bound by the nomination, however.

FRS 17   A statement that must be made in a company's accounts, mainly relating to defined benefits schemes. It requires the scheme's assets and liabilities to be valued on a 'fair value' basis with any surplus or deficit appearing in the company's balance sheet as an asset or liability. Detailed disclosure of information must also appear in the notes to the company's accounts.

Final salary scheme   A pension scheme where the benefit is calculated with reference to the member's pensionable earnings at or around retirement or leaving service.

Financial Services Authority (FSA)   The FSA is responsible for the broad framework for the regulation of investment business.

Fixed revaluation rate   The rate by which a final salary contracted-out scheme may revalue the **guaranteed minimum pension** where a member's contracted out employment ceases.

Free cover   The maximum amount of death benefit which an insurance company covering a group of lives is prepared to underwrite for each individual without requiring evidence of health.

Free standing AVC   An additional contribution, by a member of an occupational scheme, to another scheme which is completely separate. The total of the individual's contributions to both schemes is limited to 15 per cent of remuneration.

GN11 certificate   A certificate issued by the scheme actuary to the scheme trustees to show that a cash equivalent has been calculated in accordance with legislative requirements and actuarial guidance.

Guaranteed annuity option   Where the proceeds of an insurance policy may be used to buy an annuity at a rate guaranteed in the policy which may also include an open market option.

Guaranteed minimum pension (GMP)   The minimum pension which a contracted-out scheme must provide for pre-6 April 1997 service. The state benefits payable in respect of a contracted out employee are reduced by the amount of guaranteed minimum pension. Future GMPs were abolished from April 1997 and no further GMP entitlement will accrue after that date but existing GMPs will remain within schemes until members reach state pension age.

Hancock annuity   A type of immediate annuity purchased by an employer when an employee retires.

Individual Pension Account (IPA)   A new type of pension investment vehicle designed to extend the use of unit trusts and open-ended investment companies for pension saving in the post-April 2001 pension tax regime. An IPA is not an approved pension scheme.

Industry-wide schemes   Multi-member schemes set up by a number of employers operating in a similar industry, for example the printing industry. Members moving between employers within the scheme are deemed to have continuous service.

Integration   Where a pension scheme is designed to take into account part or all of the state scheme benefits.

Joint notice   A document which is completed by an individual and a pension provider and sent to the DWP stating that the personal pension scheme entered into by the individual is to be used for contracting out of SERPS and requesting the National Insurance Contributions Office to remit the minimum contribution to it.

Letter of exchange   A letter which constitutes the formal setting up of an individual pension arrangement which comes into effect when the employee acknowledges its receipt in writing.

Limited price indexation (LPI)   The requirement to guarantee pension increases in line with increases in the Retail Prices Index (RPI), subject to a maximum of 5 per cent per annum. It applies to pensions accrued in respect of service after 5 April 1997.

Low earnings threshold   In relation to the State Second Pension, an employee earning below the low earnings threshold but above the lower earnings limit is treated as earning an amount equal to the low earnings threshold.

Lower earnings limit   The lower earnings limit on which an employee's national insurance benefits are based. It is the minimum amount which must be earned before NI contributions are payable, and is approximately equal to the basic pension for a single person.

Market level indicator   An index giving a weighted comparison of values of fixed interest securities and equities, and used to adjust the amount of state scheme premiums.

Member Nominated Director (MND)   A person who is a director of a corporate trustee of an occupational pension scheme under arrangements required by the Pensions Act 1995.

Member Nominated Trustee   A person who becomes a trustee of an occupational pension scheme under arrangements required by the Pensions Act 1995.

Minimum funding requirement (MFR)   A method which a scheme actuary must use to value the assets and liabilities of a defined benefits occupational scheme. The Paul Myners Review of Institutional Investment, published in March 2001, recommended that the MFR should be replaced by a regime based on transparency and disclosure under which pension funds would report publicly on the current state of the fund and on future investment plans.

Money purchase scheme   A scheme where benefits are directly determined by the value of contributions paid in respect of each member as opposed to a scheme which provides benefits related to earnings.

New code   The code of approval of occupational pension schemes which was introduced by FA 1970, Pt II, Ch II.

Normal retirement date   The date at which a member of a pension scheme normally becomes entitled to receive his retirement benefits.

Old code   The code of approval of occupational pension schemes which applied before the passing of FA 1970: approval under the old code ended on 5 April 1980, if it had not already been replaced by new code approval.

Open market option   The option to use the proceeds of an insured pension contract to buy an annuity at a current market annuity rate from the original insurer or from another insurer.

Opra   The Occupational Pensions Regulatory Authority. Its role is to investigate schemes, to ascertain whether regulatory provisions are being complied with, and to take action to rectify non-compliance.

Paid up benefit   A preserved benefit secured for an individual member under an assurance policy where premiums have ceased to be paid in respect of that member.

Pension Schemes Office   The Inland Revenue branch which dealt with the approval of pension schemes. Now part of the Inland Revenue department, IR Savings, Pensions, Share Schemes.

Pension sharing   The splitting of a member's benefits between the member and the divorced spouse under a divorce settlement. Benefits may be split within the scheme or by means of a transfer payment.

Pensionable earnings   The earnings on which benefits and/or contributions are calculated. Pensionable earnings may differ from actual remuneration in that they may exclude various items such as bonuses, overtime, commission and directors' fees.

Pensioneer trustee   An individual widely involved with pension schemes and accepted by the Revenue as being a trustee of a small self-administered scheme.

Personal Investment Authority (PIA)   The regulatory organisation formed to replace the separate authorities LAUTRO and FIMBRA but now subsumed into the **Financial Services Authority**.

Pooled Fund   A fund (eg unit trusts and managed funds) managed by investment managers on behalf of different owners, for example scheme trustees or individual pension plan holders.

Practice notes   The vast majority of occupational pension schemes are approved by the Inland Revenue under its discretionary powers currently embodied in Practice Note IR 12 (2001) (See Appendix 2).

Further publications describe Inland Revenue practice on personal pension schemes, free-standing AVC schemes and simplified schemes.

Protected rights   That part of a personal pension scheme or contracted-out money purchase scheme that represents the fund accumulated by contributions paid by the DWP. These rights are separated from any other benefits built up by the member's or the employer's contributions, as restrictions are imposed on the options available in respect of protected rights.

Purchased life annuity   An annuity purchased privately by an individual where instalments of annuity are subject to tax only in part (ICTA 1988, s 656).

Reduction in yield (RIY)   A method used to express the charges and expenses under a personal pension plan. The RIY shows the percentage reduction in annual growth over the term of the plan.

Reference Scheme Test   The scale of benefits which a salary-related scheme must provide if it is to be used for contracting-out purposes beyond 5 April 1997. The benefits are:

- Benefits under the scheme must be payable at 65, for life.
- Benefits must be not less than one-eightieth of average qualifying earnings in the last three tax years before the end of service, multiplied by years of service.
- Qualifying earnings are to be 90 per cent of the earnings on which national insurance contributions are paid.
- Pension is not required to exceed 50 per cent of the earnings upon which pension is calculated (which effectively limits the pension to 40 years of service).
- Qualifying earnings are to be 90 per cent of the earnings between the lower and upper earnings limits.
- Spouse's pension: 50 per cent of the member's pension (based on completed service for members who die before age 65).
- All benefits for service after 6 April 1997 must increase by 5 per cent or RPI, if lower.

Relevant benefits   Any benefits given in connection with the termination of service except for benefits given only in the event of accident (see ICTA 1988, s 612).

Remuneration limit   The limit is currently £30,000 (and may be amended by a Treasury Order). Individuals who are not controlling directors may be members of an occupational pension scheme and contribute to a personal pension scheme at the same time provided their P60 earnings do not exceed £30,000.

Requisite benefits   The scale of benefits which, prior to November 1986, a pension scheme had to provide as one of the conditions to allow it to contract out.

Retained benefits   Retirement or death benefits in respect of an employee's earlier service with a former employer or an earlier period of self-employment.

SIPP   A self-invested personal pension.

SSAP 24   The abbreviation given to the accounting standard 'Statement of Standard Accounting Practice'. It refers to the statement which has been issued by the accountancy bodies concerning accounting for pension costs in company accounts: certain items of information must be disclosed about a company's pension arrangements, for example the results of the most recent actuarial valuation and the long-term contribution rate required to meet the cost of pension benefits.

S2P   An abbreviation for the State Second Pension. The State Second Pension is a reformed SERPS that will provide a more generous additional state pension for low and moderate earners.

Salary sacrifice   An agreement, normally in the form of an exchange of letters between an employer and an employee where the employee gives up part of his salary. The employer is then able to make a corresponding increase in his contribution to the pension scheme.

Section 32 policy   An insurance policy which is used to receive a transfer value from an occupational pension scheme. Sometimes called a 'buy out' plan. A s 32A policy is used to secure the protected rights of a member on the winding-up of a COMPS.

Section 67 of the Pensions Act   This restricts the ability of occupational pension scheme trustees to change any member's accrued rights without the member's consent (although there are proposals to simplify this, possibly from 6 April 2005). The actuarial value of the member's rights would still be maintained.

Section 148 orders   Orders issued each year in accordance with s 148 of the Social Security Administration Act 1992, setting out the rates of increase to be applied in the earnings factors on which the additional component and guaranteed minimum pension are based. This revaluation is based on the increase in national average earnings, and was previously known as s 21 orders.

Section 226 plan   The old name for a retirement annuity. The current legislative reference is s 620 (of ICTA 1988).

Segregated fund   An arrangement between scheme trustees and investment managers, where scheme investments are managed by the investment managers independently of other assets. The assets are typically a portfolio of individual stocks and shares, in contrast to a pooled fund.

Self-administered scheme   A scheme (usually small) where the assets are invested by the trustees in a range of media.

Special contributions   Contributions paid by the employer (or, rarely, by a member) for a limited period or as a single payment to provide augmented benefits for a member or to meet deficiencies in funding levels.

State pension age   The age from which pensions are normally payable by the state scheme, currently 60 for women and 65 for men. By 2020 state pension ages will be equalised at age 65.

Top hat scheme   An alternative term for the executive pension plan.

Transfer payment   A payment made by the trustees of one pension scheme to the trustees of another when a member leaves employment to enable the receiving pension scheme to give additional benefits. Sometimes called a 'cash equivalent'.

Trivial pension   A pension which is so small that it can be exchanged for a cash sum.

Unit-linked pension scheme   Usually an individual arrangement where the amount of retirement benefits is related to the units in an investment fund and the value of the fund varies according to the value of the units.

Upper earnings limit   The amount of earnings (approximately seven times the lower earnings limit) on which contributions are payable to the state scheme.

Vested rights   The benefits under the scheme to which a member is unconditionally entitled if he were to leave service including related benefits for dependants.

Waiting period   Period of service which an employee may have to serve before being entitled to join a pension scheme.

Whistleblower   Under the terms of the Pensions Act 1995 if the scheme actuary or scheme auditor has reasonable cause to believe that any duty relevant to the administration of the scheme is not being complied with and that the failure is likely to be of material significance to OPRA, he must report the matter to OPRA.

Winding-up   The process of terminating an occupational pension scheme and applying the scheme assets to buy annuities for scheme members and their beneficiaries, for example through **section 32 policies**.

APPENDIX 2
EXTRACT FROM OCCUPATIONAL PENSION SCHEMES PRACTICE NOTES IR 12 (2001)

(*As at July 2003*)

Insured Schemes: Loans to Employers (made on or after 1/12/99)

Background

16.61 Government policy on self-investment (i.e. the investment of pension scheme funds in the employer's business) does not preclude the use of certain pension scheme policies as security for a loan to the employer (or to any *Associated Employer* whether or not they participate in the scheme) for a genuine business purpose. Only policies (or such part thereof) taken out solely to secure benefits for a *controlling director* are suitable for this purpose and the conditions on which the loan is made must satisfy a number of Inland Revenue requirements.

Purpose of PS8 certificate

16.62 The PS 8 certificate [reproduced on pp. 312–316] is designed to enable *IR SPSS* to dispense with the need to examine documentation relating to the loan and to concentrate on monitoring the circumstances and the use of the loan itself. There is generally no requirement to provide *IR SPSS* with any related documentation but *IR SPSS* reserves the right to call for documentation in particular cases. If *IR SPSS* is satisfied with the circumstances of the loan a simple acknowledgement will be issued within 4 weeks of the receipt of the notification. Otherwise the trustees and the life office will be asked for more information or instructed to obtain immediate repayment of the loan.

Facility not to be abused

16.63   The facility of obtaining loans by using pension scheme policies as security must not be operated in such a way as to call into question the sole purpose requirement of section 590(2)(a). A succession of regular loans to bring the total loan outstanding to the maximum permitted might suggest that the employer is using the facility to only partly fund the scheme while claiming a tax deduction for the total pension contributions (see also paragraph 20.57). If such a succession is not to prejudice the approval of the scheme it should be for a genuine commercial reason and not normally extend beyond 2 years.

Conditions to be Satisfied For a Loan to be Acceptable

Loans must be commercial – what is a commercial loan?

16.64   The basic underlying principle is that the loan to the employer (or *Associated Employer*) should be made on commercial terms. In order to satisfy this basic principle the loan must:-

(a) be at a commercial rate of interest (i.e. at least Clearing Bank Base Rate + 3% will normally be accepted. See also paragraph 16.65 below)

(b) have a duration commensurate with the purpose of the loan (see paragraphs 16.66 and 16.67 below)

(c) be used for the purposes of the borrower's trading activities (see paragraph 16.68 below)

(d) not be made to companies in financial difficulties (see Update No 43 and paragraph 16.69 below)

(e) be secured against a policy (or part thereof) that is specifically and solely for the provision of benefits for a member who is a *controlling director* of the borrower and who has consented to the policy (or part thereof) being used as security for the loan, and

(f) not exceed 50% of the current value of the policy or policies used to secure the loan (if the lending takes place within 2 years of the establishment of the scheme the amount shall not exceed 25% of the current value of the policy excluding the value of any transfer values received and included therein).

Interest rate less than CBBR+3%

16.65   Where the rate of interest is less than 3% above the current base rate of a particular clearing bank (see paragraph 1(c) of the certificate) written evidence will be required to show that the borrower can obtain a loan on similar terms from an arms-length financial institution.

Duration of loan – maximum

16.66   The maximum duration for such loans is a period expiring 1 year before the *normal retirement date* of the member whose policy (or part thereof) is used as security for the loan.

(a) **Normal**
    This is, however, the maximum period for which the loan can be made and will be acceptable only in exceptional circumstances. Normally the duration of such loans would not be expected to be more than 3 to 5 years. For some purposes, e.g. the purchase of stock in trade, a duration of 1 year or less may be more appropriate.

(b) *IR SPSS* **may object to duration**
    Where the duration of the loan appears to be unusually long in the light of its stated purpose, *IR SPSS* may make enquiries and if appropriate insist that the duration of the loan be reduced to a more realistic period.

(c) **Level capital repayments**
    The duration of the loan will not be permitted to exceed 2 years unless the terms of the loan provide for level capital repayments throughout the loan period with capital repayments being made at least every 6 months.

Amendment to loan agreement

16.67   If the life office and the borrower wish to amend the terms of the loan then fresh documentation and a PS 8 certificate will be required. *IR SPSS* may require the loan to be immediately repaid unless the amendment is for acceptable commercial reasons. If the duration of the loan is to be extended, *IR SPSS* will normally expect the loan agreement to require regular repayments of capital throughout the duration of the loan as well as interest payments. It is unlikely that *IR SPSS* will accept more than two amendments to the terms of the loan.

Restriction on purpose of loan

16.68   The employer (or *Associated Employer*) may not lend the money on to someone else nor use it for some purely speculative purpose such as the purchase of shares or other investment. It may, however, be acceptable in some circumstances for a holding company to use such monies to make or manage share investments in its 50% trading subsidiaries.

Credit check required

16.69   Before the trustees of the scheme grant security for the loan, a credit check on the borrower must be undertaken and the results disclosed to *IR SPSS* when the PS 8 is submitted. There is no requirement for the credit check to take any particular form. However, the credit check should be undertaken no more than 4 weeks before the loan is made. If the credit check does not provide a rating and a financial strength indicator then it should include at least three or more years of analysed accounts (or from when the company commenced trading), the date of the latest accounts and returns filed, details of any County Court Judgements and mentions in Legal Gazette. Although there is no requirement for the credit check to include any form of rating, the inclusion of such a rating would be preferred and would significantly reduce the probability of *IR SPSS* making any further enquiries regarding the loan or requiring the loan to be repaid.

(a) **Injudicious loans**
If *IR SPSS* do not consider the granting of security to be a judicious act by the trustees *IR SPSS* may require the loan to be repaid. Clearly any loan made to an ailing or insolvent company will not be acceptable.

(b) **Information provided by trustees**
IR SPSS will take into consideration any other information that the trustees of the scheme wish to attach to the PS 8 in support of their decision to grant security for the loan, e.g. copies of the latest company accounts, cash flow projections etc.

(c) **Certainty**
If the trustees wish to have certainty that *IR SPSS* is satisfied that a loan was not injudicious then the trustees should ensure that all facts material to the financial health of the borrower are disclosed.

(d) **Acceptable level of risk**
The level of risk considered acceptable will depend on several factors including the financial health of the company, the duration of the loan and whether the terms of the loan provide for ongoing capital repayments throughout the period of the loan.

(e) **Trustees to demonstrate loan is judicious**
If there is insufficient information provided by the credit check and the trustees to determine that a loan is judicious then *IR SPSS* will require the loan to be repaid unless the trustees can justify the granting of the security.

Injudicious loan can lead to loss of approval

16.70 The PS 8 has been amended to carry a warning that the making of an injudicious loan or the securing of an injudicious loan on scheme policies or failure otherwise to comply with *IR SPSS* requirements may lead to the loss of approval of the scheme (see Part 19).

40% tax charge

16.71   Loss of approval of the scheme will give rise to a tax charge under section 591C ICTA 1988 of 40% of the scheme assets (see paragraph 19.5).

Other significant tax consequences as set out in Part 19 will also apply.

No further loans when arrears exist

16.72   No further loans may be made to an employer (or *Associated Employer*) secured on scheme policies whilst interest and/or capital is in arrears on an existing loan made to that employer or to an *Associated Employer* secured on scheme policies. This prohibition extends to loans from any other schemes of the borrower whether or not there are any arrears in respect of loans made by these schemes.

No topping up provisions

16.73   A loan agreement should not include a provision for future topping up. If an additional loan is necessary, it must be the subject of separate documentation and a separate certificate.

Waiving of interest

16.74   In some cases the growth in value of the policy used to secure the loan is linked to the interest paid on the loan. Where there is any link between the loanback and the policy returns the interest payable on the loanback may not be waived nor the rate of interest reduced. It is only permissible to waive the interest or to reduce the rate of interest payable in circumstances where this will not have any effect on the scheme policies or on the growth in value of those policies.

Restrict director's lump sum

16.75   Any reduction of benefits as a result of foreclosure will be first effected against any lump sum retirement benefits payable.

The restriction on the director's lump sum retirement benefits will be lifted to the extent of the amounts recovered by the scheme trustee(s) under the rights acquired as a result of foreclosure.

Allocation of outstanding interest when paid

16.76   Where interest is not paid by the borrower on the due and payable dates, any payments to life offices intended as repayments of interest or capital will be set off first against current and outstanding interest with any balance then being set off against capital.

PS 8 Certificate

PS 8 Certificate – Information required

16.77   The certificate PS 8 on which loans to employers (or *associated employers*) are reported must be sent to *IR SPSS* (within 90 days of the making of the loan) and requires the following information:-

(a) the identity of the borrower
(b) the results of the credit check (see paragraph 16.69 above) attached to the PS 8 together with any other information that the trustees may wish *IR SPSS* to take into account when considering whether or not the granting of security by the trustees was a judicious act
(c) certification that the policies used to secure the loan are for *controlling director*s only
(d)   certification of the purpose for which the loan is sought
(e) the duration of the loan
(f) the rate of interest chargeable on the loan and the details of when the interest becomes due and payable.

Who signs PS 8?

In addition the PS 8 and certifications should be signed by both the employer (or *Associated Employer*) and the trustees of the scheme. It is not acceptable for anyone to sign the PS 8 on behalf of the trustees and/or the employer.

If the employer is also the trustee then this may require the employer to sign twice in two separate capacities.

Consequences of Foreclosure

Trustees acquire a right of action

16.78   Where a life office has recourse to security given by the pension scheme trustees, the trustees acquire, under general law, the right to the original debt. This means that after foreclosure there will be a right of action by the trustees against the employer.

Loan judicious but borrower unable to repay loan

16.79   Where:

(a) the granting of security by the scheme trustee(s) was judicious, and
(b) repayment of the original debt has become impossible, (e.g. where the employer is in liquidation and the liquidator has indicated that there will be no dividend payable to the scheme), and

(c) *IR SPSS* is satisfied that the situation has arisen because of genuine commercial reasons,

the approval of the scheme will not be withdrawn provided that there are no other facts concerning the scheme or its administration that warrant withdrawal of approval.

No charge under s601 ICTA 1988 arises

16.80   Any rights accruing to the scheme as a result of foreclosure in the above circumstances will have no value and can be waived without giving rise to a tax charge under section 601 ICTA 1988 (see paragraph 17.38). In these circumstances the scheme will not become a self-administered scheme.

Restrict lump sum benefit

16.81   Any reduction of benefits as a result of foreclosure will be first effected against any lump sum retirement benefits payable.

Loan judicious but borrower won't pay rather than can't pay

16.82   Where the granting of security by the trustee(s) was judicious but foreclosure takes place even though the employer is capable of repaying the original debt either at the date of foreclosure or at some future date, e.g. where the employer is continuing to trade or hold assets following foreclosure, the rights acquired by the trustee(s) as a result of foreclosure have value. In this situation the waiving of those rights will be a transfer of value to the employer. This will have tax consequences under section 601 ICTA 1988 and will also be grounds for the withdrawal of the approval of the scheme.

How to avoid loss of approval

16.83   The approval of the scheme will not, however, be withdrawn where the granting of security by the trustees was judicious and, following foreclosure the rights acquired by the trustees have value, provided that *IR SPSS* is satisfied that there are no other facts concerning the scheme or its administration that warrant the withdrawal of approval and the trustees have:

(a) immediately enforced their rights against the employer, or
(b) have reached a commercial arrangement whereby the outstanding capital, together with the outstanding interest, will be paid to the scheme trustees within a reasonable period of time.

Continuation of approval will be conditional on the commercial arrangement agreed with *IR SPSS* being adhered to.

Scheme may become a SSAS

16.84   Where acceptable arrangements are made the scheme will be holding an asset which is not an insurance policy. Whether or not this is an investment will be a question of fact and the scheme may have become a self-administered scheme as a result. An approved scheme which becomes a small self-administered scheme must comply with the requirements of the "SSAS Regulations" as subsequently amended as at the time it becomes such a scheme and thereafter (see paragraph 20.1).

Restriction on benefits and how to avoid it

16.85   The reduction of the *controlling director*s benefits will be lifted to the extent of the amounts recovered by the scheme trustees from the employer under the rights acquired as a result of foreclosure. To avoid a restriction to the lump sum retirement benefits the amounts must be recovered before the lump sum retirement benefits are paid.

Injudicious loan leads to loss of approval

16.86   Where the granting of the security by the trustees was injudicious approval of the scheme will normally be withdrawn. The repayment of the loan and all interest due can usually prevent the loss of approval in these circumstances. Where foreclosure takes place even though the employer is capable of repaying the original debt, a tax charge under section 601 ICTA 1988 will also arise if the acquired rights are waived or not enforced.

How to avoid loss of approval

16.87   Where the granting of security was approved by *IR SPSS* then the withdrawal of approval of the scheme on the grounds that the loan was injudicious can only take place if *IR SPSS* demonstrates that:

(a) there was information available to the trustees relevant to the financial state of the company at the time the loan was made, which was not disclosed to *IR SPSS* with the PS 8 certificate, and which would have affected the decision made by *IR SPSS*, or

(b) the information provided to *IR SPSS* was incorrect or misleading.

Notifications Required

IR SPSS must be notified of all loans made

16.88   *IR SPSS* must be notified of all such loans within 90 days by means of a completed certificate (PS 8) that the loan and the scheme documentation meet the necessary requirements. The certificate details all the requirements which need to be certified and all the undertakings required. Customers are free to photocopy the certificate for use but must submit them to *IR SPSS* on the same coloured paper as the official form as indicated on the Appendix II specimen. Customers on our bulk forms users database will be supplied immediately with copies of the new certificate. Any customer who wants to obtain copies of the new certificate should ring *IR SPSS* Supplies Line on 0115 974 1670.

Notify *IR SPSS* of foreclosure

16.89   The lender must notify *IR SPSS* whenever foreclosure on a scheme policy takes place within 30 days of the event in question.

Notify *IR SPSS* if interest is outstanding

16.90   If interest or capital is outstanding 90 days after the due date for payment then the life office should report this to *IR SPSS* within a further 30 days.

Notify amendment

16.91   If an existing loan agreement is amended, a new PS 8 certificate should be submitted to *IR SPSS* within 90 days of the amendment.

Notify *IR SPSS* if contributions cease

16.92   If the payment of regular contributions under the scheme for the *controlling director* whose policy (or part thereof) is being used as security for the loan ceases, *IR SPSS* must be notified by the life office within 90 days of such cessation. If the life office is aware of the reason for cessation of contributions this information should be included with the notification.

Self-Managed Funds

16.93   Where an insured earmarked scheme uses a policy linked to an investment fund (usually held in the name of the insurers) exclusive to that scheme, such investment funds are regarded as self-managed funds and *IR SPSS* will, under their discretionary powers (section 591(1) ICTA 1998), require as a condition of continued approval that fund to comply with Regulations 4 to 8 of the "SSAS Regulations" as subsequently amended (see paragraph 20.1) despite the fact that the scheme is not strictly a small self-administered scheme. Such self-managed funds should therefore be managed in accordance with those Regulations and paragraphs 20.45 to 20.82 are pertinent to them. This requirement does not, however, apply to investments made before 31 December 1992.

PS 8 CERTIFICATE

DOCUMENTATION CERTIFICATE: LOAN TO EMPLOYER OR COMPANY ASSOCIATED WITH EMPLOYER

Certificate for the purposes of approval or continued approval under Chapter 1 Part XIV ICTA 1988

This certificate must be sent to IR (Savings, Pensions, Share Schemes) at [Audit & Pension Schemes Services, Yorke House, PO Box 62, Castle Meadow Road, Nottingham NG2 1BG] within 90 days of making any loan secured on scheme policies to an employer participating in the scheme or to a company associated with such an employer (*see note 1*).

IR (SPSS) reserves the right to call for a copy of the loan agreement for any particular loan.

Please remember that the making of an injudicious loan or the securing of an injudicious loan on scheme policies (*see note 2*) or failure otherwise to comply with Inland Revenue requirements may lead to the loss of approval of the scheme. This will give rise to a tax charge under s591C ICTA 1988 of 40% of the scheme assets. Other significant tax consequences will also apply as set out in Part 19 of the Practice Notes IR12 (1997).

Please read the notes overleaf before completing this form.

NAME OF PRINCIPAL EMPLOYER ⎯⎯⎯⎯⎯⎯⎯⎯⎯⎯⎯⎯⎯

NAME OF SCHEME ⎯⎯⎯⎯⎯⎯⎯⎯⎯⎯⎯⎯⎯⎯⎯⎯⎯⎯⎯

⎯⎯⎯⎯⎯⎯⎯⎯⎯⎯⎯⎯⎯⎯⎯⎯⎯⎯⎯⎯⎯⎯⎯⎯⎯⎯⎯⎯⎯⎯

SF REF NO ⎯⎯⎯⎯⎯ / ⎯⎯⎯⎯⎯⎯

LIFE OFFICE REFERENCE ⎯⎯⎯⎯⎯⎯⎯⎯⎯⎯⎯⎯⎯⎯⎯⎯⎯⎯

I certify

1. that in relation to a loan to the employer or to a company associated with the employer (the borrower) from ⎯⎯⎯⎯⎯⎯⎯ (the lender) on the security of a scheme policy, the borrower, the lender, the trustees of the scheme and the member, being a controlling director of the borrower, whose scheme benefits the policy is intended to secure have entered into a loan agreement satisfying all the following conditions:

a. that the member has agreed to his or her interest in the policy being used as security for the loan;
b. that the policies used to secure the loan are for controlling directors only;
c. that the borrower shall pay interest on the outstanding balance of the loan at a rate of interest which (subject to adjustments not being required more frequently than monthly) shall not at any time be less than either:
   i. 3 per cent greater than the base rate from time to time of a particular named clearing bank, or
   ii. such a lower rate that the borrower can obtain a loan on similar terms from

an arms-length financial institution (written evidence of the availability of such a loan must be attached to this certificate);

d. that if the interest is not paid by the borrower on the due and payable dates, any payments made by the borrower to the lender intended as repayments of interest or capital will be allocated by the lender and the borrower first against current interest and outstanding interest, any balance will then be set off against outstanding capital;

e. that there are no outstanding arrears of interest and/or capital on any existing loans secured on scheme policies to this or any associated company;

f. that if any interest is outstanding 90 days after the due date, IR (SPSS) will be notified within a further 30 days;

g. that if the terms of the loan are amended, IR (SPSS) will be notified within 90 days (*see note 3*);

h. that if the payment of regular contributions for the member ceases, IR (SPSS) will be notified within 90 days of such cessation;

i. that the borrower shall repay the loan at or before a specified date no later than twelve months before the normal retirement date specified for the member under the scheme rules;

j. that the outstanding amount of the loan together with any unpaid interest is to be immediately repayable in any of the following circumstances:
    i.   if the borrower is in breach of any of the conditions of the loan agreement, or
    ii.   if the borrower ceases to carry on business, or
    iii. if the borrower becomes insolvent, within the meaning defined in regulation 6 of The Retirement Benefit Schemes (Restriction on Discretion to Approve) (Small Self-administered Schemes) Regulations 1991 (SI 1991 No 1614), or
    iv.   on the cessation of payment of regular contributions for the member under the scheme (*see note 4*), or
    v.   if the borrower applies the loan other than for the stated business purpose of the borrower, or
    vi.   if the member dies or retires, or
    vii. if the Inland Revenue gives notice in writing that the loan is not consistent with the approval of the scheme;

k. that the lender shall in the event of default by the borrower notify IR (SPSS) within 30 days of having recourse to recovery from the value of the policy; and

2   that the rules of the scheme contain a provision enabling a scheme policy to be applied as security for a loan subject to all the following conditions:

a. that the loan is made to an employer participating in the scheme or to a company associated with such an employer (*see note 1*);

b. that any policy (or part thereof) used as security for a loan must be specifically and solely for the provision of benefits for a member who is a controlling director of the borrower and who has consented to the policy (or part thereof) being charged as security for the loan;

c. that the loan:
    i.   is for a fixed term ending not later than 12 months before the member's Normal Retirement Date,
    ii.   is to be applied entirely for the purpose of the borrower's business. In

particular it is not to be applied directly or indirectly (other than by increasing the value of the borrower's business) for the benefit of any member or any relative (or the spouse of a relative) of the member or his or her spouse,

iii. is at a commercial rate of interest, and

iv. is evidenced by an agreement in writing which contains all the conditions on which it is made and, in particular, the provisions specified in sub-paragraph d. below,

d. the provisions specified in this sub-paragraph are that the loan shall be repaid immediately in any of the following circumstances:

i. if the borrower is in breach of the conditions of the agreement, or

ii. if the borrower ceases to carry on business, or

iii. if the borrower becomes insolvent within the meaning defined in regulation 6 of the Retirement Benefits Schemes (Restriction on Discretion to Approve) (Small Self-administered Schemes) Regulations 1991 (SI 1991 No 1614), or

iv. on the cessation of payment of regular contributions for the member under the scheme (*see note 4*), or

v. if the borrower applies the loan other than for a business purpose of the borrower, or

vi. if the member dies or retires, or

vii. if the Inland Revenue gives notice in writing that the loan is not consistent with the approval of the scheme;

e. that the total amount of any loans secured on a policy under this provision shall not exceed 50% of the current value of the policy. If the lending takes place within 2 years of the establishment of the scheme the amount shall not exceed 25% of the current value of the policy excluding the value of any transfer values received and included therein,

f. should a loan not be repaid in accordance with these conditions and any amounts outstanding under the loan agreement are recovered from the value of the policy, that any consequent reduction of benefits payable under the scheme will be first effected against any lump sum retirement benefits payable,

g. the trustees of the scheme shall notify IR (SPSS) of any loan effected under this provision.

3.   that the information set out below in respect of this loan and any other such loans made in the last 5 years is both complete and correct. **A false declaration can lead to the loss of approval of the scheme.**

This certificate must be signed by the employer and (all) the trustee(s) of the scheme. (*See note 5*)

Name	Signature	Date	Capacity (Employer or Trustee)

Notes:

1.   For the purpose of this certificate companies are associated if one is controlled by the other or if both are controlled by a third person. Control shall be construed in accordance with section 840 of the Income and Corporation Taxes Act 1988 or, in the case of a close company, with section 416 of that Act.

2.   This certificate must be accompanied by a disclosure of the results of a credit check undertaken on the borrower immediately before the trustees agree to permit any policy held by the scheme to be used as security for the loan. The trustees may also attach any other information they consider relevant to their decision that they wish IR (SPSS) to take into consideration. If IR (SPSS) does not consider the granting of security by the trustees to be a judicious act, IR (SPSS) may give notice in writing that the loan is not consistent with the approval of the scheme and require the immediate repayment of the loan.

3.   IR (SPSS) is unlikely to agree to more than two amendments of a loan agreement, e.g. to extend the period of the loan. IR (SPSS) may require the loan to be repaid unless the roll-over is for acceptable commercial reasons.

4.   Immediate repayment is not necessary on suspension of regular contributions to meet Inland Revenue funding requirements or otherwise where there is a definite expectation that the contributions will be resumed within 2 years.

5.   If the employer is also the trustee of the scheme, please provide a signature in respect of each capacity.

INFORMATION ABOUT LOANS TO EMPLOYER AND ASSOCIATED COMPANIES

1	Date of loan	
2	Name of borrower and whether employer or associated company (state which (*see note 1*))	
3	Amount of loan	
4	Amount of loan outstanding	
5	Value of relevant policy at date of loan	
6	Purpose of loan	

7	Repayment date — if more than two years from the date the loan was made, please specify when level capital repayments are due and payable	
8	Rate of interest and when it is due and payable	

9.	Details of member
	i.e. Name
	      Position in company
	      National Insurance Number
	      Normal Retirement Date	

10	Policy number	

11	Details of all other outstanding loans to employers and 'associated' companies				
	Name of borrower	Employer or associated company (state which)	Date of loan	Amount of loan	Amount of loan outstanding at the date of 1 above

APPENDIX 3
EXTRACT FROM OCCUPATIONAL PENSION SCHEMES PRACTICE NOTES IR 12 (2001)

(As at July 2003)

PART 20: SMALL SELF-ADMINISTERED SCHEMES

Introduction

20.1   As the term indicates, a small self-administered scheme is a self-administered scheme with a small number of members. The Inland Revenue's discretion to approve a small self-administered scheme is limited by the Retirement Benefits Schemes (Restriction on Discretion to Approve) (Small Self-administered Schemes) Regulations 1991 (SI 1991 No 1614, as amended). References in this Part to the "SSAS Regulations" are to those Regulations and the guidance in this Part should be read in conjunction with those Regulations. The SSAS Regulations define a small self-administered scheme as a self-administered scheme with less than 12 scheme members where at least one of those members is connected with another member, or with a trustee or an employer in relation to the scheme. For the purpose of the definition of a small self-administered scheme only, "scheme member", means a member who is currently accruing benefits in the scheme as a result of service as an employee of a participating employer. It does not include deferred benefit members, pensioner members, *ex spouse* members or other beneficiaries. The Inland Revenue may also require a scheme with 12 or more members to be treated as a small self-administered scheme and to comply with the special requirements set out in this Part. An example would be a scheme established primarily for a few family directors, to whom were added some relatively low-paid employees with entitlement to a very low level of benefits, included as makeweights to bring the total membership to 12 or slightly more. Conversely it will not be necessary to apply "small scheme" treatment to a scheme with less than 12 members if all the members are at arm's length from one another, from the employer and from the trustees. An approved insured scheme which becomes a small self-administered scheme will lose its approval unless it complies with the requirements of the SSAS Regulations as at the time it becomes such a scheme and thereafter.

20.2   The reasons why the Inland Revenue consider special requirements necessary for the approval of such schemes are:

(a) Under trust law which evolved before the advent of pension schemes, a trust with one or a few beneficiaries is susceptible to being broken regardless of the terms in which the trust is constituted.
(b) The funding of a self-administered scheme for a few members is difficult because the small membership limits the extent to which statistical fluctuations can be smoothed out (e.g. for mortality).
(c) Small self-administered schemes are usually established to provide benefits for directors. Often the scheme members control the employer company and are also trustees of the scheme. This multiplicity of roles can face a trustee with a conflict of interests leading to actions concerning the scheme being taken for reasons other than the provision of benefits on retirement.

20.3   The special requirements thus fall into three categories viz.

(a) control of the format of the trust,
(b) control of funding, and
(c) control of investments.

The Trust

Pensioneer trustee

20.4   The SSAS regulations restrict the *Board*'s discretion to approve a small self-administered scheme to one whose governing documentation contains provisions requiring one of the trustees to be a "pensioneer trustee". A pensioneer trustee is an individual or body recognised by the Inland Revenue as being widely involved with small self-administered schemes and having dealings with *IR SPSS*, who has given an undertaking to the Inland Revenue. In the undertaking the pensioneer trustee agrees

- not to consent to any action that the pensioneer trustee considers infringes any approval requirement relating to a small self-administered scheme, and
- not to consent to the termination of a small self-administered scheme otherwise than in accordance with the approved terms of the winding-up rule, and

- to provide to *IR SPSS* at least annually, details of the *IR SPSS* scheme reference numbers (where allocated) together with the corresponding scheme's and sponsoring employer's names for which the pensioneer trustee acts.

20.5   An individual who acts as a pensioneer trustee has demonstrated to the Inland Revenue that he or she has a knowledge of Inland Revenue requirements concerning the approval and continued approval of small self-administered schemes and has evidenced that knowledge in relation to at least 20 small self-administered schemes. The individual can also demonstrate effective management systems and procedures which ensure that the terms of the undertaking can be met.

20.6   Where a corporate body, including an insurance company or an associated company established for the purpose of acting as a pensioner trustee, is recognised as a pensioner trustee all the directors of that corporate body have signed the undertaking given to the Inland Revenue. The corporate body can also demonstrate that a person or persons with the required experience and knowledge detailed in paragraph 20.5 holds a position of authority within the corporate body's management systems that enables the terms of the undertaking to be met.

20.7   The pensioneer trustee must, in accordance with the normal requirements of trust law, be a registered owner (along with the other trustees) of all scheme assets and a mandatory co-signatory to all scheme bank accounts (including accounts with building societies and licensed deposit takers).

20.8   Another object of the appointment of a pensioneer trustee is to block any proposal that the trust should be terminated and the funds distributed among the members. It is however accepted that the trustees have no power to resist such a proposal if all the persons having an interest under the trust are agreed in requiring this action (Saunders v Vautier 1841). Such a consensus is unlikely in the context of a typical pension scheme where, even if the number of members is small the existence of further contingent beneficiaries can rarely be excluded.

20.9   The trust provisions of an approved small self-administered scheme must be framed to allow the pensioneer trustee to fulfil his or her function. Thus a provision that allows the trustees to act on a majority rather than unanimous decision must be qualified so as not to apply in relation to the termination of the scheme. A scheme subject to Scottish law must expressly require the pensioneer trustee 's concurrence in any decision about the scheme's termination. Also, scheme documents must be drafted in such a way to permit a pensioneer trustee to become a co-signatory of scheme bank accounts and co-owner of scheme assets.

20.10   A pensioneer trustee should not act as such in any scheme of which he or she is a member. Similarly a corporate trustee should not act in that capacity for a scheme for its own employees. A pensioneer trustee must not be connected with a scheme member, any other trustee of the scheme or any employer in relation to the scheme.

20.11 The circumstances and conditions under which a pensioneer trustee's appointment in relation to a particular small self-administered scheme can be terminated are set out in Regulation 9 of the SSAS Regulations or, for schemes approved on or before 17 March 1998, paragraph 7 of Schedule 15, Finance Act 1998. A pensioneer trustee's appointment cannot be terminated unless there is an immediate replacement by another pensioneer trustee. There are some limited exceptions to this requirement, which are

- the death of the pensioneer trustee
- a court order removing the pensioneer trustee from an appointment
- the pensioneer trustee is prohibited, suspended or disqualified from being a trustee under section 3, 4 or 29 of the Pensions Act 1995 or the corresponding Order for Northern Ireland
- the loss of Inland Revenue approval to act as a pensioneer trustee
- the appointment is terminated due to the pensioneer trustee committing a fraudulent breach of the trust in relation to a scheme.

Where an appointment is terminated by virtue of any of the limited exceptions listed above, the appointment of a successor pensioneer trustee must be made no more than 30 days after the date on which the former pensioneer trustee's appointment was terminated.

A copy of the document(s) removing a pensioneer trustee and immediately appointing a replacement pensioneer trustee must be sent to *IR SPSS* within 30 days of date on which the change of pensioneer trustee took effect.

Where a pensioneer trustee's appointment is terminated without an immediate successor by virtue of any of the limited exceptions listed above, a report (together with copies of any relevant documents) must be sent to *IR SPSS* within 30 days of the terminated appointment. A successor pensioneer trustee must be appointed within 30 days of the terminated appointment and a copy of the document(s) appointing the replacement pensioneer trustee must be sent to *IR SPSS* within 30 days of the date on which the new appointment took effect.

20.12 The Inland Revenue reserves the right to withdraw pensioneer trustee status should the circumstances warrant, each case being considered on its own facts. Facts taken into account would include

- tax avoidance, for example, if the individual or corporate body or any of its directors or staff is found to be involved in or promoting tax avoidance, whether or not the avoidance relates to pension schemes

- the terms of the undertaking they have signed are not complied with
- it is apparent that there are no satisfactory systems in place to ensure that the undertaking is complied with
- action taken by Opra under section 3, 4 and 29 (3) or (4) of the Pensions Act 1995
- any disqualification under section 29 (1) Pensions Act 1995.

Pensioneer trustee status will not normally be withdrawn without prior written warning. Such a warning will explain why status as a pensioneer trustee is jeopardised, give an opportunity for problems to be rectified and for representations to be made. Pensioneer trustees involved in tax avoidance or evasion should not expect these procedures for withdrawal of pensioneer trustee status to apply.

20.13   The names of all Inland Revenue approved pensioneer trustees is published on the IR Website www.inlandrevenue.gov.uk.

Entitlement against the whole fund

20.14   It is not permissible for an approved small self-administered scheme to secure a member's benefits against particular trust assets. There is no objection to the calculation of the amount of the member's benefits being notionally linked to the value of particular assets but the trust provisions must ensure that the member's entitlement to benefit is against the funds of the trust as a whole.

Multiple small schemes

20.15   Regulation 3 of the SSAS Regulations prohibits the *Board* from approving a small self-administered scheme in respect of an employer where that employer already has such a scheme approved by the *Board* to which it was or is entitled to pay contributions, and that scheme has not been wound-up. Thus if more than one employee is to be pensioned through this medium they should all be included in one scheme. Where an employee is employed by several companies in a group of associated companies, one centralised small self-administered scheme may be established in which all the relevant companies participate (see paragraphs 21.3 and 21.4 in this context) or, alternatively, each employer may set up its own small self-administered scheme to provide benefits for the employee based on his or her salary and service with it alone.

Death benefits

20.16   The scheme rules should provide that lump sum benefits payable on death (including any lump sum payable under a pension guarantee) are, except where paragraph 11.12 applies, to be distributable at the trustee's/*administrator*'s discretion among a wide class of beneficiaries.

Further Requirements for Pensioneer Trustees

Co-ownership of scheme assets

20.17   As a trustee of the scheme, the pensioneer trustee must be a co-owner of scheme assets along with the other scheme trustees. The guiding principle is that, where it is legally possible, the pensioneer trustee should be the registered owner (along with the other trustees) of all assets owned by the schemes for which he/she/the company acts as a pensioneer trustee. The prime object is for the pensioneer trustee's name to be on the document of title. It is not acceptable for just the title "Pensioneer Trustee" put on the documentation instead of the actual name of the pensioneer trustee. If it is not possible for the pensioneer trustee's name to be put on the title document or there is no such document, there should be a legally enforceable restriction in place to prevent the assets being realised for cash without the written authority of the pensioneer trustee. Any proceeds from the sale/disposal of any assets owned by the scheme must be paid to a scheme bank account of which the pensioneer trustee is a co-signatory.

Land /property

20.18   The name of the pensioneer trustee should appear on the document evidencing any interest in land/property owned by the trustees of the SSAS along with the names of the other trustees. This should be the case for any document of title in respect of registered and unregistered land both inside and outside the UK. If there is any restriction on the number of names that can be placed on the title deed, the name of the pensioneer trustee must be included.

20.19   As an alternative to the registered co-ownership requirement explained in paragraph 20.18, there is no objection to the pensioneer trustee registering a legally binding "restriction" in respect of land/property that is held in the name of the other trustees.

20.20   For land/property registered in England and Wales a "restriction" may be registered at HM Land Registry using Form 75: "Application to register a Restriction". In the case of registered land in Northern Ireland, an "inhibition" may be registered at the Land Registers of Northern Ireland. A "caution" in respect of land/property registered at the Land Registers of Northern Ireland is not an acceptable alternative to the registered co-ownership requirement or registered "inhibition".

20.21   It is not possible to register a "restriction" in respect of land/property situated in Scotland so for such property paragraph 20.18 applies. Where a scheme owns land in Scotland or Northern Ireland and the land had been charged to secure an existing loan from a bank or other financial institution prior to 29 August 2000 it will not be necessary for the Pensioneer Trustee to become a co-owner of that land until the property ceases to be so charged.

Loans

20.22   The pensioneer trustee must be a party to the agreement evidencing loans made by the scheme trustees. Loans made before 1 October 2000 are not be subject to this requirement. Where a loan made prior to 1 October 2000 is "rolled-over", see paragraph 20.60, it is not necessary for the pensioneer trustee to be a party to the document evidencing the "roll-over" unless new money is being loaned.

All cash repayments of loans and cash payments of loan interest should be paid into a scheme bank account of which the pensioneer trustee is a mandatory co-signatory. All repayments/payments in non-cash form should be transferred into the names of all the trustees, including the pensioneer trustee.

Shares/unit trusts/loan stock/open ended investment companies

20.23   These types of assets owned by schemes should be registered to show that the pensioneer trustee is a co-owner of the asset. If there are any restrictions on the number of names that can be placed on the share certificate etc, the name of the pensioneer trustee must be included. As regards portfolios of securities the position is set out in paragraph 20.24.

Portfolio of securities/ investment management arrangements

20.24   The pensioneer trustee must be signatory to any arrangement between the trustees and fund manager/broker. This arrangement must ensure that any proceeds paid from the portfolio to the trustees is paid only into a scheme bank account of which the pensioneer trustee is a mandatory co-signatory. The pensioneer trustee does not have to be co-signatory to any nominee account that is set up by the fund manager/ broker as part of the management of the portfolio, as it should not be possible for funds held in these accounts to be accessed by anyone other than the fund manager/broker. If the trustees can access the nominee accounts the pensioneer trustee must be a co-signatory. A "fund manager/broker" is someone who is professionally engaged in the provision of investment or fund management services.

20.25   The requirements in paragraph 20.24 also apply for other management arrangements where shares are held on behalf of the trustees by a nominee and any share transactions undertaken on non-United

Kingdom stock exchanges that might require the share certificate to be registered in the name of a recognised nominee. Where shares are registered in the name of "Crest" it is acceptable for written arrangements to be put in place to the effect that the shares cannot be transferred out of the control of the duly appointed fund manager (other than in the normal course of managing investments) without the written consent of the pensioneer trustee.

Insurance policies/annuity contracts

20.26 The pensioneer trustee must be a party to insurance policies and annuity contracts taken out for the purpose of the scheme. The wording of the policies/contracts must require that any proceeds (e.g. on the surrender of the policy) are paid only if the pensioneer trustee agrees in writing to the insurance company. This requirement does not apply in respect of policies/contracts taken out before 1 October 2000.

Other assets

20.27 There should normally be a document, which evidences the trustees' ownership of the asset. Such documentation should show that the pensioneer trustee is one of the owners.

Scheme borrowings

20.28 The pensioneer trustee must be a party to all scheme borrowings undertaken on or after 1 October 2000.

Co-signatory requirements

20.29 It is the duty of a trustee to ensure, among other things, that a scheme is properly administered. Money in scheme bank accounts belongs to the trustees. In order to ensure that pensioneer trustees are in a position to carry out their trustee duties effectively, they are required to be mandatory co-signatories of scheme bank accounts. Accounts that give rise only to a liability, such as loan or overdraft accounts, do not have to be covered by this co-signatory requirement.

20.30 All money contributions paid by employers and scheme members, money transfers into the scheme and any other monies paid into a scheme must be paid into a scheme bank account to which the pensioneer trustee is a mandatory co-signatory.

20.31 There is no objection to trustees (other than the pensioneer trustee) making regular, routine, payments from a scheme bank account, provided the payments are covered by a standing order or direct debit arrangement which the pensioneer trustee has previously authorised. Such payments may include, for example, payment of pension (but not lump sums), premiums paid on insurance policies, rents, rates, standing charges for electricity, gas, telephone, mortgage/loan repayments, ground rents, bank charges. The pensioneer trustee does not have to authorise, for example, increases in pensions made to reflect cost of living increases provided the original standing order has been authorised by the pensioneer trustee. There is no objection to contributions being paid by the employer direct to an insurance company in respect of a policy provided the pensioneer trustee is aware of and in agreement with the particular arrangements. Employer contributions paid direct to a unit/investment trust can be made on the same basis. Also, the pensioneer trustee does not have to be involved with the transferring of money from one trustee bank account to another (for example, from a current account to a deposit account) provided the pensioneer trustee is aware of and in agreement with the arrangement. The pensioneer trustee must be a co-signatory to transfer payments, pension scheme refunds, benefit payments (in non-pension form) and other non-regular payments.

20.32   Where a small self-administered scheme is submitted for approval the trustees must give written confirmation that the pensioneer trustee is a mandatory co-signatory to the scheme bank accounts and co-owner of scheme assets. Where the confirmation accompanies the application it must be in respect of all scheme bank accounts open, and all assets held by the scheme, at the date of the application. Any such confirmation given at a later date must be in respect of all scheme bank accounts open, and all assets held by the scheme at that later date.

20.33   Failure to meet the co-signatory and co-ownership requirements will lead to a small self-administered scheme's tax approval status being reviewed and possibly withdrawn. A small self-administered scheme seeking approval will not be approved if it fails to meet the co-signatory and co-ownership requirements.

FUNDING

20.34   An approved small self-administered scheme, like any other approved scheme, must comply with the general funding principles set out in paragraph 13.1. The more specific requirements of Part 13 are, however, qualified as described in paragraphs 20.35 to 20.44.

Actuarial reports

20.35   An approved small self-administered scheme is required to obtain an actuarial valuation of its assets and liabilities at its inception and thereafter at intervals no greater than 3 years. A copy of each actuarial report must be submitted to *IR SPSS* not later than one year from the effective date of the valuation.

The requirement for the production and submission of an actuarial valuation report to *IR SPSS* on small self-administered schemes stands until the scheme has completed winding up. If, however, a scheme completes winding up within a year of the as at date of the actuarial valuation report in a small self-administered scheme *IR SPSS* will be prepared to dispense with the actuarial valuation report.

Contributions

20.36 No contributions are to be paid to the scheme unless justified by the latest actuarial report. It is not permissible to make contributions when money is available irrespective of the needs of the scheme (it is a popular misconception that a scheme may hold a general reserve equal to one year's *Ordinary annual contribution*).

Death benefits

20.37 All death benefits, insofar as they exceed the value of the member's interest in the fund based on his or her accrued pension and other retirement benefits, must be insured.

Purchase of annuities

20.38 To ensure that pensions from small self-administered schemes are pensions for life as required by paragraph 7.32, pensions should normally be secured from the outset by the purchase of an annuity from a life office. The annuity should be non- commutable and non-assignable. It may be purchased either in the name of the trustees or member. An annuity to secure a widow's/widower's or *dependant*'s pension (see paragraphs 20.42 and 20.43) may also be purchased in either the name of the trustees, or in the name of the widow/widower or *dependant*.

20.39 Annuity rates, however, do fluctuate and when the costs are high the immediate purchase of an annuity may not make economic sense. Rules may, therefore, provide:

- subject to paragraphs 20.40, 20.41, 20.51, 20.53, 20.56 and 20.62 for the purchase of the annuity to be deferred and the pension to be paid directly from the resources, or alternatively
- for the facility set out in Part I of Appendix XII to be adopted.

To the extent that pensions are so secured, post-retirement increases in respect of the secured pension must also be immediately secured. In the case of the second alternative, the requirements and conditions set out in Appendix XII must be applied.

20.40   Deferment of the purchase of annuities may not extend beyond the age of 75. The intention of allowing deferment is to provide scheme members with more flexibility in deciding the most opportune time to purchase the annuity rather than automatic deferral to age 75. Scheme members or survivors should be made aware of the importance of keeping the purchase of the annuity under review taking such professional advice as is considered necessary.

20.41   When pensions are paid directly out of scheme resources under paragraph 20.31 above, the scheme actuary must certify the amount of pension payable in accordance with the scheme rules and which can be maintained whilst taking account of:

(a)   any contingent widow's, widower's or *dependant*'s pension payable; and
(b)   the scheme's income and assets, particularly those notionally underpinning the provision of the member's benefits.

This certificate should compare the pension with an annuity on the same terms that could be secured on the open market at that time with the funds available. Any divergences by more than 10% between the two amounts should be explained by the actuary. The amount of any unsecured pension in payment must form part of a scheme's triennial actuarial report. Certificates should be provided to *IR SPSS* with the next actuarial valuation report, or earlier on request.

Widow's/widower's/dependant's pension

20.42   Subject to paragraph 20.43 the purchase of an annuity to secure a widow's/widower's or *dependant*'s pension payable on the member's death either while still in service or after retirement but before the member attains age 75, may be deferred until the earlier of the attaining by the widow/widower or *dependant* of age 75 or the date on which the deceased member would have attained age 75. As for deferral of members' pensions, the need to purchase an annuity for a widow/widower or *dependant* should be kept under continuous review. The requirements set out in paragraph 20.41 will apply except that when a widow's/widower's or *dependant*'s pension is in payment (a) will not be relevant and the actuarial certificate will take account under (b) only of the scheme's investments and assets underpinning the provision of the widow's/ widower's or *dependant*'s benefit. The initial certificate should compare the pension with an annuity that could have been purchased at the time of the member's death. Where the member dies in retirement on or after age 75, the widow's/widower's or *dependant*'s pension should be secured by the purchase of an annuity not later than the time of the member's death.

Widow's/widower's pension

20.43   A prospective widow's/widower's reversionary pension should be secured by the purchase of a contingent annuity at the same time as the member's own pension is so secured. If, however, the pension is payable to whichever person is the member's spouse when the member dies (i.e. the entitlement is not limited to the current spouse at the time of retirement), its purchase may be deferred in accordance with paragraph 20.42 above.

Pension increases

20.44   Any cost of living increases granted in respect of a pension already secured in accordance with paragraphs above should be secured with a life office as soon as they are awarded. Where scheme rules provide for pension increases at a fixed rate of up to 3% per annum compound (paragraph 9.4(a)), the increases should be secured when the basic pension is secured.

Investments

20.45   The Inland Revenue's interest in the investments of a small self-administered scheme flows from the statutory condition of approval that a scheme should be "bona fide established for the sole purpose of providing *relevant benefits*" (section 590(2)(a)). The concern is that tax exempt investments held for the provision of the scheme benefits should not be of a kind or used in such a way as to produce a non-relevant benefit for the beneficiaries or the employer.

Effect of Regulations

20.46   The SSAS Regulations contain requirements in relation to the power of the trustees of small self-administered schemes to:

(a) borrow money;
(b) hold certain assets as investments;
(c) lend money and purchase shares; and
(d) purchase, sell or lease assets.

The SSAS Regulations restrict the *Board*'s discretion to approve such a scheme to one whose governing documentation contains requirements complying with those Regulations in relation to (a) – (d) above.

20.47   The only exception to paragraph 20.46 is where at the date, on which the SSAS Regulations were made, the scheme was in existence and either had not been submitted to the *Board* for approval or was before the *Board* awaiting approval. In these circumstances approval will not be precluded by reason of provisions in the scheme's documentation, which allow the trustees to retain as an investment of the scheme:

(i)   personal chattels other than choses in action (see paragraph 20.75);

(ii)   residential property other than is described in paragraph 20.72); or

(iii) shares in an unlisted company which carry more than 30% of the voting power in that company or entitle the trustees to more than 30% of any dividends declared by that company (see paragraph 20.80),

Provided that such an investment was held by the trustees prior to the date on which the Regulations were made and was acceptable under previous Inland Revenue discretionary practice. Similarly, a provision in the scheme's documentation authorising the trustees to:

(iv)   continue to lend money or retain shares in an employer or any *Associated Employer*, where that money was being lent or the shares were being held prior to the date on which the SSAS Regulations were made and when the money was first lent or the shares were acquired, the scheme had been in existence for 2 years or less and the 25% restriction but not the 50% restriction described in paragraph 20.53 was exceeded; or

(v)   sell assets held by them immediately before that date to a member of the scheme or to any person connected with a member of the scheme,

will not prevent approval being given. It should be noted, however, that in relation to (v), the sale must be on an arm's length basis at full market value.

20.48   It is a condition of approval that when actuarial reports are submitted to *IR SPSS* (see paragraph 20.35) they must be accompanied by a statement detailing how the funds of the scheme are invested. This enables the Inland Revenue to monitor whether the bona fides of the scheme are being maintained.

20.49   Regulation 5 of the Information Powers Regulations requires the scheme *administrator* to provide to the *Board* information and documents relating to certain transactions within a period of 90 days of the date of the transaction. Failure to comply may lead to the imposition of a monetary penalty on the scheme *administrator* under section 98 Taxes Management Act 1970. Continued failure to furnish the information may lead to withdrawal of approval under our discretionary powers contained in section 591B.

The types of transaction involved are:

(a)   the acquisition or disposal of land including buildings and other structures;

(b)   the lending of money to an employer or an *Associated Employer*;

(c)   the acquisition or disposal of shares in an employer or an *Associated Employer*;

(d) the acquisition or disposal of shares in an unlisted company, NB an Open Ended Investment Company (OEIC) is not an unlisted company for the purposes of the Information Powers Regulations;

(e) the borrowing of money; and

(f) the purchase, sale or lease from or to an employer, or any *Associated Employer*, of any asset other than one as described in (a), (c) or (d).

The information and documents required are as may be specified on the relevant form – specimen copies are included in Appendix II.

The relevant forms are:

PS 7012 – for details of the acquisition or disposal of land (including buildings and other structures).

PS 7013 – for the lending of money to an employer or *Associated Employer*.

PS 7014 – for the acquisition or disposal of shares, in the employer, *Associated Employer*s or unlisted companies.

PS 7015 – for the borrowing of money.

PS 7016 – for the purchase from, or sale or lease to an employer, or any *Associated Employer*, of any asset other than as described in (a), (c) or (d) above.

20.50   Apart from the requirements of regulation 5 of the Information Powers Regulations, when requested, Scheme *administrator*s should provide full details of any transaction to *IR SPSS*. The following paragraphs contain details of the various restrictions which are imposed on scheme trustees by the SSAS Regulations in relation to their powers as described in (a) – (d) of paragraph 20.46 together with some guidance on Inland Revenue views and requirements on particular aspects of investment.

General principle

20.51   The Inland Revenue will not necessarily regard any form of investment as consistent with approval just because it is within the trustees' powers and not prohibited under the terms of the SSAS Regulations. In general the Inland Revenue do not interfere in the way trustees invest trust monies except:

(a) where tax avoidance is suspected; or

(b) where an investment appears to be irreconcilable with the bona fides of the scheme having regard to the sole purpose requirement and the scheme's cash needs for purchasing annuities.

For example, investment in land or buildings may be a good long-term investment when the members are many years from retirement but becomes less appropriate as their retirement approaches and, even if the purchase of a member's, widow's/widower's or *dependant*'s annuity is deferred, it is necessary to ensure that the scheme is in a position to buy an annuity between the ages of 70 and 75 without becoming involved in a forced sale of property. This is particularly so if the property purchased is an important part of the employer's own commercial premises and thus potentially difficult to realise.

Loans to members and connected persons

20.52   Regulation 6(1) of the SSAS Regulations prohibits scheme trustees from making loans to a member of the scheme or to any person, apart from an employer or any Associated Employer, who for the purposes of those Regulations is connected with a member of the scheme. For this purpose, "member of the scheme" includes members who are currently accruing benefits in the scheme as a result of service as an employee of a participating employer, deferred benefit members, pensioner members, *ex spouse* members, other beneficiaries and former scheme members who are still in the service of a participating employer. Thus if a scheme is to be approved, its trust documents should specifically preclude loans to such individuals or persons. The reason why this prohibition is considered necessary in small self-administered schemes in particular is because of the possibility (arising from the less than arm's length relationship of all the parties) that such a loan would become, in reality, a charge on the retirement benefit, or that the pension scheme would be used in this way so as to avoid the tax liability arising on loans direct from a close company to its "participators".

Self investment

20.53   Regulation 7 of the SSAS Regulations restricts trustees' investment in loans to and shares in an employer company during the first 2 years from the date the scheme was established, to 25% of the market value of its assets which are derived from contributions made to it by an employer and the members since it was established. After the end of the 2 year period the figure increases to 50% of the market value of all the assets of the scheme.

For the purpose of applying the limits in regulation 7 of the SSAS Regulations, the market value of the assets excludes:

(a) any portion of the funds notionally underpinning retired members', *ex spouses'*, widows'/widowers' or *dependants'* benefits in payment where the purchase of an annuity has been deferred (prospective widows/widowers of retired members or *ex spouse* members in receipt of a pension, whose pensions must be secured at the same

time as the retired or *ex spouse* members in accordance with paragraph 20.43 being regarded for this purpose as in receipt of a
pension), and

(b)   any sums borrowed to purchase scheme assets which are outstanding at that time and any other liabilities incurred by the trustees
which are outstanding at the time, other than liabilities to pay benefits under the scheme.

Within 5 years of the commencement of pensions to new pensioners, or
on attainment by the pensioner of age 70 if earlier, the trustees must
ensure an appropriate proportion of any loan to the employer or
Associated Employer is repaid. Where the pensioner has already attained
age 70 when payment of pension commences, repayment of the loan
must take place immediately.

20.54   Where all members of the scheme have retired/taken their pen-
sion/died, no new loans or share purchases in the employer or *associated
employer* will be permitted following the later of the first payment of the
final retiring member's pension or the final *ex spouse* member taking a
pension and the first payment of the final widow's/widower's or *dependant*'s pension (prospective widows/widowers of retired members or *ex
spouse* members in receipt of a pension, whose pensions must be secured
at the same time as the retired or *ex spouse* members' in accordance with
paragraph 20.43 being regarded for this purpose as in receipt of pension).
Existing loans and shares should be repaid or sold within 5 years of the
commencement of such pension payments or on attainment by the pensioner of age 70 if earlier. If the pensioner has already attained age 70
when payment of pension commences, such repayment or sale must take
place immediately. Where a scheme holds a policy or policies, including
a unit linked policy or policies, as part of its assets, *IR SPSS* would
regard an acceptable interpretation of the market value of such a policy
or policies to be the surrender value (calculated on the same basis as a
transfer value). In the context of regulation 7 of the SSAS Regulations
investment means both loans to, and the purchase of shares in the
employer company and any *Associated Employer* whether or not they
participate in the scheme. The Inland Revenue also applies these limits in
relation to loans to, or shares in, other persons connected with a scheme
through a member (see paragraph 20.52), trustee or an employer. It is not
possible to provide a comprehensive definition of a connected party in
this context, but broadly it includes:

(a)   an individual who is a business associate of a member of the scheme,
or of a trustee or employer in relation to the scheme (see paragraph
20.52), or who is a relative of a trustee or employer;

(b)   a partnership where one of the partners is connected as in (a) with a
member of the scheme (see paragraph 20.52), trustee or employer;
and

(c) a company in which a director or influential shareholder (i.e. one who controls 20% or more of the voting shares in the company) is connected as in (a).

20.55   An individual is connected with a corporate trustee or employer if he or she is a relative or business associate of any director or influential shareholder (as defined in (c) above) of the trustee or employer company. For practical purposes a "business associate" means a partner in a partnership, a fellow director of a company, or a fellow influential shareholder in a company. A director of a company is regarded as a business associate of an influential shareholder of the same company and vice versa. Forms PS 7013, PS 7014 and PS 7016 (headings suitably amended where necessary) should be used to provide details of loans to, shares (acquired and disposed of) in, or purchases, sales or leases from or to, connected parties other than an employer or Associated Employer. The required documentation should accompany the completed forms.

20.56   Subject to paragraph 20.53 and Department of Social Security legislation, a scheme may lend funds to an employer or any *Associated Employer* but if it is to be approved, regulation 6 of the SSAS Regulations requires that such lending may only be made for the purposes of the borrower's business (broadly an activity other than that of making or managing investments, except that a holding company is permitted to make or manage share investments in its 51% trading subsidiaries) and that the loan is:

(a) for a fixed term;
(b) at a commercial rate of interest; and
(c) evidenced by an agreement in writing which contains all the conditions on which it is made and provides for immediate repayment of the loan if the borrower:
   (i)   breaches the conditions of the agreement,
   (ii) ceases to carry on business,
   (iii) becomes insolvent, or

   if repayment is required to enable the trustees to pay benefits which have already become due under the scheme. Where the purchase of an annuity has been deferred (see paragraph 20.39) the funds necessary to purchase the whole annuity must be regarded as required to pay benefits no later than 5 years after the commencement of the pension payments or on attainment by the pensioner of age 70 if earlier. If the pensioner has already attained age 70 when payment of pension commences, the funds necessary to purchase the whole annuity must be regarded as required immediately.

The Inland Revenue will also expect these requirements to be met where a loan is made to connected persons other than an employer or *Associated Employer* as described in paragraph 20.54. The pensioneer trustee must be a party to all loans made on or after 1 October 2000 – paragraph 20.22 refers.

20.57   Loans should not be of such an amount and frequency as to suggest that the employer is only partly funding the scheme while claiming a tax deduction for the total pension contributions. Regulation 6 of the SSAS Regulations requires that a loan must be for a fixed term. The length of the term is a matter for decision between the parties to the loan agreement but it should be realistic. It is not acceptable for a series of 364 day loans to be made when in reality the intention is that the employer will not repay the loan for, say, 3 years. Nor is it acceptable for the term to be longer than necessary – scheme funds should not lodge unnecessarily with an employer.

20.58   It is an Inland Revenue requirement that a commercial rate of interest (see paragraph 20.56 (b) must be charged and paid. The commerciality of the interest will not be questioned if it is at least 3% above the Clearing Banks' Base Rate and an interest rate on this basis will be acceptable for both secured and unsecured loans. *IR SPSS* will be prepared to consider a lower rate of interest only if written evidence is produced demonstrating that the borrower can obtain a loan on similar terms from a bank or other arm's length financial institution at a rate below Clearing Banks' Base Rate + 3%.

Trustees/administrator duties in respect of loans

20.59   Quite apart from the requirements of the SSAS Regulations, *IR SPSS* require scheme trustees to act in the best interests of scheme members in their capacity as scheme members and not as employees, shareholders etc. If they fail to do so *IR SPSS* are likely to take the view that the scheme is not being properly administered and that exempt approval should be withdrawn (see Part 19). Such action may be taken if the following responsibilities, in relation to loans, are not adhered to by the trustees/*administrator*:

(a)   As a rule loans should not be made to an employer or any *Associated Employer* unless the trustees would be prepared to lend the same amount on the same terms to an unconnected party of comparable standing. All the scheme trustees, other than the pensioneer trustee, are therefore required to certify on the form PS 7013 that in the light of all the evidence before them, they are satisfied that the borrower's financial circumstances are healthy and that the loan is a prudent investment. *IR SPSS* are prepared to consider any other information that the trustees wish to submit with the PS 7013 to support their view that the loan is a prudent investment. Such information could be a copy of the borrower's most recent company accounts (together with any more recent management accounts);

(b) The scheme trustees should also ensure that where they lend money, the borrower fully honours the terms of the loan agreement. Trustees should ensure that they pursue the payment of any arrears promptly and effectively. The *administrator* is required, within 90 days of a loan default occurring, to notify *IR SPSS* in writing where the defaulted interest/capital has not been paid/repaid in the interim. Within a further 90 days of the default occurring the scheme administrator will be required to notify *IR SPSS* in writing of the steps the trustees have taken to recover the debt (including supplying copies of letters sent by the trustees and/or their legal or other representatives formally demanding repayment). A failure by scheme trustees to pursue loan arrears may jeopardise approval;

(c) Other responsibilities of the trustees include:
  (i)   ensuring that loans are not made solely to keep an ailing business afloat;
  (ii)   ensuring that loans are not made to employers who are technically insolvent; and
  (iii) taking all available legal steps to enforce the repayment of a loan to an employer in the circumstances described in paragraph 20.56 (c).

20.60   The SSAS Regulations do not prohibit an outstanding loan from being "rolled over" into a fresh loan agreement. *IR SPSS* will not, however, agree to a loan being "rolled over" more than twice nor to the "roll over" of unpaid interest into a new loan. Where a loan is "rolled over" it must satisfy the conditions described in paragraphs 20.53 – 20.58.

Back to back loans

20.61   Any attempt to circumvent the ban on loans to members (see paragraph 20.52) and connected persons or the restrictions on loans to employers by entering into arrangements whereby the scheme loans money to an unconnected party on the understanding for instance that a similar loan will be made by that party (or an associate) to the employer or a member, will almost certainly lead to withdrawal of approval from the scheme(s) involved.

Borrowing

20.62   Trustees of schemes sometimes wish to borrow funds to enable them to acquire particular assets. Regulation 4 of the SSAS Regulations restricts trustees' borrowing so that at the time of any borrowing, the aggregate amount borrowed does not exceed the total of:

(a) three times the ordinary annual contribution paid by the employers;

(b) three times the annual amount of the *basic or contractual contributions* paid by the scheme members in the year of assessment ending immediately before the time of borrowing; and

(c) 45% of the market value of the assets of the scheme*.

20.63   Any borrowing in existence when a member retires or when an *ex spouse's*, widow's/widower's or *dependant's* benefits come into payment (prospective widows/widowers of retired members or *ex spouse* members in receipt of a pension whose pensions must be secured at the same time as the retired or *ex spouse* members in accordance with paragraph 20.43 being regarded for this purpose as in receipt of benefits) must be reduced to the levels set out in (c) above within 5 years of those events or on attainment by the pensioner of age 70 if earlier. If the pensioner has already attained age 70 when payment of pension commences, any reductions in borrowing to comply with the level set out in (c) above must take place immediately.

20.64   For the purpose of regulation 4 of the SSAS Regulations, ordinary annual contribution has a different meaning to that contained in the Appendix 1 glossary. For the purpose of regulation 4 it means the smaller of:

(i)   the average annual amount of the contributions paid to the scheme by the employers in the 3 years ending at the end of the last scheme accounting period that immediately preceded the date of the borrowing or, where at that date the scheme had been established less than 3 years, the total amount of contributions paid to the scheme by the employers up to the time of the borrowing divided by the number of years since the scheme was established (a part of a year counting as one year), and

(ii)   the amount of the annual contributions which, within the period of 3 years immediately preceding the date of the borrowing, an actuary has advised in writing would have to be paid in order to secure the benefits provided under the scheme.

20.65   Monies borrowed by trustees must be used to benefit the scheme. Thus if the borrowed monies are on-lent to the employer (or any

---

*For the purpose of applying this limit, the market value of the assets excludes:

i) any portion of the funds notionally underpinning retired members', *ex spouses'*, widows'/widowers' or *dependants'* benefits in payment where the purchase of an annuity has been deferred (prospective widows/widowers of retired members or *ex spouse* members whose pensions must be secured at the same time as the retired or *ex spouse* members in accordance with paragraph 20.43 being regarded for this purpose as in receipt of benefits), and

ii) any sums borrowed to purchase scheme assets which are outstanding at that time and any other liabilities incurred by the trustees which are outstanding at the time, other than liabilities to pay benefits under the scheme.

Associated Employer) the trustees must receive a higher rate of interest than they have to pay to obtain the finance.

20.66   As an administrative relaxation, *IR SPSS* do not require notification of short term borrowings for a period not exceeding 6 months where the aggregate amount borrowed does not exceed the lesser of 10% of the market value of the fund or £50,000 and the borrowing is repaid at or before the due date. If, however, the borrowing or part of it is rolled over into a further term it must be reported.

Purchase of assets from members, connected persons or an employer

20.67   Regulation 8 of the SSAS Regulations prohibits the direct or indirect purchase by scheme trustees of an asset from a member of the scheme (see paragraph 20.52) or any person, apart from an employer or any Associated Employer, connected with a member of the scheme. For this purpose, the purchase of an asset by the trustees will not be regarded as being an indirect purchase from a member of the scheme or connected person if at the time of purchase 3 or more years have passed since the asset was owned by the member or connected person. Regulation 8 does not preclude the scheme trustees purchasing an asset from an employer or any Associated Employer but it requires that such purchase may only be made:

(a) after the trustees have obtained independent professional advice in writing, and

(b) in accordance with that advice.

20.68   Although the purchase of an asset from an employer or an Associated Employer is permissible, *IR SPSS* will need to be satisfied that it is consistent with the scheme's approval. *IR SPSS* should, whenever possible, be advised in advance of any such proposed transactions. *IR SPSS* will generally need to consult the appropriate Inspector of Taxes to determine whether tax avoidance is involved and whether the acquisition is part and parcel of a "transaction in securities" to which section 703 might apply. Trustees may wish to satisfy themselves that the vendors have obtained clearance under section 707 (from the Inland Revenue Compliance and Collection Division) before making such an acquisition. If such clearance cannot be given or if tax avoidance is involved, the transaction will not be consistent with the scheme's approval.

Sale of assets to members, connected persons or an employer

20.69   Subject to the exception explained in paragraph 20.46, regulation 8 of the SSAS Regulations prohibits the direct or indirect sale by the trustees of a scheme asset to a member of the scheme (see paragraph

20.52) or any person, apart from an employer or any Associated Employer, connected with a member of the scheme. For this purpose, the sale of a scheme asset by the trustees will not be regarded as being an indirect sale to a member of the scheme or connected person, if the purchase by the member or connected person took place 3 or more years after the sale by the trustees. Regulation 8 does not preclude the sale by the trustees of a scheme asset to an employer or any Associated Employer but such a sale may only be made subject to the conditions described in (a) and (b) of paragraph 20.67.

Lease of assets to an employer

20.70   Regulation 8 of the SSAS Regulations permits scheme documentation to provide for the lease by the trustees of scheme assets to an employer or any Associated Employer but only where the conditions described in (a) and (b) of paragraph 20.67 are satisfied. The pensioneer trustee must be a party to the documentation – paragraph 20.9 refers.

Lease of assets to members or to connected persons

20.71   Regulation 8 of the SSAS Regulations prohibits the trustees from leasing any scheme assets to a member of the scheme (see paragraph 20.52) or any person, apart from an employer or any Associated Employer, connected with a member of the scheme.

Residential property

20.72   Regulation 5 of the SSAS Regulations prohibits scheme trustees from investing in residential property other than:

(a)   residential property which is, or is to be, occupied by an employee who is not connected with his or her employer and who is required as a condition of employment to occupy the property, or

(b)   residential property which is, or is to be, occupied by a person, other than a scheme member or a person connected with a scheme member, in connection with that person's occupation of business premises (for example, a shop with an integral flat above) where those business premises are held by the trustees as a scheme asset.

In relation to (a) above, an employee is connected with his or her employer in circumstances where:

(i)   the employer is a partnership and he or she is connected with a partner (viz. is the partner's spouse, or is a relative, or the spouse of a relative, of the partner or the partner's spouse) in the partnership, or

(ii) the employer is a company and he or she or a person connected with him or her (viz. in this context the spouse, or a relative, or the spouse of a relative, of the employee or the employees' spouse) is, or at any time during the preceding 10 years has been, a *controlling director* of the company.

20.73   For the purposes of regulation 5 of the SSAS Regulations, the scheme trustees are not regarded as indirectly holding as an investment residential property other than as is described in (a) and (b) above where:

(i) they hold as investment units in a unit trust scheme:
   • which is an authorised unit trust scheme within the meaning of section 468(6), or
   • where all the unit holders would be wholly exempt from capital gains tax or corporation tax (otherwise than by reason of residence) if they disposed of their units,
   and the trustees of the unit trust scheme hold such property as an investment subject to the trusts of the scheme, or

(ii) they hold as an investment subject to the trusts of the scheme a right which confers entitlement to receive payment of any rent charge, ground annual, feu duty or other annual payment reserved in respect of, or charged on or issuing out of, that property, and the property is not occupied by a scheme member or a person connected with a scheme member.

Holiday property

20.74   Investment by scheme trustees in holiday property is not regarded as being consistent with approval.

Pride in possession articles

20.75   Regulation 5 of the SSAS Regulations prohibits scheme trustees from investing in personal chattels other than choses in action (or, in Scotland, movable property other than incorporeal movable property). A "chose in action" is something which is not corporeal, tangible, movable or visible and of which a person has not the present enjoyment but merely a right to recover it (if withheld) by action. Examples of personal chattels which are prohibited investments include works of art, jewellery, vintage cars, yachts, gold bullion etc. Examples of choses in action which are permitted investments include company shares, copyrights, financial futures etc. If scheme trustees are uncertain as to whether a particular investment would be acceptable, they should consult their professional advisers before making the investment.

Shared investments

20.76   There is no objection in principle to a scheme joining with other parties to make a single investment (e.g. In a property) provided that the other parties do not include a member of the scheme (see paragraph 20.52) or any person, apart from an employer or any Associated Employer, connected with a member of the scheme. The trustees should not, however, allow any restriction of the scheme's freedom to realise its investment how and when it wishes. The pensioneer trustee must also be a party to the documentation – paragraph 20.8 refers.

Transactions between tax approved occupational pension schemes and non-approved (or "top up") schemes

20.77   Transactions of any description between any tax approved scheme and non-approved schemes are **prohibited**. This applies in respect of any transactions between

- tax approved schemes and non-approved schemes of the same employer, and
- tax approved schemes of one employer and non-approved schemes of another employer – whether or not there is any connection between the employers or the schemes.

Non-approved schemes are generally *retirement benefits schemes* to which the provisions of sections 595 to 596C of the *Taxes Act* apply. Other than being a *retirement benefit scheme*, they do not have to adopt any particular form and there are no tax rules which govern their structure or the type, or amount, of benefits they provide.

Non-approved schemes are often known as

- FURBS (funded unapproved retirement benefit schemes)
- UURBS (unfunded unapproved retirement benefit schemes)

Non-approved schemes may also include pension schemes that

- lose tax approval – they become non-approved schemes from the effective date of withdrawal of approval
- are approved from a date later than their commencement date because of a late application for approval
- applied for approval but approval was refused.

20.78   The reason why transactions are not permitted is because there must be a clear demarcation between an employer's tax approved scheme and non-approved schemes. Otherwise, a blurring of the monies/investments held for the purposes of approved and non-approved schemes could result in tax reliefs/exemptions subsidizing the unlimited benefit provision of a non-approved scheme. There is also the possibility that conditions that might apply to the assets held for the purposes of an approved scheme can be avoided by temporarily sheltering those assets in a non-approved scheme.

20.79   The following list gives examples of prohibited transactions between tax approved schemes and non-approved schemes. This list is by no means exhaustive.

- A loan from a tax approved small self-adminstered scheme to a non-approved scheme
  - Regulation 6(1)(a) of the SSAS Regulations has the effect of prohibiting direct or indirect loans to the members (and connected persons) of tax approved SSASs. An indirect loan could occur where the trustees of a SSAS make a loan to the trustees of a non-approved scheme set up for the benefit of the member (or connected person) of the SSAS. Paragraph 20.61 contains a prohibition on "back to back" loans.

- Tax approved SSASs selling assets to non-approved schemes
  - The effect of Regulation 8(1)(a) of the SSAS Regulations is to prohibit the trustees of a tax approved SSAS from directly or indirectly selling assets to members (or connected persons) of the SSAS. An indirect sale of an asset could occur by the setting up of a non-approved scheme in respect of the SSAS member and the SSAS trustees selling the asset to the trustees of the non-approved scheme.

- Joint investment between a tax approved SSAS and a non-approved scheme

The trustees of a tax approved SSAS are able to invest in a particular asset with other parties (such as syndicated property investment) provided the other parties do no include members of the SSAS or other persons connected with a member and provided also the nature of the investment is in itself unobjectionable. A joint investment with a member of the SSAS could occur by setting up a non-approved scheme for the member of the SSAS and the trustees of the non-approved scheme entering into the joint investment on behalf of the member.

Trading

20.80   It is not necessarily inconsistent with approval for the trustees of a scheme to enter into trading activities but, as explained in paragraph 17.11, any profits are outside the protection of section 592(2). There have been, however, instances of scheme trustees either setting up a trading company or acquiring a controlling interest in such a company either directly or indirectly in order to convert non-tax exempt trading profits into tax exempt dividends. This is not consistent with approval and therefore regulation 5 of the SSAS Regulations prohibits scheme trustees from investing in the shares of an unlisted company which:

(a) carry more than 30% of the voting power in the company, or
(b) entitle the shareholder to more than 30% of any dividends declared by the company in respect of shares of the class held.

20.81   Where all members of the scheme have retired/taken their pension/died, no new investments in any stock or shares of any unlisted company will be permitted following the later of the first payment of the final retiring member's pension or the final *ex spouse* member taking a pension and the first payment of the final widow's/widower's or *dependant*'s pension (prospective widow's/widower's of retired members or *ex spouse* members in receipt of a pension, whose pensions must be secured at the same time as the retired or *ex spouse* members in accordance with paragraph 20.43 being regarded for this purpose as in receipt of pension). Existing stocks/shares should be sold within 5 years of the commencement of such pension payments or on attainment by the pensioner of age 70 if earlier. If the pensioner has already attained age 70 when payment of pension commences, such sale must take place immediately.

20.82   Where the scheme has both non-pensioners and pensioners, any portion of the funds notionally underpinning retired members', or *ex spouse* members' or widows', widowers', or *dependants*' benefits in payment where the purchase of annuity has been deferred must be excluded in determining the amount which may be used to buy stock or shares in any unlisted company. Within 5 years of the commencement of pensions to new pensioners or on attainment by the pensioner of age 70, if earlier, the trustees must ensure an appropriate proportion of the value of any stock or shares held in any unlisted company is sold. Where the pensioner has already attained age 70 when payment of pension commences, sale of an appropriate proportion of the stock/shares must take place immediately.

Other Requirements

Serious ill-health commutation

20.83   An approved small self-administered scheme may not exercise any provision for full commutation of an employee's or *ex spouse's* pension on grounds of exceptional circumstances of serious ill health without the specific prior agreement of *IR SPSS*.

Employer in liquidation

20.84   Scheme documentation should provide that, if an employer goes into liquidation without a successor, the scheme is to be wound-up or partially wound-up as appropriate. The proceeds are to be used in accordance with the documentation to purchase or transfer the accrued benefits. Any surplus is to be returned to the employer (see Part 13).

20.85   Alternatively, subject to scheme rules permitting, winding-up may be postponed and the scheme can continue as a paid - up scheme (see paragraph 14.4). The enabling provision must make such postponement subject to the agreement of the *Board* of the Inland Revenue and also subject to the such amendments or conditions as the *Board* may require.

20.86   The provisions allowing the scheme to continue must be in place before the employer goes into liquidation. If the employer that goes into liquidation is also the scheme *administrator*, the rules of the scheme should provide for a new *administrator* to succeed the liquidated employer.

APPENDIX 4
Income and Corporation Taxes Act 1988, ss 590–612, 618–655 and Schedule 23 (as amended)
(*As at July 2003*)

590 Conditions for approval of retirement benefit schemes

(1) Subject to section 591, the Board shall not approve any retirement benefits scheme for the purposes of this Chapter unless the scheme satisfies all of the conditions set out in subsection (2) below.

(2) The conditions are–

    [(a)   that the scheme is bona fide established for the sole purpose (subject to any enactment or Northern Ireland legislation requiring or allowing provision for the value of any rights to be transferred between schemes or between members of the same scheme) of providing relevant benefits in respect of service as an employee;]

    [(aa)   that those benefits do not include any benefits payable to a person other than–
        (i)   the employee or a scheme member's ex-spouse,
        (ii)   a widow, widower, child, or dependant of the employee or of a scheme member's ex-spouse, or
        (iii)   the personal representatives of the employee or of a scheme member's ex-spouse;]

    (b)   that the scheme is recognised by the employer and employees to whom it relates, and that every employee who is, or has a right to be, a member of the scheme has been given written particulars of all essential features of the scheme which concern him;

    (c)   that there is a person resident in the United Kingdom who will be responsible for the discharge of all duties imposed on the administrator of the scheme under this Chapter;

    (d)   that the employer is a contributor to the scheme;

    (e)   that the scheme is established in connection with some trade or undertaking carried on in the United Kingdom by a person resident in the United Kingdom;

    (f)   that in no circumstances, whether during the subsistence of the scheme or later, can any amount be paid by way of repayment of an employee's contributions under the scheme.

(3)   Subject to subsection (1) above, the Board shall approve a retirement benefits scheme for the purposes of this Chapter if the scheme satisfies all the conditions of this subsection, that is to say–

(a)   that any benefit for an employee is a pension on retirement at a specified age not earlier than 60 [and not later than 75], which does not exceed one-sixtieth of the employee's final remuneration for each year of service up to a maximum of 40;

(b)   that any benefit for any widow [or widower] of an employee is a pension payable on his death after retirement such that the amount payable to the widow [or widower] by way of pension does not exceed two-thirds of any pension or pensions payable to the employee;

[(ba) that any benefit for an ex-spouse, or for the widow or widower of an ex-spouse, is a benefit in relation to which the scheme satisfies the conditions set out in subsection (3A) below;

(bb)   that the scheme does not allow any rights debited to a scheme member as a consequence of a pension sharing order or provision to be replaced with any rights which that scheme member would not have been able to acquire (in addition to the debited rights) had the order or provision not been made;

(c)   that no benefits are payable under the scheme other than those mentioned in paragraphs (a), (b) and (ba) above;]

(d)   that no pension is capable in whole or in part of surrender, commutation or assignment, [except–

   (i)   for the purpose of giving effect to a pension sharing order or provision, or

   (ii)   in so far as the commutation of a benefit for an ex-spouse is allowed by virtue of subsection (3A) below, or

   (iii)] in so far as the scheme allows an employee on retirement to obtain, by commutation of [a pension provided for him],

   a lump sum or sums not exceeding in all three-eightieths of his final remuneration . . . for each year of service up to a maximum of 40;

[(da) that, in a case in which–

   (i)   a lump sum may be obtained by the commutation of a part of a pension provided for an employee, and

   (ii)   the amount of that pension is affected by the making of a pension sharing order or provision,

   the lump sum does not exceed the sum produced by multiplying by 2.25 the amount which (after effect has been given to the pension sharing order or provision) is the amount of that pension for the first year in which it is payable;]

[(e)   that, in the case of any employee who is a member of the scheme by virtue of two or more relevant associated employments, the amount payable by way of pension in respect of service in any one of them may not, when aggregated with any amount payable by way of pension in respect of service in the other or others, exceed the relevant amount;

(f)   that, in the case of any employee who is a member of the scheme by virtue of two or more relevant associated employments, the amount payable by way of commuted pension in respect of service in any one of them may not, when aggregated with any amount payable by way of commuted pension in respect of service in the other or others, exceed the relevant amount;

(g) that, in the case of any employee in relation to whom the scheme is connected with another scheme which is (or other schemes each of which is) an approved scheme, the amount payable by way of pension under the scheme may not, when aggregated with any amount payable by way of pension under the other scheme or schemes, exceed the relevant amount;

(h) that, in the case of any employee in relation to whom the scheme is connected with another scheme which is (or other schemes each of which is) an approved scheme, the amount payable by way of commuted pension may not, when aggregated with any amount payable by way of commuted pension under the other scheme or schemes, exceed the relevant amount.]

[(3A)   The conditions mentioned in subsection (3)(ba) above are–

(a) that any benefit for an ex-spouse takes the form of a pension (with or without an entitlement to commute a part of that pension);

(b) that any benefit for an ex-spouse is a pension payable only on the attainment by the ex-spouse of a specified age of not less than 60 and not more than 75;

(c) that any entitlement to commute a part of the pension is exercisable only on its becoming payable;

(d) that any benefit for the widow or widower of an ex-spouse is confined to a non-commutable pension payable on the death of the ex-spouse at a time when the ex-spouse is already entitled to receive a pension under the scheme;

(e) that any pension provided for the widow or widower of an ex-spouse is of an amount not exceeding two-thirds of the pension payable to the ex-spouse;

(f) that, in a case in which a lump sum may be obtained by the commutation of a part of a pension provided for an ex-spouse, the lump sum does not exceed the sum produced by multiplying the amount of the pension for the first year in which it is payable by 2.25.]

(4)   The conditions set out in [subsections (2) to (3A)] above are in this Chapter referred to as "the prescribed conditions".

[(4A)   In subsection (3)(c) above "benefits" does not include any benefits for whose payment the scheme makes provision in pursuance of any obligation imposed by legislation relating to social security.]

[(4B)   For the purposes of this section a benefit provided under any scheme is provided for an ex-spouse or the widow or widower of an ex-spouse, and shall be treated as not provided for an employee or the widow or widower of an employee, to the extent (and to the extent only) that–

(a) it is provided for a person who is, or is the widow or widower of, either–

(i) an employee who is an ex-spouse; or

  (ii) a scheme member's ex-spouse;
  and
(b) it is as an ex-spouse, or as the widow or widower of an ex-spouse, that that person is the person for whom the benefit is provided.

(4C) For the purposes of this section a benefit provided for any person under any scheme is provided for that person as an ex-spouse, or as the widow or widower of an ex-spouse, to the extent (and to the extent only) that–

(a) the benefit is provided in respect of rights of an ex-spouse that are or represent rights conferred on the ex-spouse as a consequence of a pension sharing order or provision; and
(b) the scheme makes provision for the benefit to be treated as provided separately from any benefits which are provided under the scheme for the same person as an employee or as the widow or widower of an employee.

(4D) In this section "scheme member", in relation to a scheme, means–

(a) an employee; or
(b) a person entitled to any relevant benefits under the scheme as a consequence of a pension sharing order or provision.

(4E) The following rules shall apply in calculating for the purposes of subsection (3)(da) or (3A)(f) above the amount of a person's pension for the first year in which it is payable–

(a) if the pension payable for the year changes, the initial pension payable shall be taken;
(b) it shall be assumed that that person will survive for the year; and
(c) the effect of commutation shall be ignored.

(4F) A pension provided for an ex-spouse who is an employee, or for the widow or widower of such an ex-spouse, shall be disregarded in any determination of whether the conditions set out in subsection (3)(e) to (h) above are satisfied or continue to be satisfied in the case of that employee.]

(5), (6) . . .

[(7) Subsections (8) to (10) below apply where the Board are considering whether a retirement benefits scheme satisfies or continues to satisfy the prescribed conditions.

(8) For the purpose of determining whether the scheme, so far as it relates to a particular class or description of employees, satisfies or continues to satisfy the prescribed conditions, that scheme shall be considered in conjunction with–

(a) any other retirement benefits scheme (or schemes) which relates (or relate) to employees of that class or description and which is (or are) approved for the purposes of this Chapter,
(b) any other retirement benefits scheme (or schemes) which relates (or relate) to employees of that class or description and which is (or are) at the same time before the Board in order for them to decide whether to give approval for the purposes of this Chapter,

    (c) any section 608 scheme or schemes relating to employees of that class or description, and

    (d) any relevant statutory scheme or schemes relating to employees of that class or description.

(9) If those conditions are satisfied in the case of both or all of those schemes taken together, they shall be taken to be satisfied in the case of the scheme mentioned in subsection (7) above (as well as the other or others).

(10) If those conditions are not satisfied in the case of both or all of those schemes taken together, they shall not be taken to be satisfied in the case of the scheme mentioned in subsection (7) above.

(11) The reference in subsection (8)(c) above to a section 608 scheme is a reference to a fund to which section 608 applies.]

[590A   Section 590: supplementary provisions]

[(1) For the purposes of section 590(3)(e) and (f) two or more employments are relevant associated employments if they are employments in the case of which–

    (a) there is a period during which the employee has held both or all of them,

    (b) the period counts under the scheme in the case of both or all of them as a period in respect of which benefits are payable, and

    (c) the period is one during which both or all of the employers in question are associated.

(2) For the purposes of section 590(3)(g) and (h) the scheme is connected with another scheme in relation to an employee if–

    (a) there is a period during which he has been the employee of two persons who are associated employers,

    (b) the period counts under both schemes as a period in respect of which benefits are payable, and

    (c) the period counts under one scheme by virtue of service with one employer and under the other scheme by virtue of service with the other employer.

(3) For the purposes of subsections (1) and (2) above, employers are associated if (directly or indirectly) one is controlled by the other or if both are controlled by a third person.

(4) In subsection (3) above the reference to control, in relation to a body corporate, shall·be construed–

    (a) where the body corporate is a close company, in accordance with section 416, and

    (b) where it is not, in accordance with section 840.]

[590B   Section 590: further supplementary provisions]

[(1) For the purposes of section 590(3)(e) the relevant amount, in relation to an employee, shall be found by applying the following formula–

$$\frac{A \times C}{60}$$

(2)   For the purposes of section 590(3)(f) the relevant amount, in relation to an employee, shall be found by applying the following formula–

$$\frac{3 \times A \times C}{80}$$

(3)   For the purposes of section 590(3)(g) the relevant amount, in relation to an employee, shall be found by applying the following formula–

$$\frac{B \times C}{60}$$

(4)   For the purposes of section 590(3)(h) the relevant amount, in relation to an employee, shall be found by applying the following formula–

$$\frac{3 \times B \times C}{80}$$

(5)   For the purposes of this section A is the aggregate number of years service (expressing parts of a year as a fraction), subject to a maximum of 40, which, in the case of the employee, count for the purposes of the scheme at the time the benefits in respect of service in the employment become payable.

(6)   But where the same year (or part of a year) counts for the purposes of the scheme by virtue of more than one of the relevant associated employments it shall be counted only once in calculating the aggregate number of years service for the purposes of subsection (5) above.

(7)   For the purposes of this section B is the aggregate number of years service (expressing parts of a year as a fraction), subject to a maximum of 40, which, in the case of the employee, count for the purposes of any of the following–

   (a)   the scheme, and
   (b)   the other scheme or schemes with which the scheme is connected in relation to him,

at the time the benefits become payable.

(8)   But where the same year (or part of a year) counts for the purposes of more than one scheme it shall be counted only once in calculating the aggregate number of years service for the purpose of subsection (7) above.

(9)   For the purposes of this section C is the permitted maximum in relation to the year of assessment in which the benefits in question become payable, that is, the figure found for that year by virtue of subsections (10) and (11) below.

(10)   For the years 1988–89 and 1989–90 the figure is £60,000.

(11)   For any subsequent year of assessment the figure is the figure found for that year, for the purposes of section 590C, by virtue of section 590C(4) [to (5A)].]

[590C   Earnings cap]

[(1)   In arriving at an employee's final remuneration for the purposes of section 590(3)(a) or (d), any excess of what would be his final remuneration (apart from this section) over the permitted maximum for the year of assessment in which his participation in the scheme ceases shall be disregarded.

(2)   In subsection (1) above "the permitted maximum", in relation to a year of assessment, means the figure found for that year by virtue of subsections (3) and (4) below.

(3)   For the years 1988–89 and 1989–90 the figure is £60,000.

(4)   For any subsequent year of assessment the figure is also £60,000, subject to [subsections (5) and (5A)] below.

(5)   If the retail prices index for the month of [September] preceding a year of assessment falling within subsection (4) above is higher than it was for the previous [September], the figure for that year shall be an amount arrived at by–

- (a)   increasing the figure for the previous year of assessment by the same percentage as the percentage increase in the retail prices index, and
- (b)   if the result is not a multiple of £600, rounding it up to the nearest amount which is such a multiple.

[(5A)   If the retail prices index for the month of September preceding a year of assessment falling within subsection (4) above is not higher than it was for the previous September, the figure for that year shall be the same as the figure for the previous year of assessment.]

(6)   The Treasury shall in the year of assessment 1989–90, and in each subsequent year of assessment, make an order specifying the figure which is by virtue of this section the figure for the following year of assessment.]

591   Discretionary approval

(1)   The Board may, if they think fit having regard to the facts of a particular case, and subject to such conditions, if any, as they think proper to attach to the approval, approve a retirement benefits scheme for the purposes of this Chapter notwithstanding that it does not satisfy one or more of the prescribed conditions; but this subsection has effect subject to subsection (5) below.

(2)   The Board may in particular approve by virtue of this section a scheme–
- (a)   which exceeds the limits imposed by the prescribed conditions as respects benefits for less than 40 years; or
- (b)   which provides pensions for the widows [and widowers] of employees on death in service, or for the children or dependants of employees; or
- [(ba)   which provides pensions for the widows and widowers of ex-spouses dying before the age at which their pensions become payable and for the children or dependants of ex-spouses; or]
- (c)   which provides on death in service a lump sum of up to four times the employee's final remuneration (exclusive of any refunds of contributions); or

(d) which allows benefits to be payable on retirement within ten years of the specified age, or on earlier incapacity; or

(e) which provides for the return in certain contingencies of employees' contributions; or

(f) which relates to a trade or undertaking carried on only partly in the United Kingdom and by a person not resident in the United Kingdom; or

(g) which provides in certain contingencies for securing relevant benefits [falling within subsection (2A) below] (but no other benefits) by means of an annuity contract . . . made with an insurance company of the employee's choice; or

(h) to which the employer is not a contributor and which provides benefits additional to those provided by a scheme to which he is a contributor.

[(2A)   Relevant benefits fall within this subsection if they correspond with benefits that could be provided by an approved scheme, and for this purpose–

(a) a hypothetical scheme (rather than any particular scheme) is to be taken, and

(b) benefits provided by a scheme directly (rather than by means of an annuity contract) are to be taken.]

[(3)   In subsection (2)(g) above "insurance company" has the meaning given by section 659B.]

(4)   In applying this section to a scheme which was in existence on 6th April 1980, the Board shall exercise their discretion, in such cases as appear to them to be appropriate, so as to preserve–

(a) benefits earned or rights arising out of service before 6th April 1980; and

(b) any rights to death-in-service benefits conferred by rules of the scheme in force on 26th February 1970.

(5)   The Board shall not approve a scheme by virtue of this section if to do so would be inconsistent with regulations made [by the Board] for the purposes of this section.

(6)   Regulations made [by the Board] for the purposes of this section may restrict the Board's discretion to approve a scheme by reference to the benefits provided by the scheme, the investments held for the purposes of the scheme, the manner in which the scheme is administered or any other circumstances whatever.

[591A   Effect on approved schemes of regulations under section 591]

[(1)   Subsection (2) below applies where on or after 17th April 1991 regulations are made for the purposes of section 591 ("section 591 regulations") which contain provisions restricting the Board's discretion to approve a retirement benefits scheme by reference to any circumstances other than the benefits provided by the scheme ("relevant provisions").

(2)   Any retirement benefits scheme approved by the Board by virtue of section 591 before the day on which the section 591 regulations come into force shall

cease to be approved by virtue of that section at the end of the period of 36 months beginning with that day if at the end of that period the scheme–

    (a)   contains a provision of a prohibited description, or

    (b)   does not contain a provision of a required description,

unless the description of provision is specified in regulations made by the Board for the purposes of this subsection.

(3)   For the purposes of this section, a provision contained in a scheme shall not be treated as being of a prohibited description by reason only of the fact that it authorises the retention of an investment held immediately before the day on which the section 591 regulations are made.

(4)   In determining for the purposes of this section whether any provision contained in a scheme is of a required description, the fact that it is framed so as not to require the disposal of an investment held immediately before the day on which the section 591 regulations are made shall be disregarded.

(5)   In this section–

    (a)   references to a provision of a prohibited description are to a provision of a description specified in the relevant provisions of the section 591 regulations as a description of provision which, if contained in a retirement benefits scheme, would prevent the Board from approving the scheme by virtue of section 591;

    (b)   references to a provision of a required description are to a provision of a description specified in the relevant provisions of the section 591 regulations as a description of provision which must be contained in a retirement benefits scheme before the Board may approve the scheme by virtue of section 591.]

[591B   Cessation of approval: general provisions]

[(1)   If in the opinion of the Board the facts concerning any approved scheme or its administration cease to warrant the continuance of their approval of the scheme, they may at any time by notice to the administrator, withdraw their approval on such grounds, and from such date (which shall not be earlier than the date when those facts first ceased to warrant the continuance of their approval or 17th March 1987, whichever is the later), as may be specified in the notice.

(2)   Where an alteration has been made in a retirement benefits scheme, no approval given by the Board as regards the scheme before the alteration shall apply after the date of the alteration unless–

    (a)   the alteration has been approved by the Board, or

    (b)   the scheme is of a class specified in regulations made by the Board for the purposes of this paragraph and the alteration is of a description so specified in relation to schemes of that class.]

[591C   Cessation of approval: tax on certain schemes]

[(1)   Where an approval of a scheme to which this section applies ceases to have effect [otherwise than by virtue of paragraph 3(2)(a) of Schedule 23ZA], tax shall be charged in accordance with this section.

(2)   The tax shall be charged under Case VI of Schedule D at the rate of 40 per cent on an amount equal to the value of the assets which immediately before the date of the cessation of the approval of the scheme are held for the purposes of the scheme (taking that value as it stands immediately before that date).

(3)   Subject to section 591D(4), the person liable for the tax shall be the administrator of the scheme . . ..

(4)   This section applies to a retirement benefits scheme in respect of which [one or more] of the conditions set out below is satisfied.

(5)   The first condition is satisfied in respect of a scheme if, immediately before the date of the cessation of the approval of the scheme, the number of individuals who are members of the scheme is less than twelve.

(6)   The second condition is satisfied in respect of a scheme if at any time within the period of one year ending with the date of the cessation of the approval of the scheme, a person who is or has been a controlling director of a company which has contributed to the scheme is a member of the scheme.

[(6A)   The third condition is satisfied in respect of a scheme if–

- (a)   at any time within the period of three years ending with the date of the cessation of the approval of the scheme, the scheme has received a transfer value in respect of any person;
- (b)   contributions made by or in respect of that person to any approved pension arrangements (whether or not those from which the transfer value was received) were represented in the transfer value; and
- (c)   the contributions so represented were made by or in respect of that person by reference to–
    - (i)   any service by him with a company of which he is or has at any time been a controlling director;
    - (ii)   any remuneration in respect of any such service; or
    - (iii)   any income chargeable to tax under Schedule D and immediately derived by him from the carrying on or exercise by him (whether as an individual or in partnership with others) of a trade, profession or vocation.]

(7)   For the purposes of [this section] a person is a controlling director of a company if he is a director of it and within section 417(5)(b) in relation to it.]

[(8)   In subsection (6A) above–

- (a)   the references to the receipt of a transfer value by a scheme are references to the transfer, so as to become held for the purposes of the scheme, of any sum or asset held for the purposes of any other approved pension arrangements; and
- (b)   the references to contributions to approved pension arrangements include references to–
    - (i)   any contributions made in accordance with, or for the purposes of, the arrangements; and
    - (ii)   anything paid by way of premium or other consideration under an annuity contract for which the arrangements provide.

(9)   In this section "approved pension arrangements" means–

   (a)   any scheme or arrangements approved for the purposes of this Chapter or Chapter IV of this Part or, in relation to a time before 6th April 1988, the corresponding provisions then in force;

   (b)   any scheme being considered for approval under this Chapter;

   (c)   any annuity contract entered into for the purposes of any scheme or arrangements falling within paragraph (a) or (b) above; or

   (d)   any contract or scheme approved for the purposes of Chapter III of this Part or, in relation to a time before 6th April 1988, the corresponding provisions then in force.]

[591D   Section 591C: supplementary]

[(1)   For the purposes of section 591C(2) the value of an asset is, subject to subsection (2) below, its market value, construing "market value" in accordance with section 272 of the 1992 Act.

(2)   Where an asset held for the purposes of a scheme a right or interest in respect of any money lent (directly or indirectly) to any person mentioned in subsection (3) below, the value of the asset shall be treated as being the amount owing (including any unpaid interest) on the money lent.

(3)   The persons are–

   (a)   any employer who has at any time contributed to the scheme;

   (b)   any company connected with such an employer;

   [(c)   any person who has at any time (whether or not before the making of the loan) been a member of the scheme;

   (d)   any person connected, at the time of the making of the loan or subsequently, with a person falling within paragraph (c) above.]

(4)   Where the administrator of the scheme constituted by persons who include a person who is an approved independent trustee in relation to a scheme, that person shall not be liable for tax chargeable by virtue of section 591C.

(5)   A person is an approved independent trustee in relation to a scheme only if he is–

   (a)   approved by the Board to act as a trustee of the scheme; and

   (b)   not connected with–

      (i)   a member of the scheme;

      (ii)   any other trustee of the scheme; or

      (iii)   an employer who has contributed to the scheme.

(6)   . . .

(7)   The reference in section 591C(1) to an approval of a scheme ceasing to have effect is a reference to–

   (a)   the scheme ceasing to be an approved scheme by virtue of section 591A(2);

   (b)   the approval of the scheme being withdrawn under section 591B(1); or

   (c)   the approval of the scheme no longer applying by virtue of section 591B(2);

and any reference in section 591C to the date of the cessation of the approval of the scheme shall be construed accordingly.

(8) For the purposes of section 591C and this section a person is a member of a scheme at a particular time if at that time a benefit–

(a) is being provided under the scheme, or

(b) may be so provided,

in respect of any past or present employment of his.

(9) Section 839 shall apply for the purposes of this section.]

592 Exempt approved schemes

(1) This section has effect as respects–

(a) any approved scheme which is shown to the satisfaction of the Board to be established under irrevocable trusts; or

(b) any other approved scheme as respects which the Board, having regard to any special circumstances, direct that this section shall apply;

and any scheme which is for the time being within paragraph (a) or (b) above is in this Chapter referred to as an "exempt approved scheme".

(2) Exemption from income tax shall, on a claim being made in that behalf, be allowed in respect of income derived from investments or deposits if, or to such extent as the Board are satisfied that, it is income from investments or deposits held for the purposes of the scheme.

(3) Exemption from income tax shall, on a claim being made in that behalf, be allowed in respect of underwriting commissions if, or to such extent as the Board are satisfied that, the underwriting commissions are applied for the purposes of the schemes and would, but for this subsection, be chargeable to tax under Case VI of Schedule D.

(4) Any sum paid by an employer by way of contribution under the scheme shall, for the purposes of Case I or II of Schedule D and of sections 75 and 76, be allowed to be deducted as an expense, or expense of management, incurred in the chargeable period in which the sum is paid [but no other sum shall for those purposes be allowed to be deducted as an expense, or expense of management, in respect of the making, or any provision for the making, of any contributions under the scheme].

(5) The amount of an employer's contributions which may be deducted under subsection (4) above shall not exceed the amount contributed by him under the scheme in respect of employees in a trade or undertaking in respect of the profits of which the employer is assessable to tax (that is to say, to United Kingdom income tax or corporation tax).

(6) A sum not paid by way of ordinary annual contribution shall for the purposes of subsection (4) above be treated, as the Board may direct, either as an expense incurred in the chargeable period in which the sum is paid, or as an expense to be spread over such period of years as the Board think proper.

[(6A) Where any sum is paid to the trustees of the scheme in or towards the discharge of any liability of an employer under section 58B of the Social Security

355

Pensions Act 1975 or section 144 of the Pension Schemes Act 1993 (deficiencies in the assets of a scheme) or under Article 68B of the Social Security Pensions (Northern Ireland) Order 1975 or section 140 of the Pension Schemes (Northern Ireland) Act 1993 (which contain corresponding provision for Northern Ireland), the payment of that sum–

(a) shall be treated for the purposes of this section as an employer's contribution under the scheme; and

(b) notwithstanding (where it is the case) that the employer's trade, profession, vocation or business is permanently discontinued before the making of the payment, shall be allowed, in accordance with subsection (4) above, to be deducted as such a contribution to the same extent as it would have been allowed but for the discontinuance and as if it had been made on the last day on which the trade, profession, vocation or business was carried on.]

[(7) Any contribution paid under the scheme shall be allowed to be deducted from employment income for the year of assessment in which the contribution is paid.

A deduction under this subsection may only be made once in respect of the same contribution.]

(8) [Subject to subsection (8A) below,] the amount allowed to be deducted by virtue of subsection (7) above in respect of contributions paid by an employee in a year of assessment (whether under a single scheme or under two or more schemes) shall not exceed 15 per cent, or such higher percentage as the Board may in a particular case prescribe, of his remuneration for that year.

[(8A) Where an employee's remuneration for a year of assessment includes remuneration in respect of more than one employment, the amount allowed to be deducted by virtue of subsection (7) above in respect of contributions paid by the employee in that year by virtue of any employment (whether under a single scheme or under two or more schemes) shall not exceed 15 per cent, or such higher percentage as the Board may in a particular case prescribe, of his remuneration for the year in respect of that employment.]

[(8B) In arriving at an employee's remuneration for a year of assessment for the purposes of subsection (8) or (8A) above, any excess of what would be his remuneration (apart from this subsection) over the permitted maximum for that year shall be disregarded.

(8C) In subsection (8B) above "permitted maximum", in relation to a year of assessment, means the figure found for that year by virtue of subsections (8D) and (8E) below.

(8D) For the year 1989–90 the figure is £60,000.

(8E) For any subsequent year of assessment the figure is the figure found for that year, for the purposes of section 590C, by virtue of section 590C(4) [to (5A)].]

(9) Relief shall not be given under section 266 or 273 in respect of any payment in respect of which an allowance can be made under subsection (7) above.

(10)   Subsection (2) of section 468 and subsection (3) of section 469 shall not apply to any authorised unit trust which is also an exempt approved scheme if the employer is not a contributor to the exempt approved scheme and that scheme provides benefits additional to those provided by another exempt approved scheme to which he is a contributor.

(11)   Nothing in this section shall be construed as affording relief in respect of any sums to be brought into account under section 438.

(12)   This section has effect only as respects income arising or contributions paid at a time when the scheme is an exempt approved scheme.

593   Relief by way of deductions from contributions

(1)   Relief under section 592(7) shall be given in accordance with subsections (2) and (3) below in such cases and subject to such conditions as the Board may prescribe by regulations under section 612(3) in respect of schemes–

   (a)   to which employees, but not their employers, are contributors; and
   (b)   which provide benefits additional to benefits provided by schemes to which their employers are contributors.

(2)   An employee who is entitled to relief under section 592(7) in respect of a contribution may deduct from the contribution when he pays it, and may retain, an amount equal to income tax at the basic rate on the contribution.

(3)   The administrator of the scheme–

   (a)   shall accept the amount paid after the deduction in discharge of the employee's liability to the same extent as if the deduction had not been made; and
   (b)   may recover an amount equal to the deduction from the Board.

(4)   Regulations under subsection (3) of section 612 may, without prejudice to the generality of that subsection–

   (a)   provide for the manner in which claims for the recovery of a sum under subsection (3)(b) above may be made;
   (b)   provide for the giving of such information, in such form, as may be prescribed by or under the regulations;
   (c)   provide for the inspection by persons authorised by the Board of books, documents and other records.

594   Exempt statutory schemes

(1)   Any contribution paid by any officer or employee under a [relevant] statutory scheme established under a public general Act [shall be allowed to be deducted from employment income for] the year of assessment in which the contribution is paid; and relief shall not be given under section 266 or 273 in respect of any contribution allowable as a deduction under this section. [A deduction under this section may only be made once in respect of the same contribution.]

(2)   [Subject to subsection (3) below,] the amount allowed to be deducted by virtue of subsection (1) above in respect of contributions paid by a person in a year of assessment (whether under a single scheme or under two or more

schemes) shall not exceed 15 per cent, or such higher percentage as the Board may in a particular case prescribe, of his remuneration for that year.

[(3)   Where a person's remuneration for a year of assessment includes remuneration in respect of more than one office or employment, the amount allowed to be deducted by virtue of subsection (1) above in respect of contributions paid by the person in that year by virtue of any office or employment (whether under a single scheme or under two or more schemes) shall not exceed 15 per cent, or such higher percentage as the Board may in a particular case prescribe, of his remuneration for the year in respect of that office or employment.]

[(4)   In arriving at a person's remuneration for a year of assessment for the purposes of subsection (2) or (3) above, any excess of what would be his remuneration (apart from this subsection) over the permitted maximum for that year shall be disregarded.

(5)   In subsection (4) above "permitted maximum", in relation to a year of assessment, means the figure found for that year by virtue of subsections (6) and (7) below.

(6)   For the year 1989–90 the figure is £60,000.

(7)   For any subsequent year of assessment the figure is the figure found for that year, for the purposes of section 590C, by virtue of section 590C(4) [to (5A)].]

Charge to tax in certain cases

595 ...

. . .

596 ...

. . .

[596A ...]

[. . .]

[596B ...]

[. . .]

[596C ...]

[. . .]

597 ...

. . .

598   Charge to tax: repayment of employee's contributions

(1)   Subject to the provisions of this section, tax shall be charged under this section on any repayment to an employee during his lifetime of any contributions (including interest on contributions, if any) if the payment is made under–

> (a)   a scheme which is or has at any time been an exempt approved scheme, or

(b) a [relevant] statutory scheme established under a public general Act.

(2)   Where any payment is chargeable to tax under this section, the administrator of the scheme shall be charged to income tax under Case VI of Schedule D and, subject to subsection (3) below, the rate of tax shall be 10 per cent.

(3)   The Treasury may by order from time to time increase or decrease the rate of tax under subsection (2) above.

(4)   The tax shall be charged on the amount paid or, if the rules permit the administrator to deduct the tax before payment, on the amount before deduction of tax, and the amount so charged to tax shall not be treated as income for any other purpose of the Tax Acts.

(5)   Subsection (1)(a) above shall not apply in relation to a contribution made after the scheme ceases to be an exempt approved scheme (unless it again becomes an exempt approved scheme).

(6)   This section shall not apply where the employee's employment was carried on outside the United Kingdom.

(7)   In relation to a statutory scheme, "employee" in this section includes any officer.

599   Charge to tax: commutation of entire pension in special circumstances

(1)   [Subject to subsection (1A) below,] where a scheme to which this section applies contains a rule allowing, in special circumstances, a payment in commutation of an employee's entire pension, and any pension is commuted, whether wholly or not, under the rule, tax shall be charged on the amount by which the sum receivable exceeds–

(a) the largest sum which would have been receivable in commutation of any part of the pension if the scheme had secured that the aggregate value of the relevant benefits payable to an employee on or after retirement, excluding any pension which was not commutable, could not exceed three-eightieths of his final remuneration (disregarding any excess of that remuneration over the permitted maximum) for each year of service up to a maximum of 40; or

(b) the largest sum which would have been receivable in commutation of any part of the pension under any rule of the scheme authorising the commutation of part (but not the whole) of the pension, or which would have been so receivable but for those special circumstances;

whichever gives the lesser amount chargeable to tax.

[(1A)   Subsection (1) above shall have effect in relation to the commutation of the whole or any part of a pension the amount of which has been affected by the making of any pension sharing order or provision as if paragraph (a) and the words after paragraph (b) were omitted.

(1B)   Where–

(a) a scheme to which this section applies contains a rule allowing, in special circumstances, a payment in commutation of the entire pension provided under the scheme for an ex-spouse, and

(b)   any pension is commuted, whether wholly or not, under the rule,

tax shall be charged on the amount by which the sum receivable exceeds the largest sum which would have been receivable in commutation of any part of the pension under any rule of the scheme authorising the commutation of a part (but not the whole) of the pension.

(1C)   A pension provided for an ex-spouse shall be disregarded when applying subsection (1) above in relation to the commutation of any pension provided for an employee.

(1D)   A pension provided for an employee shall be disregarded when applying subsection (1B) above in relation to the commutation of any pension provided for an ex-spouse.

(1E)   Subsections (4B) and (4C) of section 590 apply for the purposes of subsections (1C) and (1D) above as they apply for the purposes of that section.]

(2)   This section applies to–

(a)   a scheme which is or has at any time been an approved scheme, or

(b)   a [relevant] statutory scheme established under a public general Act.

(3)   Where any amount is chargeable to tax under this section the administrator of the scheme shall be charged to income tax under Case VI of Schedule D on that amount, and section 598(2), (3) and (4) shall apply as they apply to tax chargeable under that section.

(4)   This section shall not apply where the employee's employment was carried on outside the United Kingdom.

(5)   In relation to a statutory scheme, "employee" in this section includes any officer.

(6)   In applying paragraph (a) or (b) of subsection (1) above[, or in applying subsection (1B) above]–

(a)   the same considerations shall be taken into account, including the provisions of any other relevant scheme, as would have been taken into account by the Board in applying section 590; and

(b)   where the scheme has ceased to be an approved scheme, account shall only be taken of the rules in force when the scheme was last an approved scheme.

(7)   Where the pension has been secured by means of an annuity contract with an insurance company and the sum receivable is payable under that contract by the insurance company, the references to the administrator of the scheme in subsection (3) above and in section 598(2) and (4) as applied by that subsection are to be read as references to the insurance company.

[(8)   In subsection (7) above "insurance company" has the meaning given by section 659B.]

(9)   In relation to payments made under schemes approved or established before 17th March 1987 to employees who became members before that date, subsection (1)(a) above shall have effect with the omission of the words "(disregarding any excess of that remuneration over the permitted maximum)".

[(10)   In subsection (1)(a) above "the permitted maximum" means, as regards a charge to tax arising under this section in a particular year of assessment, the figure found for that year by virtue of subsections (11) and (12) below.

(11)   For the years 1988–89 and 1989–90 the figure is £60,000.

(12)   For any subsequent year of assessment the figure is the figure found for that year, for the purposes of section 590C, by virtue of section 590C(4) [to (5A)].]

[599A   Charge to tax: payments out of surplus funds]

[(1)   This subsection applies to any payment which is made to or for the benefit of an employee or to his personal representatives out of funds which are or have been held for the purposes of–

   (a)   a scheme which is or has at any time been an exempt approved scheme, or
   (b)   a relevant statutory scheme established under a public general Act,

and which is made in pursuance of duty to return surplus funds.

(2)   On the making of a payment to which subsection (1) above applies, the administrator of the scheme shall be charged to income tax under Case VI of Schedule D at the relevant rate on such amount as, after deduction of tax at that rate, would equal the amount of the payment.

(3)   Subject to subsection (4) below, the relevant rate shall be 35 per cent.

(4)   The Treasury may by order from time to time increase or decrease the relevant rate.

(5)   . . .

(6)   . . .

(7)   . . .

(8)   . . .

(9)   Any payment chargeable to tax under this section shall not be chargeable to tax under section 598, 599 or 600 or under the Regulations mentioned in paragraph 8 of Schedule 3 to the Finance Act 1971.

(10)   In this section–

   "employee", in relation to a relevant statutory scheme, includes any officer;

   references to any payment include references to any transfer of assets or other transfer of money's worth.]

600 ...

. . .

601   Charge to tax: payments to employers

(1)   Subsection (2) below applies where a payment is made to an employer out of funds which are or have been held for the purposes of a scheme which is or has at any time been an exempt approved scheme and whether or not the payment is made in pursuance of Schedule 22.

(2)   An amount equal to [the relevant percentage of the payment] shall be recoverable by the Board from the employer.

[(2A)   The relevant percentage is 35% or such other percentage (whether higher or lower) as may be prescribed.]

(3)   Subsection (2) above does not apply to any payment–

    (a) to the extent that, if this section had not been enacted, the employer would have been exempt, or entitled to claim exemption, from income tax or corporation tax in respect of the payment; or

    (b) made before the scheme became an exempt approved scheme; or

    (c) of any prescribed description; or

    (d) made in pursuance of the winding-up of the scheme where the winding-up commenced on or before 18th March 1986; or

    (e) made in pursuance of an application which–

        (i) was made to the Board on or before that date and was not withdrawn before the making of the payment, and

        (ii) sought the Board's assurance that the payment would not lead to a withdrawal of approval under section 19(3) of the Finance Act 1970;

(4)   Subsection (2) above does not apply where the employer is a charity (within the meaning of section 506).

(5)   Where any payment is made or becomes due to an employer out of funds which are or have been held for the purposes of a scheme which is or has at any time been an exempt approved scheme then–

    (a) if the scheme relates to a trade, profession or vocation carried on by the employer, the payment shall be treated for the purposes of the Tax Acts as a receipt of that trade, profession or vocation receivable when the payment falls due or on the last day on which the trade, profession or vocation is carried on by the employer, whichever is the earlier;

    (b) if the scheme does not relate to such a trade, profession or vocation, the employer shall be charged to tax on the amount of the payment under Case VI of Schedule D.

This subsection shall not apply to a payment which fell due before the scheme became an exempt approved scheme or to a payment to which subsection (2) above applies or would apply but for subsection (3)(a) or (4) above.

(6)   In this section–

    (a) references to any payment include references to any transfer of assets or other transfer of money's worth; and

    (b) "prescribed" means prescribed by regulations made by the Treasury.

602   Regulations relating to pension fund surpluses

(1)   In relation to an amount recoverable as mentioned in section 601(2), the Treasury may by regulations make any of the provisions mentioned in subsection (2) below; and for this purpose the amount shall be treated as if it were–

(a) an amount of income tax chargeable on the employer under Case VI of Schedule D for the year of assessment in which the payment is made; or

(b) where the employer is a company, an amount of corporation tax chargeable on the company for the accounting period in which the payment is made.

(2) The provisions are–

(a) provision requiring the administrator of the scheme or the employer (or both) to furnish to the Board, in respect of the amount recoverable and of the payment concerned, information of a prescribed kind;

(b) provision enabling the Board to serve a notice or notices requiring the administrator or employer (or both) to furnish to the Board, in respect of the amount and payment, particulars of a prescribed kind;

(c) provision requiring the administrator to deduct out of the payment the amount recoverable and to account to the Board for it;

(d) provision as to circumstances in which the employer may be assessed in respect of the amount recoverable;

(e) provision that, in a case where the employer has been assessed in respect of an amount recoverable but has not paid it (or part of it) within a prescribed period, the administrator may be assessed and charged (in the employer's name) in respect of the amount (or part unpaid);

(f) provision that, in a case where the amount recoverable (or part of it) has been recovered from the administrator by virtue of an assessment in the employer's name, the administrator is entitled to recover from the employer a sum equal to the amount (or part);

(g) provision enabling the employer or administrator (as the case may be) to appeal against an assessment made on him in respect of the amount recoverable;

(h) provision as to when any sum in respect of the amount recoverable is payable to the Board by the administrator or employer and provision requiring interest to be paid on any sum so payable;

(j) provision that an amount paid to the Board by the administrator shall be treated as paid on account of the employer's liability under section 601(2).

(3) For the purpose of giving effect to any provision mentioned in subsection (2)(c) to (j) above, regulations under this section may include provision applying (with or without modifications) provisions of the enactments relating to income tax and corporation tax.

(4) Subject to any provision of regulations under this section–

(a) a payment to which section 601(2) applies shall not be treated as a profit or gain brought into charge to income tax or corporation tax and shall not be treated as part of the employer's income for any purpose of this Act; and

(b) the amount recoverable shall not be subject to any exemption or reduction (by way of relief, set-off or otherwise) or be available for set-off against other tax.

(5) If the employer is a company and a payment to which section 601(1) and (2) applies is made at a time not otherwise within an accounting period of the com-

pany, an accounting period of the company shall for the purposes of subsection (1)(b) above be treated as beginning immediately before the payment is made.

603   Reduction of surpluses

Schedule 22 (which provides for the reduction of certain pension fund surpluses) shall have effect.

Supplementary provisions

604   Application for approval of a scheme

(1)   An application for the approval for the purposes of this Chapter of any retirement benefits scheme shall be made in writing by [the appropriate applicant] to the Board before the end of the first year of assessment for which approval is required, and shall be accompanied by–

- (a)   two copies of the instrument or other document constituting the scheme; and
- (b)   two copies of the rules of the scheme and, except where the application is being sought on the setting up of the scheme, two copies of the accounts of the scheme for the last year for which such accounts have been made up; and
- (c)   such other information and particulars (including copies of any actuarial report or advice given to the [appropriate applicant,] administrator or employer in connection with the setting up of the scheme) as the Board may consider relevant.

[(1A)   In subsection (1) above "the appropriate applicant" means–

- (a)   in the case of a trust scheme, the trustee or trustees of the scheme; and
- (b)   the case of a non-trust scheme, the scheme sponsor or scheme sponsors;

and subsection (9) of section 611AA applies for the purposes of this subsection as it applies for the purposes of that section.]

(2)   The form in which an application for approval is to be made, or in which any information is to be given, in pursuance of this section may be prescribed by the Board.

605   Information

[(1A)   The Board may by regulations make any of the following provisions–

- (a)   provision requiring prescribed persons to furnish to the Board at prescribed times information relating to any of the matters mentioned in subsection (1B) below;
- (b)   provision enabling the Board to serve a notice requiring prescribed persons to furnish to the Board, within a prescribed time, particulars relating to any of those matters;
- (c)   provision enabling the Board to serve a notice requiring prescribed persons to produce to the Board, within a prescribed time, documents relating to any of those matters;
- (d)   provision enabling the Board to serve a notice requiring prescribed

persons to make available for inspection on behalf of the Board books, documents and other records, being books, documents and records which relate to any of those matters;

(e) provision requiring prescribed persons to preserve for a prescribed time books, documents and other records, being books, documents and records which relate to any of those matters.

(1B)   The matters referred to in subsection (1A) above are–

[(a) a scheme which is or has been an approved scheme;]

(b) a relevant statutory scheme;

(c) an annuity contract by means of which benefits provided under an approved scheme or a relevant statutory scheme have been secured;

(d) a retirement benefits scheme which is not an approved scheme but in relation to which an application for approval for the purposes of this Chapter has been made.

(1C)   A person who fails to comply with regulations made under subsection (1A)(e) above shall be liable to a penalty not exceeding £3,000.

(1D)   Regulations under subsection (1A) above may make different provision for different descriptions of case.

(1E)   In subsection (1A) above "prescribed" means prescribed by regulations made under that subsection.]

(1), (2)   . . .

(3)   It shall be the duty of every employer–

(a) if there subsists in relation to any of his employees a retirement benefits scheme to which he contributes and which is neither an approved scheme nor a [relevant] statutory scheme, to deliver particulars of that scheme to the Board within three months beginning with the date on which the scheme first comes into operation in relation to any of his employees, and

(b) when required to do so by notice given by the Board, to furnish within the time limited by the notice such particulars as the Board may require with regard to–

(i) any retirement benefits scheme relating to the employer which is neither an approved scheme nor a [relevant] statutory scheme; and

(ii) the employees of his to whom any such scheme relates.

(4)   It shall be the duty of the administrator of a retirement benefits scheme which is neither an approved scheme nor a [relevant] statutory scheme, when required to do so by notice given by the Board, to furnish within the time limited by the notice such particulars as the Board may require with regard to the scheme.

[605A   False statements, etc]

[(1)   A person who fraudulently or negligently makes a false statement or false representation on making an application for the approval for the purposes of this Chapter of–

(a) a retirement benefits scheme, or

(b) an alteration in such a scheme,

shall be liable to a penalty not exceeding £3,000.

(2) In a case where–

(a) a person fraudulently or negligently makes a false statement or false representation, and

(b) in consequence that person, or any other person, obtains relief from or repayment of tax under this Chapter,

the person mentioned in paragraph (a) above shall be liable to a penalty not exceeding £3,000.]

[606   Default of administrator, etc]

[(1) This section applies in relation to a retirement benefits scheme if at any time–

(a) there is no administrator of the scheme, or

(b) the person who is, or all of the persons who are, the administrator of the scheme cannot be traced, or

(c) the person who is, or all of the persons who are, the administrator of the scheme is or are in default for the purposes of this section.

(2)   If the scheme is a trust scheme, then–

(a) if subsection (1)(b) or (c) above applies and at the time in question the condition mentioned in subsection (3) below is fulfilled, the trustee or trustees shall at that time be responsible for the discharge of all duties imposed on the administrator under this Chapter (whenever arising) and liable for any tax due from the administrator in the administrator's capacity as such (whenever falling due);

(b) if subsection (1)(a) above applies, or subsection (1)(b) or (c) above applies and at the time in question the condition mentioned in sub-section (3) below is not fulfilled, the employer shall at that time be so responsible and liable;

and paragraph (b) above shall apply to a person in his capacity as the employer even if he is also the administrator, or a trustee, of the scheme.

(3) The condition is that there is at least one trustee of the scheme who–

(a) can be traced,

(b) is resident in the United Kingdom, and

(c) is not in default for the purposes of this section.

(4) If the scheme is a non-trust scheme, then–

(a) if subsection (1)(b) or (c) above applies and at the time in question the condition mentioned in subsection (5) below is fulfilled, the scheme sponsor or scheme sponsors shall at that time be responsible for the discharge of all duties imposed on the administrator under this Chapter (whenever arising) and liable for any tax due from the administrator in the administrator's capacity as such (whenever falling due);

(b) if subsection (1)(a) above applies, or subsection (1)(b) or (c) above applies and at the time in question the condition mentioned in subsection (5) below is not fulfilled, the employer shall at that time be so responsible and liable;

and paragraph (b) above shall apply to a person in his capacity as the employer even if he is also the administrator of the scheme, or a scheme sponsor.

(5) The condition is that there is at least one scheme sponsor who–

    (a) can be traced,

    (b) is resident in the United Kingdom, and

    (c) is not in default for the purposes of this section.

(6) Where at any time–

    (a) paragraph (b) or (c) of subsection (1) above applies in relation to a scheme, and

    (b) a person is by virtue of this section responsible for the discharge of any duties, or liable for any tax, in relation to the scheme,

then at that time the person or persons mentioned in paragraph (b) or (as the case may be) paragraph (c) of subsection (1) above shall not, by reason only of being the administrator of the scheme, be responsible for the discharge of those duties or liable for that tax.

(7) Where the scheme is a trust scheme and the employer is not a contributor to the scheme, subsection (2) above shall have effect as if–

    (a) for "the employer", in the first place where those words occur, there were substituted "the scheme sponsor or scheme sponsors", and

    (b) for "the employer", in the second place where those words occur, there were substituted "scheme sponsor".

(8) Where the scheme is a non-trust scheme and the employer is not a contributor to the scheme, subsection (4) above shall have effect as if paragraph (b) and the words after that paragraph were omitted.

(9) No liability incurred under this Chapter [or Chapter 2 of Part 6 of ITEPA 2003 (benefits from non-approved pension schemes)]–

    (a) by the administrator of a scheme, or

    (b) by a person by virtue of this section,

shall be affected by the termination of a scheme or by its ceasing to be an approved scheme or to be an exempt approved scheme.

[(9A) Where by virtue of this section any person is the person, or one of the persons, responsible for the discharge of the duties of the administrator of a scheme, any power or duty by virtue of this Part to serve any notice on, or to do any other thing in relation to, the administrator may be exercised or performed, instead, by the service of that notice on that person or, as the case may be, by the doing of that other thing in relation to that person.]

(10) Where by virtue of this section a person becomes responsible for the discharge of any duties, or liable for any tax, the Board shall, as soon as is reasonably practicable, notify him of that fact; but any failure to give such notification shall not affect that person's being responsible or liable by virtue of this section.

(11) A person is in default for the purposes of this section if–

    (a) he has failed to discharge any duty imposed on him under this Chapter, or

    (b) he has failed to pay any tax due from him by virtue of this Chapter [or Chapter 2 of Part 6 of ITEPA 2003 (benefits from non-approved pension schemes)],

and (in either case) the Board consider the failure to be of a serious nature.

[(11A) In determining for the purposes of this section–

    (a) whether all of the persons who are the administrator of a scheme are at any time in default in respect of an amount of tax chargeable by virtue of section 591C, or

    (b) whether a trustee of a scheme is in default in respect of any amount of tax so chargeable,

the persons who at that time are trustees of the scheme or hold appointments in relation to the scheme under section 611AA(4) to (6) shall be deemed not to include any person who by virtue of section 591D(4) is not liable for that tax.]

(12) References in this section to a trust scheme, a non-trust scheme, trustees and scheme sponsors shall be construed in accordance with section 611AA.

(13) References in this section to the employer include, where the employer is resident outside the United Kingdom, references to any branch or agent of the employer in the United Kingdom, and in this subsection "branch or agent" has the meaning given by section 118(1) of the Management Act.

(14) This section does not apply for the purposes of sections 602 and 603 and Schedule 22.]

[606A   Recourse to scheme members]

[(1) This section applies where–

    (a) an approval of a retirement benefits scheme has ceased to have effect;

    (b) a person ("the employer") has become liable by virtue of section 606 to any tax chargeable on the administrator of the scheme under section 591C;

    (c) the employer has failed, either in whole or in part, to pay that tax; and

    (d) a person falling within subsection (2) below ("the relevant member") was a member of the scheme at the time ("the relevant time") immediately before the date of the cessation of its approval.

(2) A person falls within this subsection in relation to any tax chargeable under section 591C if–

    (a) at the relevant time or at any time before that time he was a controlling director of the employer; or

    (b) he is a person by or in respect of whom any contributions were made by reference to which the condition in subsection (6A) of that section has been satisfied for the purpose of the charge to that tax.

(3) Subject to subsection (4) below, if in a case where this section applies–

(a) the employer has ceased to exist, or

(b) the Board notify the relevant member that they consider the failure of the employer to pay the unpaid tax to be of a serious nature,

the relevant member shall be treated as included in the persons on whom the unpaid tax was charged and shall be assessable accordingly.

(4)   The amount of tax for which the relevant member shall be taken to be assessable by virtue of this section shall not exceed the amount determined by–

(a) taking the amount equal to 40 per cent of his share of the scheme; and

(b) subtracting from that amount his share of any tax charged under section 591C that has already been paid otherwise than by another person on whom it is treated as charged in accordance with this section.

(5)   For the purposes of this section the relevant member's share of the scheme is the amount equal to so much of the value of the assets held for the purposes of the scheme at the relevant time (taking the value at that time) as, on a just and reasonable apportionment, would have fallen to be treated as the value at that time of the assets then held for the purposes of the provision under the scheme of benefits to or in respect of the relevant member.

(6)   For the purposes of this section the relevant member's share of an amount of tax already paid is such sum as bears the same proportion to the amount paid as is borne by his share of the scheme to the total value at the relevant time of the assets then held for the purposes of the scheme.

(7)   The reference in subsection (5) above to the provision of benefits to or in respect of the relevant member includes a reference to the provision of a benefit to or in respect of a person connected with the relevant member.

(8)   For the purposes of this section a person is a controlling director of a company if he is a director of the company and is within section 417(5)(b) in relation to the company.

(9)   A notification given to any person for the purposes of subsection (3)(b) above may be included in any assessment on that person of the tax to which he becomes liable by virtue of the notification.

(10)   An assessment to tax made by virtue of this section shall not be out of time if it is made within three years after the date on which the tax which the employer has failed to pay first became due from him.

(11)   Subsections (1) to (3) of section 591D shall apply to the determination of the value at any time of an asset held for the purposes of a scheme as they apply for the purposes of section 591C(2).

(12)   Subsections (7) and (8) of section 591D shall apply for the purposes of this section as they apply for the purposes of subsection (1) of section 591C and section 591C, respectively.

(13)   Section 839 (connected persons) shall apply for the purposes of this section.]

607   Pilots' benefit fund

(1)   The Board may, if they think fit, and subject to such conditions as they think proper to attach to the approval, approve a pilots' benefit fund for the purposes

of this Chapter as if it were a retirement benefits scheme and notwithstanding that it does not satisfy one or more of the conditions set out in section 590(2) and (3).

(2)   If a fund is approved by virtue of this section–

> (a)   sections 592, [598 to 599A] and 604 to 606 shall have effect in relation to the fund with the modifications specified in subsection (3) below;
>
> (b)   pensions paid out of the fund and any sums chargeable to tax in connection with the fund [in accordance with section 584 of ITEPA 2003 (unauthorised payments)] shall be treated for the purposes of the Income Tax Acts as earned income; and
>
> (c)   Chapter III of this Part shall have effect as if a member of the fund were the holder of a pensionable office or employment and his earnings as a pilot (estimated in accordance with the provisions of Case II of Schedule D) were remuneration from such an office or employment.

(3)   The modifications referred to in subsection (2)(a) above are as follows–

> [(a)   in section 592–
>
> > (i)   subsections (4) to (6) shall be omitted; and
> >
> > (ii)   for subsection (7) there shall be substituted–

"(7)   Any contribution paid under the scheme by a member of the fund shall, in assessing tax under Schedule D, be allowed to be deducted as an expense.";]

> (b)   in [sections 598 to 599A and sections 604 to 606]–
>
> > (i)   for references to an employee there shall be substituted references to a member or former member of the fund;
> >
> > (ii)   in section 599(1)(a) for the reference to a year of service there shall be substituted a reference to a year as a pilot licensed by a pilotage authority or authorised by a competent harbour authority;
> >
> > (iii)   [section 606(2)(b), (4)(b), (7), (8) and (13)] and so much of any other provision as applies to an employer shall be omitted; . . .
> >
> > (iv)   . . ..

(4)   In this section "pilots' benefit fund" means a fund established under section 15(1)(i) of the Pilotage Act 1983 or any scheme supplementing or replacing any such fund.

608   Superannuation funds approved before 6th April 1980

(1)   This section applies to any fund which immediately before 6th April 1980 was an approved superannuation fund for the purposes of section 208 of the 1970 Act if–

> (a)   it has not been approved under this Chapter (or under Chapter II of Part II of the Finance Act 1970); and
>
> (b)   no sum has been paid to it by way of contribution since 5th April 1980.

(2)   Subject to subsection (3) below, exemption from income tax shall, on a claim being made in that behalf, be allowed to a fund to which this section applies in respect of–

(a) income derived from investments or deposits of the fund;

(b) any underwriting commissions which apart from this subsection would be chargeable to tax under Case VI of Schedule D; and

(c) any profits or gains which (apart from this subsection) would be chargeable to tax under Case VI of Schedule D by virtue of section 56(1)(a) and (2);

if, or to such extent as the Board are satisfied that, the income, commissions, profits or gains are applied for the purposes of the fund.

(3) No claim under subsection (2) above shall be allowed unless the Board are satisfied that the terms on which benefits are payable from the fund have not been altered since 5th April 1980.

(4) . . .

609 Schemes approved before 23rd July 1987

Schedule 23 to this Act, which makes provision with respect to retirement benefit schemes approved before 23rd July 1987, shall have effect.

610 Amendments of schemes

(1) This section applies to any amendment of a retirement benefits scheme proposed in connection with an application for the Board's approval for the purposes of this Chapter which is needed in order to ensure that approval is so given, or designed to enhance the benefits under the scheme up to the limits suitable in a scheme for which approval is sought.

(2) A provision, however expressed, designed to preclude any amendment of a scheme which would have prejudiced its approval under section 208 or 222 of the 1970 Act shall not prevent any amendment to which this section applies.

(3) In the case of a scheme which contains no powers of amendment, the administrator of the scheme may, with the consent of all the members of the scheme, and of the employer (or of each of the employers), make any amendment to which this section applies.

611 Definition of "retirement benefits scheme"

(1)   In this Chapter "retirement benefits scheme" means, subject to the provisions of this section, a scheme for the provision of benefits consisting of or including relevant benefits, but does not include

[(a)] any national scheme providing such benefits[; or

(b) any scheme providing such benefits which is an approved personal pension scheme under Chapter IV of this Part].

(2) References in this Chapter to a scheme include references to a deed, agreement, series of agreements, or other arrangements providing for relevant benefits notwithstanding that it relates or they relate only to–

(a) a small number of employees, or to a single employee, or

(b) the payment of a pension starting immediately on the making of the arrangements.

371

(3)   The Board may, if they think fit, treat a . . . scheme relating to [scheme members] of two or more different classes or descriptions as being for the purposes of this Chapter [and Chapter IV of this Part] two or more separate . . . schemes relating respectively to such one or more of those classes or descriptions of those [scheme members] as the Board think fit.

(4)   For the purposes of this section, and of any other provision of this Chapter–

> (a)   [scheme members] may be regarded as belonging to different classes or descriptions if they are employed by different employers; and
> (b)   a particular class or description of [scheme member] may consist of a single [scheme member], or any number of [scheme members], however small.

(5)   Without prejudice to subsections (3) and (4) above, the Board may continue to treat as two different schemes, for the purposes of this Chapter, any retirement benefits scheme which, in pursuance of paragraph 5 of Schedule 3 to the Finance Act 1971 (schemes in existence before 5th April 1973), they treated, immediately before the coming into force of this Chapter, as two separate schemes for the purposes of Chapter II of Part II of the Finance Act 1970.

[(6)   In this section "scheme member", in relation to a scheme means–

> (a)   an employee; or
> (b)   a person whose rights under the scheme derive from a pension sharing order or provision[; or
> (c)   if the scheme is an approved personal pension scheme under Chapter IV of this Part, any other person who is a member of the scheme].]

[611AA   Definition of the administrator]

[(1)   In this Chapter references to the administrator, in relation to a retirement benefits scheme, are to the person who is, or the persons who are, for the time being the administrator of the scheme by virtue of the following provisions of this section.

(2)   Subject to subsection (7) below, where–

> (a)   the scheme is a trust scheme, and
> (b)   at any time the trustee, or any of the trustees, is or are resident in the United Kingdom,

the administrator of the scheme at that time shall be the trustee or trustees of the scheme.

(3)   Subject to subsection (7) below, where–

> (a)   the scheme is a non-trust scheme, and
> (b)   at any time the scheme sponsor, or any of the scheme sponsors, is or are resident in the United Kingdom,

the administrator of the scheme at that time shall be the scheme sponsor or scheme sponsors.

(4)   At any time when the trustee of a trust scheme is not resident in the United Kingdom or (if there is more than one trustee) none of the trustees is so resident, the trustee or trustees shall ensure that there is a person, or there are persons–

(a) resident in the United Kingdom, and

(b) appointed by the trustee or trustees to be responsible for the discharge of all duties relating to the scheme which are imposed on the administrator under this Chapter.

(5) At any time when the scheme sponsor of a non-trust scheme is not resident in the United Kingdom or (if there is more than one scheme sponsor) none of the scheme sponsors is so resident, the scheme sponsor or scheme sponsors shall ensure that there is a person, or there are persons–

(a) resident in the United Kingdom, and

(b) appointed by the scheme sponsor or scheme sponsors to be responsible for the discharge of all duties relating to the scheme which are imposed on the administrator under this Chapter.

(6) Without prejudice to subsections (4) and (5) above–

(a) the trustee or trustees of a trust scheme, or

(b) the scheme sponsor or scheme sponsors of a non-trust scheme,

may at any time appoint a person who is, or persons who are, resident in the United Kingdom to be responsible for the discharge of all duties relating to the scheme which are imposed on the administrator under this Chapter.

(7) Where at any time there is or are a person or persons–

(a) for the time being appointed under subsection (4), (5) or (6) above as regards a scheme, and

(b) resident in the United Kingdom,

the administrator of the scheme at that time shall be that person or those persons (and no other person).

(8) Any appointment under subsection (4), (5) or (6) above–

(a) must be in writing, and

(b) if made after the time when the scheme is established, shall constitute an alteration of the scheme for the purposes of section 591B(2).

(9) In this section–

(a) references to a trust scheme are to a retirement benefits scheme established under a trust or trusts;

(b) references to the trustee or trustees, in relation to a trust scheme and to a particular time, are to the person who is the trustee, or the persons who are the trustees, of the scheme at that time;

(c) references to a non-trust scheme are to a retirement benefits scheme not established under a trust or trusts, and

(d) references to the scheme sponsor or scheme sponsors, in relation to a retirement benefits scheme and to a particular time, are references to any person who established the scheme and is in existence at that time or, if more than one, all such persons.]

[611A Definition of relevant statutory scheme]

[[(1) In this Chapter any reference to a relevant statutory scheme is to–

(a)   a statutory scheme established before 14th March 1989, or

(b)   a statutory scheme established on or after that date and entered in the register maintained by the Board for the purposes of this section, or

(c)   a parliamentary pension scheme.]

(2)   The Board shall maintain a register for the purposes of this section and shall enter in it the relevant particulars of any statutory scheme established on or after 14th March 1989 which is reported to the Board by the authority responsible for establishing it as a scheme the provisions of which correspond with those of an approved scheme.

(3)   The reference in subsection (2) above to the relevant particulars, in relation to a scheme, is a reference to–

(a)   the identity of the scheme,

(b)   the date on which it was established,

(c)   the authority responsible for establishing it, and

(d)   the date on which that authority reported the scheme to the Board.

(4)   Where the Board enter the relevant particulars of a scheme in the register maintained by them for the purposes of this section, they shall inform the authority responsible for establishing the scheme of the date of the entry.

[(5)   In subsection (1)(c) "parliamentary pension scheme" means–

(a)   the Parliamentary pension scheme within the meaning of the Parliamentary and other Pensions Act 1987;

(b)   any pension scheme established for members of the Scottish Parliament under section 81(4) of the Scotland Act 1998;

(c)   any pension scheme established for members of the Welsh Assembly under section 18(2) of the Government of Wales Act 1998;

(d)   any pension scheme established for members of the Northern Ireland Assembly under section 48(2) of the Northern Ireland Act 1998;

(e)   the pension scheme established for members of the European Parliament under section 4 of the European Parliament (Pay and Pensions) Act 1979;

(f)   the pension scheme established under section 3 of the Ministerial Salaries and Members' Pensions Act (Northern Ireland) 1965;

(g)   the pension scheme established under the Assembly Pensions (Northern Ireland) Order 1976.]]

612   Other interpretative provisions, and regulations for purposes of this Chapter

(1)   In this Chapter, except where the context otherwise requires–

. . .

"approved scheme" means a retirement benefits scheme for the time being approved by the Board for the purposes of this Chapter;

"director" in relation to a company includes–

(a)   in the case of a company the affairs of which are managed by a board of directors or similar body, a member of that board or body,

(b)   in the case of a company the affairs of which are managed by a single director or similar person, that director or person,

(c) in the case of a company the affairs of which are managed by the members themselves, a member of that company;

and includes a person who is to be or has been a director;

"employee"–

(a) in relation to a company, includes any officer of the company, any director of the company and any other person taking part in the management of the affairs of the company, and

(b) in relation to any employer, includes a person who is to be or has been an employee;

and "employer" and other cognate expressions shall be construed accordingly;

"exempt approved scheme" has the meaning given by section 592(1);

"final remuneration" means the average annual remuneration of the last three years' service;

"pension" includes annuity;

"the permitted maximum" has the meaning given by section 590(3);

"relevant benefits" means any pension, lump sum, gratuity or other like benefit given or to be given on retirement or on death[, or by virtue of a pension sharing order or provision], or in anticipation of retirement, or, in connection with past service, after retirement or death, or to be given on or in anticipation of or in connection with any change in the nature of the service of the employee in question, except that it does not include any benefit which is to be afforded solely by reason of the disablement by accident of a person occurring during his service or of his death by accident so occurring and for no other reason;

"remuneration" does not include–

(a) anything [which is chargeable to tax as employment income and] arises from the acquisition or disposal of shares or an interest in shares or from a right to acquire shares; or

(b) anything in respect of which tax is chargeable by virtue of [Chapter 3 of Part 6 of ITEPA 2003 (payments and benefits on termination of employment etc)];

"service" means service as an employee of the employer in question and other expressions, including "retirement", shall be construed accordingly; and

"statutory scheme" means a retirement benefits scheme established by or under any enactment–

(a) the particulars of which are set out in any enactment, or in any regulations made under any enactment, or

(b) which has been approved as an appropriate scheme by a Minister or government department (including the head of a Northern Ireland department or a Northern Ireland department).

(2) Any reference in this Chapter[, in relation to a scheme,] to the provision of relevant benefits, or of a pension, for employees [or ex-spouses] includes a reference to the provision of relevant benefits or a pension by means of a contract between the administrator or the employer or the employee [or ex-spouse] and a

third person; and any reference to pensions or contributions paid, or payments made, under a scheme includes a reference to pensions or contributions paid, or payments made, under such a contract entered into for the purposes of the scheme.

[(2A)   In subsection (2) above the reference to the employer is a reference to the person who is the employer in relation to the scheme.]

(3)   The Board may make regulations generally for the purpose of carrying the preceding provisions of this Chapter into effect.

618   Termination of relief under this Chapter, and transitional provisions

(1)   Nothing in this Chapter shall apply in relation to–

- (a) a contract made or trust scheme established on or after [1st July] 1988; or
- (b) a person by whom contributions are first paid on or after that date under a trust scheme established before that date.

(2)   Subject to subsection (4) below, the terms of a contract made, or the rules of a trust scheme established, on or after 17th March 1987 and before [1st July] 1988 and approved by the Board under section 620 shall have effect (notwithstanding anything in them to the contrary) as if they did not allow the payment to the individual by whom the contract is made, or an individual paying contributions under the scheme, of a lump sum exceeding £150,000 or such other sum as may for the time being be specified in an order under section 635(4).

(3)   Subject to subsection (5) below, the rules of a trust scheme established before 17th March 1987 and approved by the Board under section 620 shall have effect (notwithstanding anything in them to the contrary) as if they did not allow the payment to any person first paying contributions under the scheme on or after 17th March 1987 of a lump sum such as is mentioned in subsection (2) above.

(4)   Subsection (2) above shall not apply–

- (a) to a contract if, before the end of January 1988, the persons by and to whom premiums are payable under it jointly give notice to the Board that subsection (2) is not to apply; or
- (b) to a scheme if, before the end of January 1988, the trustees or other persons having the management of the scheme give notice to the Board that subsection (2) is not to apply;

and where notice is given to the Board under this subsection, the contract or scheme shall, with effect from the date with effect from which it was approved, cease to be approved.

(5)   Subsection (3) above shall not apply in the case of any person paying contributions under a scheme if, before the end of January 1988, he and the trustees or other persons having the management of the scheme jointly give notice to the Board that subsection (3) is not to apply; and where notice is given to the Board, the scheme shall cease to be approved in relation to the contributor with effect from the date on which he first paid a contribution under it or (if later) the date with effect from which it was approved.

619   Exemption from tax in respect of qualifying premiums

(1)   Where in any year of assessment an individual is (or would but for an insufficiency of profits or gains be) chargeable to income tax in respect of relevant earnings from any trade, profession, vocation, office or employment carried on or held by him, and pays a qualifying premium, then–

(a)   relief from income tax shall be given under this section in respect of that qualifying premium, but only on a claim made for the purpose, and where relief is to be so given, the amount of that premium shall, subject to the provisions of this section, be deducted from or set off against his relevant earnings for the year of assessment in which the premium is paid; and

(b)   any annuity payable to the same or another individual shall be treated as earned income of the annuitant to the extent to which it is payable in return for any amount on which relief is so given.

Paragraph (b) above applies only in relation to the annuitant to whom the annuity is made payable by the terms of the annuity contract under which it is paid.

(2)   Subject to the provisions of this section and section 626, the amount which may be deducted or set off in any year of assessment (whether in respect of one or more qualifying premiums, and whether or not including premiums in respect of a contract approved under section 621) shall not be more than $17\frac{1}{2}$ per cent of the individual's net relevant earnings for that year.

(3)   Subject to the provisions of this section, the amount which may be deducted or set off in any year of assessment in respect of qualifying premiums paid under a contract approved under section 621 (whether in respect of one or more such premiums) shall not be more than 5 per cent of the individual's net relevant earnings for that year.

(4)   An individual who pays a qualifying premium in a year of assessment (whether or not a year for which he has relevant earnings) may [on or before the 31st January next following] that year elect that the premium shall be treated as paid–

(a)   in the last preceding year of assessment; or

(b)   if he had no net relevant earnings in the year referred to in paragraph (a) above, in the last preceding year of assessment but one;

and where an election is made under this subsection in respect of a premium the other provisions of this Chapter shall have effect as if the premium had been paid in the year specified in the election and not in the year in which it was actually paid.

(5)   Where relief under this section for any year of assessment is claimed and allowed (whether or not relief then falls to be given for that year), and afterwards there is made any assessment, alteration of an assessment, or other adjustment of the claimant's liability to tax, there shall be made also such adjustments, if any, as are consequential thereon in the relief allowed or given under this section for that or any subsequent year of assessment.

(6)   Where relief under this section is claimed and allowed for any year of assessment in respect of any payment, relief shall not be given in respect of it

under any other provision of the Income Tax Acts for the same or a later year of assessment nor (in the case of a payment under an annuity contract) in respect of any other premium or consideration for an annuity under the same contract; and references in the Income Tax Acts to relief in respect of life assurance premiums shall not be taken to include relief under this section.

(7)   If any person, for the purpose of obtaining for himself or any other person any relief from or repayment of tax under this section, knowingly makes any false statement or false representation, he shall be liable to a penalty not exceeding [£3,000].

620   Qualifying premiums

(1)   In this Chapter "qualifying premium" means, subject to subsection (5) below, a premium or other consideration paid by an individual–

- (a)   under an annuity contract for the time being approved by the Board under this section as having for its main object the provision for the individual of a life annuity in old age, or
- (b)   under a contract for the time being approved under section 621.

(2)   Subject to subsection (3) and (4) below, the Board shall not approve a contract under this section unless it appears to them to satisfy the conditions that it is made by the individual with a person lawfully carrying on in the United Kingdom the business of granting annuities on human life, and that it does not–

- (a)   provide for the payment by that person during the life of the individual of any sum except sums payable by way of annuity to the individual; or
- (b)   provide for the annuity payable to the individual to commence before he attains the age of 60 or after he attains the age of 75; or
- (c)   provide for the payment by that person of any other sums except sums payable by way of annuity to the individual's widow or widower and any sums which, in the event of no annuity becoming payable either to the individual or to a widow or widower, are payable by way of return of premiums, by way of reasonable interest on premiums or by way of bonuses out of profits; or
- (d)   provide for the annuity, if any, payable to a widow or widower of the individual to be of a greater annual amount than that paid or payable to the individual; or
- (e)   provide for the payment of any annuity otherwise than for the life of the annuitant;

and that it does include provision securing that no annuity payable under it shall be capable in whole or in part of surrender, commutation or assignment.

(3)   A contract shall not be treated as not satisfying the requirements of subsection (2) above by reason only that it–

- (a)   gives the individual the right to receive, by way of commutation of part of the annuity payable to him, a lump sum not exceeding three times the annual amount of the remaining part of the annuity, taking, where the annual amount is or may be different in different years, the initial annual amount, and

    (b)   makes any such right depend on the exercise by the individual of an election at or before the time when the annuity first becomes payable to him.

(4)   The Board may, if they think fit, and subject to any conditions they think proper to impose, approve, under this section, a contract otherwise satisfying the preceding conditions, notwithstanding that the contract provides for one or more of the following matters–

    (a)   for the payment after the individual's death of an annuity to a dependant not the widow or widower of the individual;

    (b)   for the payment to the individual of an annuity commencing before he attains the age of 60, if the annuity is payable on his becoming incapable through infirmity of body or mind of carrying on his own occupation or any occupation of a similar nature for which he is trained or fitted;

    (c)   if the individual's occupation is one in which persons customarily retire before attaining the age of 60, for the annuity to commence before he attains that age;

    (d)   for the annuity payable to any person to continue for a term certain (not exceeding ten years), notwithstanding his death within that term, or for the annuity payable to any person to terminate, or be suspended, on marriage (or re-marriage) or in other circumstances;

    (e)   in the case of an annuity which is to continue for a term certain, for the annuity to be assignable by will, and in the event of any person dying entitled to it, for it to be assignable by his personal representatives in the distribution of the estate so as to give effect to a testamentary disposition, or to the rights of those entitled on intestacy, or to an appropriation of it to a legacy or to a share or interest in the estate.

(5)   Subject to section 621(5), section 619 and subsections (1) to (4) above shall apply in relation to a contribution under a trust scheme approved by the Board as they apply in relation to a premium under an annuity contract so approved, with the modification that, for the condition as to the person with whom the contract is made, there shall be substituted a condition that the scheme–

    (a)   is established under the law of any part of, and administered in, the United Kingdom; and

    (b)   is established for the benefit of individuals engaged in or connected with a particular occupation (or one or other of a group of occupations), and for the purpose of providing retirement annuities for them, with or without subsidiary benefits for their families or dependants; and

    (c)   is so established under irrevocable trusts by a body of persons comprising or representing a substantial proportion of the individuals so engaged in the United Kingdom, or of those so engaged in England, Wales, Scotland or Northern Ireland;

and with the necessary adaptations of other references to the contract or the person with whom it is made.

(6)   Exemption from income tax shall be allowed in respect of income derived from investments or deposits of any fund maintained for the purpose mentioned

in subsection (5)(b) above under a scheme for the time being approved under that subsection.

(7)   The Board may at any time, by notice given to the persons by and to whom premiums are payable under any contract for the time being approved under this section, or to the trustees or other persons having the management of any scheme so approved, withdraw that approval on such grounds and from such date as may be specified in the notice.

(8)   Nothing in sections 4 and 6 of the Policies of Assurance Act 1867 (obligations of assurance companies in respect of notices of assignment of policies of life assurance) shall be taken to apply to any contract approved under this section.

(9)   For the purposes of any provision applying this subsection "approved annuities" means–

(a)   annuities under contracts approved by the Board under this section, being annuities payable wholly in return for premiums or other consideration paid by a person who (when the premiums or other consideration are or is payable) is, or would but for an insufficiency of profits or gains be, chargeable to tax in respect of relevant earnings from a trade, profession, vocation, office or employment carried on or held by him; and

(b)   annuities or lump sums under approved personal pension arrangements within the meaning of Chapter IV of this Part.

621   Other approved contracts

(1)   The Board may approve under this section–

(a)   a contract the main object of which is the provision of an annuity for the wife or husband of the individual, or for any one or more dependants of the individual,

(b)   a contract the sole object of which is the provision of a lump sum on the death of the individual before he attains the age of 75.

(2)   The Board shall not approve the contract unless it appears to them that it is made by the individual with a person lawfully carrying on in the United Kingdom the business of granting annuities on human life.

(3)   The Board shall not approve a contract under subsection (1)(a) above unless it appears to them to satisfy all the following conditions, that is to say–

(a)   that any annuity payable to the wife or husband or dependant of the individual commences on the death of the individual,

(b)   that any annuity payable to the individual commences at a time after the individual attains the age of 60, and, unless the individual's annuity is one to commence on the death of a person to whom an annuity would be payable under the contract if that person survived the individual, cannot commence after the time when the individual attains the age of 75;

(c)   that the contract does not provide for the payment by the person contracting with the individual of any sum, other than any annuity payable to the individual's wife or husband or dependant, or to the individual, except, in the event of no annuity becoming payable under the contract, any sums payable by way of return of premiums, by way of reasonable interest on premiums or by way of bonuses out of profits;

(d) that the contract does not provide for the payment of any annuity otherwise than for the life of the annuitant;

(e) that the contract does include provision securing that no annuity payable under it shall be capable in whole or in part of surrender, commutation or assignment.

(4)   The Board may, if they think fit, and subject to any conditions that they think proper to impose, approve a contract under subsection (1)(a) above notwithstanding that, in one or more respects, they are not satisfied that the contract complies with the provisions of paragraphs (a) to (e) of subsection (3) above.

(5)   The main purpose of a trust scheme, or part of a trust scheme, within section 620(5) may be to provide annuities for the wives, husbands and dependants of the individuals, or lump sums payable on death and in that case–

(a) approval of the trust scheme shall be subject to subsections (1) to (4) above with any necessary modifications, and not subject to section 620(2) to (4);

(b) the provisions of this Chapter shall apply to the scheme or part of the scheme when duly approved as they apply to a contract approved under this section; and

(c) section 620(6) shall apply to any duly approved trust scheme, or part of a trust scheme.

(6)   Except as otherwise provided in this Chapter (and in particular except in section 620), any reference in the Tax Acts to a contract or scheme approved under that section shall include a reference to a contract or scheme approved under this section.

622   Substituted retirement annuity contracts

(1)   The Board may, if they think fit, and subject to any conditions they think proper to impose, approve an annuity contract under section 620 notwithstanding that the contract provides that the individual by whom it is made–

(a) may agree with the person with whom it is made that a sum representing the value of the individual's accrued rights under it should be applied as the premium or other consideration either under another annuity contract made between them and approved by the Board under section 620, or under personal pension arrangements made between them and approved by the Board under Chapter IV of this Part; or

(b) may require the person with whom it is made to pay such a sum to such other person as the individual may specify, to be applied by that other person as the premium or other consideration either under an annuity contract made between the individual and him and approved by the Board under section 620, or under personal pension arrangements made between the individual and him and approved by the Board under Chapter IV of this Part.

(2)   References in subsection (1) above to the individual by whom the contract is made include references to any widow, widower or dependant having accrued rights under the contract.

(3)   Where in pursuance of any such provision as is mentioned in subsection (1) above of an annuity contract approved under section 620, or of a corresponding provision of a contract approved under section 621(1)(a), a sum representing the value of accrued rights under one contract ("the original contract") is paid by way of premium or other consideration under another contract ("the substituted contract"), any annuity payable under the substituted contract shall be treated as earned income of the annuitant to the same extent that an annuity payable under the original contract would have been so treated.

623   Relevant earnings

(1)   ...

(2)   ... "relevant earnings", in relation to any individual, means, for the purposes of this Chapter, any income of his chargeable to tax for the year of assessment in question, being either–

- (a)   income arising in respect of remuneration from an office or employment held by him other than a pensionable office or employment; or
- (b)   income from any property which is attached to or forms part of the emoluments of any such office or employment held by him; or
- (c)   income which is chargeable under ... Schedule D and is immediately derived by him from the carrying on or exercise by him of his trade, profession or vocation either as an individual or, in the case of a partnership, as a partner personally acting therein; or
- (d)   income treated as earned income by virtue of section 529;

but does not include any remuneration as director of a company whose income consists wholly or mainly of investment income [(that is to say, income which, if the company were an individual, would not be earned income)], being a company of which he is a controlling director.

(3)   For the purposes of this Chapter, an office or employment is a pensionable office or employment if, and only if, service in it is service to which a sponsored superannuation scheme relates (not being a scheme under which the benefits provided in respect of that service are limited to a lump sum payable on the termination of the service through death or disability before the age of 75 or some lower age); but references to a pensionable office or employment apply whether or not the duties are performed wholly or partly in the United Kingdom or the holder is chargeable to tax in respect of it.

(4)   Service in an office or employment shall not for the purposes of subsection (3) above be treated as service to which a sponsored superannuation scheme relates by reason only of the fact that the holder of the office or employment might (though he does not) participate in the scheme by exercising or refraining from exercising an option open to him by virtue of that service.

(5)   For the purposes of relief under section 619, an individual's relevant earnings are those earnings before giving effect to any capital allowances, other than deductions allowable in computing profits or gains, but after taking into account the amounts on which charges fall to be made under [the Capital Allowances Act (including enactments which under this Act are to be treated as contained in that Act)]; and references to income in the following provisions of this section (other than references to total income) shall be construed similarly.

(6)   Subject to the following provisions of this section "net relevant earnings" means, in relation to an individual, the amount of his relevant earnings for the year of assessment in question, less the amount of any deductions falling to be made from the relevant earnings in computing for the purposes of income tax his total income for that year, being–

- (a) deductions which but for section 74(m), (p) or (q) could be made in computing his profits or gains; or
- (b) deductions in respect of relief under Schedule 9 of the Finance Act 1981 (stock relief); or
- (c) deductions in respect of losses or capital allowances arising from activities profits or gains of which would be included in computing relevant earnings of the individual ...

(7)   Where in any year of assessment for which an individual claims and is allowed relief under section 619–

- (a) there falls to be made in computing the total income of the individual ... a deduction in respect of any such loss or allowance of the individual as is mentioned in subsection (6)(c) above; and
- (b) the deduction or part of it falls to be so made from income other than relevant earnings,

the amount of the deduction made from that other income shall be treated as reducing the individual's net relevant earnings for subsequent years of assessment (being deducted as far as may be from those of the immediately following year, whether or not he claims or is entitled to claim relief under this section for that year, and so far as it cannot be so deducted, then from those of the next year, and so on).

(8)   An individual's net relevant earnings for any year of assessment are to be computed without regard to any relief which falls to be given for that year under section 619 ... to that individual . . .

(9)   An individual's relevant earnings, in the case of partnership profits, shall be taken to be his share of the partnership income, estimated in accordance with the Income Tax Acts, but the amount to be included in respect of those earnings in arriving at his net relevant earnings shall be his share of that income after making therefrom all such deductions (if any) in respect of payments made by the partnership or of relief given to the partnership under Schedule 9 of the Finance Act 1981 (stock relief) or in respect of capital allowances falling to be made to the partnership as would be made in computing the tax payable in respect of that income.

624   Sponsored superannuation schemes and controlling directors

(1)   In section 623 "a sponsored superannuation scheme" means a scheme or arrangement–

- (a) relating to service in particular offices or employments, and
- (b) having for its objects or one of its objects to make provision in respect of persons serving in those offices or employments against future retirement or partial retirement, against future termination of service through death or disability, or against similar matters,

being a scheme or arrangement under which any part of the cost of the provision so made is or has been borne otherwise than by those persons by reason of their service (whether it is the cost or part of the cost of the benefits provided, or of paying premiums or other sums in order to provide those benefits, or of administering or instituting the scheme or arrangement).

(2)   For the purposes of subsection (1) above a person shall be treated as bearing by reason of his service the cost of any payment made or agreed to be made in respect of his service, if that payment or the agreement to make it is treated under the Income Tax Acts as increasing his income, or would be so treated if he were chargeable to tax under [section 15 of ITEPA 2003 in respect of his general earnings] from that service.

(3)   In section 623 "controlling director" means a director of a company, the directors of which have a controlling interest in the company, who is the beneficial owner of, or able either directly or through the medium of other companies or by any other indirect means to control, more than 5 per cent of the ordinary share capital of the company; and for the purposes of this definition–

> "company" means one within the Companies Act 1985 or the Companies (Northern Ireland) Order 1986; and
> "director" means–

- (a)   in relation to a body corporate the affairs of which are managed by a board of directors or similar body, a member of that board or similar body;
- (b)   in relation to a body corporate the affairs of which are managed by a single director or similar person, that director or person;
- (c)   in relation to a body corporate the affairs of which are managed by the members themselves, a member of the body corporate;

and includes any person who is to be or has been a director.

625   Carry-forward of unused relief under section 619

(1)   Where–

- (a)   in any year of assessment an individual is (or would but for an insufficiency of profits or gains be) chargeable to income tax in respect of relevant earnings from any trade, profession, vocation, office or employment carried on or held by him, but
- (b)   there is unused relief for that year, that is to say, an amount which would have been deducted from or set off against the individual's relevant earnings for that year under subsection (1) of section 619 if–
  - (i)   he had paid a qualifying premium in that year; or
  - (ii)   the qualifying premium or premiums paid by him in that year had been greater;

then, subject to section 655(1)(b), relief may be given under that section, up to the amount of the unused relief, in respect of so much of any qualifying premium or premiums paid by the individual in any of the next six years of assessment as exceeds the maximum applying for that year under subsection (2) of that section.

(2)   Relief by virtue of this section shall be given for an earlier year rather than a later year, the unused relief taken into account in giving relief for any year being deducted from that available for giving relief in subsequent years and unused relief derived from an earlier year being exhausted before unused relief derived from a later year.

(3)   Where a relevant assessment to tax in respect of a year of assessment becomes final and conclusive more than six years after the end of that year and there is an amount of unused relief for that year which results from the making of the assessment–

>   (a)   that amount shall not be available for giving relief by virtue of this section for any of the six years following that year, but
>   (b)   the individual may, within the period of six months beginning with the date on which the assessment becomes final and conclusive, elect that relief shall be given under section 619, up to that amount, in respect of so much of any qualifying premium or premiums paid by him within that period as exceeds the maximum applying under subsection (2) of that section for the year of assessment in which they were paid;

and to the extent to which relief in respect of any premium or premiums is given by virtue of this subsection it shall not be given by virtue of subsection (1) above.

(4)   In this section "a relevant assessment to tax" means an assessment on the individual's relevant earnings or on the profits or gains of a partnership from which the individual derives relevant earnings.

626   Modification of section 619 in relation to persons over 50

In the case of an individual whose age at the beginning of a year of assessment is within a range specified in the first column of the Table set out below, section 619(2) shall have effect for that year with the substitution for the reference to $17\frac{1}{2}$ per cent of a reference to the relevant percentage specified in the second column of the Table.

TABLE

Age range	Percentage
51 to 55	20
56 to 60	$22\frac{1}{2}$
61 or more	$27\frac{1}{2}$

627   . . .

. . .

628   Partnership retirement annuities

(1)   Where a person ("the former partner") has ceased to be a member of a partnership on retirement, because of age or ill-health or on death and, under–

>   (a)   the partnership agreement; or
>   (b)   an agreement replacing the partnership agreement or supplementing it or supplementing an agreement replacing it; or
>   (c)   an agreement made with an individual who acquires the whole or part of the business carried on by the partnership;

annual payments are made for the benefit of the former partner or [a widow, widower or dependant of the former partner] and are for the purposes of income tax income of the person for whose benefit they are made, the payments shall be treated as earned income of that person, except to the extent that they exceed the limit specified in subsection (2) below.

(2)   The limit mentioned in subsection (1) above is 50 per cent of the average of the amounts which, in the best three of the relevant years of assessment, were the former partner's shares of the relevant profits or gains; and for this purpose–

(a)   the former partner's share in any year of the relevant profits or gains is, subject to subsection (3) below, so much of the relevant profits or gains as fell to be included in a return of his income for that year; and

(b)   the relevant profits or gains are the profits or gains of any trade, profession or vocation on which the partnership or any other partnership of which the former partner was a member was assessed to income tax; and

(c)   the relevant years of assessment are the last seven years of assessment in which he was required to devote substantially the whole of his time to acting as a partner in the partnership or those partnership; and

(d)   the best three of the relevant years of assessment are those three of them in which the amounts of his shares of the relevant profits were highest;

but where, in any of the relevant years, the circumstances were such that any of the profits or gains of a partnership were not assessable to income tax, paragraphs (a), (b) and (d) above shall apply as they would apply had those profits or gains been so assessable.

(3)   If the retail prices index for the month of December in the last of the seven years referred to in paragraph (c) of subsection (2) above is higher than it was for the month of December in any of the other years referred to in that paragraph, the amount which, for that other year, was the former partner's share of the relevant profits or gains shall be treated for the purposes of that subsection as increased by the same percentage as the percentage increase in that index.

(4)   If the retail prices index for the month of December preceding a year of assessment after that in which the former partner ceased to be a member of the partnership is higher than it was for the month of December in the year of assessment in which he ceased to be such a member, the amount which under subsection (2) above is the limit for the first-mentioned year of assessment shall be treated as increased by the same percentage as the percentage increase in that index.

(5)   Where the former partner ceased to be a member of the partnership before the year 1974–75, subsection (4) above shall have effect as if he had ceased to be a member in that year.

629   Annuity premiums of Ministers and other officers

(1)   For the purposes of this Chapter so much of any salary which–

(a)   is payable to the holder of a qualifying office who is also a Member of the House of Commons, and

(b)   is payable for a period in respect of which the holder is not a participant in relation to that office in arrangements contained in the

Parliamentary pension scheme but is a participant in relation to his membership of the House of Commons in any such arrangements, or for any part of such a period,

as is equal to the difference between a Member's pensionable salary and the salary which (in accordance with any such resolution as is mentioned in subsection (3)(a) below) is payable to him as a Member holding that qualifying office shall be treated as remuneration from the office of Member and not from the qualifying office.

(2) In this section–

"Member's pensionable salary" means a Member's ordinary salary under any resolution of the House of Commons which, being framed otherwise than as an expression of opinion, is for the time being in force relating to the remuneration of Members or, if the resolution provides for a Member's ordinary salary thereunder to be treated for pension purposes as being at a higher rate, a notional yearly salary at that higher rate;

"qualifying office" means an office mentioned in section 2(2)(b), (c) or (d) of the Parliamentary and other Pensions Act 1987;

"the Parliamentary pension scheme" has the same meaning as in that Act;

and without prejudice to the power conferred by virtue of paragraph 13 of Schedule 1 to that Act, regulations under section 2 of that Act may make provision specifying the circumstances in which a person is to be regarded for the purposes of this section as being or not being a participant in relation to his Membership of the House of Commons, or in relation to any office, in arrangements contained in the Parliamentary pension scheme.

(3) In subsection (2) above "a Member's ordinary salary", in relation to any resolution of the House of Commons, means–

(a) if the resolution provides for salary to be paid to Members at different rates according to whether or not they are holders of particular offices, or are in receipt of salaries or pensions as the holders or former holders of particular offices, a Member's yearly salary at the higher or highest rate; and

(b) in any other case, a Member's yearly salary at the rate specified in or determined under the resolution.

Chapter IV

Personal pension schemes

Preliminary

630 Interpretation

[(1)] In this Chapter–

"approved"–

(a) in relation to a scheme [(other than an approved retirement benefits scheme)], means approved by the Board under this Chapter; and

    (b) in relation to arrangements, means

        [(i)] made in accordance with a scheme which is for the time being, and was when the arrangements were made, an approved scheme; [or

        (ii) made in accordance with a scheme which is for the time being an approved converted scheme but which was, when the arrangements were made, an approved retirement benefits scheme;]

but does not refer to cases in which approval has been withdrawn;

["approved converted scheme" means an approved personal pension scheme which is such a scheme by virtue of paragraph 3(2)(b) of Schedule 23ZA;";

"approved retirement benefits scheme" means a retirement benefits scheme approved under Chapter I of this Part;]

["authorised insurance company" has the meaning given by section 659B;]

["the earnings threshold" for any year of assessment is £3,600;]

["higher level contributions", in the case of any year of assessment, means contributions in excess of the earnings threshold for the year;]

["income withdrawal" means a payment of income, under arrangements made in accordance with a personal pension scheme, otherwise than by way of an annuity;]

"member", in relation to a personal pension scheme, means an individual who makes arrangements in accordance with the scheme;

["pension date", in relation to any personal pension arrangements, means [(subject to section 638ZA)] the date determined in accordance with the arrangements on which–

    (a) an annuity such as is mentioned in section 634 is first payable, or

    (b) the member elects to defer the purchase of such an annuity and to make income withdrawals in accordance with section 634A;]

"personal pension arrangements" means arrangements made by an individual in accordance with a personal pension scheme;

["the personal pension fund", in the case of any personal pension arrangement and an individual, means the accrued rights to which the individual is entitled conferring prospective entitlement to benefits under the arrangement;]

"personal pension scheme" means a scheme whose sole purpose is the provision of annuities[, income withdrawals] or lump sums under arrangements made by individuals in accordance with the scheme;

["retirement benefits scheme" has the same meaning as in Chapter I of this Part (see section 611);]

"scheme administrator" means the person referred to in section 638(1)

[and references to an employee or to an employer include references to the holder of an office or to the person under whom an office is held].

[(1A) The Treasury may by order amend the definition of "the earnings threshold" in subsection (1) above for any year of assessment by varying the amount there specified.]

[(2)   For the purposes of this Chapter the annual amount of the annuity which would have been purchasable by a person on any date shall be calculated by reference to–

(a)   the value on that date, determined by or on behalf of the scheme administrator, of the [personal pension fund] under the arrangements in question, and

(b)   the current published tables of rates of annuities prepared for the purposes of this Chapter by the Government Actuary.

[Where a lump sum falls to be paid on the date in question, the reference is to the value of the personal pension fund after allowing for that payment.]

(3)   ...

(4)   The Board may make provision by regulations as to the basis on which the tables mentioned in subsection (2)(b) above are to be prepared and the manner in which they are to be applied.]

631   Approval of schemes

(1)   An application to the Board for their approval of a personal pension scheme shall be in such form, shall contain such information, and shall be accompanied by such documents, in such form, as the Board may prescribe.

(2)   The Board may at their discretion grant or refuse an application for approval of a personal pension scheme, but their discretion shall be subject to the restrictions set out in sections 632 to [638A] [(and, where applicable, Schedule 23ZA)].

[(2A)   An application for approval of a personal pension scheme may, if the Board think fit, be granted subject to conditions.]

(3)   The Board shall give notice to the applicant of the grant or refusal of an application; and

[(a)   in the case of a grant subject to conditions, the notice shall state that the grant is so subject and shall specify the conditions; and

(b)]   in the case of a refusal the notice shall state the grounds for the refusal.

(4)   If an amendment is made to an approved scheme without being approved by the Board, their approval of the scheme shall cease to have effect.

[631A   Conversion of certain approved retirement benefits schemes]

[Schedule 23ZA to this Act (which makes provision for or in connection with the conversion of certain retirement benefits schemes approved under Chapter I of this Part into personal pension schemes approved under this Chapter) shall have effect.]

Restrictions on approval

632   Establishment of schemes

(1)   [Subject to subsection (1A), the] Board shall not approve a personal pension scheme established by any person other than–

(a)   a person who [has permission under Part 4 of the Financial Services and Markets Act 2000 to effect or carry out contracts of long-term insurance or to manage unit trust schemes authorised under section 243 of that Act];

[(aa) an EEA firm of the kind mentioned in paragraph 5(d) of Schedule 3 to the Financial Services and Markets Act 2000 which–

      (i)   has permission under paragraph 15 of that Schedule (as a result of qualifying for authorisation under paragraph 12 of that Schedule) to effect or carry out contracts of long-term insurance; and

     (ii) fulfils any one of the requirements under subsections (5), (6) or (7) of section 659B;

(ab) a firm which has permission under paragraph 4 of Schedule 4 to the Financial Services and Markets Act 2000 (as a result of qualifying for authorisation under paragraph 2 of that Schedule) to manage unit trust schemes authorised under section 243 of that Act;

(ac) a person who qualifies for authorisation under Schedule 5 to the Financial Services and Markets Act 2000;]

(b)   a building society within the meaning of the Building Societies Act 1986;

[(bb) . . .]

[(c)   a person falling within section 840A(1)(b);]

[(cc) a body corporate which is a subsidiary or holding company of [a person falling within section 840A(1)(b)], or is a subsidiary of the holding company of [such a person];]

(d)   . . .

[(e)   an institution which–

      [(i)   is an EEA firm of the kind mentioned in paragraph 5(a), (b) or (c) of Schedule 3 to the Financial Services and Markets Act 2000,

     (ii) qualifies for authorisation under paragraph 12(1) or (2) of that Schedule, and

    (iii) has permission under that Act to manage portfolios of investments]].

[(1A)   The Board may approve a personal pension scheme established by any person other than a person mentioned in subsection (1)(a) to (e) if the scheme is established under a trust or trusts.]

[(2)   In subsection (1)(a) above "contracts of long-term insurance" means contracts which fall within Part II of Schedule 1 to the Financial Services and Markets Act 2000 (Regulated Activities) Order 2001.]

[(2A)   In subsection 1(cc) above "holding company" and "subsidiary" are to be construed in accordance with section 736 of the Companies Act 1985 or Article 4 of the Companies (Northern Ireland) Order 1986.]

[(2B) . . .]

(3)   Subsection (1) above shall not apply in relation to a scheme approved by the Board by virtue of section 620(5) if it was established before [1st July] 1988.

(4)   The Treasury may by order amend this section as it has effect for the time being.

[632A   Eligibility to make contributions]

[(1)   The Board shall not approve a personal pension scheme if it permits, in relation to arrangements made by a member in accordance with the scheme, the acceptance of–

  (a)   contributions by the member, or
  (b)   contributions by an employer of the member,

at a time when the member is not eligible to make contributions.

(2)   The Board shall not approve a personal pension scheme unless it makes provision for ensuring, in relation to any such arrangements, that any contributions accepted at a time when the member is not eligible to make contributions are repaid–

  (a)   to the member, to the extent of his contributions; and
  (b)   as to the remainder, to his employer.

(3)   The following provisions of this section, and the provisions of section 632B, have effect for determining for the purposes of subsections (1) and (2) above the times at which a member is eligible to make contributions (and, for those purposes, a member is not eligible to make contributions at any other time).

(4)   A member is eligible to make contributions at any time during a year of assessment for which he has actual net relevant earnings.

(5)   A member who does not have actual net relevant earnings for a year of assessment ("the relevant year") is eligible to make contributions at any time during that year if–

  (a)   for at least some part of the year he does not hold an office or employment to which section 645 applies; and
  (b)   the condition in any of subsections (6) to (9) below is satisfied.

(6)   Condition A is that at some time in the relevant year the member is resident and ordinarily resident in the United Kingdom.

(7)   Condition B is that the member–

  (a)   at some time during the five years of assessment preceding the relevant year, has been resident and ordinarily resident in the United Kingdom; and
  (b)   was resident and ordinarily resident in the United Kingdom when he made the personal pension arrangements in question.

(8)   Condition C is that at some time in the relevant year the member is a person who performs duties which, by virtue of section 132(4)(a), are treated as being performed in the United Kingdom.

(9)   Condition D is that at some time in the relevant year the member is the spouse of a person who performs such duties as are mentioned in subsection (8) above.]

[632B   Eligibility to make contributions: concurrent membership]

[(1)   A member who would not, apart from this section, be eligible to make contributions during a year of assessment shall be eligible to make contributions at any time during that year if–

(a) throughout the year he holds an office or employment to which section 645 applies;

(b) the condition in any of subsections (6) to (9) of section 632A is satisfied in his case as respects the year;

(c) he is not, and has not been, a controlling director of a company at any time in the year or in any of the five years of assessment preceding it;

(d) for at least one of the five years of assessment preceding the year, the aggregate of his grossed-up remuneration from each office and each employment held on 5th April in that preceding year does not exceed the remuneration limit for the relevant year; and

(e) the total relevant contributions made in the year do not exceed the earnings threshold for the year.

(2)   For the purposes of paragraphs (c) and (d) of subsection (1) above, no account shall be taken of any year of assessment earlier than the year 2000–01.

(3)   For the purposes of paragraph (c) of subsection (1) above, a person is a controlling director of a company at any time if at that time–

(a) he is a director, as defined by section 612(1); and

(b) he is within paragraph (b) of section 417(5) in relation to the company.

(4)   For the purposes of paragraph (d) of subsection (1) above–

(a) "grossed up", in relation to a person's remuneration from an office or employment, means increased by being multiplied by a figure determined in accordance with an order made by the Treasury (or left unchanged, if that figure is unity);

(b) "remuneration" shall be construed in accordance with an order made by the Treasury;

(c) "the remuneration limit" for any year of assessment is £30,000;

(d) "the relevant year" means the year of assessment first mentioned in subsection (1) above.

The Treasury may by order amend the definition of "the remuneration limit" in paragraph (c) above for any year of assessment by varying the amount there specified.

(5)   For the purposes of paragraph (e) of subsection (1) above and the following provisions of this section, "the total relevant contributions", in the case of a year of assessment, means the aggregate amount of the contributions made in the year–

(a) by the member in question, and

(b) by any employer of his,

under arrangements made by the member under the scheme in question, together with the aggregate amounts of such contributions under other approved personal pension arrangements made by that member.

(6)   If–

   (a)   in the case of a member, the total relevant contributions in a year of assessment, apart from this subsection, exceed the earnings threshold for the year, and

   (b)   but for that, the member would be eligible to make contributions by virtue of subsection (1) above at any time in that year,

the repayment required by subsection (2) of section 632A is repayment of the relevant excess contributions only (so that the condition in subsection (1)(e) above becomes satisfied).

(7)   In subsection (6) above "the relevant excess contributions" means–

   (a)   to the extent that a contribution is the first which caused the total relevant contributions in the year to exceed the earnings threshold for the year, that contribution; and

   (b)   all subsequent contributions in the year.

(8)   The Treasury may by order make provision requiring any person who claims to be eligible to make contributions by virtue of this section to provide to–

   (a)   the Board,

   (b)   an officer of the Board, or

   (c)   the scheme administrator of the personal pension scheme concerned,

such declarations, certificates or other evidence in support of the claim as may be specified or described in, or determined in accordance with, the order.

(9)   A person shall only be eligible to make contributions by virtue of this section in a year of assessment if he complies with any requirements imposed by order under subsection (8) above.]

633   Scope of benefits

(1)   The Board shall not approve a personal pension scheme which makes provision for any benefit other than–

   (a)   the payment of an annuity satisfying the conditions in section 634 [or income withdrawals with respect to which the conditions in section 634A are satisfied];

   (b)   the payment to a member of a lump sum satisfying the conditions in section 635;

   (c)   the payment after the death of a member of an annuity satisfying the conditions in section 636 [or income withdrawals with respect to which the conditions in section 636A are satisfied];

   (d)   the payment on the death of a member of a lump sum satisfying [the conditions in section 637 (death benefit);]

   [(e)   the payment on or after the death of a member of a lump sum [with respect to which the conditions in section 637A (return of contributions) are satisfied].]

(2)   . . .

634 Annuity to member

(1)   The annuity must be payable by an authorised insurance company which may be chosen by the member.

(2)   Subject to subsection (3) below, the annuity must not commence before the member attains the age of 50 or after he attains the age of 75.

(3)   The annuity may commence before the member attains the age of 50 if–

  (a)   it is payable on his becoming incapable through infirmity of body or mind of carrying on his own occupation or any occupation of a similar nature for which he is trained or fitted; or
  (b)   the Board are satisfied that his occupation is one in which persons customarily retire before that age.

(4)   Subject to subsection (5) below, the annuity must be payable to the member for his life.

(5)   The annuity may continue for a term certain not exceeding ten years, notwithstanding the member's death within that term; and for this purpose an annuity shall be regarded as payable for a term certain notwithstanding that it may terminate, after the death of the member and before expiry of that term, on the happening of any of the following–

  (a)   the marriage of the annuitant;
  (b)   his attaining the age of 18;
  (c)   the later of his attaining that age and ceasing to be in full-time education.

(6)   The annuity must not be capable of assignment or surrender, [except that–

  (a)   an annuity may be assigned or surrendered for the purpose of giving effect to a pension sharing order or provision; and
  (b)]   an annuity for a term certain may be assigned by will or by the annuitant's personal representatives in the distribution of his estate so as to give effect to a testamentary disposition, or to the rights of those entitled on an intestacy, or to an appropriation of it to a legacy or to a share or interest in the estate.

[634A   Income withdrawals by member]

[(1)   Where a member elects to defer the purchase of an annuity such as is mentioned in section 634, income withdrawals may be made by him during the period of deferral, subject as follows.

[(1A)   The Board shall not refuse to approve a personal pension scheme by reason only that it makes provision for arrangements under the scheme which enable a member who makes such an election as is mentioned in subsection (1) above to apply different parts of the personal pension fund at different times in the purchase of different annuities satisfying the conditions in section 634 (whether commencing on the same day or on different days).]

(2)   Income withdrawals must not be made before the member attains the age of 50, unless–

  (a)   they are available on his becoming incapable through infirmity of body or mind of carrying on his own occupation or any occupation of a similar nature for which he is trained or fitted, or

(b) the Board are satisfied that his occupation is one in which persons customarily retire before that age.

(3)   Income withdrawals must not be made after the member attains the age of 75.

(4)   The aggregate amount of income withdrawals by a member in each successive period of twelve months [in each valuation period] must be not less than 35 per cent or more than 100 per cent of the annual amount of the annuity which would have been purchasable by him

[(a) in the case of the initial period, on the relevant reference date; and

(b) in the case of any subsequent valuation period,

[(i)] on a particular day in the period of sixty days ending with the relevant reference date][, or

(ii) immediately after the last qualifying annuitisation,

whichever is the later].

[(4A)   For the purposes of subsection (4) above–

(a) "annuitisation" means the application of part of the personal pension fund in the purchase of an annuity satisfying the conditions in section 634; and

(b) an annuitisation is a "qualifying annuitisation", in relation to any such period of twelve months as is mentioned in subsection (4) above, if it has taken place–

(i) in an earlier such period, but

(ii) since the relevant reference date.]

[(5)   For the purposes of this section, in the case of any arrangements the relevant reference date–

(a) for the period beginning with the member's pension date ("the initial period"), is that pension date; and

(b) for each succeeding period, is the first day of the period;

and, subject to subsection (5D) below, any period mentioned in paragraph (a) or (b) above (a "valuation period") is a period of three years.]

[(5A)   Where–

(a) a member has made an election under subsection (1) above in respect of two or more personal pension arrangements under the same personal pension scheme, and

(b) in the case of one or more of those arrangements, the relevant reference date for any valuation period after the initial period would not, apart from this subsection, coincide with a date which is (or, but for the ending of the period of deferral, would be) the relevant reference date for a valuation period in the case of the arrangements with the earliest pension date,

the relevant reference date for any valuation period other than the initial period, and the valuation period to which that date relates, shall, if the scheme or the arrangements so require, be determined in the case of all those arrangements on the assumption that the pension date is in each case the same as in the case of the arrangements with the earliest pension date.

(5B)   In determining in accordance with subsection (5A) above the relevant reference date and the valuation period to which it relates, in the case of any arrangements ("the relevant arrangements"), there shall be left out of account any arrangements in whose case the period of deferral ended–

(a)   before the actual pension date in the case of the relevant arrangements; or

(b)   before the date on which the relevant arrangements first become subject to such a requirement as is mentioned in subsection (5A) above.

(5C)   But where, in the case of any arrangements,–

(a)   the relevant reference date for any valuation period falls to be determined, in accordance with the assumption in subsection (5A) above, by reference to the pension date for any other arrangements, and

(b)   the period of deferral in the case of those other arrangements comes to an end,

the same pension date shall continue to be assumed under that subsection for that and any subsequent valuation period, notwithstanding the coming to an end of the period of deferral in the case of those other arrangements (and references in subsection (5A) to the arrangements with the earliest pension date shall be construed accordingly).

(5D)   Where, in the case of any personal pension arrangements, in consequence of subsection (5A) above the relevant reference date for any valuation period ("the later date") falls less than three years after the relevant reference date for the previous valuation period ("the earlier date")–

(a)   the valuation period beginning with the earlier date shall end with the day before the later date; and

(b)   [subsections (4) and (4A)] above shall apply in relation to any portion of the period which remains after the completion of any successive periods of twelve months as if it were a period of twelve months.]

(6)   The right to income withdrawals must not be capable of assignment or surrender[, except for the purpose of giving effect to a pension sharing order or provision].]

635   Lump sum to member

(1)   The lump sum must be payable only if the member so elects on or before [his pension date under the arrangements in question].

(2)   The lump sum must be payable [on the date which is his pension date under the arrangements in question].

[(3)   The lump sum must not exceed one quarter of the difference between–

(a)   the total value, at the time when the lump sum is paid, of the benefits provided for by [the arrangements in question], and

(b)   the value, at that time, of such of the member's rights [under those arrangements] as are protected rights for the purposes of the [Pension Schemes Act 1993] or the [Pension Schemes (Northern Ireland) Act 1993].]

(4) ...

(5) The right to payment of the lump sum must not be capable of assignment or surrender[, except for the purpose of giving effect to a pension sharing order or provision].

636 Annuity after death of member

(1) The annuity must be payable by an authorised insurance company which may be chosen by the member or by the annuitant.

(2) The annuity must be payable to the surviving spouse of the member, or to a person who was at the member's death a dependant of his.

(3) The aggregate annual amount (or, if that amount varies, the aggregate of the initial annual amounts) of all annuities to which this section applies and which are payable under the same personal pension arrangements shall not exceed–

  (a) where before his death the member was in receipt of an annuity under the arrangements, the annual amount (or, if it varied, the highest annual amount) of that annuity; or

  (b) where paragraph (a) does not apply, the highest annual amount of the annuity that would have been payable under the arrangements to the member (ignoring any entitlement of his to commute part of it for a lump sum) if it had [been purchased] on the day before his death.

[(3A) The references in subsection (3) above–

  (a) to the annual amount or highest annual amount of an annuity of which the member was in receipt before his death, and

  (b) to the highest annual amount of an annuity that would have been payable if it had been purchased on the day before the member's death,

shall each be construed in a case where payments of that annuity were or would have been affected by the making of any pension sharing order or provision as if the only payments of that annuity to be taken into account were those that have been or would have been so affected.]

(4) Subject to subsections (5) to (9) below, the annuity must be payable for the life of the annuitant.

(5) Where the annuity is payable to the surviving spouse of the member and at the time of the member's death the surviving spouse is under the age of 60, the annuity may be deferred to a time not later than–

  (a) the time when the surviving spouse attains that age; or

  (b) where the member's annuity is payable to the surviving spouse for a term certain as mentioned in section 634(5) and the surviving spouse attains the age of 60 before the time when the member's annuity terminates, that time.

(6)　The annuity may cease to be payable on the marriage of the annuitant.

(7)　Where the annuity is payable to the surviving spouse of the member, it may cease before the death of the surviving spouse if–

  (a)　the member was survived by one or more dependants under the age of 18 and at the time of the member's death the surviving spouse was under the age of 45; and

  (b)　at some time before the surviving spouse attains that age no such dependant remains under the age of 18.

(8)　Where the annuity is payable to a person who is under the age of 18 when it is first payable, it must cease to be payable either–

  (a)　on his attaining that age; or

  (b)　on the later of his attaining that age and ceasing to be in full-time education,

unless he was a dependant of the member otherwise than by reason only that he was under the age of 18.

(9)　The annuity may continue for a term certain not exceeding ten years, notwithstanding the original annuitant's death within that term; and for this purpose an annuity shall be regarded as payable for a term certain notwithstanding that it may terminate, after the death of the original annuitant and before the expiry of that term, on the happening of any of the following–

  (a)　the marriage of the annuitant to whom it is payable;

  (b)　his attaining the age of 18;

  (c)　the later of his attaining that age and ceasing to be in full-time education.

(10)　The annuity must not be capable of assignment or surrender, [except that–

  (a)　an annuity may be assigned or surrendered for the purpose of giving effect to a pension sharing order or provision; and

  (b)] an annuity for a term certain may be assigned by will or by the annuitant's personal representatives in the distribution of his estate so as to give effect to a testamentary disposition, or to the rights of those entitled on an intestacy, or to an appropriation of it to a legacy or to a share or interest in the estate.

[636A　Income withdrawals after death of member]

[(1)　Where a person entitled to such an annuity as is mentioned in section 636 elects to defer the purchase of the annuity, income withdrawals may be made by him during the period of deferral, subject as follows.

[(1A)　The Board shall not refuse to approve a personal pension scheme by reason only that it makes provision for arrangements under the scheme which enable a person who makes such an election as is mentioned in subsection (1) above to apply different parts of the personal pension fund at different times in the purchase of different annuities satisfying the conditions in section 636 (whether commencing on the same day or on different days).]

(2)   No such deferral may be made, and accordingly income withdrawals may not be made, if the person concerned elects in accordance with section 636(5)(a) to defer the purchase of an annuity.

(3)   Income withdrawals must not be made after the person concerned if he had purchased such an annuity as is mentioned in section 636 would have ceased to be entitled to payments under it.

(4)   Income withdrawals must not in any event be made after the member would have attained the age of 75 or, if earlier, after the person concerned attains the age of 75.

(5)   The aggregate amount of income withdrawals by a person in each successive period of twelve months beginning with the date of the member's death must be not less than 35 per cent or more than 100 per cent of the annual amount of the annuity which would have been purchasable by him

[(a) in the case of the first period of three years, on the relevant reference date; and

(b) in the case of any succeeding period of three years,
[(i)] on a particular day in the period of sixty days ending with the relevant reference date] [or
(ii) immediately after the last qualifying annuitisation,
whichever is the later].

[(5A)   For the purposes of subsection (5) above–

(a) "annuitisation" means the application of part of the personal pension fund in the purchase of an annuity satisfying the conditions in section 636; and

(b) an annuitisation is a "qualifying annuitisation", in relation to any such period of twelve months as is mentioned in subsection (5) above, if it has taken place–
(i) in an earlier such period, but
(ii) since the relevant reference date.]

(6)   For the purposes of this section the relevant reference date for the first three years is the date of the member's death, and for each succeeding period of three years is the first day of that period.

(7)   The right to income withdrawals must not be capable of assignment or surrender[, except for the purpose of giving effect to a pension sharing order or provision].]

[637   Death benefit]

[The lump sum–

(a) must be payable on the death of the member before he attains the age of 75, and

(b) must be payable by an authorised insurance company.]

[637A   Return of contributions on or after death of member]

[(1)   The lump sum payable under the arrangements in question (or, where two or more lump sums are so payable, those lump sums taken together) must represent no more than the return of contributions together with reasonable interest on contributions or bonuses out of profits, after allowing for–

 (a) any income withdrawals, and

 (b) any purchases of annuities such as are mentioned in section 636.

To the extent that contributions are invested in units under a unit trust scheme, the lump sum (or lump sums) may represent the sale or redemption price of the units.

(2) A lump sum must be payable only if, in the case of the arrangements in question–

 (a) no such annuity as is mentioned in section 634 has been purchased by the member;

 (b) no such annuity as is mentioned in section 636 has been purchased in respect of the relevant interest; and

 (c) no election in accordance with subsection (5)(a) of section 636 has been made in respect of the relevant interest.

(3) Where the member's death occurs after the date which is his pension date in relation to the arrangements in question, a lump sum must not be payable more than two years after the death unless, in the case of that lump sum, the person entitled to such an annuity as is mentioned in section 636 in respect of the relevant interest–

 (a) has elected in accordance with section 636A to defer the purchase of an annuity; and

 (b) has died during the period of deferral.

(4) In this section "the relevant interest" means the interest, under the arrangements in question, of the person to whom or at whose direction the payment in question is made, except where there are two or more such interests, in which case it means that one of them in respect of which the payment is made.

(5) Where, under the arrangements in question, there is a succession of interests, any reference in subsection (2) or (3) above to the relevant interest includes a reference to any interest (other than that of the member) in relation to which the relevant interest is a successive interest.]

638 Other restrictions on approval

(1) The Board shall not approve a personal pension scheme unless they are satisfied that there is a person resident in the United Kingdom who will be responsible for the management of the scheme.

(2) The Board shall not approve a personal pension scheme unless it makes such provision for the making, acceptance and application of transfer payments as satisfies any requirements imposed by or under regulations made by the Board.

(3) The Board shall not approve a personal pension scheme unless it makes provision, in relation to arrangements made in accordance with the scheme, for ensuring that–

 (a) the aggregate amount of the contributions that may be made in a year of assessment by the member and an employer of his under the arrangements, together with the aggregate amounts of such contributions under other approved personal pension arrangements made by that member, does not exceed [the earnings threshold for that year or, if greater,] the permitted maximum for that year; and

(b) any excess is repaid to the member to the extent of his contributions and otherwise to his employer.

(4) In subsection (3) above "the permitted maximum" for a year of assessment means an amount equal to . . .–

(a) the relevant percentage of the member's net relevant earnings for the year; . . .

(b) . . .

and references in subsection (3) to contributions by the member do not include references to contributions treated by virtue of section 649(3) as paid by him.

(5) In subsection (4) above "the relevant percentage" means 17.5 per cent or, in a case where section 640(2) applies, the relevant percentage there specified.

(6) The Board shall not approve a personal pension scheme which permits the acceptance of contributions other than–

(a) contributions by members;

(b) contributions by employers of members;

(c) minimum contributions paid by the [Board] under [section 43 of the Pension Schemes Act 1993] or . . . under [section 39 of the Pension Schemes (Northern Ireland) Act 1993].

[(7) The Board shall not approve a personal pension scheme which permits the acceptance of minimum contributions paid as mentioned in subsection (6)(c) above in respect of an individual's service as director of a company, if his [general earnings] as such are within section 644(5).

[(7A) The Board shall not approve a personal pension scheme unless it prohibits, except in such cases as may be prescribed by regulations made by the Board–

(a) the acceptance of further contributions, and

(b) the making of transfer payments,

after the date which is the member's pension date in relation to the arrangements in question.]

[(7B) Subsection (7A) above shall have effect subject to and in accordance with section 638ZA.]

(8) A personal pension scheme which permits the acceptance of minimum contributions paid as mentioned in subsection (6)(c) above in respect of an individual's service in an office or employment to which section 645 applies may be approved by the Board only if–

(a) the scheme does not permit the acceptance of contributions from the individual or from the person who is his employer in relation to that office or employment; or

    (b)   at the time when the minimum contributions are paid the individual is not serving in an office or employment to which section 645 applies.]

[(9)   The Board may only approve a personal pension scheme if it prohibits the acceptance of contributions in any form other than–

    (a)   the payment of monetary sums; or

    (b)   the transfer, subject to the conditions in subsection (12) below, of eligible shares in a company;

and any reference in this Chapter to the payment of contributions includes a reference to the making of contributions in accordance with paragraph (b) above.

(10)   For the purposes of this Chapter, the amount of a contribution made by way of a transfer of shares shall be the aggregate market value of the shares at the date of the transfer.

(11)   For the purposes of subsection (9)(b) above, "eligible shares" means shares–

    (a)   which the member has exercised the right to acquire, or

    (b)   which have been appropriated to the member,

in accordance with the provisions of [an SAYE option scheme], an approved profit-sharing scheme or [a share incentive plan].

(12)   The conditions mentioned in subsection (9)(b) above are–

    (a)   in relation to shares which the member has exercised his right to acquire in accordance with the provisions of [an SAYE option scheme], that the transfer of the shares as contributions under the personal pension scheme takes place before the expiry of the period of 90 days following the exercise of that right;

    (b)   in relation to shares appropriated to the member in accordance with the provisions of an approved profit-sharing scheme or [a share incentive plan], that the transfer of the shares as contributions under the personal pension scheme takes place before the expiry of the period of 90 days following the date when the member directed the trustees of the approved profit-sharing scheme or [share incentive plan] to transfer the ownership of the shares to him or, if earlier, the release date in relation to the shares.

(13)   In this section–

    "approved profit-sharing scheme" has the same meaning as in section 186;

    . . .

    "market value" shall be construed in accordance with section 272 of the Taxation of Chargeable Gains Act 1992;

    ["SAYE option scheme" has the same meaning as in the SAYE code (see section 516 of ITEPA 2003 (approved SAYE option schemes)), and

    "share incentive plan" has the same meaning as in the SIP code (see section 488 of that Act (approved share incentive plans))].]

[638ZA   Personal pension arrangements with more than one pension date etc]

[(1)   This section applies where a personal pension scheme makes provision for a personal pension arrangement under the scheme to make provision–

    (a)   for the payment of more than one annuity satisfying the conditions in section 634 or 636 (a "qualifying annuity") and for different such annuities to commence, or be capable of commencing, on different days;

    (b)   for elections such as are mentioned in section 634A(1) or 636A(1) ("elections for deferral") to be capable of being made at different times in relation to different portions of the personal pension fund; and

    (c)   for a qualifying lump sum to be payable in connection with–

        (i)   each qualifying annuity (other than one purchased pursuant to section 634A, 636 or 636A); and

        (ii)   each election for deferral such as is mentioned in section 634A(1).

(2)   The Board shall not refuse to approve a personal pension scheme by reason only that it makes such provision as is mentioned in subsection (1) above if they are satisfied that it makes provision in conformity with the provisions of this section.

(3)   In this section–

    "income withdrawal fund" means a portion of the personal pension fund which is specified or described in an election for deferral as the portion of that fund to which the election relates;

    "qualifying lump sum" means a lump sum satisfying the conditions of section 635 (as that section has effect by virtue of and in accordance with this section);

    "the relevant date", in relation to any qualifying annuity or election for deferral, means the date determined in accordance with the arrangement on which–

    (a)   the qualifying annuity commences; or

    (b)   the member makes the election for deferral.

(4)   In the application of section 635 in relation to a qualifying lump sum, for the condition in subsection (3) there shall be substituted the conditions in subsections (5) and (6) below (as read with subsection (7) below).

(5)   The first condition is that the lump sum must not exceed one-third of–

    (a)   the difference between–

        (i)   the value of the portion of the personal pension fund applied in the provision of the qualifying annuity in connection with which the lump sum is paid, determined as at the date on which that portion is so applied, and

        (ii)   the value, determined as at that date, of so much of that portion as represents protected rights, or

    (b)   the value, as at the relevant date, of the income withdrawal fund which relates to the election for deferral in connection with it is paid,

as the case may be.

(6)   The second condition is that the lump sum must not represent any of the value, at the time when the lump sum is paid, of any protected rights.

(7)   In subsections (5) and (6) above, "protected rights" means any of the member's rights under the personal pension arrangement which are protected rights for the purposes of the Pension Schemes Act 1993 or the Pension Schemes (Northern Ireland) Act 1993.

(8)   Where a qualifying annuity commences, this Chapter and the personal pension scheme concerned shall have effect, as from the relevant date, as if there had been a separate personal pension arrangement and–

(a)   the annuity, and any qualifying lump sum payable in connection with it, were benefits provided for by that separate arrangement (instead of by the personal pension arrangement by which it was actually provided (in this subsection referred to as "the relevant arrangement"));

(b)   the portion of the personal pension fund applied in the provision of the annuity, together with the amount of any qualifying lump sum payable in connection with the annuity, had been the personal pension fund in the case of that separate arrangement (and were excluded from the personal pension fund in the case of the relevant arrangement);

(c)   any election for the annuity, or for such a qualifying lump sum, had been made under that separate arrangement (instead of under the relevant arrangement); and

(d)   except in the case of an annuity satisfying the conditions in section 636, the relevant date were the pension date in relation to that separate arrangement (and were not, by reference to that annuity, the pension date in relation to the relevant arrangement).

(9)   Where, in the case of any personal pension arrangement (in this subsection referred to as "the relevant arrangement"), an election for deferral is made, this Chapter and the personal pension scheme concerned shall have effect, as from the relevant date, as if there had been, and continued to be, a separate personal pension arrangement and–

(a)   the income withdrawal fund which relates to the election, together with the amount of any qualifying lump sum payable in connection with the election, had been the personal pension fund in the case of that separate arrangement (and were excluded from the personal pension fund in the case of the relevant arrangement);

(b)   the election for deferral, and any election for such a qualifying lump sum, had been made under that separate arrangement (instead of under the relevant arrangement);

(c)   the election for deferral had been made in respect of the whole of the income withdrawal fund which relates to the election; and

(d)   except in the case of an election such as is mentioned in section 636A(1), the relevant date were the pension date in relation to that separate arrangement (and were not, by reference to that election, the pension date in relation to the relevant arrangement).]

[638A Power to prescribe restrictions on approval]

[(1) The Board–

(a) may by regulations restrict their discretion to approve a personal pension scheme; and

(b) shall not approve any such scheme if to do so would be inconsistent with any regulations under this section.

(2) The restrictions that may be imposed by regulations under this section may be imposed by reference to any one or more of the following, that is to say–

(a) the benefits for which the scheme provides;

(b) the investments held for the purposes of the scheme;

(c) the manner in which the scheme is administered;

(d) any other circumstances whatever.

(3) The following provisions of this section apply where–

(a) any regulations are made under this section imposing a restriction ("the new restriction") on the Board's discretion to approve a personal pension scheme;

(b) the new restriction did not exist immediately before the making of the regulations; and

(c) that restriction is one imposed by reference to circumstances other than the benefits for which the scheme provides.

(4) Subject to subsections (5) and (6) below, a personal pension scheme which is an approved scheme immediately before the day on which the regulations imposing the new restriction come into force shall cease to be approved at the end of the period of 36 months beginning with that day if, at the end of that period, the scheme–

(a) contains a provision of a prohibited description, or

(b) does not contain every provision which is a provision of a required description.

(5) The Board may by regulations provide that subsection (4) above is not to apply in the case of the inclusion of such provisions of a prohibited description, or in the case of the omission of such provisions of a required description, as may be specified in the regulations.

(6) For the purposes of subsection (4) above–

(a) a provision contained in a scheme shall not be treated as being of a prohibited description to the extent that it authorises the retention of an investment held immediately before the day of the making of the new regulations; and

(b) so much of any provision contained in a scheme as authorises the retention of an investment held immediately before that day shall be disregarded in determining if any provision of the scheme is of a required description.

(7) In this section–

(a) references to a provision of a prohibited description are references to a provision of a description which, by virtue of the new restriction, is

405

a description of provision which, if contained in a personal pension scheme, would prevent the Board from approving it; and

(b) references to a provision of a required description are references to a provision of a description which, by virtue of the new restriction, is a description of provision which must be contained in a personal pension scheme before the Board may approve it.]

Tax reliefs

639 Member's contributions

[(1) An individual who pays a contribution under approved personal pension arrangements made by him shall be entitled to relief under this section in respect of the contribution.

(1A) Subsection (1) above is subject to the other provisions of this Chapter.

(1B) The total amount of contributions in respect of which relief may be given to an individual under this section for any year of assessment must not exceed–

(a) the permitted maximum for the year, as defined in section 638(4), or
(b) the earnings threshold for the year,

whichever is the greater.

(2) Any relief under this section shall be given in accordance with–

(a) subsections (3) and (4) below, and
(b) where applicable, subsection (5A) below.

(2A) Relief in accordance with subsections (3) and (4) below shall be subject to such conditions as the Board may prescribe in regulations.]

[(3) An individual who is entitled to relief under this section in respect of a contribution shall be entitled, on making the payment, to deduct and retain out of it a sum equal to income tax on the contribution at the basic rate for the year of assessment in which the payment is made.]

[(4) Where a sum is deducted under subsection (3) above from a contribution–

(a) the scheme administrator shall allow the deduction on receipt of the residue;
(b) the individual paying the contribution shall be acquitted and discharged of so much money as is represented by the deduction as if the sum had been actually paid; and
(c) the sum deducted shall be treated as income tax paid by the scheme administrator.]

[(4A) Where payment of a contribution under approved personal pension arrangements is received–

(a) the scheme administrator shall be entitled to recover from the Board, in accordance with regulations, an amount which by virtue of subsection (4)(c) above is treated as income tax paid by him; and
(b) any amount so recovered shall be treated for the purposes of the Tax Acts in like manner as the payment of the contribution to which it relates.]

(5)   Regulations under this section may make provision for carrying subsections [(3) to (4A)] above into effect and, without prejudice to the generality of that, may provide–

(a)   for the manner in which claims for the recovery of a sum under subsection [(4A)(a)] may be made;

(b)   for the giving of such information, in such form, as may be prescribed by or under the regulations;

(c)   for the inspection by persons authorised by the Board of books, documents and other records.

[(5A)   Where–

(a)   an individual is entitled to relief under this section in respect of contributions paid in any year of assessment, and

(b)   apart from this subsection, income tax at the higher rate is chargeable in respect of any part of his total income for the year,

the basic rate limit for that year shall in his case be increased by the addition of the amount of the contributions in respect of which he is entitled to relief under this section.

(5B)   Relief in accordance with subsection (5A) above shall be given only on a claim made for the purpose.]

(6)   Where relief under this section for any year of assessment is claimed and allowed (whether or not it then falls to be given for that year), and afterwards an assessment, alteration of an assessment, or other adjustment of the claimant's liability to tax is made, there shall also be made such consequential adjustments in the relief allowed or given under this section for that or any subsequent year as are appropriate.

(7)   Where relief [is given under this section] for any year of assessment in respect of a contribution, relief shall not be given in respect of it under any other provision of the Income Tax Acts for the same or any subsequent year, nor (in the case of a contribution under an annuity contract) in respect of any other premium or consideration for an annuity under the same contract.

(8)   References in the Income Tax Acts to relief in respect of life assurance premiums shall not be taken to include relief under this section.

640   Maximum amount of deductions

(1)   The maximum amount [of contributions in respect of which relief may be given] in any year of assessment by virtue of section 639(1) shall be

[(a)   an amount equal to the earnings threshold for that year; or

(b)   if greater,] 17.5 per cent of the individual's net relevant earnings for that year.

(2)   In the case of an individual whose age at the beginning of the year of assessment is within a range specified in the first column of the following table, subsection (1) above shall have effect with the substitution for 17.5 per cent of the relevant percentage specified in the second column.

[36 to 45	20 per cent
46 to 50	25 per cent
51 to 55	30 per cent
56 to 60	35 per cent
61 or more	40 per cent.]

[(3)   Without prejudice to subsection (1) above, where any contributions are paid in a year of assessment by an individual to secure benefits satisfying the conditions in section 637, the maximum amount of those contributions in respect of which relief may be given by virtue of section 639(1)] [shall be an amount equal to 10 per cent of the aggregate amount of the relevant pension contributions made in that year by the individual and an employer of his].

[(3A)   In subsection (3) above "relevant pension contribution" means a contribution paid towards securing benefits falling within paragraph (a), (b) or (c) of section 633(1) under arrangements made under a personal pension scheme on or after 6th April 2001.]

(4)   Where personal pension arrangements are made by an employee whose employer makes contributions under the arrangements, the maximum amount [of contributions in respect of which relief may be given by virtue of section 639(1)] in any year of assessment shall be reduced by the amount of the employer's contributions in the year.

(5)   Any minimum contributions treated by virtue of section 649(3) as paid by the individual in respect of whom they are paid shall be disregarded for the purposes of this section.

[640A   Earnings cap]

[(1)   In arriving at an individual's net relevant earnings for a year of assessment for the purposes of section 640 above, any excess of what would be his net relevant earnings for the year (apart from this subsection) over the allowable maximum for the year shall be disregarded.

(2)   In subsection (1) above "the allowable maximum" means, as regards a particular year of assessment, the figure found for that year by virtue of subsections (3) and (4) below.

(3)   For the year of assessment 1989–90 the figure is £60,000.

(4)   For the year of assessment 1990–91 and any subsequent year of assessment the figure is the figure found for that year, for the purposes of section 590C, by virtue of section 590C(4) [to (5A)].]

641   . . .

. . .

[641A   Election for contributions to be treated as paid in previous year]

[(1)   A person who pays a contribution under approved personal pension arrangements on or before the 31st January in any year of assessment may, at or before the time when he pays the contribution, irrevocably elect that the contribution, or part of it, shall be treated as paid in the preceding year of assessment.

(2)   Where an election is made under this section in respect of a contribution or

part of a contribution, the other provisions of this Chapter shall have effect as if the contribution or part had been paid in the year specified in the election and not in the year in which it was actually paid.]

642 ...

...

643 Employer's contributions and personal pension income etc

(1) ...

(2) Income derived by a person from investments or deposits held by him for the purposes of an approved personal pension scheme shall be exempt from income tax.

(3) An annuity payable under approved personal pension arrangements shall be treated as earned income of the annuitant.

(4) Subsection (3) above applies only in relation to the annuitant to whom the annuity is made payable by the terms of the arrangements.

[(5) Income withdrawals under approved personal pension arrangements . . . shall be treated as earned income of the recipient.]

644 Meaning of "relevant earnings"

(1) In this Chapter, "relevant earnings", in relation to an individual, means any income of his which is chargeable to tax for the year of assessment in question and is within subsection (2) below.

(2) Subject to subsections (3) to [(6F)] below, income is within this subsection if it is–

  (a) [general earnings] from an office or employment held by the individual;
  (b) income from any property which is attached to or forms part of the [earnings from] an office or employment held by him;
  (c) income which is chargeable under Schedule D and is immediately derived by him from the carrying on or exercise by him of his trade, profession or vocation (either as an individual or as a partner acting personally in a partnership);
  (d) income treated as earned income by virtue of section 529.

(3) Where section 645 applies to an office or employment held by the individual, neither [general earnings] from the office or employment nor income from any property which is attached to it or forms part of its [general earnings] are within subsection (2) above.

(4) The following are not income within subsection (2) above–

  (a) anything in respect of which tax is chargeable under [ITEPA 2003] and which arises from the acquisition or disposal of shares or an interest in shares or from a right to acquire shares;
  (b) anything in respect of which tax is chargeable by virtue of [Chapter 3 of Part 6 of ITEPA 2003 (payments and benefits on termination of employment etc)].

(5) [General earnings] of an individual as director of a company are not income within subsection (2) above if–

    (a) the income of the company consists wholly or mainly of investment income; and

    (b) the individual, either alone or together with any other persons who are or have been at any time directors of the company, controls the company;

and section 840 shall apply for the purposes of this subsection.

(6)   For the purposes of subsection (5) above–

"director" includes any person occupying the position of director by whatever name called; and

["investment income" means income which, if the company were an individual, would not be earned income.]

[(6A) [General earnings] of an individual as an employee of a company are not income within subsection (2) above if–

    (a) he is a controlling director of the company at any time in the year of assessment in question or has been a controlling director of the company at any time in the ten years immediately preceding that year of assessment, and

    (b) any of subsection (6B) to (6E) below applies in his case.

(6B) This subsection applies in the case of an individual if–

    (a) at any time in the year of assessment in question he is in receipt of benefits under a relevant superannuation scheme, and

    (b) the benefits are payable in respect of past service with the company.

(6C) This subsection applies in the case of the individual if–

    (a) at any time in the year of assessment in question he is in receipt of benefits under a personal pension scheme,

    (b) the scheme has received a transfer payment relating to him from a relevant superannuation scheme, and

    (c) the transfer payment is in respect of past service with the company.

(6D) This subsection applies in the case of an individual if–

    (a) at any time in the year of assessment in question he is in receipt of benefits under a relevant superannuation scheme,

    (b) the benefits are payable in respect of past service with another company,

    (c) the [general earnings] are for a period during which the company mentioned in subsection (6A) above has carried on a trade or business previously carried on by the other company, and

    (d) the other company carried on the trade or business at any time during the period of service in respect of which the benefits are payable.

(6E) This subsection applies in the case of the individual if–

    (a) at any time in the year of assessment in question he is in receipt of benefits under a personal pension scheme,

(b) the scheme has received a transfer payment relating to him from a relevant superannuation scheme,

(c) the transfer payment is in respect of past service with another company,

(d) the [general earnings] are for a period during which the company mentioned in subsection (6A) above has carried on a trade or business previously carried on by the other company, and

(e) the other company carried on the trade or business at any time during the period of service in respect of which the transfer payment was made.

[(6EA) Where–

(a) there is a time at which a person would be in receipt of any benefits under a scheme but for any debit to which any of his rights under that scheme became subject by virtue of any pension sharing order or provision, and

(b) the benefits he would be in receipt of are benefits payable in respect of past service with a company,

that person shall be deemed for the purposes of subsections (6A) to (6E) above to be in receipt at that time of benefits under that scheme and the benefits which he is deemed to be in receipt of shall be deemed to be benefits in respect of past service with that company.]

(6F) For the purposes of subsections (6A) to [(6EA)] above–

(a) a person is a controlling director of a company if he is a director (as defined by section 612(1)), and he is within paragraph (b) of section 417(5), in relation to the company;

(b) "relevant superannuation scheme" has the same meaning as in section 645(1);

(c) references to benefits payable in respect of past service with a company include references to benefits payable partly in respect of past service with the company [but do not include references to benefits which (within the meaning of section 590) are provided for him as an ex-spouse]; and

(d) references to a transfer payment in respect of past service with a company include references to a transfer payment partly in respect of past service with the company [but do not include references to any transfer payment made for the purpose of giving effect to a pension sharing order or provision].]

(7) . . .

645 Earnings from pensionable employment

(1) This section applies to an office or employment held by an individual if–

(a) service in it is service to which a relevant superannuation scheme relates; and

(b) the individual is a participant in the scheme; and

(c) [subsection (4) below does not apply] to his participation in the scheme.

(2)   This section applies whether or not the duties of the office or employment are performed wholly or partly in the United Kingdom or the individual is chargeable to tax in respect of it.

(3)   In subsection (1) above "a relevant superannuation scheme" means a scheme or arrangement–

(a)   the object or one of the objects of which is the provision, in respect of persons serving in particular offices or employments, of relevant benefits within the meaning of section 612; . . .

(b)   which is established by a person other than the individual [. . .

(c)   which is of a description mentioned in [section 387(2) of ITEPA 2003 (meaning of non-approved retirement benefits scheme)] [; and

(d)   which is not an approved converted scheme].]

(4)   This subsection applies to an individual's participation in a scheme if the scheme provides no benefits in relation to him other than–

(a)   an annuity payable to his surviving spouse or a dependant of his;

(b)   a lump sum payable on his death in service.

[(4A)   Where the [earnings] from an office or employment held by an individual are [earnings and amounts treated as earnings to which subsection (4B) applies], this section shall have effect with the substitution of the following for paragraph (c) of subsection (3) above–

"(c)   which corresponds to a scheme of a description mentioned in [section 387(2) of ITEPA 2003 (meaning of non-approved retirement benefits scheme)].]

[(4B)   This subsection applies to earnings and amounts treated as earnings for a year of assessment if–

(a)   the employee or office-holder is not domiciled in the United Kingdom in that year, and

(b)   the employment is with a foreign employer.

(4C)   If there is a dispute as to whether the employee or office-holder is not domiciled in the United Kingdom, sections 42 and 43 of ITEPA 2003 (Board to determine dispute as to domicile) apply to the dispute as they apply to a dispute mentioned in section 42(1) of that Act.

(4D)   In this section– ˙

"earnings and amounts treated as earnings" means earnings and amounts treated as earnings which constitute employment income (see section 7(2)(a) or (b) of ITEPA 2003);

"foreign employer" has the meaning given by section 721 of ITEPA 2003.]

(5)   . . .

646   Meaning of "net relevant earnings"

(1)   Subject to subsections (3) to (7) below [and section 646A], in this Chapter "net relevant earnings", in relation to an individual, means the amount of his relevant earnings for the year of assessment in question, less the amount of any

deductions within subsection (2) below which fall to be made from the relevant earnings in computing for the purposes of income tax his total income for that year.

(2)   Deductions are within this subsection if they are–

(a)   deductions which but for section 74(m), (p) or (q) could be made in computing the profits or gains of the individual;

[(b)   deductions made by virtue of section 232, 336, 343, 344 or 351 of ITEPA 2003 (mileage allowance, expenses, professional membership fees, annual subscriptions, ministers of religion);

(ba)   travelling or subsistence expenses deducted by virtue of Part 5 of that Act;

(bb)   deductions made by virtue of section 332(3) of this Act;]

(c)   deductions in respect of relief under Schedule 9 to the Finance Act 1981 (stock relief);

(d)   deductions in respect of losses or capital allowances, being losses or capital allowances arising from activities profits or gains of which would be included in computing relevant earnings of the individual
. . .

(3)   For the purposes of this section, an individual's relevant earnings shall be taken to be those earnings before giving effect to any capital allowances, other than deductions allowable in computing profits or gains, but after taking into account the amounts on which charges fall to be made [under [the Capital Allowances Act (including enactments which under this Act are to be treated as contained in that Act)]]; and in subsections (4) and (5) below, references to income (other than references to total income) shall be construed similarly.

(4)   In the case of an individual's partnership profits, the amount to be included in arriving at his net relevant earnings shall be his share of the partnership income (estimated in accordance with the Income Tax Acts) after making from it any such deductions in respect of–

(a)   payments made by the partnership;

(b)   relief given to the partnership under Schedule 9 to the Finance Act 1981; or

(c)   capital allowances falling to be made to the partnership,

as would be made in computing the tax payable in respect of that income.

(5)   Where, in a year of assessment for which [the basic rate limit is increased in accordance with section 639(5A) in the case] of an individual–

(a)   a deduction in respect of such a loss or allowance of the individual as is mentioned in subsection (2)(d) above falls to be made in computing the total income of the individual . . . ; and

(b)   the deduction or part of it falls to be so made from income other than relevant earnings;

the amount of the deduction made from that other income shall be treated as reducing the individual's net relevant earnings for subsequent years of assessment in accordance with subsection (6) below.

(6)   The deduction shall be made so far as possible from the individual's net relevant earnings for the first of the subsequent years of assessment (whether or not

413

he is entitled to relief [in accordance with section 639(5A)] for that year), and then, so far as it cannot be so made, from those of the next year, and so on.

(7) . . .

[646A Earnings from associated employments]

[(1) This section applies where in the year of assessment in question–

    (a) an individual holds two or more offices or employments which are associated in that year,

    (b) one or more of them is an office or employment to which section 645 applies ("pensionable job"), and

    (c) one or more of them is an office or employment to which that section does not apply ("non-pensionable job").

(2) Where the [general earnings] for that year from the pensionable job (or jobs) are equal to or exceed the allowable maximum for that year, section 646(1) shall have effect in the case of the individual as if the references to relevant earnings were references to relevant earnings not attributable to the non-pensionable job (or jobs).

(3) Where the allowable maximum for that year exceeds the [general earnings] for that year from the pensionable job (or jobs), the individual's net relevant earnings, so far as attributable to the non-pensionable job (or jobs), shall not be greater than the amount of the excess.

(4) For the purposes of this section two or more offices or employments held by an individual in a year of assessment are associated in that year if the employers in question are associated at any time during it.

(5) For the purposes of subsection (4) above, employers are associated if (directly or indirectly) one is controlled by the other or if both are controlled by a third person.

(6) In subsection (5) above the reference to control, in relation to a body corporate, shall be construed–

    (a) where the body corporate is a close company, in accordance with section 416, and

    (b) where it is not, in accordance with section 840.

(7) In this section "the allowable maximum" has the same meaning as in section 640A(1).]

[646B Presumption of same level of relevant earnings etc for 5 years]

[(1) This section applies where an individual (the "relevant member") who is or becomes a member of a personal pension scheme provides to the scheme administrator the requisite evidence of the relevant amounts for any year of assessment (the "basis year").

(2) For the purposes of this section, the "relevant amounts" for any year of assessment are the amounts which need to be known in order to calculate the relevant member's net relevant earnings for that year.

(3) The basis year need not be a year of assessment in which the relevant member is a member of the personal pension scheme concerned.

(4)   Where this section applies, it shall be presumed for the purposes of this Chapter in the case of the relevant member and the personal pension scheme concerned that, for each of the five years of assessment following the basis year, the relevant amounts (and, accordingly, the relevant member's net relevant earnings) are the same as for the basis year.

(5)   Subsection (4) above is subject to–

   (a)   subsections (6) to (9) below; and
   (b)   such conditions or exceptions as may be prescribed.

(6)   For the purposes of this section, the requisite evidence provided for a later basis year (the "later basis year") supersedes the requisite evidence provided for an earlier basis year (the "earlier basis year").

(7)   Subsection (6) above has effect subject to, and in accordance with, subsections (8) and (9) below.

(8)   If–

   (a)   the actual net relevant earnings for the later basis year, exceed

   (b)   the actual net relevant earnings for the earlier basis year,

the supersession effected by subsection (6) above has effect as respects the later basis year and subsequent years of assessment (and subsection (4) above applies accordingly).

(9)   Where the condition in subsection (8) above is not satisfied, the supersession effected by subsection (6) above has effect only as respects years of assessment later than the last of the five years of assessment following the earlier basis year (and subsection (4) above applies accordingly).

(10)   It is immaterial for the purposes of this section whether the requisite evidence for a later year of assessment is provided before or after, or at the same time as, the requisite evidence for an earlier year of assessment.

(11)   This section is subject to section 646D.]

[646C   Provisions supplementary to section 646B]

[(1)   In this section and section 646B, "requisite evidence" means evidence–

   (a)   of such a description as may be prescribed;
   (b)   in such form as may be prescribed; and
   (c)   satisfying such conditions as may be prescribed.

(2)   Regulations may make further provision in connection with requisite evidence.

(3)   The provision that may be made by regulations under subsection (2) above includes provision for or in connection with the provision, use, retention, production or inspection of, or of copies of,–

   (a)   requisite evidence;
   (b)   books, documents or other records relating to any requisite evidence; or
   (c)   extracts from requisite evidence or from such books, documents or other records.

(4)   Any power to make regulations under this section or section 646B includes power to make different provision for different cases or different purposes.

(5)   In this section and section 646B–

"prescribed" means specified in or determined in accordance with regulations;

"regulations" means regulations made by the Board.]

[646D   Higher level contributions after cessation of actual relevant earnings: modification of section 646B]

[(1)   This section applies where a member of a personal pension scheme–

(a)   has no actual relevant earnings in a year of assessment (the "break year"); but

(b)   had actual relevant earnings in the preceding year of assessment (the "cessation year"); and

(c)   was entitled to make higher level contributions under arrangements under the scheme in any one or more of the six years of assessment preceding the break year (the "reference years").

(2)   In the application of the presumption in subsection (4) of section 646B for any qualifying post-cessation year, in a case where this section applies, the basis year may be any one of the reference years for which the member provides or has provided the requisite evidence–

(a)   notwithstanding anything in subsections (6) to (9) of that section; and

(b)   whether or not the qualifying post-cessation year is included among the five years of assessment following the basis year.

(3)   If the member provides or has provided the requisite evidence for two or more of the reference years, he may by notice in writing to the scheme administrator nominate that one of those years which is to be the basis year by virtue of subsection (2) above.

(4)   In this section "post-cessation year", in the case of the member concerned, means any of the five years of assessment following the cessation year.

(5)   For the purposes of this section any post-cessation year is a "qualifying" post-cessation year unless–

(a)   it is a year for which the member has any actual relevant earnings;

(b)   it is a year throughout which the member holds an office or employment to which section 645 applies; or

(c)   it immediately follows a post-cessation year which is not a qualifying post-cessation year.

(6)   Subsection (5) above is without prejudice to the further application of this section in relation to the member if the conditions in subsection (1) above are again fulfilled.

(7)   In this section–

"the basis year" shall be construed in accordance with section 646B;

"the requisite evidence" has the same meaning as in that section.]

647 ...

...

648 ...

...

[648A ...]

[...]

[648B   Return of contributions after pension date]

[(1)   Tax shall be charged under this section on any payment to a person under approved personal pension arrangements of such a lump sum as is mentioned in section 637A in a case where the member's death occurred after his pension date in relation to the arrangement in question.

(2)   Where a payment is chargeable to tax under this section, the scheme administrator shall be charged to income tax under Case VI of Schedule D and, subject to subsection (3) below, the rate of tax shall be 35 per cent.

(3)   The Treasury may by order from time to time increase or decrease the rate of tax under subsection (2) above.

(4)   The tax shall be charged on the amount paid or, if the rules of the scheme permit the scheme administrator to deduct the tax before payment, on the amount before deduction of tax; and the amount so charged to tax shall not be treated as income for any other purpose of the Tax Acts.]

Miscellaneous

649   Minimum contributions under Social Security Act 1986

(1)   Where under [section 43 of the Pension Schemes Act 1993] the [Board pay] minimum contributions for the purposes of approved personal pension arrangements, the amount of the employee's share of those contributions shall, instead of being the amount provided for in that Part, be the grossed-up equivalent of the amount so provided for.

(2)   For the purposes of this section–

["the employee's share" of minimum contributions is the amount that would be the minimum contributions if, for the reference in section 45(1) of the Pension Schemes Act 1993 to the appropriate age-related percentage, there were substituted a reference to the percentage mentioned in section 41(1A)(a) of that Act];

"the grossed-up equivalent" of an amount is such sum as, after deduction of income tax at the basic rate in force for the year of assessment for which the contributions are paid, is equal to that amount.

(3)   The employee's share of minimum contributions paid for a year of assessment by the [Board] for the purposes of approved personal pension arrangements shall be treated for the purposes of income tax–

    (a)   as the income for that year of the individual in respect of whom it is paid; and

    (b)   as contributions paid in that year by that individual under those arrangements.

(4)   The Board may make regulations–

    (a) . . .

    (b) . . .

    (c)   prescribing circumstances in which this section or any provision of it shall not apply;

    (d)   making such provision as appears to the Board to be necessary or expedient for the purposes of supplementing the provisions of this section.

[(5)   The Board shall pay into the National Insurance Fund out of money provided by Parliament the amount of any increase attributable to this section in the sums paid out of that Fund under the Pension Schemes Act 1993.]

(6)   In relation to Northern Ireland, this section shall have effect as if–

    (a)   . . .

    (b)   references to [section 43, section 45(1) and section 41(1)(a) of the Pension Schemes Act 1993] were references to [sections 39, 41(1) and 37(1)(a) of the Pension Schemes (Northern Ireland) Act 1993];

    [(bb) references to sections 45(1) and 41(1A)(a) of the Pension Schemes Act 1993 were references to sections 41(1) and 37(1A)(a) of the Pension Schemes (Northern Ireland) Act 1993, respectively;] and

    (c)   references to the National Insurance Fund were references to the Northern Ireland National Insurance Fund.

650   Withdrawal of approval

(1)   If in the opinion of the Board the facts concerning an approved personal pension scheme or its administration or arrangements made in accordance with it do not warrant the continuance of their approval of the scheme, they may at any time by notice given to the scheme administrator withdraw their approval of the scheme.

(2)   If in the opinion of the Board the facts concerning any approved personal pension arrangements do not warrant the continuance of their approval in relation to the arrangements, they may at any time by notice given to the individual who made them and to the scheme administrator withdraw their approval in relation to the arrangements.

(3)   Without prejudice to the generality of subsection (2) above, the Board may withdraw their approval in relation to any personal pension arrangements if they are of the opinion that securing the provision of benefits under the arrangements was not the sole purpose of the individual in making them.

(4)   A notice under subsection (1) or (2) above shall state the grounds on which, and the date from which, approval is withdrawn.

(5)   The Board may not withdraw their approval from a date earlier than the date when the facts were first such that they did not warrant the continuance of their

approval (so, however, that in a case within subsection (3) above their approval may be withdrawn from the day the arrangements in question were made).

[(6)   The power of the Board under this section to withdraw their approval in relation to any arrangements made under a personal pension scheme shall be exercisable for the purposes of section 650A notwithstanding that the time from which the approval is withdrawn is a time from which, by virtue of section 631(4) or 638A(4), the whole scheme ceases to be an approved scheme.]

[650A   Charge on withdrawal of approval from arrangements]

[(1)   Where any personal pension arrangements cease to be approved arrangements by virtue of the exercise by the Board of their power under section 650(2), tax shall be charged in accordance with this section.

(2)   The tax shall be charged under Case VI of Schedule D at the rate of 40 per cent on an amount equal to the value (taking that value at the relevant time) of the appropriate part of the assets held at that time for the purposes of the relevant scheme.

(3)   In subsection (2) above–

"the appropriate part", in relation to the value of any assets, is so much of those assets as is properly attributable, in accordance with the provisions of the scheme and any just and reasonable apportionment, to the arrangements in question; and

"the relevant time" means the time immediately before the date from which the Board's approval is withdrawn.

(4)   Subject to subsection (5) below, the person liable for the tax charged under this section shall be the scheme administrator for the relevant scheme.

(5)   If, in any case where an amount of tax has been charged under this section and has not been paid–

(a)   there is at any time no person who, as the scheme administrator for the relevant scheme, may be assessed to that amount of tax, or is liable to pay it,

(b)   the scheme administrator for that scheme cannot for the time being be traced,

(c)   there has been such a failure by the scheme administrator for that scheme to meet a liability to pay that amount as the Board consider to be a failure of a serious nature, or

(d)   it appears to the Board that a liability of the scheme administrator for that scheme to pay that amount of tax is a liability that he will be, or (were there an assessment) would be, unable to meet out of assets held in accordance with the scheme for the purposes of those arrangements,

the Board shall be entitled to assess the unpaid tax on the person who made the arrangements in question as if the tax charged under this section, to the extent that it is unpaid, were assessable under this section on that person, instead of on the scheme administrator.

(6)   An assessment to tax made by virtue of subsection (5)(c) above shall not be out of time if it is made within three years after the date on which the tax which the scheme administrator has failed to pay first became due from him.

(7)   For the purposes of this section the value of an asset is, subject to subsection (8) below, its market value, construing "market value" in accordance with section 272 of the 1992 Act.

(8)   Where an asset held for the purposes of a scheme is a right or interest in respect of any money lent (directly or indirectly) to any person mentioned in subsection (9) below, the value of the asset shall be treated as being the amount owing (including any unpaid interest) on the money lent.

(9)   Those persons are–

    (a)   the person who (whether or not before the making of the loan) made the arrangements in relation to which the Board's approval has been withdrawn;

    (b)   any other person who has at any time (whether or not before the making of the loan) made contributions under those arrangements; and

    (c)   any person connected, at the time of the making of the loan or subsequently, with a person falling within paragraph (a) or (b) above.

(10)   In this section "the relevant scheme", in relation to any personal pension arrangements, means the scheme in accordance with which those arrangements were made.

(11)   Section 839 shall apply for the purposes of this section.]

651   Appeals

(1)   Where the Board–

    (a)   refuse an application by notice under section 631 [or paragraph 3 of Schedule 23ZA]; or

    (b)   withdraw an approval by notice under section 650;

the person to whom the notice is given may appeal to the Special Commissioners against the refusal or, as the case may be, the withdrawal.

(2)   An appeal under this section shall be made by notice stating the grounds for the appeal and given to the Board before the end of the period of 30 days beginning with the day on which the notice of refusal or withdrawal was given to the appellant.

(3)   On an appeal under this section against the withdrawal of an approval, the Special Commissioners may, instead of allowing or dismissing the appeal, order that the withdrawal shall have effect from a date other than that determined by the Board.

(4)   The bringing of an appeal under this section shall not affect the validity of the decision appealed against pending the determination of the proceedings.

[651A   Information powers]

[(1)   The Board may by regulations make any of the following provisions–

    (a)   provision requiring prescribed persons to furnish to the Board, at prescribed times, information relating to any of the matters mentioned in subsection (2) below;

    (b)   provision enabling the Board to serve a notice requiring prescribed persons to furnish to the Board, within a prescribed time, particulars relating to any of those matters;

(c) provision enabling the Board to serve a notice requiring prescribed persons to produce to the Board, within a prescribed time, documents relating to any of those matters;

(d) provision enabling the Board to serve a notice requiring prescribed persons to make available for inspection on behalf of the Board books, documents and other records, being books, documents and records which relate to any of those matters;

(e) provision requiring prescribed persons to preserve for a prescribed time books, documents and other records, being books, documents and records which relate to any of those matters.

(2) The matters referred to in subsection (1) above are–

(a) any personal pension scheme which is or has been approved; and

(b) any personal pension arrangements which are or have been approved.

(3) A person who fails to comply with regulations made under subsection (1)(e) above shall be liable to a penalty not exceeding £3,000.

(4) Regulations under this section may make different provision for different descriptions of case.

(5) In this section "prescribed" means prescribed by regulations made under this section.]

652 . . .

. . .

653 Information: penalties

A person who knowingly makes a false statement or false representation on making an application under section 631 or for the purpose of obtaining for himself or any other person any relief from or repayment of tax under this Chapter shall be liable to a penalty not exceeding [£3,000].

[653A Notices to be given to scheme administrator]

[(1) Where–

(a) the Board, or any officer of the Board, is authorised or required by or in consequence of any provision of this Chapter to give a notice to the person who is the scheme administrator of a personal pension scheme, but

(b) there is for the time being no scheme administrator for that scheme or the person who is the scheme administrator for that scheme cannot be traced,

that power or duty may be exercised or performed by giving that notice, instead, to the person specified in subsection (2) below.

(2) That person is–

(a) the person who established the scheme; or

(b) any person by whom that person has been directly or indirectly succeeded in relation to the provision of benefits under the scheme.

(3)   The giving of a notice in accordance with this section shall have the same effect as the giving of that notice to the scheme administrator and, without prejudice to section 650A(5), shall not impose an additional obligation or liability on the person to whom the notice is actually given.]

654   Remuneration of Ministers and other officers

(1)   This section applies to any salary–

- (a)   payable to the holder of a qualifying office who is also a Member of the House of Commons; and
- (b)   payable for a period in respect of which the holder is not a participant in relation to that office in arrangements contained in the Parliamentary pension scheme but is a participant in relation to his membership of the House of Commons in any such arrangements, or for any part of such a period.

(2)   So much of any salary to which this section applies as is equal to the difference between a Member's pensionable salary and the salary which (in accordance with any such resolution as is mentioned in subsection (4)(a) below) is payable to him as a Member holding that qualifying office, shall be treated for the purposes of this Chapter as remuneration from the office of Member and not from the qualifying office.

(3)   In this section–

> "Member's pensionable salary" means a Member's ordinary salary under any resolution of the House of Commons which, being framed otherwise than as an expression of opinion, is for the time being in force relating to the remuneration of Members or, if the resolution provides for a Member's ordinary salary thereunder to be treated for pension purposes as being at a higher rate, a notional yearly salary at that higher rate;
>
> "qualifying office" means an office mentioned in paragraph (b), (c) or (d) of subsection (2) of section 2 of the Parliamentary and other Pensions Act 1987;
>
> "the Parliamentary pension scheme" has the same meaning as in that Act;

and, without prejudice to the power conferred by virtue of paragraph 13 of Schedule 1 to that Act, regulations under section 2 of that Act may make provision specifying the circumstances in which a person is to be regarded for the purposes of this section as being or not being a participant in relation to his membership of the House of Commons, or in relation to any office, in arrangements contained in the Parliamentary pension scheme.

(4)   In subsection (3) above "a Member's ordinary salary", in relation to any resolution of the House of Commons, means–

- (a)   if the resolution provides for salary to be paid to Members at different rates according to whether or not they are holders of particular offices or are in receipt of salaries or pensions as the holders or former holders of particular offices, a Member's yearly salary at the higher or highest rate; and

(b) in any other case, a Member's yearly salary at the rate specified in or determined under the resolution.

655 Transitional provisions

(1) Where approved personal pension arrangements are made by an individual who pays qualifying premiums within the meaning of section 620(1)–

   (a) the amount [of contributions in respect of which relief may be given] by virtue of section 639(1) in any year of assessment shall be reduced by the amount of any qualifying premiums which are paid in the year by the individual and in respect of which relief is given for the year under section 619(1)(a); and

   (b) the relief which, by virtue of section 625, may be given under section 619 by reference to the individual's unused relief for any year shall be reduced by the amount of any contributions paid by him in that year under the approved personal pension arrangements.

(2) Where an individual elects under section 641 that a contribution or part of a contribution shall be treated as paid in the year of assessment [1985–86, 1986–87 or 1987–88], the payment shall be treated as the payment of a qualifying premium for the purposes of Chapter III of this Part; and in such a case references in section 641 to an amount of unused relief shall be construed in accordance with section 625.

(3) The references in section 642 to unused relief for any year are, for years of assessment before [1988–89], references to unused relief within the meaning of section 625.

(4) The Board shall not grant any application under section 631 so as to approve a scheme with effect from a date earlier than [1st July] 1988.

(5) The Board may by regulations make provisions for applications for approval of personal pension schemes to be granted provisionally . . . notwithstanding that the Board have not satisfied themselves that the schemes comply with the requirements of sections 632 to 638; and such regulations may, in particular, provide–

   (a) for the contents and form of certificates or other documents which the Board may require the applicant to give them before they grant an application provisionally;

   (b) for the making of such amendments of the rules of the scheme after the provisional grant of an application as are necessary to enable the scheme to comply with the requirements of sections 632 to 638, and for those amendments to have effect as from the date of approval of the scheme;

   (c) for the withdrawal of approval of the scheme as from that date if it does not comply with the requirements of sections 632 to 638 and such amendments as are mentioned in paragraph (b) above are not made;

and may make such supplementary provision as appears to the Board to be necessary or expedient.

SCHEDULE 23

OCCUPATIONAL PENSION SCHEMES

SCHEMES APPROVED BEFORE 23RD JULY 1987

Section 609

Preliminary

1.—(1)   This Schedule shall be deemed to have come into force on 17th March 1987 and, subject to sub-paragraphs (2) and (3) below, applies in relation to any retirement benefits scheme approved by the Board before the passing of the Finance (No. 2) Act 1987 (23rd July 1987).

[(2)   The Board may by regulations provide that, in circumstances prescribed in the regulations, this Schedule or any provision of it shall not apply or shall apply with such modifications as may be so prescribed.

(2A)   Regulations under sub-paragraph (2) above–

- (a)   may include provision authorising the Board to direct that this Schedule or any provision of it shall not apply in any particular case where in the opinion of the Board the facts are such that its application would not be appropriate;
- (b)   may take effect (and may authorise any direction given under them to take effect) as from 17th March 1987 or any later date;
- (c)   may make such supplementary provision as appears to the Board to be necessary or expedient.]

(3)   This Schedule shall not apply to a retirement benefits scheme if, before the end of 1987, the administrator of the scheme gave notice to the Board that it is not to apply.

(4)   Where a notice is given to the Board under sub-paragraph (3) above, the scheme shall, with effect from 17th March 1987 or (if later) the date with effect from which it was approved, cease to be approved.

Accelerated accrual

2.—(1)   This paragraph applies where an employee becomes a member of the scheme on or after 17th March 1987.

(2)   Notwithstanding anything to the contrary in the rules of the scheme, they shall have effect as if they did not allow the provision for the employee of a pension exceeding one-thirtieth of his relevant annual remuneration for each year of service up to a maximum of 20.

3.—(1)   This paragraph applies where an employee becomes a member of the scheme on or after 17th March 1987 and the scheme allows him to commute his pension or part of it for a lump sum or sums.

(2)   If the employee's full pension (that is, the pension before any commutation) is equal to or less than a basic rate commutable pension, the rules of the scheme shall have effect (notwithstanding anything in them to the contrary) as if they did not allow him to obtain by way of commutation a lump sum or sums exceeding in all a basic rate lump sum.

(3)   If the employee's full pension is greater than a basic rate commutable pension but less than a maximum rate commutable pension, the rules of the scheme shall have effect (notwithstanding anything in them to the contrary) as if they did not allow him to obtain by way of commutation a lump sum or sums exceeding in all the aggregate of–

- (a) a basic rate lump sum, and
- (b) an amount equal to the relevant percentage of the difference between a basic rate lump sum and a maximum rate lump sum.

(4)   In this paragraph, as it applies in relation to an employee–

- (a) a "basic rate commutable pension" means a pension of one-sixtieth of his relevant annual remuneration for each year of service up to a maximum of 40;
- (b) a "maximum rate commutable pension" means a pension of one-thirtieth of his relevant annual remuneration for each year of service up to a maximum of 20;
- (c) a "basic rate lump sum" means a lump sum of three-eightieths of his relevant annual remuneration for each year of service up to a maximum of 40;
- (d) a "maximum rate lump sum" means a lump sum of such amount as may be determined by or under regulations made by the Board for the purposes of this paragraph and paragraph 4 below;
- (e) "the relevant percentage" means the difference between a basic rate commutable pension and the employee's full pension expressed as a percentage of the difference between a basic rate commutable pension and a maximum rate commutable pension.

4.—(1)   This paragraph applies where an employee becomes a member of the scheme on or after 17th March 1987 and the scheme provides a lump sum or sums for him otherwise than by commutation of his pension or part of it.

(2)   If the employee's pension is equal to or less than a basic rate non-commutable pension, the rules of the scheme shall have effect (notwithstanding anything in them to the contrary) as if they did not allow the payment to him, otherwise than by way of commutation, of a lump sum or sums exceeding in all a basic rate lump sum.

(3)   If the employee's pension is greater than a basic rate non-commutable pension but less than a maximum rate non-commutable pension the rules of the scheme shall have effect (notwithstanding anything in them to the contrary) as if they did not allow the payment to him, otherwise than by way of commutation, of a lump sum or sums exceeding in all the aggregate of–

- (a) a basic rate lump sum, and
- (b) an amount equal to the relevant percentage of the difference between a basic rate lump sum and a maximum rate lump sum.

(4)   In this paragraph, as it applies in relation to an employee–

- (a) a "basic rate non-commutable pension" means a pension of one-eightieth of his relevant annual remuneration for each year of service up to a maximum of 40,

    (b) a "maximum rate non-commutable pension" means a pension of one-fortieth of his relevant annual remuneration for each year of service up to a maximum of 20,

    (c) "basic rate lump sum" and "maximum rate lump sum" have the same meanings as in paragraph 3 above, and

    (d) "the relevant percentage" means the difference between a basic rate non-commutable pension and the employee's actual pension expressed as a percentage of the difference between a basic rate non-commutable pension and a maximum rate non-commutable pension.

Final remuneration

5.—(1) This paragraph applies where an employee who is a member of the scheme retires on or after 17th March 1987.

(2) The rules of the scheme shall have effect as if they provided that in determining the employee's relevant annual remuneration for the purpose of calculating benefits, no account should be taken of anything excluded from the definition of "remuneration" in section 612(1).

(3) In the case of an employee–

    (a) whose employer is a company and who at any time in the last ten years of his service is a controlling director of the company, or

    (b) whose relevant annual remuneration for the purpose of calculating benefits, so far as the remuneration is ascertained by reference to years beginning on or after 6th April 1987, would (apart from this Schedule) exceed the permitted maximum,

the rules of the scheme shall have effect as if they provided that his relevant annual remuneration must not exceed his highest average annual remuneration for any period of three or more years ending within the period of ten years which ends with the date on which his service ends.

(4) In the case of an employee within paragraph (b) of sub-paragraph (3) above who retires before 6th April 1991, the rules of the scheme shall have effect as if they provided that his relevant annual remuneration must not exceed the higher of–

    (a) the average annual remuneration referred to in that sub-paragraph, and

    (b) his remuneration (within the meaning given by section 612(1)) assessable to income tax under Schedule E for the year of assessment 1986–87.

(5) For the purposes of this paragraph a person is a controlling director of a company if–

    (a) he is a director (as defined in section 612), and

    (b) he is within paragraph (b) of section 417(5),

in relation to the company.

Lump sums

6.—(1) This paragraph applies where an employee becomes a member of the scheme on or after 17th March 1987.

(2)   If the rules of the scheme allow the employee to obtain, (by commutation of his pension or otherwise), a lump sum or sums calculated by reference to his relevant annual remuneration, they shall have effect as if they included a rule that in calculating a lump sum any excess of that remuneration over the permitted maximum should be disregarded.

Additional voluntary contributions

7.—(1)   This paragraph applies where–

- (a)   the rules of the scheme make provision for the payment by employees of voluntary contributions, and
- (b)   on or after 8th April 1987 an employee enters into arrangements to pay such contributions.

(2)   Notwithstanding anything in the rules of the scheme, they shall have effect as if they did not allow the payment to the employee of a lump sum in commutation of a pension if or to the extent that the pension is secured by the voluntary contributions.

8   . . .

Supplementary

9.   In this Schedule "relevant annual remuneration" means final remuneration or, if the scheme provides for benefits to be calculated by reference to some other annual remuneration, that other annual remuneration.

[SCHEDULE 23ZA

CONVERSION OF CERTAIN APPROVED RETIREMENT BENEFITS SCHEMES]

[Interpretation

1.—(1)   In this Schedule–

> "the date of the change" shall be construed in accordance with paragraph 3(2) below;
> "eligible scheme" shall be construed in accordance with paragraph 2(4) below;
> "the personal pension provisions of this Act" means this Schedule and the other provisions of Chapter IV of Part XIV;
> "prescribed" (except in paragraph 2(3)(c)) means specified in, or determined in accordance with, regulations;
> "regulations" means regulations made by the Board.

(2)   Any power conferred by this Schedule to make regulations includes power to make different provision for different cases or different purposes.

Eligible schemes

2.—(1)   This Schedule applies to any retirement benefits scheme which is for the time being approved under Chapter I of Part XIV.

(2)   Sub-paragraph (1) above is subject to the following provisions of this paragraph.

(3)   This Schedule applies to a retirement benefits scheme only if–

    (a)   it is an occupational pension scheme, as defined in section 1 of the Pension Schemes Act 1993 or section 1 of the Pensions Schemes (Northern Ireland) Act 1993;

    (b)   it is a money-purchase scheme, as defined in section 181 of the Pension Schemes Act 1993 or section 176 of the Pensions Schemes (Northern Ireland) Act 1993;

    (c)   any documents relating to the scheme which are prescribed under section 631(1) are such that, subject to approval under paragraph 3 below, the scheme is capable of being an approved personal pension scheme for the purposes of Chapter IV of Part XIV as from the date of the change; and

    (d)   such other conditions as may be prescribed are satisfied in the case of the scheme.

(4)   Any retirement benefits scheme to which this Schedule applies is referred to in this Schedule as an "eligible scheme".

Approval of eligible schemes as approved personal pension schemes

3.—(1)   The trustees of an eligible scheme may at any time on or after 1st October 2000 apply to the Board for approval of the scheme under this paragraph.

(2)   If an application under sub-paragraph (1) above is granted, the eligible scheme shall, as from such date as the Board may specify in granting the application (the "date of the change"),–

    (a)   irrevocably cease to be approved, and to be capable of approval, under Chapter I of Part XIV; and

    (b)   become an approved personal pension scheme (and subject accordingly to section 631(4) and the other provisions of Chapter IV of Part XIV).

(3)   The date of the change must not be earlier than 6th April 2001.

(4)   An application under sub-paragraph (1) above shall be in such form, shall contain such information, and shall be accompanied by such documents, in such form, and prepared as at such time, as the Board may prescribe.

(5)   The Board may at their discretion grant or refuse an application under sub-paragraph (1) above.

(6)   The Board's discretion under sub-paragraph (5) above shall be subject to the restrictions set out in sections 632 to 638A and this Schedule.

(7)   The Board shall give notice to the applicant of the grant or refusal of an application.

(8)   A notice under sub-paragraph (7) above shall, in the case of a refusal, state the grounds for the refusal.

(9)   If, at any time after the making of an application under sub-paragraph (1) above, the eligible scheme concerned ceases to be approved under Chapter I of Part XIV otherwise than by virtue of the operation of sub-paragraph (2)(a) above, the scheme shall not, by virtue of that application, become an approved personal pension scheme.

Excessive funding of certain individual members

4.—(1)   The Board may refuse or withhold approval under paragraph 3 above in the case of an eligible scheme of a prescribed description if or so long as they are not satisfied that prescribed requirements will be fulfilled with respect to–

  (a)   the value of any prescribed benefits which may be provided for or in respect of an individual member of a prescribed description, and
  (b)   the value of the assets held for the purpose of providing benefits for or in respect of that member,

if approval under paragraph 3 above is granted.

(2)   Regulations may make provision for or in connection with cases where the value mentioned in paragraph (b) of sub-paragraph (1) above exceeds, or exceeds by more than a prescribed percentage, the value mentioned in paragraph (a) of that sub-paragraph.

(3)   The provision that may be made by virtue of sub-paragraph (2) above includes provision for or in connection with eliminating or reducing any such excess within a prescribed period by one or more prescribed methods.

(4)   Regulations may make provision for the purposes of this paragraph for or in connection with–

  (a)   the valuation of benefits; or
  (b)   the valuation of assets.

(5)   The provision that may be made by virtue of sub-paragraph (4)(a) or (b) above includes provision with respect to, or in connection with,–

  (a)   the person by whom any such valuation is to be made;
  (b)   the method or principles of valuation to be used;
  (c)   certification of any such valuations and of any prescribed matters relating to or connected with them;
  (d)   any facts, matters or assumptions by reference to which any such valuation is to be made;
  (e)   any tables to be used for the purpose of making any such valuation;
  (f)   the basis on which any such tables are to be prepared;
  (g)   the manner in which any such tables are to be applied.

(6)   The methods or principles of valuation and the tables that may be prescribed by virtue of sub-paragraph (5) above include methods or principles or, as the case may be, tables published by the Government Actuary for any purposes of the personal pension provisions of this Act.

Directions as to contributions between valuation and date of change etc

5.—(1)   The Board may give directions for or in connection with–

(a) prohibiting the making of contributions during the post-valuation period, or

(b) restricting the amount of the contributions that may be made during that period,

by or in respect of members of a converting scheme.

(2) Directions under sub-paragraph (1) above–

(a) may be given in respect of schemes generally, schemes of a particular description or any particular scheme or schemes; and

(b) may make different provision in relation to different schemes or different members.

(3) Any directions under sub-paragraph (1) above must be complied with by–

(a) the trustees and managers, or administrators, of any scheme to which the directions relate;

(b) any member of such a scheme to whom the directions relate; and

(c) any person who is the employer of such a member.

(4) If there is any contravention of, or failure to comply with, directions under sub-paragraph (1) above, the Board may–

(a) refuse or withhold approval of the conversion application in question; or

(b) revoke or vary any approval granted or any conditions pending the satisfaction of which approval is withheld.

(5) Sub-paragraph (4) above is without prejudice to any other powers of the Board.

(6) In this paragraph–

"conversion application", in the case of a converting scheme, means the application under paragraph 3(1) above in respect of the scheme;

"converting scheme" means a scheme in respect of which an application under paragraph 3(1) above has been made and not withdrawn or finally refused;

"the post-valuation period", in the case of a converting scheme, means the period which–

(a) begins with the day as at which any valuation for the purposes of paragraph 4 above is made in connection with the conversion application; and

(b) ends with the day preceding the date of the change (or, if earlier, the date on which the conversion application is withdrawn or finally refused).

(7) For the purposes of this paragraph, an application is "finally refused" when it has been refused by the Board and–

(a) the time for appealing under section 651 against the refusal has expired without such an appeal being made; or

(b) an appeal under that section against the refusal has been withdrawn or finally disposed of in a way which affirms refusal of the application.

(8) Any directions under this paragraph must be given in writing.

Scheme rules to allow changes for purpose of conversion

6.   An approved retirement benefits scheme shall be taken to include provisions allowing the making of changes to any provisions of the scheme for the purpose of enabling the scheme to become an eligible scheme, notwithstanding anything to the contrary in any provision of the scheme.]

INDEX

All references are to paragraph numbers.